AF334017

HONG KONG ART

Culture and Decolonization

DAVID CLARKE

DUKE UNIVERSITY PRESS
2002

First published 2001 in the United Kingdom by

Reaktion Books Ltd
79 Farringdon Road
London, EC1M 3JU UK

and in 2002 in the United States by

Duke University Press
Box 90660
Durham, NC 27708 USA

Library of Congress Cataloging-in-Publishing Data

Clarke, David J. (David James), 1954–
    Hong Kong art: culture and decolonization / David Clarke.
        p. cm.
    ISBN 0-8223-2905-0 (cloth: alk. paper) – ISBN 0-8223-2920-4 (pbk: alk. paper)
    1. Art, Chinese–China–Hong Kong–20th century. 2. East and West: in art. I. Title

    N7346_H66 C58 2002
    709'.5125'0945–dc21

                                                          2001045106

Series design by Ron Costley
Printed and bound in Singapore by CS Graphics

Contents

Introduction, 7
1 Varieties of Cultural Hybridity, 13
2 Living in the Shadow of the Future, 38
3 Para/Site Art Space, 70
4 Carving Public Space, 100
5 The Visual Production of a Transition, 151
Epilogue, 203
References, 211
Bibliography, 232
Acknowledgements, 237
Photographic Acknowledgements, 238
Index of Personal and Place Names, 239

Introduction

Art history as practised in the Western world has characteristically marginalized non-Western visual culture. The very popular American college textbook *Gardner's Art Through the Ages*, for instance, seems so unaware of the basic facts of Chinese history that its ninth edition (published in 1991) has a subheading in its only chapter on Chinese art that reads 'Ming, Ch'ing, and Later Dynasties'. There were no 'later dynasties', of course, and a mind-set is revealed that wants to subsume modern Chinese history into that which had preceded it, to emphasize continuity over change. By placing the chapter on Chinese art in the section prior to the one in which European Renaissance art and the narrative of Western art's subsequent development are treated, the authors create a picture of Chinese art as static and homogeneous. The notion that progress is the monopoly of Western culture is thereby sustained. Thus ignorance about non-Western art is structural, as it were, not accidental. Ernst Gombrich's *The Story of Art* also relegates discussion of East Asian art to a pre-Giotto section. In the fourteenth edition (1984), we move from an illustration of a Hidenobu woodcut dated to the early nineteenth century at the end of one chapter to a section of the eleventh-century Bayeux Tapestry at the beginning of the next. The position from which the narrative is being told is signalled by the title of the earlier chapter: since we are 'Looking Eastwards', we are clearly assumed to have a Western standpoint.

In recent years, this Western master narrative of art history has been undermined to some degree. Its Greenbergian incarnation, which found in European and American painting a linear development towards greater formal purity, has lost its former dominance in accounts of twentieth-century art.[1] More contextual approaches to the writing of art history have become popular, and a larger and more distinct place has been found in these for the analysis of art by women and by members of previously marginalized minorities. This fragmentation has been very beneficial, on the whole, but one should not overestimate what has been achieved. The writing of art history is still largely being done from Western sites, and modern and contemporary Asian art – for instance – still largely falls into the blind spot of European and American academic discourse.

A parallel can be made between writing about non-Western art and writing about the art of women, or of minorities within Western culture defined in terms of ethnicity or sexual orientation. In each case, it is not simply a quantitative matter of including more extensive coverage of previously marginalized art, but of opening up new perspectives on the whole of art. Only when a multiplicity of perspectives exists, with none granted any particular priority, can we talk of art history as having become globalized as a discipline. Globalization requires an insight into the local nature of meaning that rules out the possibility of a panoptic mastering viewpoint. The present study aims to play a small part in furthering such a process by offering a contextual analysis of Hong Kong art around the time of its 1997 return to Chinese rule. A cosmopolitan art which has displayed an increasing concern with the local is examined in a text which also aspires to be aware of the specific possibilities of its chosen vantage point.

The local-ness of recent Hong Kong art is not a quality that has accrued to it by default as the result of some provincial isolation. In a city as fully a part of globalized flows of capital, goods and people as any other, the development of a local orientation has been actively sought in response to particular circumstances. At a certain historical conjuncture, Hong Kong artists no longer felt the need to refer back to what was happening in New York and other Western metropolises as the measure of contemporaneity. Instead, they chose to address themselves primarily to a local audience, even if Western artistic language remained a useful resource. At the same time, this local turn was a rejection of the Chinese national frame of reference, and of the artistic culture and traditional resources through which it was expressed. A psychic decolonization occurred which marked out a distance from both of these larger contexts without simply denying either.

The primary impetus for this development was of course the approach of the 1997 handover of sovereignty. Whereas the usual path beyond the colonial has tended to involve a development of national consciousness and a moment of liberation in which national autonomy (however compromised in practice) has become a constitutional fact, in the case of Hong Kong the end of the colonial era offered absorption into a larger entity with an alien political system. In this atypical circumstance, assertions of autonomy needed to be as sceptical of national, as of any other, rhetorics, and the psychic or cultural dimension of the quest for autonomy took on particular importance.

The emergence of this politicized concern for the local is documented throughout the following pages, but in Chapter 1 a contrast is offered to the art of an earlier period in which both Western modernist and Chinese national frameworks were valorized. Even in this earlier phase, a culturally hybrid art was created, but it differs from that which developed later as belief in these conflicting master narratives weakened. Two very different paths to the local are examined in some detail. The painter Luis Chan took a route that gave the unconscious a major role in the creative process, allowing it to work transformatively on visual material of both Western and Chinese origin. The sculptor Antonio Mak, on the other hand, opted for ironic distance, carving out a Hong Kong viewpoint in the process.

Neither Chan nor Mak, unfortunately, was to live to see the 1997 handover, but as the date of this pre-arranged appointment with history approached, a great many other Hong Kong artists developed a concern for the expression of local identity. Examples of their art will be considered in Chapter 2, which discusses a number of works that looked towards the approaching event itself in various ways. Retrospection was also a major theme of this pre-handover phase and of the handover period as well, and a number of works with this backward-glancing quality will be examined.

A concern with history, in particular the recent history of memory and lived personal experience, plays a major role in the difficult project of Hong Kong identity, and most of the artists treated in Chapter 3 share this concern with the past and the erasure of its traces. Installation art, which became very popular in Hong Kong in the years leading up to the handover, particularly among younger artists, is the theme of that chapter. The focus is on the artists associated with Para/Site, one of the most prominent art spaces to emerge during this fertile period. Its exhibitions before, during and after the handover period are considered in sequence.

In Chapter 4, a systematic consideration is made of the role of public sculpture in Hong Kong, and again both the pre- and post-handover periods are treated. The emphasis here is on issues of display and reception, and the attempts of both the colonial regime and its successor to use public sculpture as a means to project state ideology are analysed. The critical reception of such sculpture is discussed, as well as the introduction into public space of artworks carrying oppositional meanings. Corporate use of public sculpture is examined, as is the relationship between sculptural meaning and architectural context.

In the first four chapters, the focus is primarily on visual art as it is narrowly understood, but in the final chapter other types of visual production are also considered. In particular, there is a study of the handover's impact on architecture, fashion, graphic design and graffiti. The response of artists to these other kinds of visual production is also discussed, with identity issues again coming to the fore.

The approach throughout the following pages is contextual, offering an examination of the relationship of art to the particular time and space in which it came into being. The major events of Hong Kong's history between 1984 to 2000 will thus be introduced in the course of discussion, even if an investigation of political history in its own terms remains beyond the scope of this study. Also beyond its scope is an examination of Hong Kong art history as a whole.[2] Instead of such a chronological survey, an investigation is made of a particular historical moment in which Hong Kong art came into its own, which is capable of being understood in its own terms without extensive reference back to earlier artistic eras. Chapter 1 does, however, consider examples of work from an earlier moment of high ambition beginning in the late 1960s, when an attempt was made to create works that were both modern and Chinese in flavour. Key to this phase was the artistic and pedagogic work of Lui Shou-kwan, who became the prime mover in what has been termed the New Ink Painting movement.[3] The work of Wucius Wong, one of the most significant painters of this movement, is investigated, and Lui's own work is also discussed, as is the sculpture of Van Lau. These painters and sculptors, along with their counterparts in Taiwan and the overseas Chinese community, were producing the most challenging Chinese art of that period, open to cosmopolitan influences at a time when the People's Republic was more or less closed to cultural dialogue with the wider world.[4]

Although more recent work has on occasion engaged critically with the art of this earlier phase, it is hard to discover cross-generational stylistic continuities in Hong Kong art. Many of the artists discussed in the following pages gained their art education overseas (a consequence of both the paucity of local opportunities for training and Hong Kong's increasing prosperity) and employ a visual language whose roots can be found in Western modernist or post-modernist practice rather than in the Chinese brushwork traditions that provided the primary frame for New Ink Painting. Likewise, New Ink Painting's project of creating a modern yet recognizably Chinese art has no precedent in earlier Hong Kong artistic practice. Instead, its roots are in the artistic experiments that took place in mainland China (especially in Shanghai) during the 1920s and 1930s, when similar problems of integrating Western stylistic influences into a consciously national art were faced.[5] Indeed, since Hong Kong's population grew more by immigration (following the end of the Second World War and the founding of the People's Republic in 1949) than by the natural increase of an indigenous population, post-war Hong Kong artists were not alone in having more cultural links to mainland China than to their adopted home.

Of the generation of artists active in Hong Kong during the pre-

Second World War period, the only one to be considered in this study is Luis Chan. The work he produced during that phase of his career is indebted to Western realist examples, as is that of several other prominent artists based in Hong Kong during the same time such as Yee Bon, Lee Byng and Li Tiefu. These last three artists gained their technical grounding through overseas study and were among the earliest Chinese artists to obtain a Western art education, but Luis Chan learned his craft in Hong Kong itself. Hong Kong at that time provided an inhospitable environment for ambitious artists, but Chan chose to base himself there for the whole of his long life. His late work, which broke radically with his early realist production, is one of the earliest expressions of a local spirit in Hong Kong art, and one of the first indications of a move beyond the Chinese national framework which preoccupied New Ink Painting. Like other more recent art discussed in this study, it has little in common with earlier Hong Kong work – even though it was created by an artist who had himself been participating in local artistic life since the 1930s.

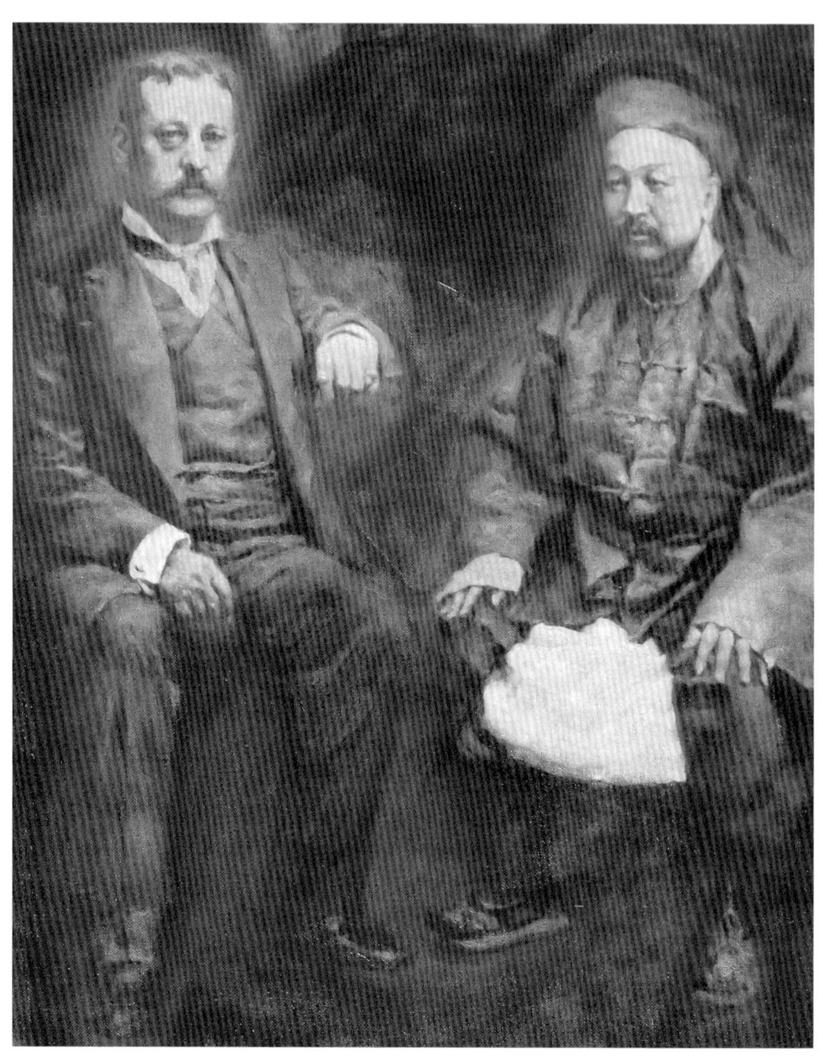

1 Detail of illus. 35.

1 Varieties of Cultural Hybridity

Both Western modernist and Chinese traditionalist cultural narratives have been active in Hong Kong cultural space. While there have been individuals who have attempted to adhere to one or the other, many ambitious artists seem to have felt that neither narrative could simply be dismissed. They apparently recognized that to ignore an increasingly internationalized art world in which Western definitions of the modern or contemporary were hegemonic would have meant condemning themselves to marginality, while to embrace Western modernism without equivocation would have meant running the risk of losing a sense of their own cultural identity, of appearing to be mere mimics or belated followers of Western trends. Hybrid art has been the consequence of this dilemma, and artists such as Lui Shou-kwan and Van Lau made an explicit relationship in their works to both the narrative of Western modernism and that of Chinese traditional culture, even though they are irreconcilable. The problem challenging these artists was to make both narratives legible to the spectator, but at the same time to prevent their incompatibility from becoming apparent, lest their work failed to hold together and the task of becoming an artist who was both 'modern' and 'Chinese' appeared impossible to achieve.

At a time when the notion of hybridity is being much explored in critical theory and given largely positive associations, it is valuable to note how problematic hybrid art works can be.[1] The following discussion shows how certain consciously hybrid works produced in Hong Kong anxiously attempt to reconcile the incompatible. It also seeks to demonstrate that hybridity can collude with the notion of cultural essence, which it is often taken to be undermining. The work of Wucius Wong rather than Lui Shou-kwan or Van Lau will serve to represent the first generation of artists in Hong Kong to attempt to create a consciously modernist art. Wong's work is particularly worthy of examination since he is more willing to acknowledge visually the incompatibility between Western modernist and Chinese traditionalist narratives.

Although Wong and other artists of his generation seemed to want to hold on to both narratives, there was a later moment when both of them began to fall into disrepute. Luis Chan and Antonio Mak, artists from very different age groups, attained their maturity in this moment. Neither Chan nor Mak attempted to find a space outside the dominant narratives; both seemed to recognize that these were too powerful simply to be ignored. Nevertheless, neither artist seemed to take either narrative seriously, and both may be viewed as having produced works which are at least implicitly critical of those Hong Kong artists who do. The art of Chan and Mak is also hybrid in nature, but differs from that of Wong or Lui in that it happily erodes both of the narratives with which it engages instead of attempting to uphold them. Chan and Mak, although their solutions were different, can each be said to have produced art that makes a Hong Kong viewpoint possible. Taking elements from both cultural narratives, but without being in thrall to either, they produced a variety of hybrid art with greater liberatory potential – one that helped to create a more explicitly local cultural space.

In juxtaposing the work of Chan and Mak with that of Wong, we can identify differences and even antagonisms between various artistic phenomena to which the term *hybrid* might be applied, and thus highlight some dangers in the indiscriminate or blanket use of the term. Hong Kong paintings and sculptures invite scepticism about the notion of hybridity, and in such a particular, relatively defined cultural and historical context we can see more clearly how hybrid artworks function. The cultural narratives which artists employ are not wholly given to them: at a certain level, they choose to engage with those narratives in their work, and for particular purposes. Nevertheless, artists do always find themselves in cultural or discursive landscapes that are largely not of their own making. A particular cultural locus may only sustain certain strategies of hybridity at any one time. This at any rate seems to have been the case in Hong Kong, with the emergence of Wong's hybrid style belonging to the moment of modernism's appearance in Hong Kong visual culture, while Chan and Mak's emergence as mature artists belonged to the post-modern moment. While the two moments might for the sake of convenience be characterized as 'modern' and 'post-modern', they should not be conceived in narrowly artistic terms, but rather as moments of broader cultural change, even as moments when the colonial government underwent crises of legitimation.

The broader preconditions for these two moments are alluded to in the pages that follow and are also explored here in a schematic way. The first moment was arguably precipitated by the development of Hong Kong's manufacturing sector, giving rise, for instance, to a heightened sense of inequalities, but also leading to a greater openness to external intellectual and cultural frames of reference. The vast influx of refugees in the post-war period was also a destabilizing factor.

Demographically, the second moment occurred when the children of those refugees reached adulthood, constituting a generation that took Hong Kong as its horizon and knew China only as a foreign country, the border having been closed by that time.[2] Political factors that helped to precipitate this second moment were the Sino-British Joint Declaration on the Future of Hong Kong of 1984 (which set the clock running for the handover of the territory to China) and the brutal crackdown of the Beijing student democracy movement in 1989 (which intensified fears over 1997). Concern for cultural identity in art since that time has been paralleled by political demands for greater local democracy.

Wucius Wong

Wucius Wong seems to feel caught between an allegiance to Western modernism and one to Chinese tradition, wishing in some sense to affirm both. Rather than allowing his work to suffer from his inability to harmonize these two conflicting narratives, however, Wong takes some degree of control over his situation by making opposition the theme of his work. The conflict is not resolved by this decision, but is at least given expression, dramatized.

In a work such as *Cloud Harmony No. 1* (illus. 2), Wong shows his desire to retain a link to Chinese cultural narratives by his adoption of a hanging-scroll format, but also, more directly, by his reference to the misty-mountain subject matter of classical Chinese painting. Whereas Lui Shou-kwan and his followers in the Hong Kong New Ink Painting movement made use of Chinese ink and absorbent paper, thereby producing works that claim an allegiance to traditional Chinese technique, Wong has commonly used acrylic. Subject matter thus becomes the primary site where Chineseness is signified in his painting. The sculptor Van Lau, working in metal and thus unable to effect links at the level of technique to literati culture, is similarly constrained to signify Chineseness through subject matter. He does this, for instance, in his sculptures on the theme of bamboo (such as *Windy Form* and *Autumn Leaves* [both 1985]), executed in a manner indebted to the Constructivists of the West (illus. 3).

For Wong, unlike a straightforward traditionalist artist, a mere declaration of allegiance to literati modes is not enough: Chinese references must be counterbalanced by signs of modernity. Such claims to contemporaneity are made by the introduction of a grid-like structure which serves to partition the surface of the image. Wong would have encountered this Constructivist vocabulary (also found in more recent

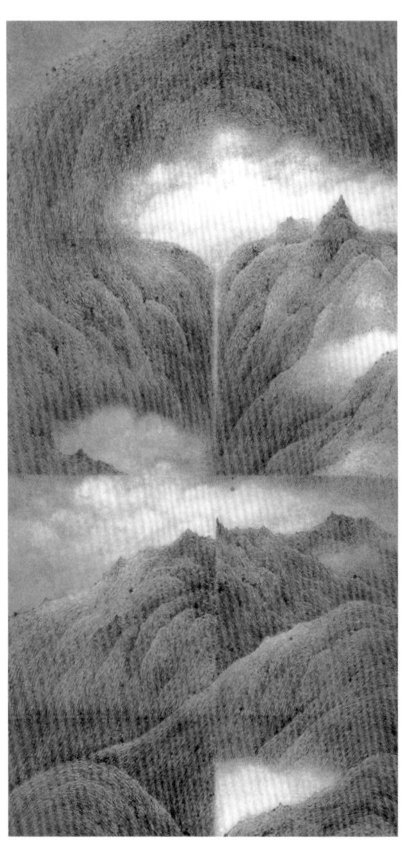

2 Wucius Wong, *Cloud Harmony No. 1*, 1978, ink and colour on paper. Hong Kong Museum of Art.

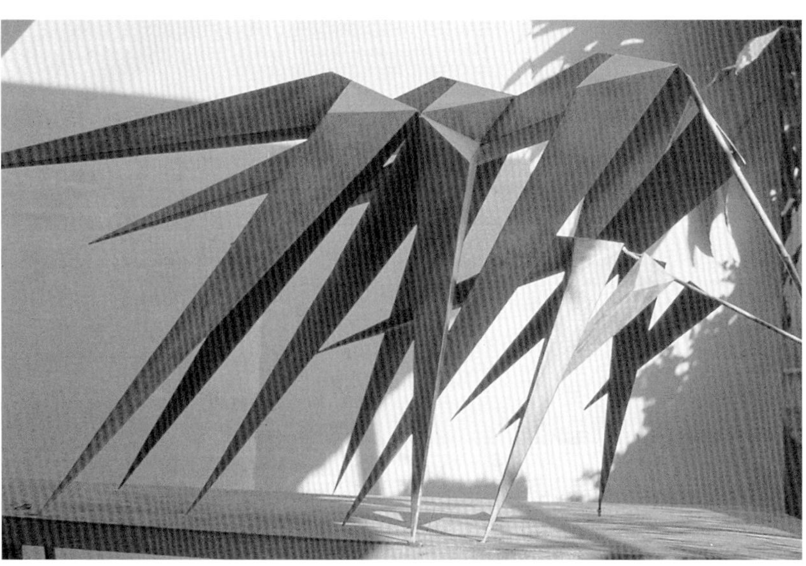

3 Van Lau, *Autumn Leaves*, 1985, bronze. Hong Kong Museum of Art.

paintings such as *Agitated Waters No. 5* [1989]) through his involvement with design. Wong worked at one time as a lecturer at the design school of Hong Kong Polytechnic (now Hong Kong Polytechnic University), and he is also the author of several widely disseminated manuals on two- and three-dimensional design in which a Bauhaus educational model is presented.

In *Cloud Harmony No. 1*, the organic and the geometric are both present, but each retains a large degree of autonomy. Visual harmony becomes largely a matter of balancing opposing or incommensurable forces. The painting opens up a symbolic arena in which Chinese (traditional) elements and Western (modern) elements are allowed their different voices. In this respect, *Cloud Harmony No. 1* differs from such New Ink Painting works as Lui Shou-kwan's *Zhuangzi* (illus. 4), which also balances these aspects but which wishes to avoid any sense that the modernization of ink painting is a problematic project. In *Zhuangzi*, the allusion to European and American gestural abstraction is meant to be noticed (in order to give the work its claim of contemporaneity), but an attempt is made to play down the differ-

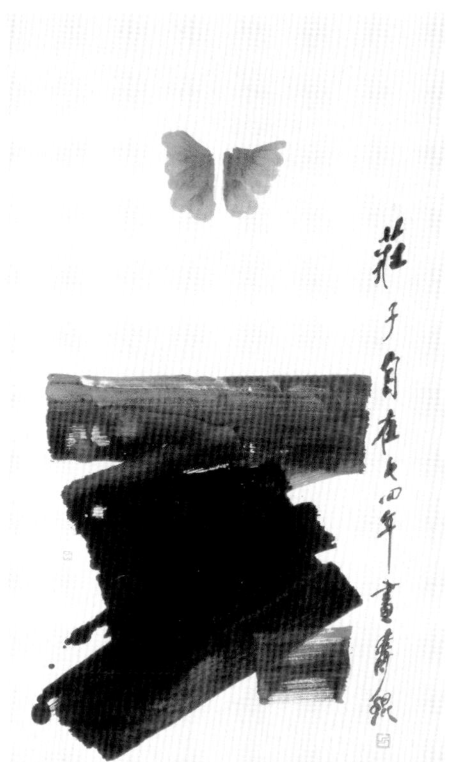

4 Lui Shou-kwan, *Zhuangzi*, 1974, vertical scroll, ink on paper. Hong Kong Museum of Art.

ences between the two cultural narratives invoked, in order to present an aesthetically unified whole. Abstract Expressionism and its European counterpart arguably offered particular possibilities to Chinese artists at the time when it was the most up-to-date signifier of Western modernism available in the international arena, because its gestural nature had superficial similarities with the foregrounded brushwork of classical Chinese painting and calligraphy, and because the Abstract Expressionists were often themselves interested in East Asian brushwork.[3] By choosing a hard-edged formal vocabulary instead of engaging with Abstract Expressionism like his one-time teacher Lui, Wong must have consciously decided to accentuate rather than blur the East/West distinctions in his painting. Geometry, with its associations to rationality and the West, serves there as the 'yang' in opposition to the 'yin' of the organic, the natural and the Chinese.

Although Wong may be understood as producing a kind of muted allegory of the situation of Hong Kong in works such as *Cloud Harmony No. 1*, it is an allegory that tends towards treating the Chinese and the Western as necessary complementary parts of a larger whole. It points away from political and historical frameworks of interpretation towards a metaphysical one. His mode of painting has something of a double-voiced quality, acknowledging difference but ending up reducing both Chinese and Western cultures to (diametrically opposed) essences in a way that is not all that different from the position of the traditionalist. Indeed, China is represented in his paintings only in terms of tradition, modernity always being placed outside Chineseness. Because of this restriction, a rigidity enters: the signs of Chineseness become exaggerated clichés, repetitive caricatures of literati traits. Hybridity proves capable of co-existing with a notion of cultural essence, and even of entrenching it.

Luis Chan

Although Luis Chan developed his mature style at a later date than Lui Shou-kwan (and, indeed, partly as a response to the challenge of such early Hong Kong modernists as Lui), he was a much older man. Chan had already worked for some years in the academic realist manner adopted by a number of other Hong Kong artists of his own generation, such as Lee Byng and Yee Bon.[4] None of these artists appear to have felt any pressing need to forge connections with Chinese cultural traditions, and all were seemingly unaware of Western modernist discourse. Indeed, Chan's early work seems a striking instance of art created within a kind of colonial mentality. Since his mature work offers a radical departure from such a frame of mind, and shares with that of the other artists considered here a certain self-awareness about the cultural situation in which it finds itself, a brief consideration of his earlier work offers a valuable counterpoint.

Luis Chan differed from Wong and Mak in that he did not have any overseas training.[5] Born in Panama in 1905, he moved to Hong Kong in 1910, remaining there until his death in 1995. Apart from a painting trip to Beijing and other mainland Chinese cities in 1936 and a sojourn in Macau during the Japanese occupation, he hardly seems to have left Hong Kong at all. Because of the absence of opportunities for formal art education in the territory (there is no art academy even today), Chan relied on correspondence courses, turning to the colonial power, Britain, as the source of information and standards. *The Studio*, the leading British art magazine of the time, was an important frame of reference for Chan, who was subscribing to it by 1927. The style he developed was a fluent naturalism indebted to British models: he favoured landscape as his subject matter and generally preferred to use watercolour, working directly from nature and paying particular attention to light effects (illus. 5). Although his style of this time can hardly be described as innovative, Chan did achieve a degree of local recognition and status. Not only did he gain some attention from the Hong Kong colonial élite; he even received it from the colonial power itself. Chan must have felt a sense of achievement when in 1954 he wrote an article on his own work and that of other Hong Kong artists for *The Studio*, thereby featuring in the very publication which had given him his initial point of artistic reference.[6] A more official form of British recognition came in 1960, when Chan was invited, along with David Kwok and Zhao Shao'ang, two Chinese media artists, to represent Hong Kong at the British Commonwealth Exhibition in London.

Only a year after this triumph, however, Chan was faced with a catastrophe. His work was excluded from a major exhibition organized at the new Hong Kong City Hall on the grounds that it was 'out of date'. Chan seems to have discovered his marginality as a result of this rejection, his insight into his real situation as a colonial artist leading to a loss of artistic security. For a great part of the 1960s, his art was in crisis: one modern style after another appeared in the work of an artist who had once seemed so confident about his way of painting, but none was able to provide a stable basis for a distinctive individual idiom. Once naturalism was no longer acceptable, the issue of style was inevitably foregrounded, but there seemed to be no criteria Chan could adopt to choose among the plethora of possible artistic identities. While not all works of this period are failures, one senses that Chan

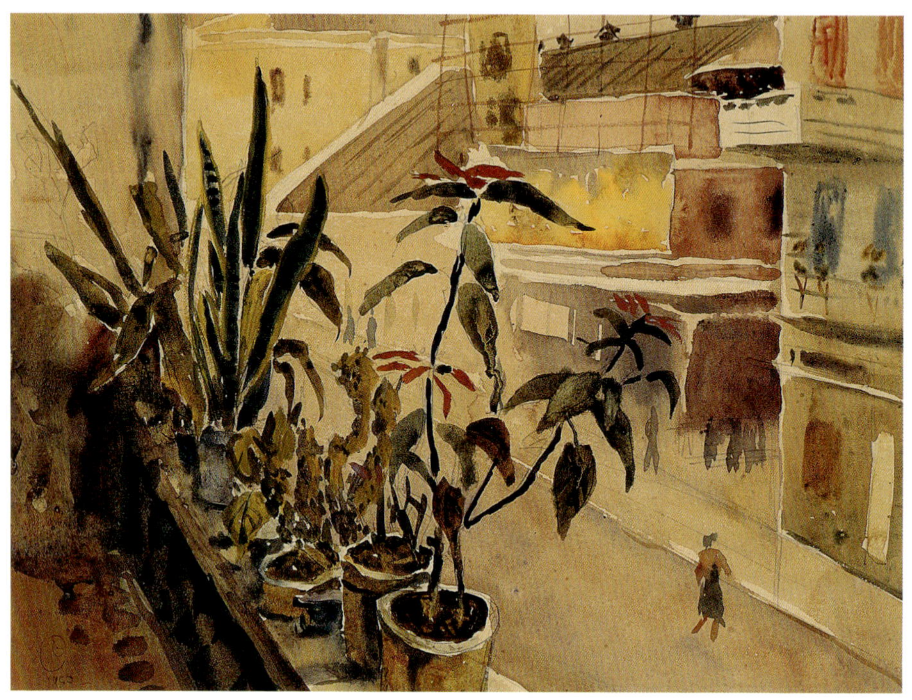

5 Luis Chan, *The Theatre, Kowloon City*, 1950, watercolour on paper. Private collection.

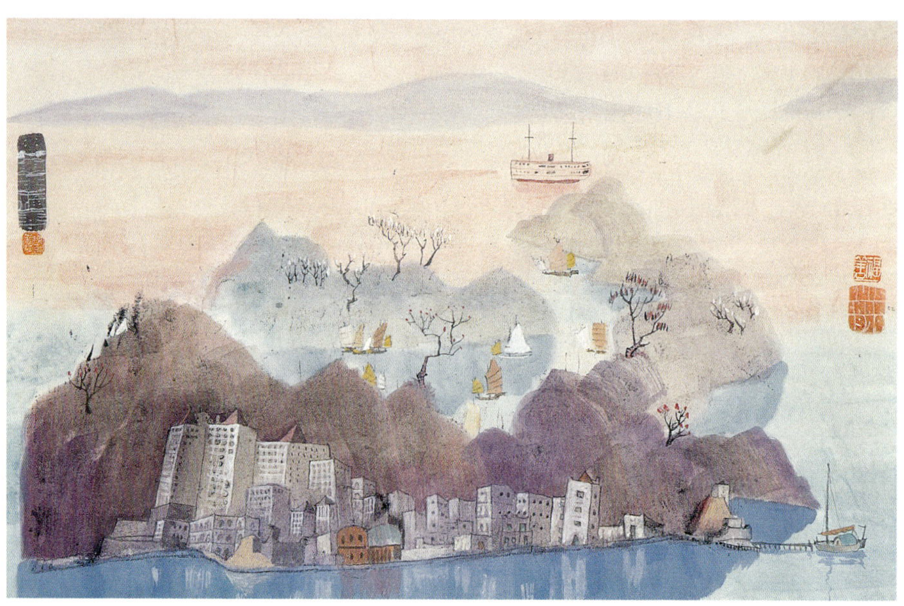

6 Luis Chan, *City by the Sea*, 1974, water-based media on paper. Collection Hanart TZ Gallery, Hong Kong.

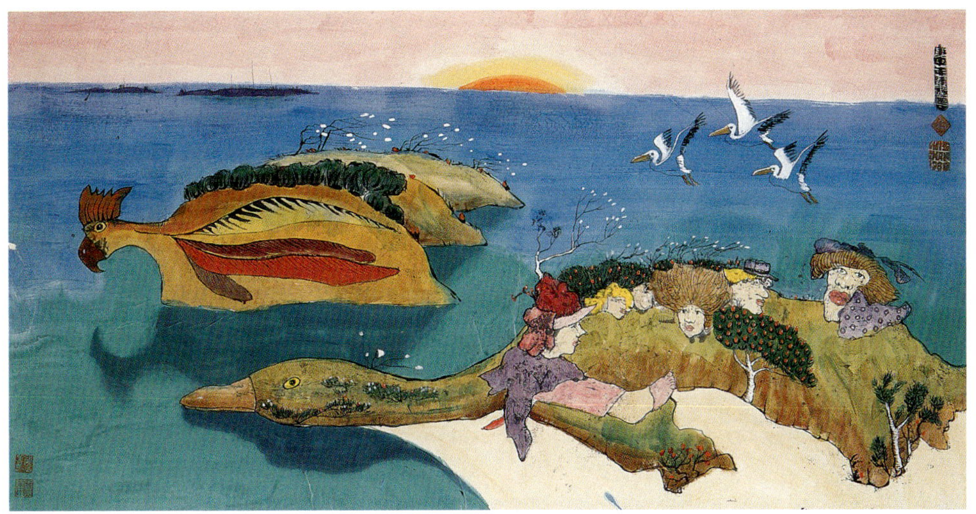

7 Luis Chan, *Duck and Rooster Island*, 1980, water-based media on paper. Collection Hanart TZ Gallery, Hong Kong.

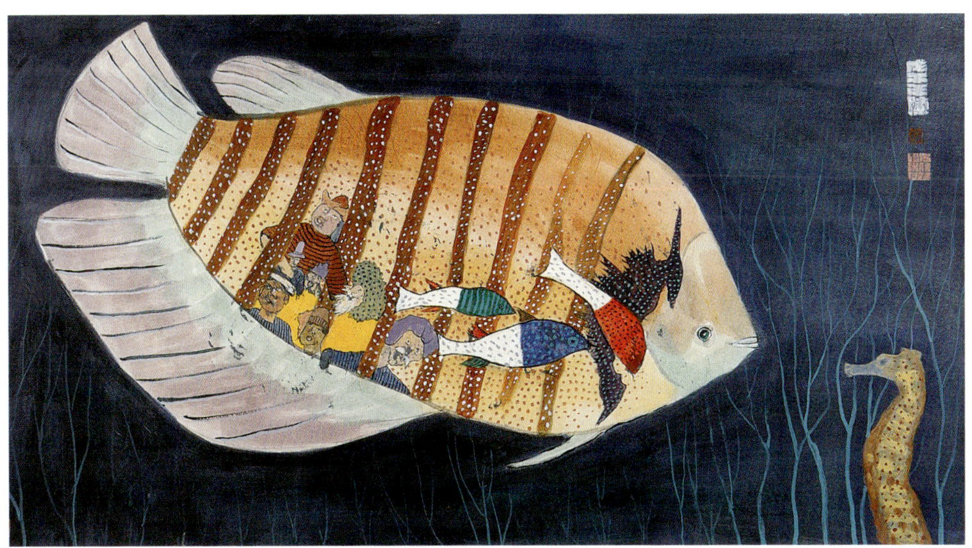

8 Luis Chan, *Seahorse Meeting a Fish*, water-based media on paper. Collection Hanart TZ Gallery, Hong Kong.

was playing with styles he did not fully understand: Cubist or Pointillist idioms, for instance, are present in a partial and largely decorative way, the artist having been condemned to the role of mimic.

Chan was to find a way of coming to terms with his marginality in relation to Western modernism after seeing a demonstration of monotype technique by the French artist Jacques Halpern. Halpern seems to have favoured a non-geometric abstract idiom of an *art informel* kind, but it is perhaps important that Chan did not chose to imitate his style. Discovery of an automatist method of working was more important to Chan than the encounter with abstraction, since it provided him with a specific technique for initiating a dialogue with the unconscious. His new works may have started as abstract pattern-making, but this was followed by a crucial second phase in which he studied the marks produced with the assistance of chance. Illusory images were found in them which were then further specified. This fantasy art has much in common with the *decalcomania* technique employed by Max Ernst in paintings such as *Europe After the Rain II* (1940–42) or Henri Michaux's ink experiments (of which Chan as an extremely well-read artist was certainly aware), but only at the level of method. At the level of content, they are highly original, and no longer in the shadow of Western modernist examples: in the seventh decade of his life, Chan had finally discovered his 'mature' style.

Landscape predominates in these works, as it had done in Chan's earlier paintings, and water is frequently to be seen. Although we no longer find exact topographical description, it is still possible to recognize in a work such as *City by the Sea* (illus. 6) the island and sea topography of Hong Kong, rather than the mountain and river landscape of the Chinese heartland favoured by traditional ink painting. The animal, vegetal and mineral realms are no longer distinct. Faces may appear in rocks (*Peach Garden* [1977]), or islands may metamorphose into birds (*Duck and Rooster Island* [illus. 7]). We may be taken underwater to visit a rich and strange world of tropical fish (a recurrent subject for Chan), but then encounter a crowd of human faces as if trapped behind the bars along a fish's side (*Seahorse Meeting a Fish* [illus. 8]). There is much that is visually ravishing (particularly because of Chan's growing confidence as a colourist), and the mood is frequently whimsical, but darker notes do intrude, *Death as a Skater* (1980) and *Execution* (illus. 9) being two examples of this.

References to Chinese mythology may be found on occasion (as in *Rise of the Drowned Poet* [1980]), but while Chan in this phase of his art welcomed inspiration from all sources (Chinese or Western, high or popular), he was never a servant to them. His very openness inoculated

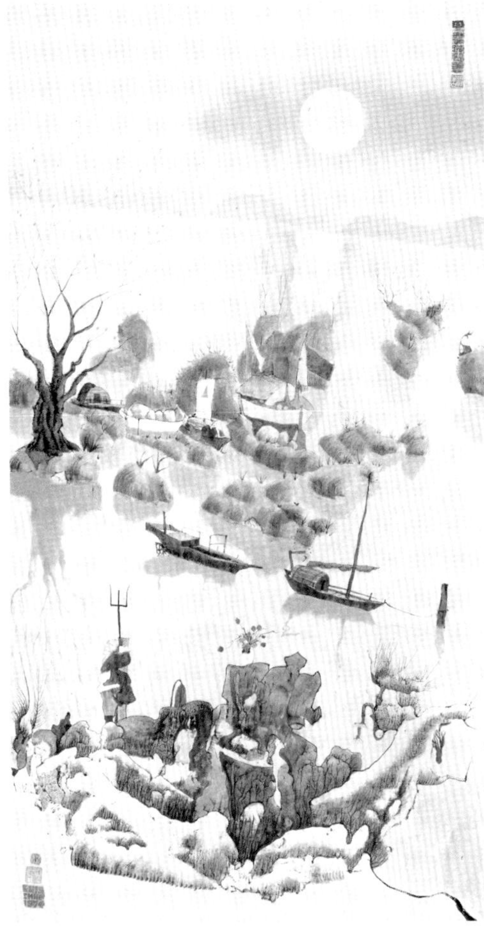

9 Luis Chan, *Execution*, 1974, ink and colour on paper. Hong Kong Museum of Art.

him against the danger of being either a Chinese traditionalist or a provincial imitator of Western modernism, and all sources faced transformation on entering the world of his paintings. *Rise of the Drowned Poet*, for instance, is based on the story of the poet-statesman Chu Yuan, whose drowning is commemorated in early summer by the Dragon Boat Festival. Chan's personal and perhaps even autobiographical reworking of the traditional story introduces the theme of rebirth.

Whereas his earlier works showed no relationship at all to premodern Chinese painting, Chan was now willing to adopt both hanging-scroll and handscroll formats on occasion, referring to such works as his 'modern Chinese paintings'.[7] His lack of hang-ups about tradition (unlike Wong or Lui, he seems not to have been anxious about the difficulties of being both Chinese and modern) is revealed in his matter-of-fact statement that a painting by him was Chinese if it had been done on Chinese paper. Lui's *Zhuangzi* anxiously counterbalances its engagement with the modernism of Adolph Gottlieb and Pierre Soulages by a reference to a traditionally sanctioned Chinese text in which the philosopher of the title dreams of being a butterfly. When Chan produced a work on the same theme (*Butterfly Dream* [1986]), his approach was recognizably more playful and accepting of heterogeneity. In a work that must surely have been undertaken with the intention of conducting a dialogue with Lui's, Chan employed both collage (his butterfly is a real one) and a pouring technique which clearly invokes Jackson Pollock (like Lui, Chan brought together Chinese and Abstract Expressionist influences, but whereas Lui sinicized the reference to Abstract Expressionism by rendering it in Chinese ink, Chan left his quotation in a Western medium). This Pollock-like pouring appears in other works by Chan and is used in an uninhibited way without worry over what meaning the technique might have had in its original context. Letting his unconscious be the guide to what may be given meaning in his own work, the skeins of paint start to suggest faces, and circles are added to indicate eyes (*Untitled* [1987]). The theme of transformation in the *Zhuangzi* text is embodied by Chan even at the level of creative method. Although his treatment may initially appear less reverential than Lui's, Chan perhaps displayed a deeper engagement with their shared textual source.

Chan not only appropriated or resignified elements of the stylistic vocabulary of other artists in his own work, he also seemed to be doing something similar when in the role of spectator. He talked for instance of the possibility of seeing illusory images of people or creatures in the paintings of Cézanne and Zhang Daqian. The traces of this very idiosyncratic mode of reception can be seen on the copies of the art magazines to which he subscribed: often a face had been 'discovered' in an image, and specified by a ballpoint pen mark. Even the austere abstract paintings of Kenneth Noland were given this treatment. Far more than most Western artists of the same period, he relied on reproductions for information, but the subservient attitude towards Western sources adopted in his early years had now manifestly disappeared. His relationship to them became more active and confident, as his graffiti-like additions to the magazine illustrations attest. Rather than treating them as role models, he offered them up to his unconscious as raw material, interpreting them from his own (Hong Kong) viewpoint.

As well as effortlessly incorporating elements from both Chinese and

Western high art traditions, Chan also found a place for references to popular culture. In addition to his life-long interest in art magazines, Chan turned to television for inspiration in his later phase. 'I still do life studies – I watch T.V.!' he once quipped in answer to an interviewer's question. Both political figures and fictional characters from television entered his paintings, but only if his unconscious found their presence appropriate. At a time when television was giving a lot of coverage to events in the Middle East, Chan was surprised to discover 'the figure of Arafat boxed in the corner of a half-finished painting' (*Magic Carpet* [1981]).

Another media event which found its way into a painting was the Silver Jubilee celebration for Queen Elizabeth II of England (*H.M. Queen Elizabeth's Silver Jubilee* [1977]). The monarch's head appears as a collage item (on Hong Kong-issue stamps attached to the painting's surface), and the British Union Jack – in black and red rather than red, white and blue – is also included. What at first might appear to be an act of homage in fact turns out to be a gently subversive statement about the colony's mother country. Gentle, perhaps, because (after all) Britain had been the most important source of cultural information in Chan's early years as an artist, and because his growing autonomy as a painter permitted a degree of magnanimity that might not have prevailed had he failed to transcend his earlier state of cultural provincialism. Having decolonized his psyche, Luis Chan could look more with humour than with anger at the signifiers of colonial power.

Antonio Mak

By the time of his tragic early death in 1994, Antonio Mak had created an extensive body of sculpture, working primarily in bronze cast from wax originals. The human figure was his principal subject (with animals such as horses and tigers also being of great interest), and the style in which he worked owed more to Rodin (and indeed to even earlier sculptural traditions) than it did to contemporary trends. Undertaking his studies at a later date than Wong, Mak seems to have been aware that the Western narrative of modernist progress was losing its credibility. So, although he used a recognizably Western visual language, he therefore chose not to make a futile attempt to be more up to the minute than artists being fêted in Western metropolitan centres. His relatively 'old-fashioned' idiom was put to the service of an acute intellect; one might see him as a sort of conceptual artist. Marcel Duchamp and Bruce Nauman were both artists to whom Mak responded positively, as was René Magritte, the most conceptual of the painters associated with Surrealism.

Although he did not represent Hong Kong subjects directly or promote Hong Kong cultural identity in any positive sense, Mak's art can be said to offer a Hong Kong viewpoint. This is achieved by the ironic, distanced way in which he made references to both Western and Chinese culture – often both within the same work. These two great cultural influences were quoted by Mak (rather than simply employed); he even treated the issue of their interaction (oppositions of various kinds being a key theme in his work). Most other Hong Kong artists who seek to make use of both Western and Chinese references seem concerned to bring them into harmony (Wong's *Cloud Harmony No. 1* and Lui's *Zhuangzi* have already been discussed), but Mak emphasized disparities. It is extremely common to describe Hong Kong as the place where 'East meets West'; this cliché reduces the place to a mere gateway or bridge through or over which Chinese and Western influences pass, denying it any separate identity. Rather than illustrating this well-worn notion, Mak seemed determined to undermine or expose it. In his work, Hong Kong gained a measure of autonomy as the site where incredulity towards grand narratives from elsewhere was allowed to develop. Irony opened up a space.

Verbal associations (either made in the title or alluded to in other ways) are important to Mak's art and offer one of the means by which

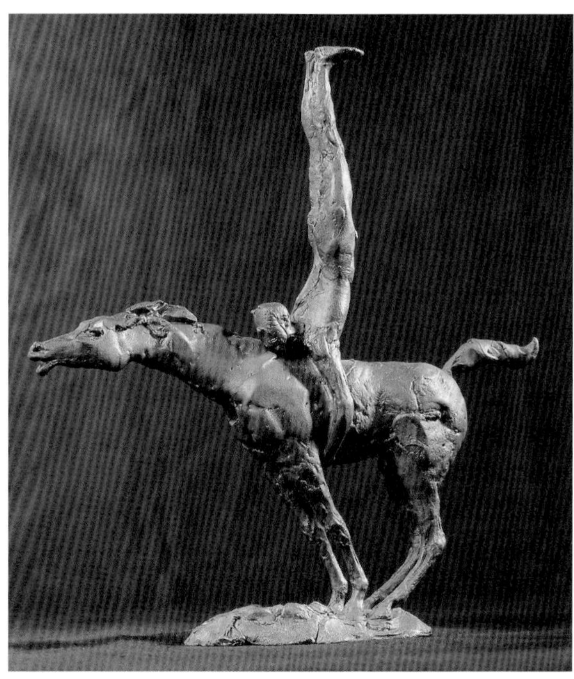

10 Antonio Mak, *Horse Lover Goes West*, 1992, bronze. Private collection.

his ironic perspective is developed. Both Chinese and Western (that is, English) verbal associations may exist within the same work, an example being *Horse Lover Goes West* (illus. 10). This title seems to point us towards an Occidental interpretation of the sculpture or, more specifically, an American one: 'Go West young man.' The Western reference in the title is confirmed by the visual evidence of the sculpture: a horse is a key prop of the Wild West lifestyle (at least as it is depicted in movies). In terms of artistic reference, one thinks of the tacky horse paintings and sculptures of Frederic Remington, Charles Marion Russell and their followers, all propagators of the cowboy myth.

Despite the strong gesture this work seems to be making towards the West, there is also a contradictory signposting towards the East. The Chinese version of its title (*Mami Xiyouji*) brings completely different associations into play, *Xiyouji* being the Chinese title of the literary classic *Journey to the West*. In the gap between these narratives, local Hong Kong meanings of a less exalted nature are allowed to develop. To a Hong Kong Cantonese speaker, the characters rendered as *xiyou* in Putonghua (the standard pronunciation of Chinese used on the mainland) evoke a colloquial phrase that specifies bullshitting, the telling of fanciful stories. Given the context of horses and horse lovers, we might be correct in imagining a reference to the many fans of racing

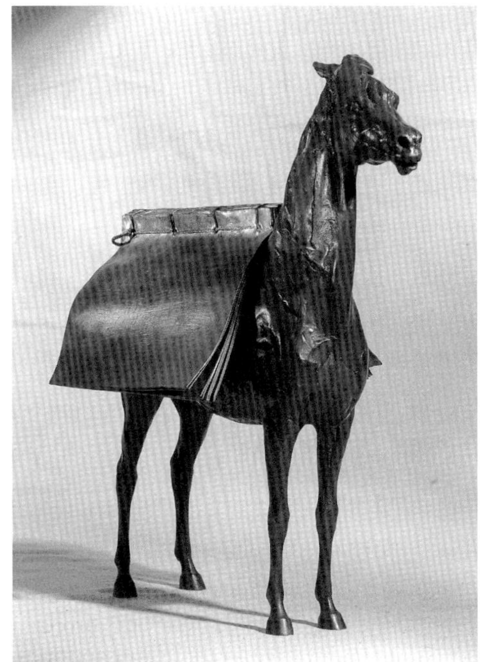

11 Antonio Mak, *Bible from Happy Valley*, 1992, bronze and lead. Collection Susan Fong.

in Hong Kong. Mak himself grew up near the racetrack in Happy Valley and referred to that location in another work, *Bible from Happy Valley* (illus. 11), which also represents a horse. In this case, the bronze horse has an open book made of lead on its back in place of a rider. The verbal dimension that is so often an important part of Mak's work helps us to come to terms with the incongruity of this combination of elements, although in this case the title gives only an oblique clue. It points us to the racetrack, and to betting, and thus to bookmakers, who *keep books on horses*. We are still in the world of *Horse Lover Goes West*: the pages of the book are arranged over the horse's back rather like wings, but by using lead as his material Mak seems to have wanted to mock the grand dreams of gamblers. Flight will never be possible: this Pegasus (a literary or 'bookish' horse) is being brought down to earth. Verbal associations underline the point: in both Cantonese and Putonghua, the verb used to describe losing at gambling has exactly the same sound as that of the word *book*. For this reason, in fact, superstitious Hong Kong Cantonese gamblers use an alternate term when referring to form books, which Mak has referenced by its common English translation 'bible'. This particular homophony between the words *book* and *lose* leads to other verbal avoidance and punning by Cantonese speakers as well.[8]

Attempts to juxtapose Chinese and Western references within the same work occurred as early as 1972. *West meets East* (illus. 12), a large collage from that year, has as its central image a photo of Richard Nixon shaking hands with Chairman Mao on the occasion of his then recent ground-breaking visit to China. In choosing such an image, Mak was denying the depoliticized framework in which the 'meeting of East and West' was generally presented in colonial Hong Kong, and his reversal of the order in which the two compass points are usually paired verbally was another signal that he wished to disrupt clichéd thinking. A further reversal in this work helps to hint at Mak's cynicism concerning the historic meeting of opposites he was depicting: Mao the leftist appears on the right of the photo, while the rightist Nixon is shown on the left. Apparent opposites can actually be on the *same side*, Mak seems to have been suggesting: 'Tricky Dick' may have been a *dexterous* or *adroit* politician, but *on the other hand* that Vietnam War-era President had his *sinister* side.

Colonial Hong Kong might have been the ideal place to see through both American free-world rhetoric and its Maoist counterpart, and Mak continued to make reference to the encounter between Communism and capitalism, albeit obliquely. Several of his sculptures of tigers and men can be read as allegories of that subject. *Last Tango With*

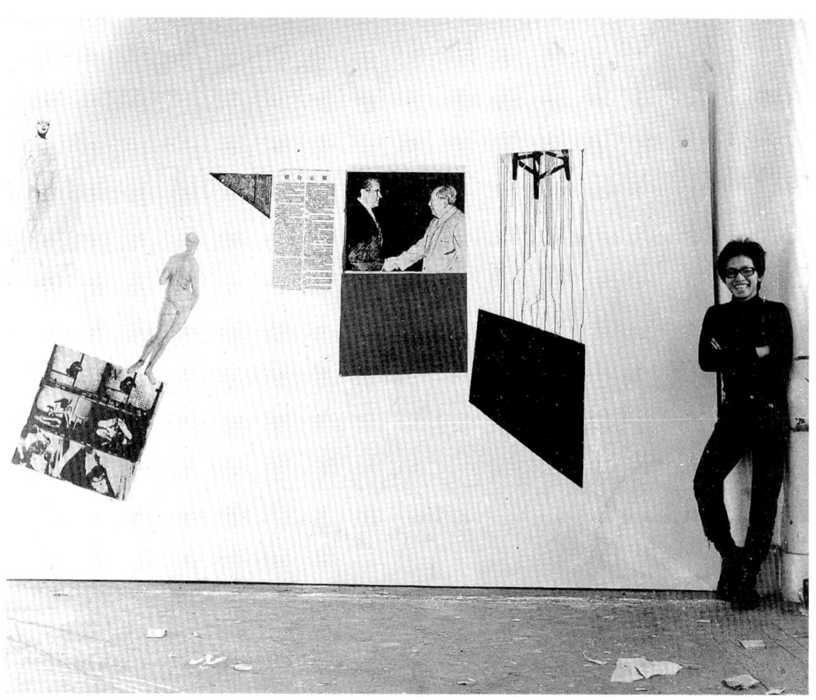

12 Antonio Mak, *West meets East*, 1972, collage. Presumed destroyed.

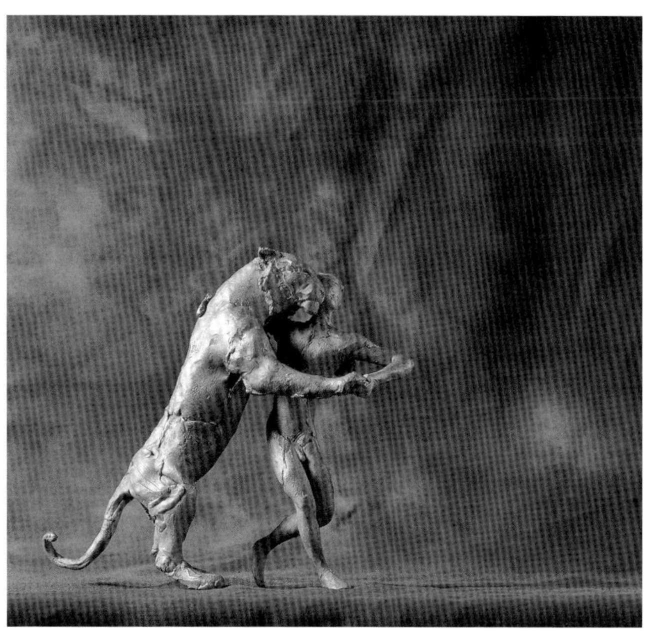

13 Antonio Mak, *Last Tango With Tiger*, 1993, bronze.
Private collection.

Tiger (illus. 13), for instance, shows a man dancing with a tiger, and seems to represent those businessmen and others in capitalist Hong Kong who have so assiduously courted the Communist Chinese government in the period since the 1984 Joint Declaration agreeing Hong Kong's return to Chinese sovereignty. 'That guy is really in trouble, but he doesn't know it' was Mak's own comment on this work: a tiger is unlikely to sustain such behaviour as dancing on its hind legs for long before its own nature reasserts itself, so the human is deeply mistaken if he thinks he is in control of the situation. As the title indicates, the dancing will soon be over, and then what? Mak was aware of a Chinese saying that compares serving a ruler to serving a tiger, in that they both might harm you; and our dancer faces a similar danger. This, after all, is no paper tiger.

Sleepwalker II (illus. 14) can also be read as a political allegory. Again, the tiger seems to represent China, and the work as a whole

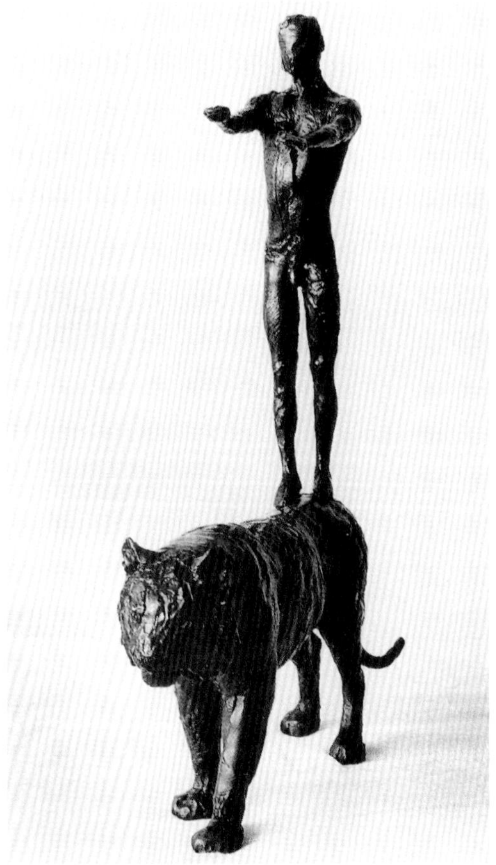

14 Antonio Mak, *Sleepwalker II*, 1991, bronze. Collection Susan Fong.

seems a meditation on Hong Kong's relation to it in the run-up to the 1997 handover. The formula 'one country, two systems' (which described the supposed relationship between the post-handover Hong Kong Special Administrative Region and the rest of the People's Republic, and which was much-promulgated between 1984 and 1997) was apparently being invoked, but ironically. The peaceful co-existence of opposites is a precarious one, made possible by the lack of wakefulness in the figure on the tiger's back. About this work Mak commented: 'So long as he doesn't wake up he'll be all right.' But can sleepwalking really be a positive thing, even if it shields us from realities?[9] Since the somnambulist as well as the tiger is in forward motion, it looks as if he is going to fall off the front of his mount, in which case his protective sleep will surely come to an end. The moment of waking seems already to have arrived in *Good Morning II* (1993). Here, the outstretched arms, albeit similar to those of a sleepwalker, and reminiscent of a diver about to take the plunge, seem (because of the context given by the title) to refer to someone stretching in order to throw off the drowsiness of the night.

In *Heaven and Hell*, an installation piece of 1993, Mak again explored his interest in the theme of opposites. He made use of a mirror, an element that had appeared in many of his earlier sculptural pieces, in part because of the way in which reflections offer opportunities for treatment of the theme of opposition. Mak combined the mirror with a flight of steps, another frequently utilized element, which like the mirror can symbolize a threshold to another realm. *Heaven and Hell* is set into the ground, the steps leading down to a mirrored surface set at an angle, in which the viewer's reflection becomes visible. In an earlier work, *Inside Out* (1974–82), a human figure appears to be walking into the illusory space of the mirror at the same time as a figure from within the mirror walks out (part of the bronze section of the sculpture represents the 'penetrating' figure, part the 'emerging' one). In *Heaven and Hell*, however, the spectator takes the place of the figure moving to meet its double in the mirror.

Because of the steps, the oppositions offered by the mirror are supplemented by an opposition between up and down (the directions metaphorically associated with Heaven and Hell). But because of the possibilities of the mirror there is a reversal, and in walking down into the work we seem to be descending into the (reflected) sky, rather than into the earth. We can interpret this as a statement about the unstable nature of the relationship between opposites, a reading that could gain support from a consideration of *Root* (1990). That sculpture also seems concerned with a confusion or similarity between opposites, specifically between the roots and branches of a tree, which are represented as more or less indistinguishable.

From a certain angle of approach, one has the strong illusion in *Heaven and Hell* of a doorway below ground level leading to an unbounded empty space. Steps lead down into what seems to be a void that has been discovered below the earth's surface. The strength of this illusion is tempered only when one gets close enough for one's own reflection to appear, thus identifying the plane of the mirror's surface and laying bare the mechanics of the work. Mak, if he does offer an intimation of the numinous, is quick to undermine it, and perhaps the whole notion of walking down towards heaven could be read in a similarly ironic way as a comment on human delusions. We are being quite literally brought down to earth, and this happens at the very same moment as we appear to ascend into the heavens. Metaphysical pretensions may be being deflated here, but so, one feels, are all kinds of utopian thought. Grand narratives of progress are being thrown into doubt, whether they offer an artistic Holy Grail of formal purity and autonomy, or a social or material paradise to be attained if we could only make one 'great leap forward'.

Because of its title, we may be led to see an influence from William Blake's *The Marriage of Heaven and Hell* on Mak's installation piece. The theme of contraries is treated explicitly in Blake's text, which tells us to accept them as necessary to human existence. 'Without contraries is no progression' is one statement of this principle in the poem, which also asserts that 'opposition is true friendship'. If one wanted to, one could find further resonances between Blake's text and Mak's *Heaven and Hell*: the artist's opening up of an illusory void beneath the earth could be related to Blake's lines about 'melting apparent surfaces away, and displaying the infinite which was hid', as well as to the passage where the narrating voice describes being led through a cavern by an angel until 'a void boundless as a nether sky appear'd beneath us'.

As with so much else in Mak's art, however, one can also find a Chinese dimension to *Heaven and Hell*: the notion of yin and yang as dynamically interacting polarities underlying all phenomena is at least as valuable a source for the idea of complementaries as anything Blake could offer. This Chinese philosophical source, which Mak was happy to acknowledge, is perhaps most clearly influential on *Walking Figure I* (1977), a body constructed of two separate elements which intertwine (like the dark and light areas of the yin/yang diagram) to create a whole. Since in *Walking Figure I*, the right side of the head is linked to the left side of the torso (and vice versa), one is also reminded of the

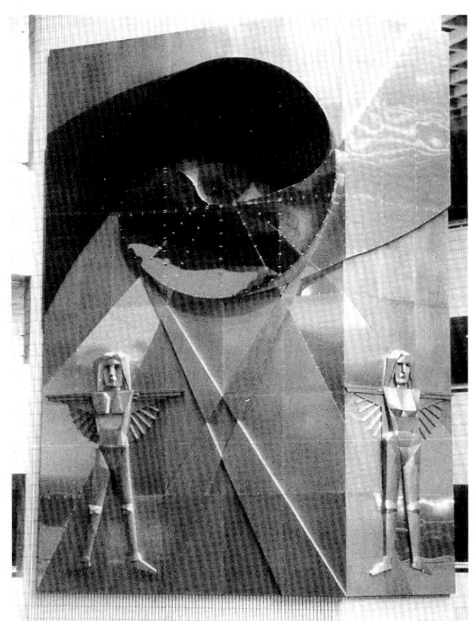

15 Van Lau, *The Meeting of Yin and Yang*, 1989, metallic sculptural relief. Property of the Hong Kong Special Administrative Region Government, installed in the Hong Kong Cultural Centre.

discovery that the two sides of our bodies are controlled by the opposite sides of our brains: a reversal and an opposition built into our biological hardware.

Useful as it is to note the culturally diverse range of sources employed by Mak, a mere cataloguing of them is insufficient and may even be misleading. What is crucial is the work he has done on his sources in *Heaven and Hell*. Rather than merely being 'influenced by' Blake, Mak offered a commentary on him (as much as Blake himself offered one on Dante and the other authors he chose to illustrate). Again, Mak was invoking both Western and Chinese culture while marking a degree of distance from both. He refused to reconcile opposites by treating them as binary essences. Opposites were not necessary parts of a metaphysical whole, but rather differences which could not be reconciled, yet which might collapse into sameness.

Mak's concern with the theme of opposition, and the particular position he took regarding it, must be seen as (in part at least) a critical, parodic response to the way in which other Hong Kong artists have treated the theme. A concern with the doctrine of yin/yang, for instance, can be found in a great number of works by first-generation Hong Kong modernists, including Irene Chou, Hon Chi-fun, Aries Lee and Van Lau. In the works of many such artists, it functions as a 'traditional' reference, a compensatory invocation of Chinese culture at the level of subject matter in paintings and sculptures that are deeply involved with Western modernism at the level of style. In certain works, however, the notion of yin/yang seems to be used as a way of thinking about that complex question of East/West interaction itself, offering a comforting philosophical framework in which to think about the potentially troublesome issue of the clash between cultural narratives. In Van Lau's relief for the foyer of the Hong Kong Cultural Centre, *The Meeting of Yin and Yang* (illus. 15), there even appears to be an attempt to allude to the political aspect of the meeting of China and the West. Depicting male and female figures standing side by side, but not interacting even to the extent of looking at one another, it seems to represent allegorically the 'one country, two systems' motto of the post-Joint Declaration era which Mak's works poke fun at.

Wucius Wong and other artists of his generation (in particular, those of the New Ink Painting tendency, of whom Lui Shou-kwan is the most significant representative) were the first artists in Hong Kong to engage seriously with the project of producing modernist art. Whereas the most interesting artists of the previous (the early Luis Chan, Yee Bon etc.) and younger (represented here by Antonio Mak) generations worked mainly in Western media, taking their primary conceptual framework from the West, Wong and the artists of the middle generation tended to make Chinese culture their principal frame of reference. Their project of modernization became problematic because they were never willing to critique the image they had of that culture, instead merely juxtaposing signifiers of the Western and modern to those of Chineseness. There is no point of purchase within their work for an interrogation of tradition, which survives unchallenged – and possibly even intensified in order to anxiously counterbalance the Western references. I see Wong's misty-mountain subject matter or Van Lau's choice of bamboo as a subject for his sculptures as examples of this desire to claim a cultural rootedness.

Tradition, often synonymous in everyday parlance with the past, is really only a modern way of looking at it, a kind of perspectival image of the past on the two-dimensional surface of the present. Despite appearances to the contrary, traditionalists (as well as artists like Wong who wish to preserve tradition in tandem with modernity) actually prevent us from investigating and recovering the past in new and meaningful ways. A precondition for such an investigation would be an awareness of the autonomy and heterogeneity of the past, of the absence of any cultural essence which continues in existence over time.

One can only begin to critique notions of tradition when one is able to see supposedly traditional references as having particular present meanings and functions. Bamboo may have been a favoured subject of literati painters, symbolizing (because of the way in which it combines flexibility and strength) the virtues to which this social élite aspired, but in Van Lau's sculpture bamboo's primary signification is 'Chineseness'.[10] The same signification can be said to be carried by Wong's mountain landscapes (the presence of 'Western' elements in these images only serves to highlight the fact that this is the case). Such nationalistic meanings predominate in a great deal of 'traditional' art, to the point where we might wish to think of traditionalism as an aspect of the specifically modern phenomenon of nationalism, as the historian Eric Hobsbawm did in his ground-breaking study of the phenomenon.[11] Signs of modernity and of tradition are semiotic acts occurring in the same present tense, although the latter can be characterized as wishing to erase our awareness of their contemporaneity (and thereby gain a spurious authority as inheritors of the past), whereas the former wish to foreground (or to claim) novelty. The kind of sign which is able to signify modernity is constantly changing: at one moment, it may be a reference to the visual language of Abstract Expressionism, at another it may define someone's work as passé because the game has moved on. Tradition, on the other hand, tends to be signified through the investment of new meaning in pre-existing signs. The meaning may be quite radically new, but continuity at the level of the signifier helps to disguise that fact.[12]

In this chapter, the earlier work of Luis Chan has been used to exemplify art that is unaware of any possible conflict between narratives of modernism and tradition. Wucius Wong represents those artists who are aware of a problem and who seek to resolve or manage it symbolically through a form of hybrid art. The later paintings of Chan, and the sculptures of Antonio Mak, have been offered as instances of art that attempts to escape from the binary thinking that plagued artists of Wong's generation. Both also engaged with the art of that generation in their works, albeit obliquely. Mak concerned himself extensively with the theme of opposites, but did so more consciously and playfully than Wong, and ended up both unexpectedly deflating oppositions and exacerbating them until they become unmanageable difference. Chineseness is not merely represented in terms of the past in his work – and since China is thought of as Mao as much as Tao, the political is not excluded from consideration. Mak's conceptual response (a move towards greater artistic self-consciousness) was quite different from that of Chan, who turned instead to the unconscious as a resource for moving beyond the East/West dilemma. Instead of an anxious search for signifiers of ever-greater modernity, Chan let the unconscious work in its own way on material taken from a variety of sources, high and low, Chinese and Western. Elements prised from the grand narratives of both (Western) modernism and (Chinese) tradition can still be identified in his images, but transformed by fantasy. There is heterogeneity, but the strong unconscious element to the creative process ensures some degree of psychic resolution. In different ways, both Mak and Chan made use of a kind of active playfulness to open up a Hong Kong position.

The cultural construction of such a position tends always to be fragile or tentative, as the cases of Chan and Mak show. Although, as the following chapters will demonstrate, other artists of Mak's generation were also interested in the question of Hong Kong cultural identity – particularly in the years approaching the handing back of the territory to China – they did not find it easy to express that identity in positive terms. Oblique strategies for evoking a sense of the local predominated. Unlike most narratives of identity, Hong Kong-ness cannot draw upon either religious, national or ethnic discourse for support. Indeed, the latter two of this trio (powerful props for the assertion of identity because they can appear as essential truths or natural distinctions) are actively ranged against the narrative of Hong Kong-ness, and in favour of the competing narrative of Chineseness. In the case of Hong Kong, nationalism is a discourse in the service of annexation, not of libera-tion. Hong Kong-ness has as a value its distance from or scepticism about grand narratives – it is a species of rootless, non-essentializing or post-modern identity which might usefully be considered by those concerned with cultural identity politics elsewhere – but it is always in danger of being unable to sustain itself in relation to the more powerful Chinese nationalist narrative to which notions of tradition are allied.

Even during the colonial period, there were attempts to interpellate Hong Kong people as Chinese national subjects, and in the cultural sphere tradition has been one of the masks employed by nationalist ideology. Strong forms of traditionalism, however, have faced difficul-ties in gaining a widespread appeal in Hong Kong, and even official Chinese political rhetoric of the post-Joint Declaration era was expedi-ent enough to acknowledge 'two systems' at the same time as it proclaimed 'one country'. That is, an ideology of hybridity was adopted at the political level as the principle governing Hong Kong's post-handover life, and in the period after 1984 it was actively promoted by the British colonial regime as much as by the Chinese government. Artworks such as Van Lau's previously mentioned *Meeting of Yin and Yang* are its visual expression.

Even prior to the Joint Declaration, in fact, the colonial government had already elevated a somewhat different but not unrelated conception of cultural hybridity to the level of a civic ideology, and since hybridity has often been thought of in cultural theory as being associated with positive values, it is particularly salutary to note this. Wucius Wong's paintings, together with those of Lui Shou-kwan and the other artists of the New Ink Painting movement, are well represented in the collection of the Hong Kong Museum of Art, and figured prominently in both its permanent displays and travelling exhibits during the late colonial era. This institutional privileging occurred because the concern that artists showed for combining the Chinese and the Western (and the apolitical way in which they did so) made it quite a suitable visual culture for a colonial government to promote. After the riots of the late 1960s, old-style colonial policy was given something of a rethink, and a conscious modernity with suitably Chinese trimmings was the result. An image of Hong Kong as a place where 'East meets West' was the perfect veil for the realities of colonial life.[13]

While the hybrid art of Wong, Lui and other artists of their generation was accepted by the cultural institutions of the colonial government as consonant with their aims, the work of artists from Mak's generation was ignored for a long time, and was only reluctantly admitted to institutional space as a consequence of pressure from the arts community, generated primarily through the media.[14] One reason for this institutional exclusion must surely have been that it is a type of hybrid art which offers meanings that are difficult for civic ideology to appropriate. It functions to undermine the very art which that ideology has embraced, and so can be seen as positively injurious to it, as offering a viewpoint from which its closures begin to become visible. Indeed, on occasion Mak even ridiculed the 'one country, two systems' notion in a fairly direct way.

Two varieties of hybrid art, then, which came into being at two different historical moments, can be seen as competing for cultural space in late colonial Hong Kong. This competition, more than just a question of aesthetic rivalry, was also a matter of broader political import. One occasion on which this was made clear even to actors on the Hong Kong political stage was when a commercial gallery, holding an exhibit of Mak's work after his death, invited Zhang Junsheng, Deputy Director of the New China News Agency (China's unofficial embassy in Hong Kong during the colonial period) to be a guest of honour at the exhibition. Zhang accepted, but a news report immediately prior to the occasion pointed out that this instance of capitalists courting Communists was exactly the kind of curious hybridity which works like Mak's *Last Tango With Tiger* were making fun of. No doubt made aware of the report, Zhang never turned up for his engagement.[15]

2 Living in the Shadow of the Future

The 1997 reunification of Hong Kong and China was clearly an occasion of some historical importance. As such, it offers a useful opportunity to study the response of artists to a major socio-political event. Such investigations have been conducted before, but they have tended to be studies of events more distant in time, about which documentary evidence is more scarce. T. J. Clark's study of Courbet and the Revolution of 1848 in *Image of the People* (London, 1982) comes to mind, as does Ronald Paulson's *Representations of Revolution* (New Haven and London, 1983).

The transfer of sovereignty over Hong Kong should be considered not simply because of its historical magnitude and temporal proximity. The event has distinctive characteristics of its own, such as the fact that its occurrence was fixed so far in advance (at least, that is, since the Sino-British Joint Declaration of 1984). Political events frequently cast their shadows before them, but rarely quite so far or so distinctly. Pre-knowledge made the Hong Kong handover different from the reunification of Germany or the break-up of the Soviet Union, and conditioned artistic responses to the event in a profound way. 'Handover art' occurred before the event itself, for instance, not just during or after it, and artistic responses were more conscious than they might otherwise have been.

Examples of Hong Kong artworks made prior to the actual handover period, but which were influenced by its approach, as well as those which local artists produced or exhibited during the handover period itself are presented here. All the works discussed are in some way marked by a concern with temporality, either because they involved attempts to envisage the approaching future, or because they looked back towards the past. While a concern with the future was almost exclusively a characteristic of the pre-handover years, retrospection was not confined to the post-handover period, and was a prominent feature of art produced in the years immediately before the transfer of sovereignty.

Prior to the analysis of individual artworks, brief consideration will be given to the way in which events in Hong Kong and the People's Republic of China during the period between the signing of the Joint Declaration and the handover led to a crisis of political legitimacy, and thus also to challenges to the existing cultural order. During this rela-

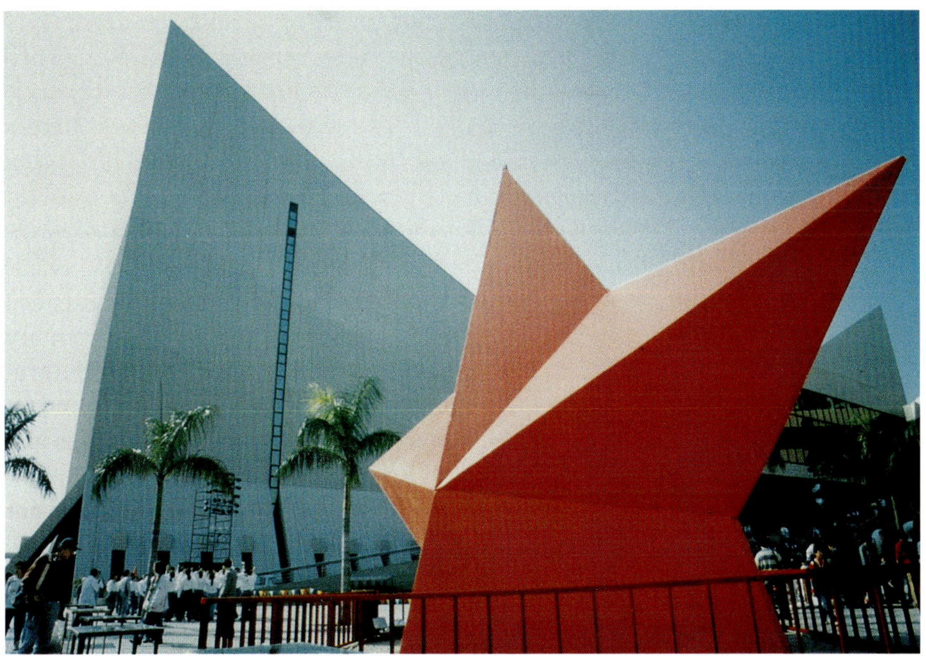

16 Danny Yung, *The Star* (retitled *The Wishing Star*), 1994, mixed-media construction installed outside the Hong Kong Cultural Centre and subsequently dismantled.

tively long period the meaning of the future handover was to change and become more problematic for Hong Kong people, artists included. In the face of the territory's imminent absorption into China a greater sense of Hong Kong's autonomy emerged, and in art this was often expressed as a sense of local cultural identity. Art about the handover was often critical art, contesting officially promulgated interpretations of the event.

A Crisis of Legitimacy: The Changing Meaning of the Handover

The Joint Declaration of 1984 set the clock ticking for Hong Kong's transfer to Chinese sovereignty at midnight on 30 June 1997, and it may therefore be considered as having initiated a new era in the territory's history. Despite its unprecedented nature, the agreement to hand over one of the capitalist world's leading cities to Communist rule did not provoke widespread public opposition in Hong Kong at the time of its signing. While resentment at having one's future decided by external parties was commonly felt, the agreement was mostly regarded as a fait accompli. In June 1989, however, after the bloody suppression of the democracy movement in Beijing, things changed dramatically. Hong Kong people took to the streets in large-scale demonstrations, and fears about a loss of freedom after Hong Kong's return to Chinese rule became widespread. China under Deng Xiaoping had theretofore seemed to be on a convergence course with Hong Kong, experiencing a large measure of economic liberalization. But now memories of the Cultural Revolution were awakened.[1]

A consequence of this shift in local perspective was a degree of political crisis for the colonial regime: the relatively paternalistic approach practiced up to that point was no longer viable. Organized political groups with pro-democratic agendas began to appear in the territory.[2] London's response was to appoint a politician as the final British governor of Hong Kong (rather than a foreign service professional, as had previously been usual). In order to retain credibility in a suddenly politicized environment, the new governor Chris Patten (who took office on 9 July 1992) inevitably had to make concessions, and in due course the first wholly elected and more or less democratic legislature in the colony's history came into existence in 1995. As a direct consequence of Patten's granting of a degree of political autonomy to Hong Kong, Sino-British relations went into a steep decline, and the possibility of a 'through train', a smoothly managed transition of sovereignty, was sacrificed.

Emerging demands for greater political self-determination in the period after 1989 had parallels in the cultural arena with a growing concern for Hong Kong cultural identity. Much of this locally addressed art made use of styles and media borrowed from Western art, partly to distance itself from the Chinese media work of those artists who had gained pre-eminence in the pre-1984 period, and who mostly identified culturally with China rather than with the territory itself. Whereas these latter artists were able to invoke the resources of 'tradition' (albeit that allusions to it were often anxiously combined with consciously 'modern' references as earlier discussion of the art of Lui Shou-kwan and Wucius Wong has demonstrated), the more Hong Kong-centred artists lacked obvious props for use in their project of representing a Hong Kong identity. The national and ethnic narratives most commonly used in fashioning cultural identity were not available to Hong Kong-ness, and indeed were ranged against it in what had now become a fractured field of competing cultural paradigms. More oblique strategies for invoking a sense of local autonomy in cultural terms therefore came to predominate.

Past Attempts at Envisioning the Future

Uncertainty about future eventualities is an experience common to all humanity. What distinguished those in Hong Kong following 1989 from people elsewhere with similar concerns, was that their uncertainties were tied up with a certainty, namely the known date of the handover. Temporality was foregrounded in Hong Kong from the time of the Joint Declaration, everyone learning to live with an enhanced awareness of time's passage in the form of a countdown. Rather than 'passing by', time 'ran out' in pre-handover Hong Kong. A sense of an imminent ending was immensely strong – the millennium was arriving a few years early.

Although the date of the transition was fixed a long time in advance, there was, of course, no way of knowing in advance what that event would bring in its wake. Only its form was fixed and knowable, not its content. This combination of circumstances led a number of artists to produce works that might be taken as attempting to pre-envision post-handover Hong Kong, as attempting to describe it in advance in a future perfect tense.

The least interesting among such works were quasi-realistic representations such as Liu Yuyi's *Liangchen (Festive Day)* of 1993–7 which can be taken as offering an official idealization of the handover ceremony itself. Deng Xiaoping, still alive at the time the work was begun, although not at the time represented, is depicted among an extensive but carefully selected group of PRC and pro-PRC political figures shown celebrating the handover.[3] Like most paintings that attempt to include large numbers of recognizable portraits, this work suffers from compositional infelicities, and lack of dramatic unity. The wall of faces is awkwardly placed in front of a composite landscape background that shows both Chinese landmarks on the left and Hong Kong ones on the right. Tiananmen is clearly visible, as is the Convention and Exhibition Centre Extension in which the handover ceremony took place.

The problem of later developments discrediting a work that attempts to foresee the future is more liable to occur when that work employs a rhetoric of realism. In contrast to *Liangchen*, which embodied official Chinese rhetoric concerning the handover, works by avant-garde Hong Kong artists that attempted to refer to it in advance tended to avoid claiming to know fully the content of a future eventuality. This is the case, for instance, with Danny Yung's *The Star* (illus. 16), which instead made ironic employment of Cultural Revolution (or at least Communist Chinese) references in order to allude to fears about the transfer of sovereignty. This work can be taken as wishing to mentally prepare Hong Kong people for the future by a deliberately exaggerated

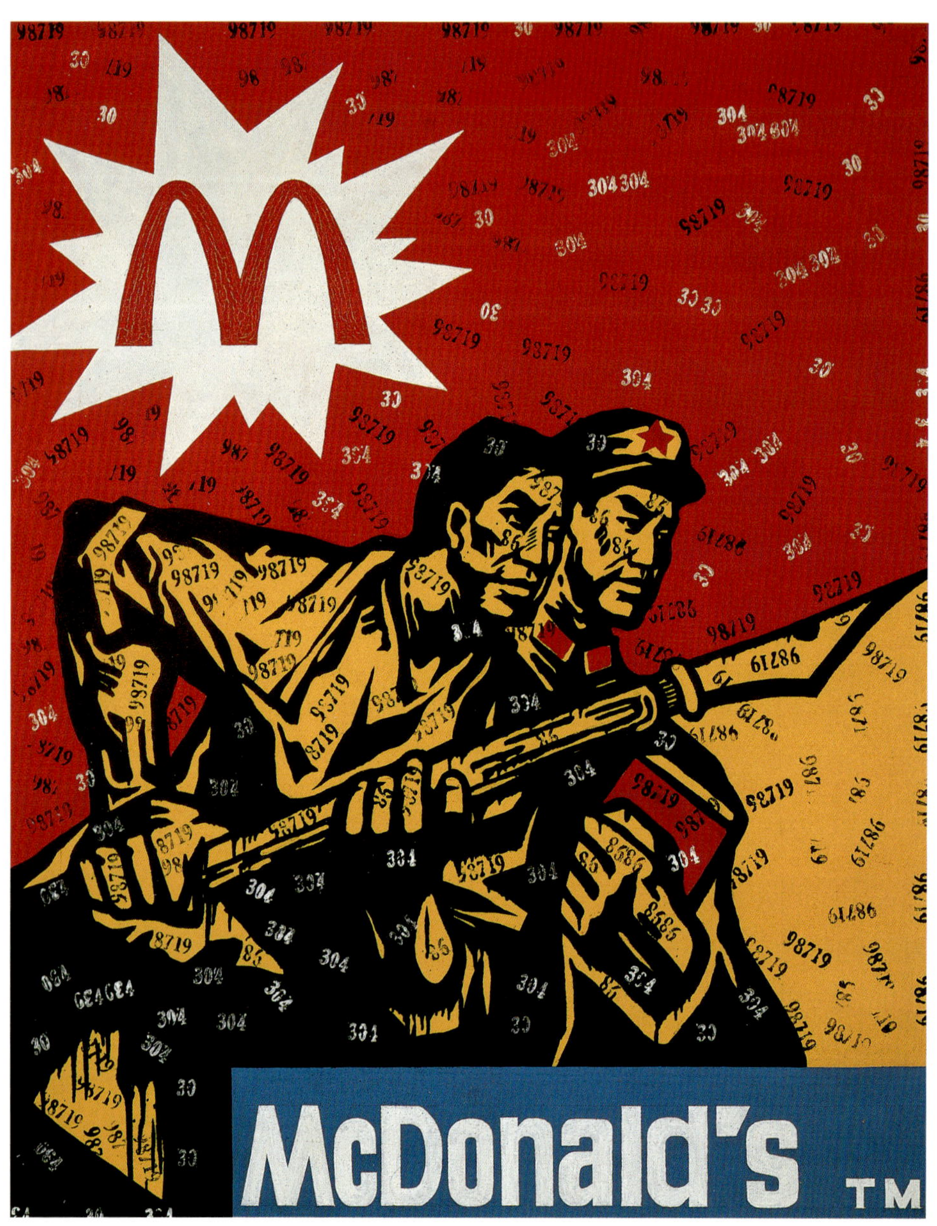

17 Wang Guangyi, *Great Criticism Series: McDonald's*, 1992, enamel on canvas. Collection Hanart TZ Gallery, Hong Kong.

representation of what it might contain, while at the same time attempting to defuse apprehension through humour and ambivalence.

The Star is a 12-metre tall truncated five-point star form in red which reads ambiguously as either rising from or descending into the ground. Its temporary one-month installation in a prominent waterfront site between the Hong Kong Cultural Centre and the Hong Kong Museum of Art during January and February 1994 gave it a clear identity as an alien, invasive presence that it would not have possessed had it been exhibited in the bare white cube of a gallery space. Clearly its meaning was enhanced by its chosen site of display, but also by the time of its display. Unlike Liu Yuyi's *Liangchen*, Yung's *The Star* was created to be seen before the handover itself, and not afterwards. It functioned as a premonition, or a fake advance party, rather than as a commemoration.

The Star can be compared with the work of the various 'Political Pop' artists from the People's Republic, such as Wang Guangyi (illus. 17), Yu Youhan or Li Shan, who similarly manipulated Maoist imagery in the early 1990s.[4] There is, however, a difference of intention in that the mainland Political Pop artists referenced Maoist imagery deconstructively in order to comment on and move definitively beyond a past through which they had lived, whereas Yung dealt primarily with fears concerning a possible Hong Kong future. His primary temporal reference is in a different direction from theirs.

A related appropriation of Chinese Communist symbolism with the future in mind can be found in Chan Yuk-keung's *Absolute Stability* (illus. 18), a wall-mounted installation included in Hanart TZ Gallery's handover period show, *Exhibition 6.30* (20–30 June 1997). The primary form of the work is taken from the same Communist five-pointed red star symbol that Yung's *The Star* employs. In Chan's case, however, the symbol is much transformed, having been constructed from wooden rulers, a reference that requires a detour into English to decode. Knives are included in the installation, seeming to support the star (and thereby perhaps symbolizing a state power dependent on violence). A deflated balloon introduces handover references, in part because it has the form of a teardrop, but also because it evokes a Cantonese idiom concerning the feeling of impotence. Language plays a part in this work as a way of producing a local meaning, of eroding the official associations of the quoted form.

Lee Ka-sing also introduced the Communist five-pointed star symbol in certain of his images (for example *Yellow Star*, illus. 19), again using visual/verbal punning to introduce a reference that is both local and personal.[5] In Cantonese pronunciation (but not really in Putonghua,

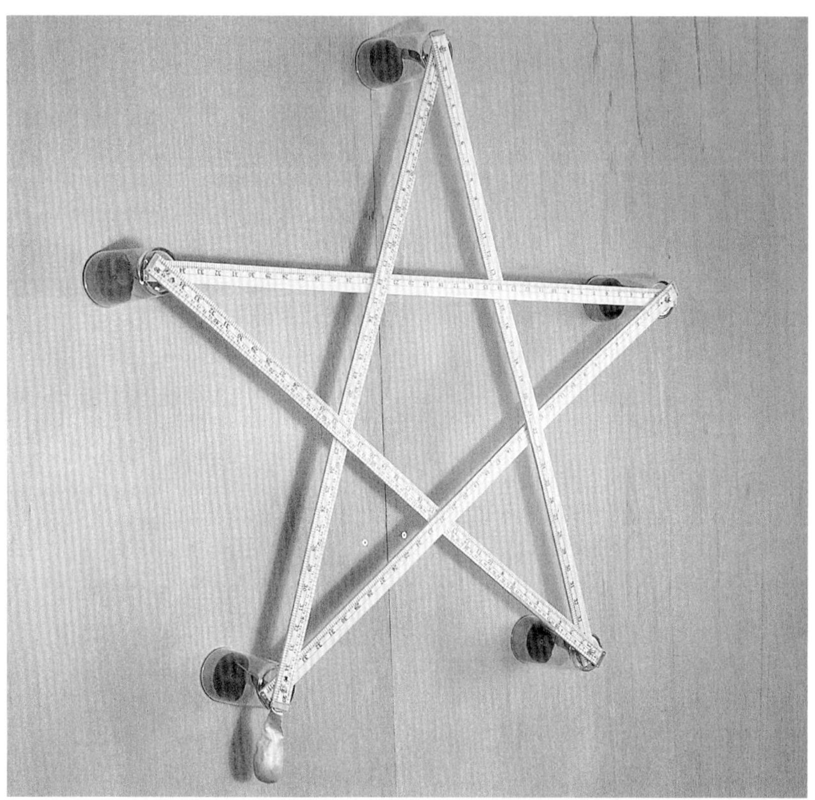

18 Chan Yuk-keung, *Absolute Stability*, 1997, mixed-media construction. Collection of the artist.

the official national spoken language) the Chinese character for 'star' has the same sound as the last character of the artist's own given name. Such a discovery of private meanings only apparent within the linguistic space of Cantonese reads as a defusing of an alien symbol and a rejection of the ideology it represents. Less verbal means were employed to subvert a Communist symbol in another work of the same year, *The Hero Playing with a Red Rubber Band* (illus. 20). Here Mao Zedong is represented by a statuette, of the kind mass-produced on the mainland during the days of the former leader's cult status. Since the statuette appears to be lying flat, it reads as having been toppled, and thus as having lost its power. A residual degree of ambiguity remains, however, given both the empty or undefined nature of the background (which makes orientation unclear) and the absence of markers of scale. Instead of looking down on a small and manipulable Mao we could perhaps be in a subservient position at the feet of a large

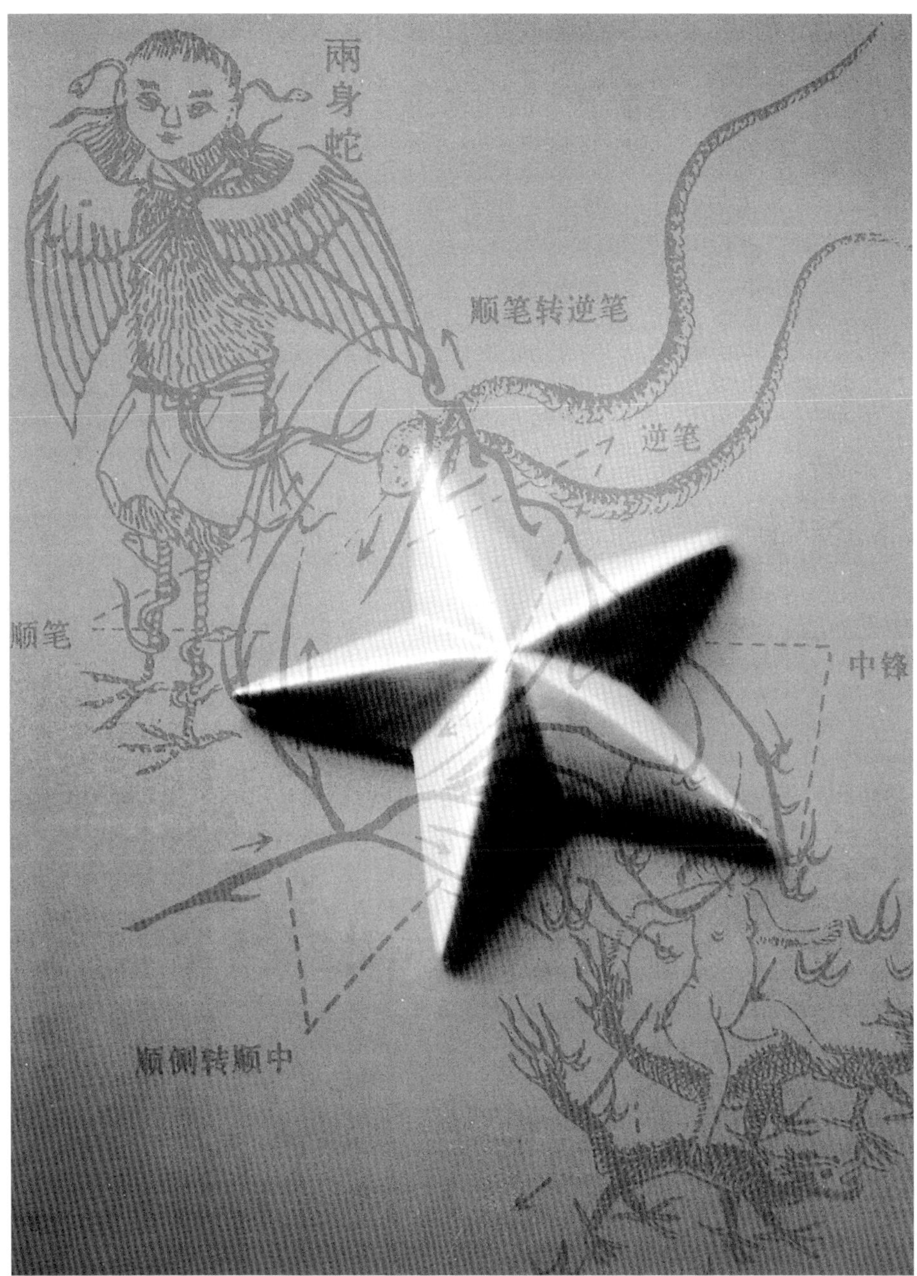

19 Lee Ka-sing, *Yellow Star*, 1995, digital print. Private collection.

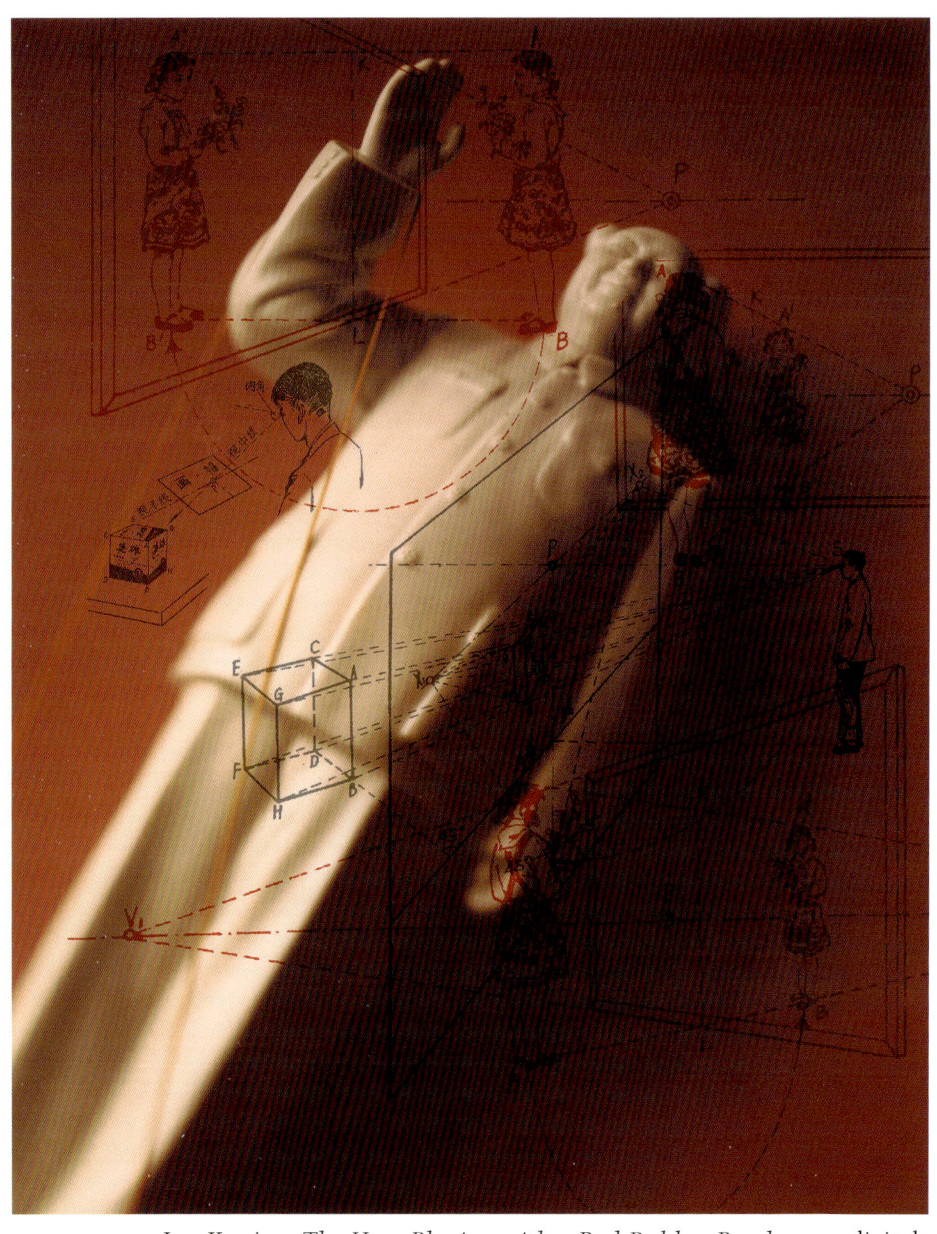

20 Lee Ka-sing, *The Hero Playing with a Red Rubber Band*, 1995, digital print. Collection of the artist.

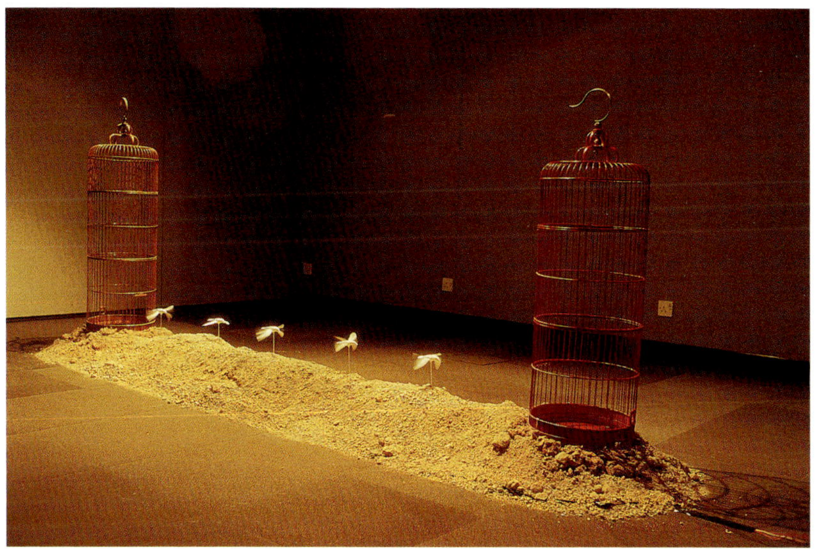

21 Desmond Kum Chi-keung, *Transition Space*, 1995, mixed-media construction. Collection of the artist.

one. As with Yung's *The Star*, we are offered the possibility that China's Cultural Revolution past could be Hong Kong's post-1997 future, even if this sense is not the dominant one here.

Mainland-trained artist Pun Sing Lui, resident in Hong Kong since 1992, also manipulated PRC symbols in works of the late colonial period produced with the return of sovereignty in mind. For example, in 1995 he created photographic images of himself wearing a jacket with the design of the Communist Chinese flag on the back, posing in front of various Hong Kong landmarks. This ironic 'pre-envisioning' of Hong Kong life under Chinese rule was also present when, in the same year, he did a humorously intended performance piece (again adopting a 'mainlander' role)[6] in which he taught Putonghua, the national dialect, to an audience of Cantonese speakers. The texts used in his classroom (actually the gallery space of the Fringe Club) were from the Basic Law of the post-handover Hong Kong Special Administrative Region, which was being promulgated at that time.

Desmond Kum Chi-keung – like many other younger Hong Kong artists – favours using installation as his medium and he frequently employs birdcages as major elements in his pieces. The keeping of birds is a popular pastime in the territory and it is not uncommon, for instance, to see men strolling outdoors, cage in hand. Kum's use of these cages may therefore be taken as an explicitly local reference (no matter whether analogous practices exist in other Chinese communities). In the absence of a separate high art tradition, Hong Kong-ness can perhaps be more easily indexed in this way by objects from popular or material culture – a theme explored further in Chapter 3 where installation art is considered at greater length.

In certain of Kum's works the cages enabled him to comment upon emigration (the response to fears of the approaching handover which a great many Hong Kong people made), or the overheated local housing market (which was to see a dramatic collapse of prices in the economic downturn which occurred in the period following the transfer of sovereignty). On occasion Kum stacked birdcages to resemble tower blocks, commenting on the cramped mode of living that is the norm in the territory's high density urban areas. In *Transition Space* (illus. 21), however, the handover itself was addressed, in straightforwardly allegorical terms. Mechanical birds are represented as moving from one cage to another identical one, a clear comment on the absence of any independence for Hong Kong at the end of its colonial era, and an expression of the fear that Chinese rule would approximate to a neo-colonialism. In addition to suggesting that the future may look like the past, Kum was also attempting to specify the nature of the late colonial period in which the work was made, and to which the title

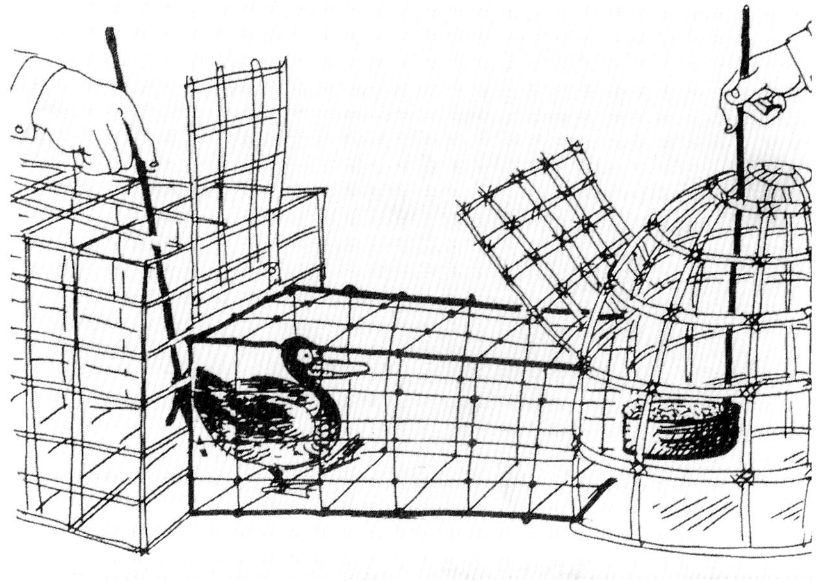

22 Zunzi, Untitled cartoon, 23 July 1984, graphic media on paper.
Collection of the artist.

referred. Because of the constitutional reforms of the Patten era, Hong Kong did briefly experience a wholly elected and more or less democratic legislature, a kind of decolonization *avant la lettre* which it was clear at the time would never be allowed to continue under Chinese sovereignty. The space between the two cages, in which the mechanical birds are to be found, specifies this albeit temporary experience of relative autonomy.

In political rhetoric, too, the limited degree of enfranchisement envisioned for Hong Kong in the post-handover period was frequently referred to as 'birdcage democracy' (a freedom within strict limits), and the use of this term makes a politicized reading of Kum's *Transition Space* easier for the local viewer to understand.[7] Cages are such ready symbols of oppression or lack of freedom that they appeared in other images around the handover period as well. In fact, a remarkably similar conception to Kum's can be seen in a considerably earlier image by Zunzi, a prominent local cartoonist whose works appear in daily newspapers as well as in weekly magazines, and who also on occasion displays his work in art world contexts. A Zunzi cartoon of 23 July 1984 (illus. 22) shows a duck being prodded out of one cage and into another (where a material inducement in the form of some food is being offered). Unlike Kum's work there is no attempt to specify a transition phase of illusory freedom – the two cages are linked by a caged corridor. At the time when this image was made, just prior to the Sino-British Joint Declaration on Hong Kong's future, no such temporary experience of democracy for Hong Kong people was envisaged, and an unproblematic political 'through train' was desired by both sovereign powers.

Wong Shun-kit's *Waiting* of 1996 (illus. 23), as the title suggests, deals with the artist's feelings concerning the approach of the handover. Unlike Kum he emphasized the personal consequences of this historical event, making use of self-portraiture as his means. Although made and exhibited some time before the transfer of sovereignty, this painting is set in the future, being an attempt to visualize the artist himself in the very last minutes before the handover. A calendar open at 30 June 1997 and a clock whose hands are at ten minutes to twelve make this clear. We see the artist's head and shoulders reflected in a mirror, and can also catch sight of his hands in the foreground, at work with a drawing pad. The image seems to be making the point that creative work is the only avenue left to the artist to assert subjecthood and come to terms with an event over which he has no control. Immobility of everything but the hands is emphasized since the artist is clearly seated in a barber's chair. Passivity is further

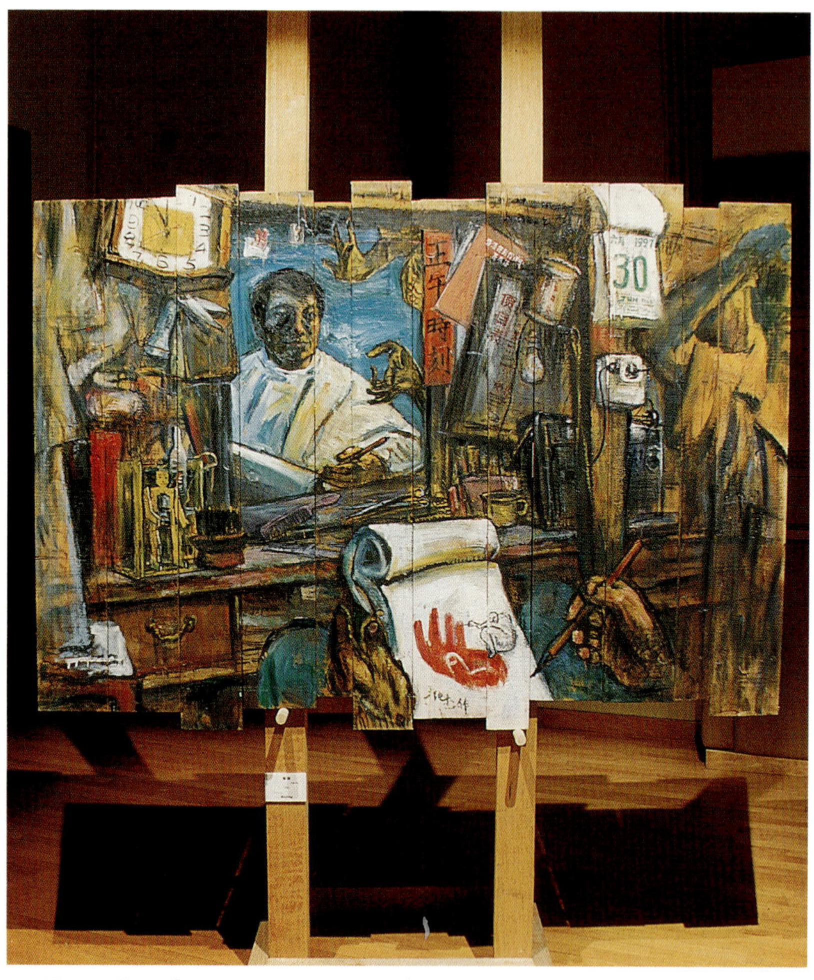

23 Wong Shun-kit, *Waiting*, 1996, oil on canvas. Hong Kong Museum of Art.

underlined by the reflection in the mirror of two rather threatening hands (presumably belonging to the invisible barber), which approach the artist's head. The *mise-en-scène* the artist has employed to convey an idea of the handover as something that is being done to Hong Kong people (and not by them as active agents of their own destiny) is indeed rather unusual. It may be more clearly understood, however, when one remembers that it is customary for Chinese people to get haircuts immediately prior to Chinese New Year, the ritual transition between old and new in the customary calendar which the handover most closely resembles.

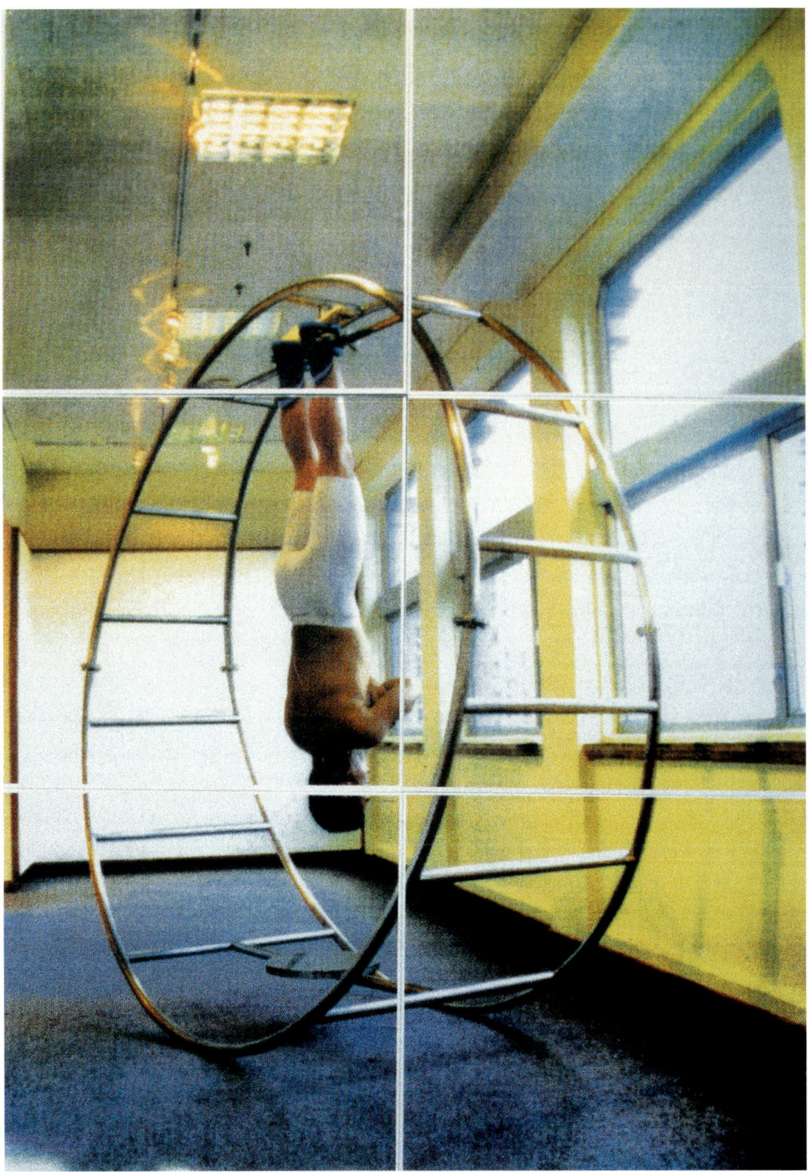

24 Ho Siu Kee, *Gravity Hoop*, 1996, mixed-media installation.
Collection of the artist.

Whereas Wong, Pun and Yung created artworks which were intended to help visualize the transition and the changes it might bring, Ho Siu Kee took preparation one step further by inventing devices to help train himself (and by implication others) for life in the coming era. His project involved as much irony, humour and deconstructive intent as Yung's, but differed by adopting the rhetoric of science (so closely associated with notions of smooth progress), and never made any direct allusion to the handover itself. Whereas Yung's manipulation of a political symbol invoked the public, political realm, Ho retreated back to a concern with the body, perhaps because of a feeling of impotence in relation to broader political events.

Ho's *Gravity Hoop* (illus. 24) consists of a stainless steel hoop form and a digital print showing the artist in the process of employing it. He hangs upside-down from the top of the hoop in what looks like a topsy-turvy parody of Leonardo's 'Vitruvian man', preparing himself for looking at things from a very different perspective. Like other prosthetic objects that Ho constructs, *Gravity Hoop* initially disables the body rather than extending its power. Perhaps in the longer run, however, it might aid in a somatic preparation for reversals in the world around which the transfer of sovereignty might bring.

In *Walking on Two Balls* (illus. 25) a video is presented of a performance in which Ho is attempting to progress forward while balancing precariously on two ball-shaped sculptural objects he has constructed. Ho's concern is not merely allegorical, but this work could be viewed as representing the situation of someone attempting to acquire the responsiveness and fine sense of balance required to operate in the hybrid and ungrounded cultural space of Hong Kong. Although official rhetoric from the time of the Joint Declaration constantly emphasized that 'stability and prosperity' would prevail in post-handover Hong Kong (despite the anomaly of it being a capitalist city in a Communist country), perhaps keeping your equilibrium and getting ahead would in fact require special skills.

Ellen Pau's video installation *Pik-Lai Chu (Dressing Room: Pledge)* (illus. 26) presented at the Fringe Club as part of the 1994 Hong Kong Installation Art Festival, has certain features in common with the two works by Ho discussed above. In her case as well there is a use of the artist's own body within the work, a retreat to the somatic in order to comment on public or political forces beyond the artist's control. Pau's primary medium is video, and when using it in an installation she commonly, as with this work, prefers projection to the use of monitors. Also typical is the use of a space closed off from its surroundings, and the presentation of a single image sequence only. Her interest in the human

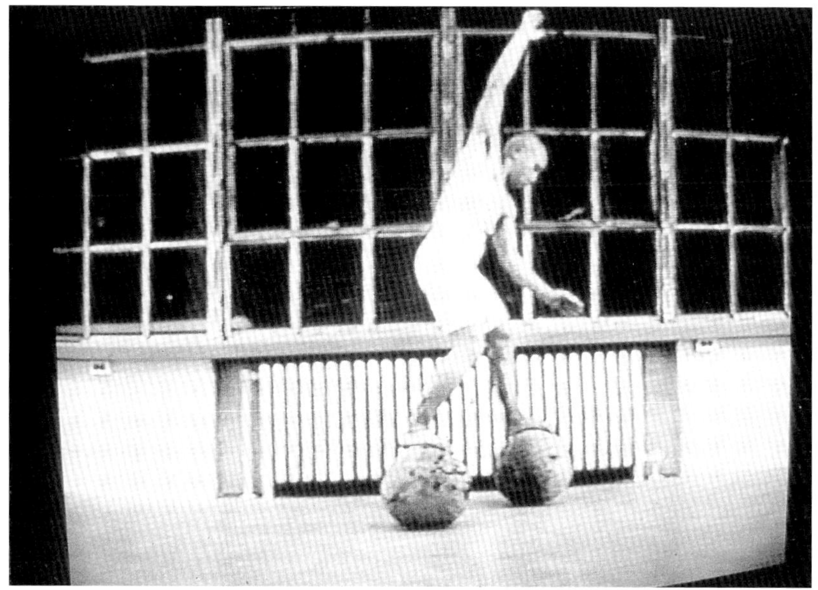

25 Ho Siu Kee, *Walking on Two Balls*, 1995, video still from a mixed-media installation. Collection of the artist.

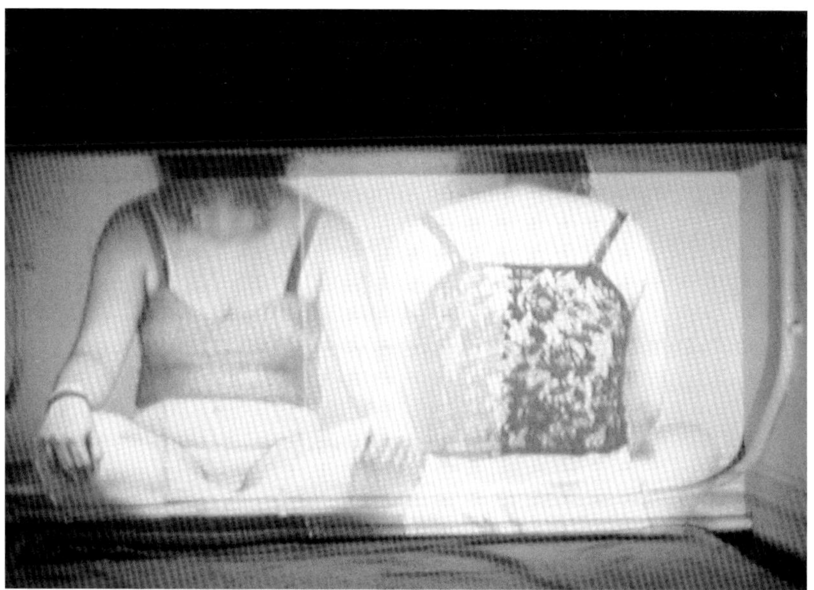

26 Ellen Pau, *Pik-Lai Chu (Dressing Room: Pledge)*, 1994, still from a temporary site-specific video projection installed at the Fringe Club, Hong Kong.

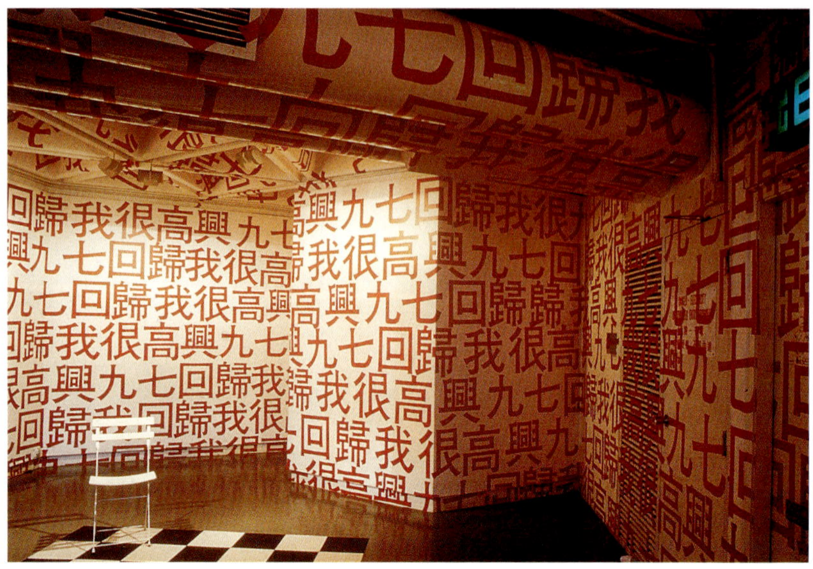

27 Phoebe Man, *Reunification with China, I am happy. Reunification with China, I am happy. Reunification with China, I am happy. Reunification with China, I am happy. Reunification with China, I am happy...*, 1997, mixed-media installation temporarily installed in the Pao Galleries, Hong Kong Arts Centre.

body in motion as a subject stems from her earlier involvement with performance, and in particular with the avant-garde dance collective Zuni Icosahedron, whose minimalist aesthetic has much in common with her own. In *Pik-Lai Chu (Dressing Room: Pledge)* Pau makes use of front and back images of her own body projected side by side. The image was recorded in the location in which it was projected, and in response to the original function of the space as a theatre dressing room she has stripped down to her underwear. The movement of the figure in the confined space conveys a feeling of entrapment, and the piece may be taken as expressing feelings about the approaching handover.

At the time of the handover the façades of many waterfront buildings in Hong Kong were covered in illuminated messages celebrating reunification. Even Jardine House, headquarters of the trading company most reviled by the Chinese government on account of its links to the opium trade, was a participant in this politic display of enthusiasm by the business community. Naturally such unnuanced optimism about the future was a target of those whose own response was more mixed, and Phoebe Man adopted the strategy of mimicry in an installation included in the Hong Kong Arts Centre's handover show (*Museum 97:*

History, Community, Individual, 23 June–12 July). All the local artists so far discussed perhaps envisioned the approaching handover in a somewhat negative way – Man by contrast pretended to be looking forward to it happily. She filled the entire wall-space – and even the ceiling – of a small gallery room with large-scale Chinese characters repeating over and over again the message *'Wo hen gaoxing jiuqi huigui'* ('I am very happy about the '97 return [of Hong Kong to China]'). Repetition, together with the over-exaggerated parody of enthusiasm displayed in covering every inch of available surface, works against the meaning conveyed by the words themselves (illus. 27). The title has some of the same qualities: *Reunification with China, I am happy. Reunification with China, I am happy. Reunification with China, I am happy. Reunification with China, I am happy. Reunification with China, I am happy ....* An obvious insincerity works to question the supposed sincerity of other patriotic and celebratory signs we may encounter.

Looking Back with the Future in Mind

When the handover period finally came, the task of mental preparation became largely redundant. The future had arrived to overtake its images, as it were. Of course, reference to what the post-handover period might bring still had a place, but much of the art exhibited at that time was concerned instead with retrospection. There was a widespread artistic engagement with a past that was on the point of disappearing: a search for identity in the face of its imminent potential loss. Indeed, a retrospective attitude was as prevalent outside the artistic community as within during the handover period, and television documentaries and mass-reproduced souvenirs were as much its consequence as art works. That nostalgia for earlier periods of Hong Kong life had been a common theme of local popular culture since at least the early 1990s indicates that the concern of artists for the past should not be thought of as diametrically opposed to the previously examined concern with the future: to mourn the absorption of Hong Kong into China so far ahead of its occurrence was to imagine oneself into a future vantage point, looking back.

Given the widespread interest in looking to the past for signifiers of the local, and particularly to a recent past of memory and lived experience as opposed to the past of official written history, it is unsurprising that photography became prominent as an artistic medium in Hong Kong with the approach of the handover. Well suited for the task of remembrance because of its established role as a truthful witness with

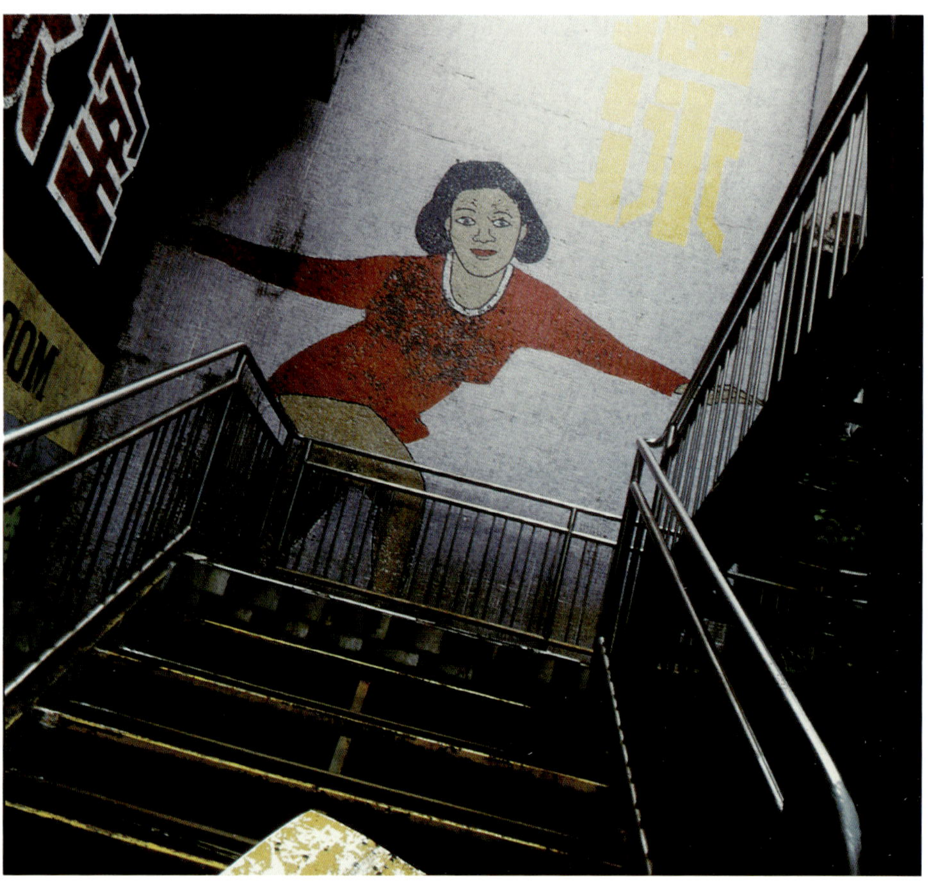

28 Wong Wobik, *Ice Skating, Lai Yuen Amusement Park (now demolished)*, 1997, colour photographic print. Collection of the artist.

a concern for concrete particularities, photography also helps convey anxieties about loss through its characteristic of speaking in the present tense about a moment that has already passed by the time of viewing. This innate property of the medium, deriving from an indexical relation between photographic images and their subjects established at the moment of exposure, is frequently exacerbated by Hong Kong photographers through a choice of subjects that are explicitly threatened with disappearance.

Several artists have been drawn to produce works documenting the amusement park at Lai Chi Kok, a long-established if somewhat faded Hong Kong icon. Characteristically represented as already evacuated of human presence and subject to dilapidation (as in the works of Wong Wobik such as *Ice Skating, Lai Yuen Amusement Park (now demol-*

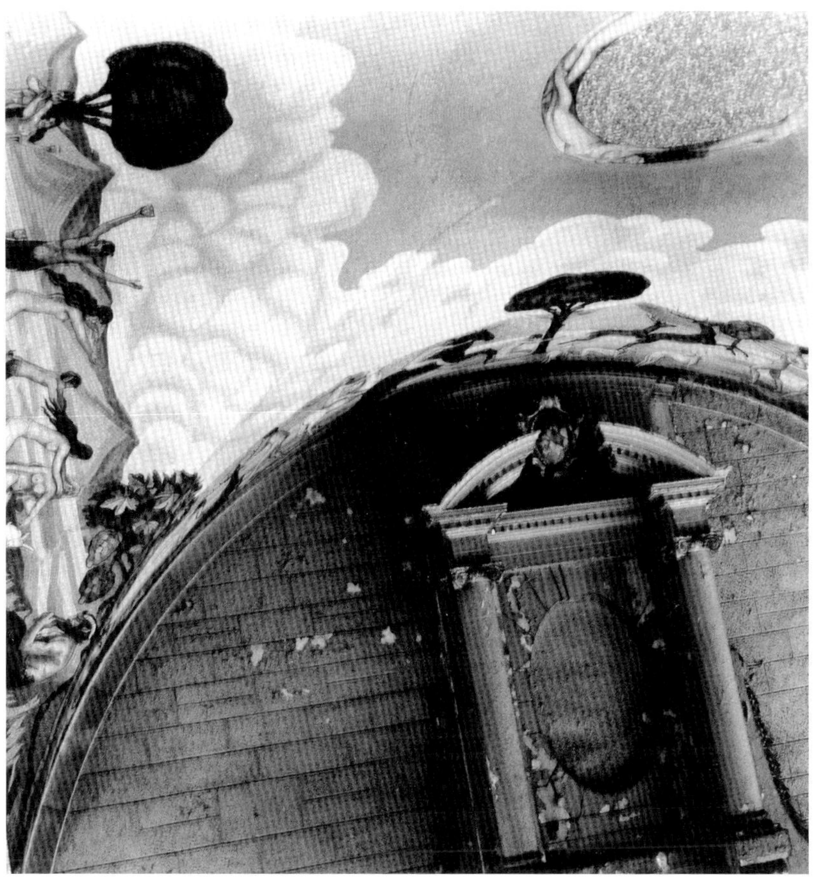

29 Wong Wobik, *Euston, Bonham Road, Hong Kong*, 1984, colour photographic print. Collection of the artist.

ished) of 1997 [illus. 28]), the park readily functions as a symbol of local cultural identity under threat of erasure. One of the first local photographers to produce work in dialogue with international avant-garde trends, Wong (who trained at the Tyler School of Art in Philadelphia between 1977 and 1979) took an early interest in recording old Hong Kong structures on the point of disappearance. Always more than straight documentation, her images allude to a building's former occupants even as they demonstrate their absence. In *Euston, Bonham Road, Hong Kong* (illus. 29), for example, human presence is alluded to by means of the figures in a mosaic.[8] Although this structure, a luxurious private residence, was demolished many years ago, the closure of the Lai Chi Kok amusement park occurred only a few months before the handover itself, and thus was easily associated with it metaphorically.

Such broader associations easily accrue in the case of another location popular with Hong Kong photographic artists in the period around the handover, Rennie's Mill. Here the political dimension of the handover is particularly highlighted. A distinct community settled by pro-Taiwanese Guomindang supporters who had arrived as refugees following the establishment of Communist rule in China, Rennie's Mill was cleared during the summer of 1996, ostensibly to enable urban renewal. Undoubtedly, however, the dispersal of the settlement was a politically motivated attempt to avoid potential embarrassment and confrontation after the change of sovereignty. Chan Yiu Hung's images of Rennie's Mill, made at night with carefully manipulated light effects, are consciously emptied of human presence in order to allude to the clearance of residents. So Hing Keung (illus. 30) and Raymond Chan, on the other hand, adopt a rather more photo-documentary tone in their images, and show aspects of the residents' lives as the deadline for the destruction of the settlement approaches. Both also show Taiwanese flags or symbols, which could be found all over Rennie's Mill.[9]

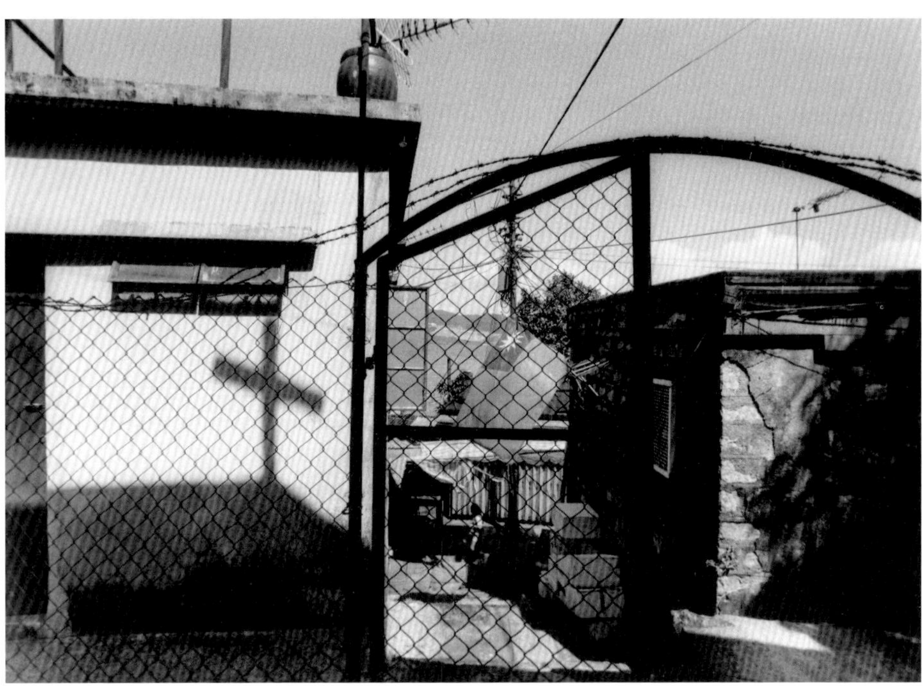

30 So Hing Keung, *Rennie's Mill*, 1993, black-and-white photographic print. Collection of the artist.

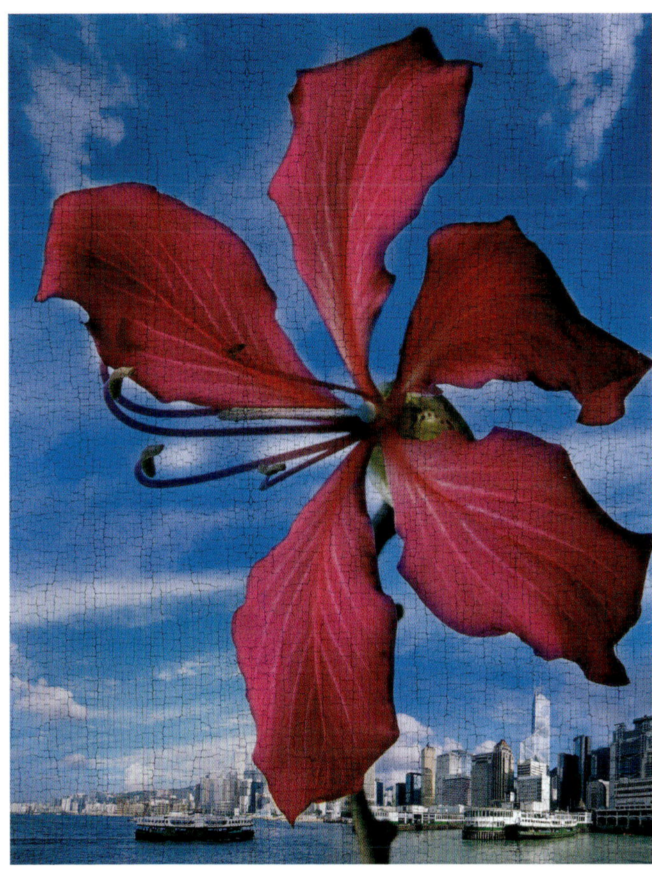

31 Holly Lee, *Bauhinia, in front of Hong Kong Harbour,
circa 1997*, 1997, digital print. Collection of the artist.

While So and Chan exploit the camera's reputation for honesty, Holly
Lee seeks to undermine it by digital manipulation of her chosen photographic source imagery. Among the works in which this occurs is
Bauhinia, in front of Hong Kong Harbour, circa 1997 (illus. 31), a
handover-related work which involves both retrospection and a
concern with the future. It was included in *Souvenir 97: A Design
Project*, an Arts Centre exhibition held in April 1997 just as the run-up
to the handover was beginning, with overseas news teams starting to
make their appearance in Hong Kong. Although the exhibition as a
whole was targeted more at commercial souvenirs of the transition
than at official symbols associated with it, Lee chose to engage with the
stylized Bauhinia flower emblem that appears on the flag and official
seal of the Hong Kong Special Administrative Region. Lee's work, a fake

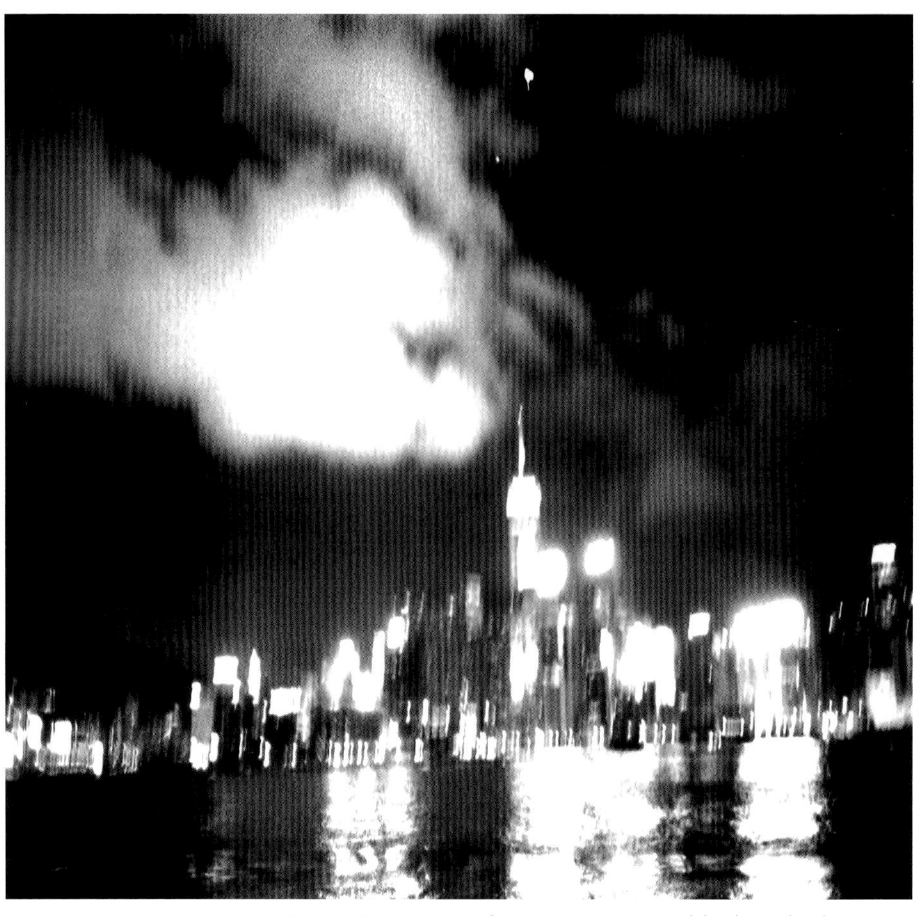

32 Lee Ka-sing, *Hong Kong, Someday in 1997*, 1997, black-and-white photographic print. Collection of the artist.

old-master image of a Bauhinia flower against the contemporary Hong Kong skyline, although not overtly subversive, nevertheless implicitly challenges the stylized abstractness of the official symbol, offering us by contrast a Bauhinia flower in all its concrete natural detail. The retrospective reference in the title (with its mimicking of art historical language), as well as an imitation of the network of cracks that might be found on the surface of an old oil painting, indicate that this is a further case of a Hong Kong artist attempting to envision the future. Whereas Wong Shun-kit envisions the (then) future handover moment in *Waiting* itself, Lee encourages the spectator to imagine that he or she is viewing an object produced during the handover in some moment a long time after it has occurred. An approaching historical event is

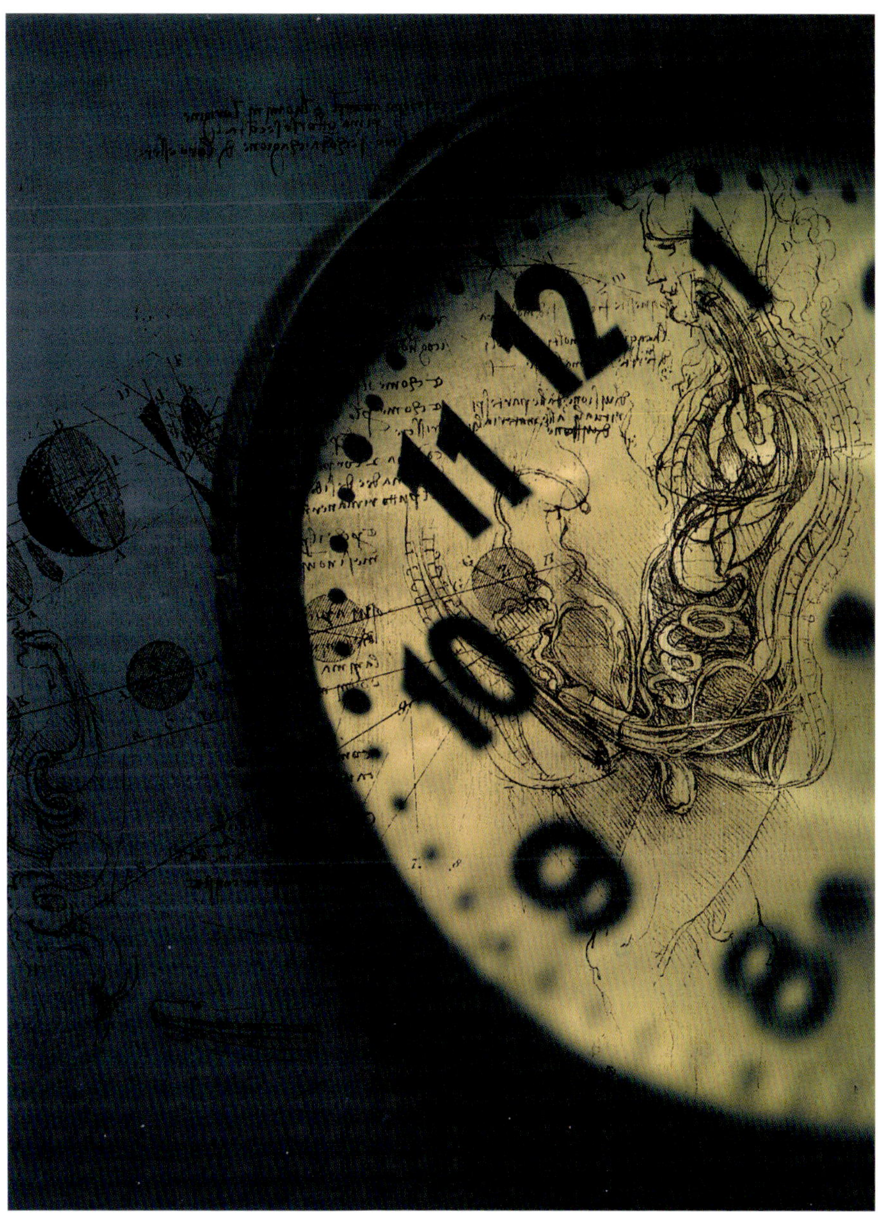

33 Lee Ka-sing, *The Clock and a Classical Interpretation of Time*, 1995, digital print. Collection of the artist.

regarded *sub specie aeternitatis*, as it were.

A similar pretended vagueness about date to that introduced by the 'circa 1997' in Holly Lee's title is also found in Lee Ka-sing's *Hong Kong, Someday in 1997* (illus. 32), a black-and-white photographic image of the Hong Kong skyline. To be unconcerned about a date in a year that supposedly saw a great transformation (particularly in the case of a photograph, which has such a strong indexical connection to the time of its exposure) is to make a particular point of refusing the significance of the handover moment as a great watershed in Hong Kong experience. Elsewhere Lee also seems to express a desire to escape the sense of a countdown with which Hong Kong people lived in the pre-handover period. His *The Clock and a Classical Interpretation of Time* of 1995 (illus. 33) shows a clock face from which the hands have been removed, stilling the inexorable march of time towards Hong Kong's predetermined moment of destiny. The internal mechanism of the clock has also been dismantled, its spring appearing as a major element of another work from the same year, *Clockwork Movement.*[10]

Film offers some of the same possibilities of retrospection as still photography, and Ellen Pau explores old film images in certain of her video works that deal with Hong Kong themes. *Diversion* (illus. 34), for instance, makes use of old film stock from the Hong Kong Public Record Office. Pau's interest is more particularly in the moment of editing than in the moment of shooting and video facilitates this in a way that she feels comfortable with. Slow-motion and repeat are common elements of her visual syntax. Applied to pre-existing historical material, as in this case, her editorial manipulation has the effect of subverting the documentary realism of the colonial government propaganda footage. Whereas Nam-June Paik often undermines the information content of his borrowed imagery by a strategy of overload, Pau achieves the same end by moving in the opposite direction. Her minimal and often slow-moving videos foreground rhythmic and formal concerns, and explore poetic dimensions. An earlier, apparently more innocent Hong Kong is presented to view, and offered up for meditation on contemporary cultural identity.

With painter Wang Hai's *Cultural Relics: Hong Kong History Series (Section 4)* of 1990 (illus. 1, 35) there is the same feeling as with Pau's *Diversion* that historical materials are not always easy to incorporate into a local narrative of identity, that they need to be subjected to artistic manipulation before they can be made serviceable. Like Pau, Wang makes use of pre-existing imagery, albeit photographic rather than filmic, and his manipulation of it is by means of a collage-like princi-

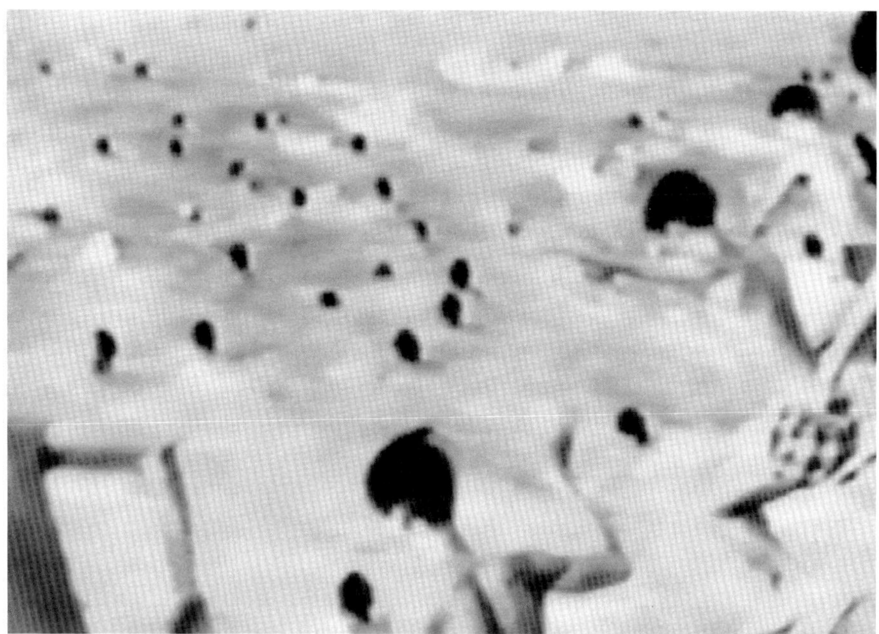

34 Ellen Pau, *Diversion*, 1990, video still. Collection of the artist.

ple. The resulting loss of coherent illusory space undermines any possibility of an unmediated realism, which photography would otherwise encourage. Instead of a coherent colonial narrative of history we are presented with a consciously fragmented and discontinuous local story fabricated from old colonial images. The visual history employed is laid bare as one which embodies an alien viewpoint, recording its Chinese subjects either incidentally as servants, or more consciously as ethnographic types.

A similar recognition that history and its physical relics are difficult to appropriate to a local narrative of identity appears to lie behind a display arranged over the handover period by the Hong Kong Arts Centre, *The Prehistoric Hong Kong Museum*. Part of the larger multi-faceted exhibition titled *Museum 97: History, Community, Individual*, it offered a fabricated history of Hong Kong in order to provoke questions about local identity at the point of transition of sovereignty. In the face of a feeling that textbook history belongs to either colonial or Chinese national narratives, an invented origin myth for Hong Kong people was presented, sometimes incorporating fragments from existing legends and historical data. Hong Kong people were said to have descended from half-human, half-fish hybrids called Lo Ting, perhaps a

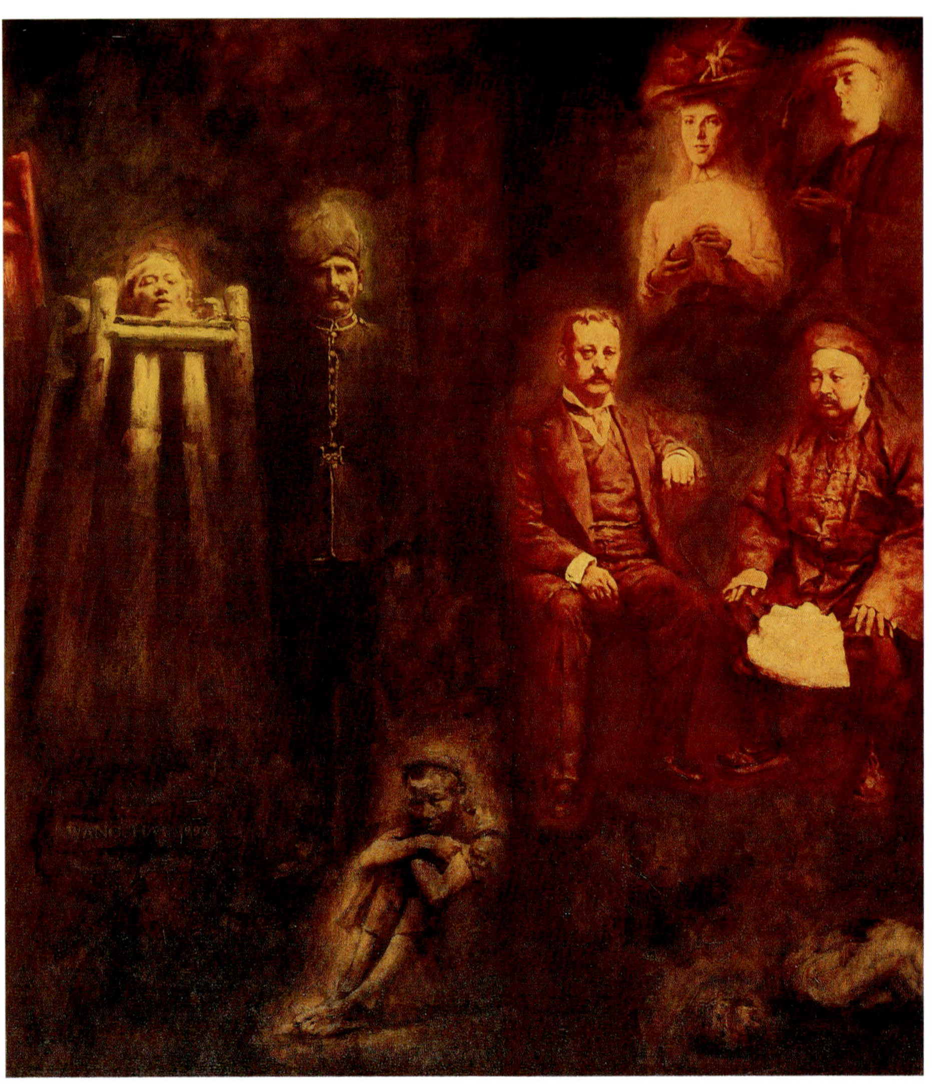

35 Wang Hai, *Cultural Relics: Hong Kong History Series (Section 4)*, 1990, oil on canvas. Collection of the artist.

reference to the water-dwelling fishing population who occupied the region in the pre-colonial era, and who were often harshly treated by the Chinese imperial authorities. Various Hong Kong artists involved with the project created museum-style dioramas and pseudo-archaeological relics as visual 'evidence' to supplement the wall texts, which mimicked the neutral official tone that might be expected in a history museum (illus. 36, 37). Indeed, *The Prehistoric Hong Kong Museum*

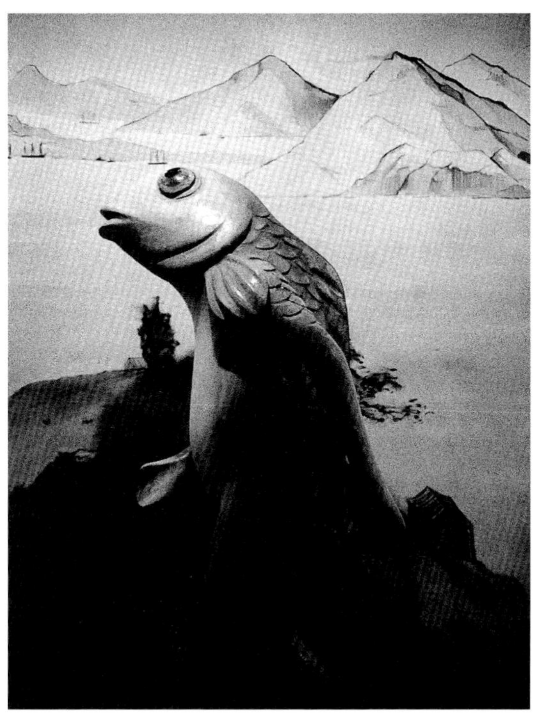

36 Detail of a diorama made by Jimmy Keung for *The Prehistoric Hong Kong Museum* (one part of *Museum 97: History, Community, Individual*, exhibition at the Pao Galleries, Hong Kong Arts Centre, 1997), mixed media. The work no longer exists.

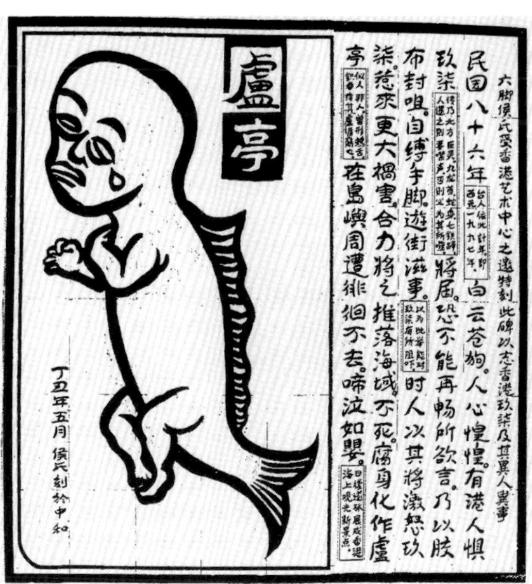

37 *Lo Ting: New Discovery on 1197 Massacre*, contribution by Taiwanese artist Hou Chun-ming to *The Prehistoric Hong Kong Museum* (one part of *Museum 97: History, Community, Individual*, exhibition at the Pao Galleries, Hong Kong Arts Centre, 1997).

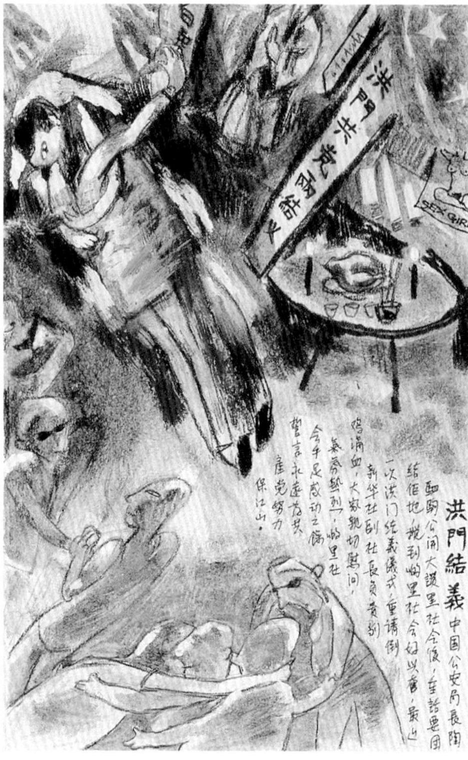

38 Oscar Ho, *Brotherhood with the Triad*, 1993, mixed graphic media on paper. Collection of the artist.

might be taken as parodying quite directly the official narratives of Hong Kong and its culture found in local museums, which tend to place the territory's history within the context of Chinese history.[11]

The curator of *The Prehistoric Hong Kong Museum* was Oscar Ho, Exhibition Director of the Arts Centre, and the strategy of fabrication he adopted in that show is also found in many of his own artworks. Since 1991 he has been creating a series of works on paper titled *Stories Around Town*, which illustrate invented tales about Hong Kong. These works have gradually accumulated into an historical narrative of the territory, fictional and discontinuous though it may be. Fashioned on the model of urban myths, and sharing their supernatural dimension, the *Stories Around Town* also incorporate information culled from actual news reports, which can be equally hard to believe, even when true.[12] *Brotherhood with the Triad* (illus. 38), for instance, was inspired by press reports of a secret meeting in a Hong Kong hotel during the early 1990s between local Sun Yee On triad bosses and officials from the Public Security Bureau of the People's Republic, during which an understanding was said to have been reached between the two sides.

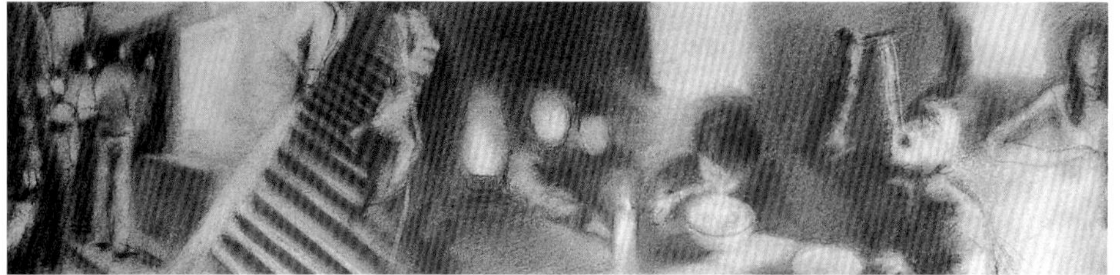

39 Sze Yuen, Detail from *Daily News (6)*, 1995, charcoal on paper. Collection of the artist.

Like Antonio Mak's *Last Tango With Tiger*, which dates from the same year, this work by Ho deals with the co-existence of unlikely opposites.

As well as using newspapers as a source, Ho also turned to the press as a way of disseminating his work. During the days of the handover itself, a sequence of images from the *Stories Around Town* series were reproduced in a newspaper, *The Hong Kong Economic Journal.* Unlike earlier works in the series these were produced at short notice as comments on topical events, and have less of a fabricated quality about them than many of their predecessors. One example is *Anecdote About Chinese Dress* (illus. 103), which makes fun of a patriotic Dress Chinese Day held just after the handover on 3 July 1997, which was sponsored by Shanghai Tang, a store which specializes in marketing nostalgic Chinese clothes and design items.

Ho's use of newspapers (as an avidly consumed source of information about the troubled psyche of Hong Kong in the shadow of the handover, and as a site for a politicized engagement) contrasts sharply with that of Sze Yuen. Starting from photojournalistic representations of often traumatic news events culled from newspapers, Sze has in the last few years been concerned to construct long, scroll-like montages of graphic images (illus. 39). The harsh clarity of news photographs becomes blurred as she translates them into drawn equivalents, their narrative specificity becoming lost in the process of being appropriated as personal property. Such a way of working may well have been inspired by a sense of powerlessness in relation to the events of the period leading towards the handover, being a retreat to the personal (given drawing's status as a more private medium) that paralleled Ho Siu Kee's move towards a body-centred art. Something public is taken into a private space where it can be transmuted by artistic manipulation and thus made less threatening. Something topical can be detached from the flow of temporality and taken into a context where a relationship to time's forward rush is no longer apparent.

In the handover period itself, Sze again adopted the approach of getting personal in order to deal with the changes in public life. She documented the life of 'Grandma Cheung', a lady of advancing years who earned her living from a street shoe repair stall. Photographs of her subject at work were displayed in the Arts Centre's *Museum 97: History, Community, Individual* alongside shoes and a text produced by transcribing their conversations. Because of her relative poverty, Mrs Cheung felt that the handover would not have any great consequences for her, good or bad. The position of immunity from the traumas of public life that Sze seems to search for through her art was found in someone so devoid of a stake in Hong Kong's burgeoning prosperity that she had little to lose.

From Objecthood to Subjecthood

Nationalist rhetoric tended to predominate in official Chinese interpretations of the handover of sovereignty. Since Communist ideology no longer has a widespread appeal in China, nationalism has become a unifying force, and the narrative of national wholeness recovered which the 'return' of Hong Kong allowed was fully exploited in the mainland. Nationalist rhetoric was also aimed at Hong Kong during the handover, but although most people in the territory strongly identify themselves as Chinese ethnically, they also have a cultural identification with Hong Kong which makes them less susceptible to PRC definitions of nationhood. The artworks I have analysed here are expressions of such scepticism about the incorporation of Hong Kong into China, and mark out some distance from national narratives.

The very lack of a national frame for discourse about Hong Kong identity means that oblique strategies predominated in the politically sensitized art that has been discussed here, making it somewhat different from most political art elsewhere. Appropriation (of symbols or images, from either Chinese Communist or colonial sources), mimicry, fabrication, or a retreat to the private, the personal and the somatic are all strategies adopted by these artists. Reference to popular culture and lived experience on the point of disappearance has also been noted, and photography has been discovered to offer particular possibilities for this. Strategies identified in the previously discussed case of Antonio Mak have again been observed: the ironic self-consciousness and deflationary quality of his work have been paralleled, and the Cantonese spoken language, alluded to from within a visual domain, has again been shown to be an effective marker of the local. The political subject discovered in these works is not a unified,

self-transparent actor. It differs for instance from the classical Marxist conception of the proletariat as the bearer of historical agency. No vision is offered of an end-point in which political struggle will be complete, and liberation achieved (independence, the characteristic goal of colonial struggles, could never have been a realistic political aspiration in the case of Hong Kong). Although looking forward to the future has been shown to be a major preoccupation of the art discussed here, the future (that is, the post-handover period) has been viewed as the potential bringer of loss, not plenitude, and this sense of loss has been the theme of much of the more retrospective art produced.

Looked at more positively, one might see these works as revealing a post-essentialist political subject of a particularly contemporary kind.[13] Responding to a situation in which Hong Kong people felt they were being made the passive objects of history, these artists found a measure of subjecthood by commenting on their plight. In a world of social facts and meanings not of their own making, they nevertheless discovered effective ways of fashioning a contestatory social identity.

3 Para/Site Art Space

The Rise of Installation Art

Modern art in Hong Kong had been primarily the creation of artists utilizing Chinese ink painting techniques, albeit with an awareness of Abstract Expressionist brushwork, as demonstrated by the work of Liu Shou-kwan and Wucius Wong. These artists, alongside their counterparts in Taiwan such as Liu Guosong, were responsible for creating the first Chinese modern art of international ambition. They had come to maturity at a time when mainland China was still culturally and intellectually closed because of the Cultural Revolution, and almost completely lacking in space for free artistic experiment.[1]

In the late 1980s a new generation of artists came to the fore in Hong Kong, and in contrast to their predecessors they chose to employ techniques and stylistic languages more directly related to those of Western art. This shift at the level of medium and language can be partly explained in demographic terms. The earlier modernists were often immigrants from mainland China, whereas members of this younger generation were mostly locally born, and brought up during a time when the border with China was closed. Often they had been educated in Europe or North America, because to the lack of opportunities for art training locally. The return of these cosmopolitan, overseas-educated artists was a precondition for the subsequent evolution of a contemporary art scene, although the particular form it took, as well as the timing of its appearance, was more influenced by events in the political domain. The Joint Declaration of 1984 and the brutal suppression of the Beijing democracy movement in 1989, were both factors that encouraged artistic preoccupation with the local, and made cultural identity into a major concern.

The coming to maturity of this younger generation of artists has already been characterized in Chapter 1 as the moment of the 'post-modern' in Hong Kong art. It should be emphasized, however, that many of the artists involved did not produce work with strong visual similarity to that of Western 'post-modernists'. Rather than mimicking the look of contemporary European or American art, these artists often found less 'up-to-date' Western idioms more useful for their purposes. Although it might seem paradoxical at first, a shift towards local meaning and intended audience was actually an escape from provincialism. The post-modern moment for Hong Kong was that in which Western

narratives of art's development lost their credibility (even if European and North America post-modernists themselves were not feeling a strong sense of cultural relativization and dethronement).

Artists such as Antonio Mak, Oscar Ho, Danny Yung, Wong Wobik and Lee Ka-sing, prominent members of this generation that helped create a locally addressed contemporary art scene, faced the customary obstacles of all pioneers. Opportunities to put their work before a broader public were often hard to come by at first, and the situation only really improved appreciably after the establishment of the Hong Kong Arts Development Council in 1995. Brought into being largely as a result of grass-roots pressure from the local arts community, it made public funding available to innovative visual arts projects for the first time (replacing a previous non-statutory body, the Council for Performing Arts). Partly as a result of this newly supportive financial environment, a great number of younger artists came to prominence as the handover began to approach. These younger cultural workers share the local orientation displayed by artists such as Mak and Ho, and have an equal concern with the issue of cultural identity, but have displayed a much stronger interest in installation art.

The marked popularity of installation as a medium in the second half of the 1990s seems due to a number of factors. The lack of a developed market for local contemporary art meant that there was no incentive for artists to produce objects which could function as commodities. The high cost of studio and storage space in a compact and crowded city also discouraged work in more traditional media. It was a practical solution to the space problem to create works which only existed during the time of their exhibition. Installation has a much shorter history as a medium than oil paint or bronze, and this lack may be perceived as an advantage by artists coming from outside the centres of artistic power. Installation is less securely a Western cultural possession than oil painting, the canonical examples of which are European. Since women were beginning to play a more prominent role in this phase of Hong Kong art than in any earlier one, it is important to note that installation is also much less male-dominated than more established media. It came to prominence in an era when women were already winning for themselves much wider social freedoms, and thus it has no long history of service to patriarchy.

One reason why younger Hong Kong artists have engaged more directly with Western art than their predecessors has been a desire to find mediums of expression which are less 'Chinese' in connotation. The Chineseness of ink painting, produced by the medium's associations with the great ink painting heritage, makes it a problematic tool for artists who wish to emphasize the local. An artist using it inevitably projects a certain 'Chinese' identity, yet it is from a generalized or essentialized Chineseness that artists concerned with Hong Kong cultural identity most wish to distinguish themselves. Installation enables Hong Kong artists to connect to a history which is local rather than framed as national, since it opens up the possibility of appropriating objects from markedly local popular and material culture as part of the artwork. The textbook narrative of national history may be perfectly able to subsume high cultural artefacts to its purpose, but objects from everyday life that are beneath its disdain may become tools for a fragile alternative history – a history based on memory and personal lived experience.

To the extent that it is site-specific, installation art has a relation to the particularities of local space that other more portable art forms do not have. This gives it a resource for referencing the local not available to film, say, and may be one factor accounting for its popularity. Hong Kong movies are now quite well known in many parts of the world, and feature prominently in academic analysis of Hong Kong culture, but it could be argued that the portability of film (especially in video format), and the ease with which identically valid copies may be made, tends to erode its relation to Hong Kong itself. A movie by a Hong Kong director might be filmed in Argentina and viewed and written about in the United States.

Given the peculiar sense of time that existed in Hong Kong during the countdown to the handover, the temporally specific nature of installation art became as important as its site specificity. The transient nature of installations enabled them to belong to and comment on a particular moment of local significance in a way that more durable artworks could not. Photography, because of its indexical relationship to the space and time of the negative's exposure, was also (as the works by Wong Wobik and others have shown) a medium that came into its own in Hong Kong during this period, where artists were interested in referencing the local and evoking a sense of living at the end of time. But photographs, because of their durability, outlive the moments they are forever tied to (and indeed because of the time-lag of development and printing can only be seen after that moment has already passed). They speak in a present tense, but of something that has passed before the time of viewing commences, and thus offer expressive possibilities somewhat different from those of installation art. Certain of the installation artists to be discussed below seem well aware of photography's particular potential as a marker of a now-lost time, and either employ it as a second area of

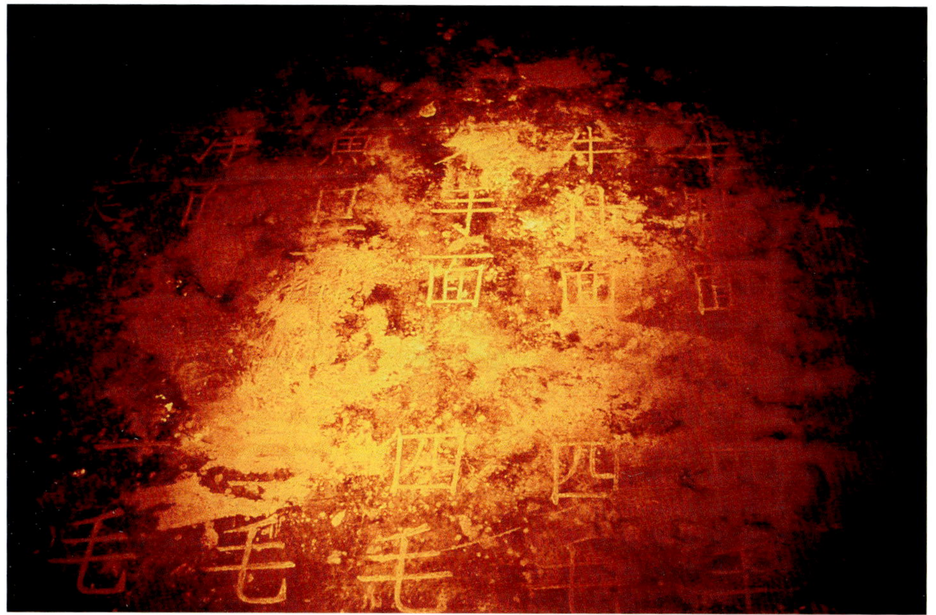

40 Warren Leung, Detail from *Dream of a Path*, 1996, a temporary site-specific mixed-media installation.

artistic activity or even make use of photographs as an element within their installation works.

In Hong Kong, museums have shown more interest in pre-modern Chinese ink painting, ceramics or bronzes than in contemporary art. These objects have been utilized to construct displays embodying ideological narratives of continuous national culture (a parallel or supplement to the textbook versions), and the modern and contemporary has been marginalized because it is potentially disruptive of such atemporal cultural essentialism. Finding no sympathetic home in institutional spaces, local contemporary artists have become used to playing the role of curator for their own shows, which often take place in marginal sites. Absence of an institutional public sphere for challenging art has led to a premium on the private, in content and in site of display (on occasion artists have even shown art by holding open days at their homes).[2] Given the experience of artists with curating, with taking responsibility for the whole space in which their work is displayed, it is hardly surprising that installation art should be popular. Both curators and installation artists deal with ready-made objects, bringing them into temporary juxtaposition in meaningful ways, thus the transition from one activity to the other is not so great. Indeed,

Hong Kong artists have sometimes played productively with the vagueness of the boundary between them.

Artists in Western

As well as organizing their own shows, Hong Kong artists have in recent years moved one step further and created their own alternative exhibition spaces. This became possible after Arts Development Council funding came on stream in 1995. Among the artist-run spaces to have opened since that time are 1A Space and the OP Fotogallery, but one of the first – and certainly one of the most interesting – is Para/Site Art Space. From the time of its earliest exhibition in January 1996 Para/Site has provided a venue for installation art, and although more recently it has made a conscious effort to accommodate other types of art production as well it is still closely associated with that medium. All of its founding members – Lisa Cheung (*b.* 1969), Patrick Lee (*b.* 1949), Leung Mee (*b.* 1961), Warren Leung Chi Wo (*b.* 1968), Phoebe Man Ching Ying (*b.* 1969), Kith Tsang Tak-ping (*b.* 1959) and Sara Wong (*b.* 1968) – have made installations, and for several it is the primary medium.

Para/Site has occupied two different locations. During 1996 it was based in the area of Hong Kong Island called Western, and its first series of shows (titled *Artists in Western*) took place there. In 1997 it moved to nearby Sheung Wan, where it has been based since. Both locations were originally shop spaces, located in older established areas of the city which, although not immune to the effects of urban redevelopment, are yet to feel its full force. While the lower rents to be found in such districts have no doubt influenced the choice of site, there seems also to have been a deliberate decision to locate in an area where the traces of Hong Kong history have not yet been erased. A diversity of small businesses survive in the current neighbourhood of Para/Site: one can encounter stores selling the dried ingredients for Chinese medicine and a workshop producing Chinese-style coffins, for instance. The memoryless homogeneity of the high-rise Central business district is absent, even if it is only a short distance away. To reach that earnestly contemporary section of the city requires a walk up Hollywood Road, a long street dominated by antique shops (which become increasingly up-market as one progresses), so history and its loss is already thematized in this part of the urban landscape, even if the antique stores are concerned with relics of China's past rather than Hong Kong's.

As well as indexing the local in installation works by making use of objects and materials with strong Hong Kong associations, the Para/Site artists have used the existing associations of the neighbourhood and their rented space as a resource for their art. In this sense their installations have been more site-specific than is often the case in Hong Kong. Many other local installation art pieces have a homeless or displaced quality, looking as though they are camping out in their space of exhibition, but in Para/Site installations there can be some allusion to the neighbourhood, and the traces of the space's previous functions can be incorporated into the work. Inevitably this latter strategy has become less available over time, however, because repeated artistic use of the space gradually obliterates its pre-existing characteristics.

The first show to be held at the original location of Para/Site was *Relic/Image* (January 1996), which featured works by Patrick Lee, Warren Leung and Kith Tsang. In many ways this show set the tone for later Para/Site exhibitions by its emphasis on installation as a means and its concern to recover a sense of Hong Kong-ness through attention to the surviving traces of vernacular history. In Leung's *Dream of a Path* (illus. 40), for instance, the names and prices of food dishes (taken from a street stall menu of the 1960s) were engraved directly on the floor of the former shop space, at a much enlarged scale. In this way Leung produced a sort of fake relic of a earlier time when such stalls were a common sight in this older Chinese residential district, and drew attention to the process of 'urban renewal' which, Haussmann-like, has erased these previous forms of life. The disparity between the prices shown and those now current in Hong Kong served to underline the passage of time, which an act of stone engraving (given its monumental and even memorial associations) seemed as if attempting to arrest. The sense of disparity between the 'low' or trivial content and the 'high' or serious presentation was further underlined when Leung made a paper rubbing of the inscription (a sort of relic of a relic), and turned this into an independent artwork. *Untitled (After Dream of a Path)* (illus. 41) recalls the ancient Chinese practice of making rubbings of important inscriptions or samples of distinguished calligraphy.

Tsang's contribution to the same show also attempted to bring the neighbourhood environment into the gallery. His primary materials were bamboo and sheets of galvanized iron, out of which he fashioned a structure at the far end of the gallery space. Even in contemporary Hong Kong bamboo is a widely used scaffolding material (being light and cheap), but in combination with this kind of sheet metal it evokes the construction of temporary (so-called 'matshed') theatres for outdoor performances of Chinese opera. Such performances tend to

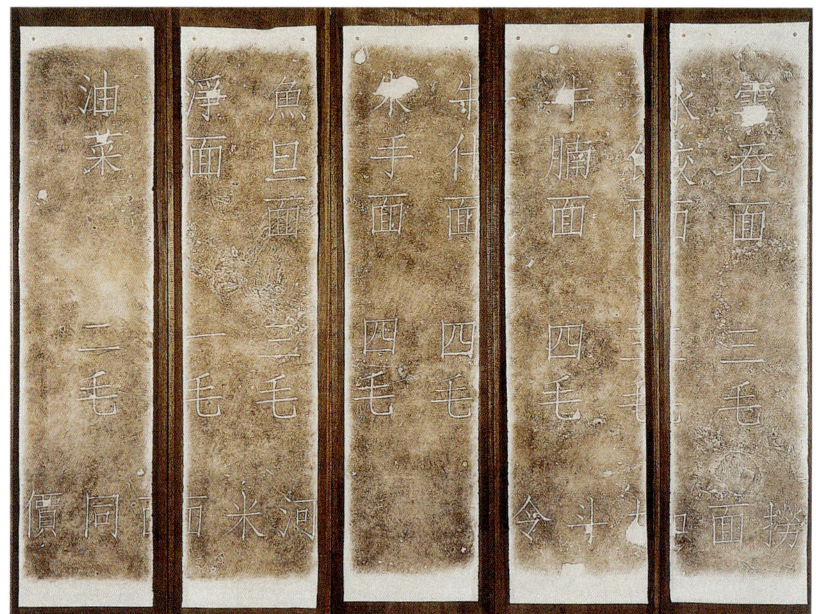

41 Warren Leung, *Untitled (After Dream of a Path)*, 1996, oil colour on paper, plexiglass and wood. Hong Kong Museum of Art.

take place on the occasion of particular festivals in the Chinese lunar calendar, such as the 'Hungry Ghost Festival' held at the end of summer, and although still widespread they have the flavour of being residual expressions of an earlier cultural world. The word 'opera', although customarily used in English translation, brings the wrong associations into play, since the audience for these performances are not drawn from the social élite. Instead they attract a primarily local audience, with older people from the poorer strata of society predominating – the very people who are most excluded from the burgeoning consumer culture that dominates the city's more contemporary spaces. Tsang has taken a strong interest in matshed opera performance – a part of his experience since childhood – making a study of it as part of the work for his MA degree in an active exploration of possible local counterparts to the Western high art practice of installation art. The temporary stages for opera performance are characteristically set up in the older residential districts of Hong Kong, and this easy integration of art and life, or sculpting of social space, is as much an inspiration to Tsang as the transience of the structures and the bricolage of their construction.

Tsang's installation (*Hello! Hong Kong – Part 3* [illus. 42, 43])

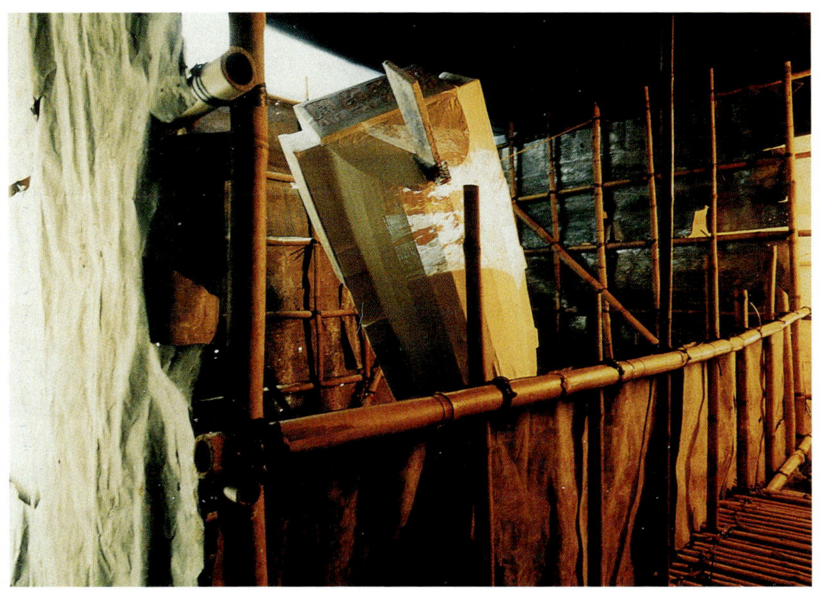

42 Kith Tsang, Detail from *Hello! Hong Kong – Part 3*, 1996, temporary site-specific mixed-media installation.

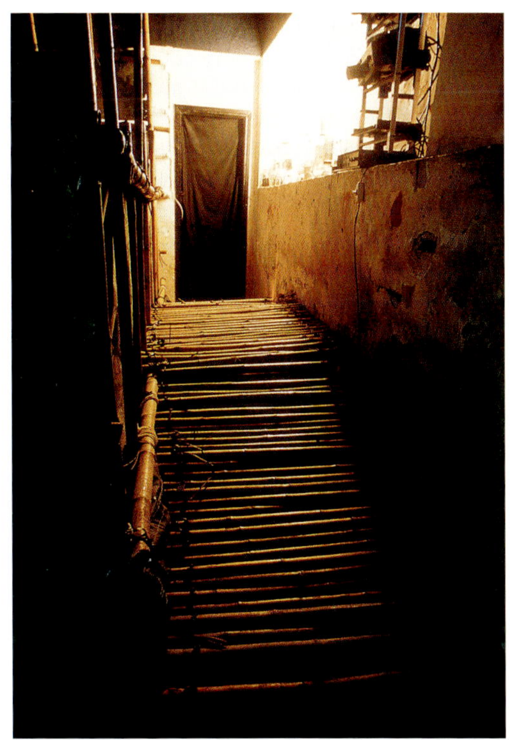

43 Kith Tsang, Detail from *Hello! Hong Kong – Part 3*, 1996, temporary site-specific mixed-media installation.

consisted of a small bamboo and galvanized iron sheet structure, with a bamboo bridge to one side of it which spectators could use as a viewing position. From here they could see a 2-metre-long papier maché boat which had been placed – partially inverted – in the matshed space, above a few centimetres of water. Lighting effects were carefully manipulated, and from the opposite side of the bridge a pair of slide projectors coupled with a dissolve unit projected a sequence of photographic images onto the side of the boat. One projector showed coloured slides of weathered wall surfaces and advertisements, while the other showed blurred black and white images of construction in progress along the waterfront of Hong Kong harbour, thus continuing the theme of bringing the environment into the gallery itself. Both sets of slides were projected simultaneously (but with different time intervals), and the projected images were allowed to overlap. On the same side of the bridge as the projector was a miscellaneous collection of clear glass bottles, almost all of which contained transparent black-and-white photographic images of the harbour, and which were filled with water. A faintly audible recording of Nanyin (a style of southern Chinese improvizational music) infiltrated from an adjoining space, further developing the allusion to folk performance which the matshed materials introduced.

Tsang's work had a strong resonance of the past, of a Hong Kong of living memory now increasingly difficult to discern in day-to-day experience. In addition to the already discussed associations of bamboo and metal sheeting, the papier maché boat was also a reference to local craft skills whose survival is endangered as older practitioners fail to find apprentices to continue their trade. Nanyin too is a vanishing tradition, and although the audience would not have known that Tsang was inspired to place the source of the music outside of the main exhibition space by childhood memories of this music infiltrating though thin partition walls from a neighbour's radio, they would have been able to pick up a melancholy tone which reinforces the sense of loss conveyed by the work's visual elements. The lyrics of the chosen song, *Sorrows on an Autumn Trip*, conveyed a sense of uncertainty about the future which for Tsang echoed the mood of Hong Kong people in the run-up to the 1997 handover of sovereignty.[3]

The fragile upturned boat – a wrecked or marooned vessel, above rather than in the water – recalled Hong Kong's harbour, which has seen dramatic changes in the last few years, with reclamation altering its whole physical appearance. The weathered surfaces shown in the projected images brought further associations with the past and its loss or erosion, while the changing appearance of the harbour, the unstable or ungraspable nature of the present moment, was conveyed by the blurred quality of the photographs that recorded it. In contrast to all these significations of loss or the ephemeral (which the temporary nature of installation art itself helps to underline) was the gesture of preservation implied by placing photographs of the harbour into bottles. This recalls the traditional method used for preserving beancurd and other food products, although in this case the water in the bottles gradually peeled off the emulsion to create a further image of the past's erasure. Such destructive embalming had a precedent in Choi Yan-chi's installation pieces such as *Drowned II* (illus. 44) and *Drowned III* (1993, Asia-Pacific Triennial, Queensland Art Gallery, Brisbane), in which piles of books were submerged in tanks of water or oil.

Preservation and decay were also themes of Lee's installation for *Relic/Image*. Titled *Walk On*, it contained (among other items) a stuffed bird and a stuffed deer (such as might belong in some natural history museum display),[4] and also a roast pig (such as might be seen hanging in many restaurants in the surrounding area). This latter item, as one would predict, decayed during the course of the exhibition, losing its benign identity as a food item. The theme of decay returned – more wistfully – with *Ah Keung*, Lee's contribution to the show *Bad Rice* (curated at 1A Space by Hiram To, December 1998 to January 1999). Waxed roses (similar to the flowers Lee preserved in his elegant black-

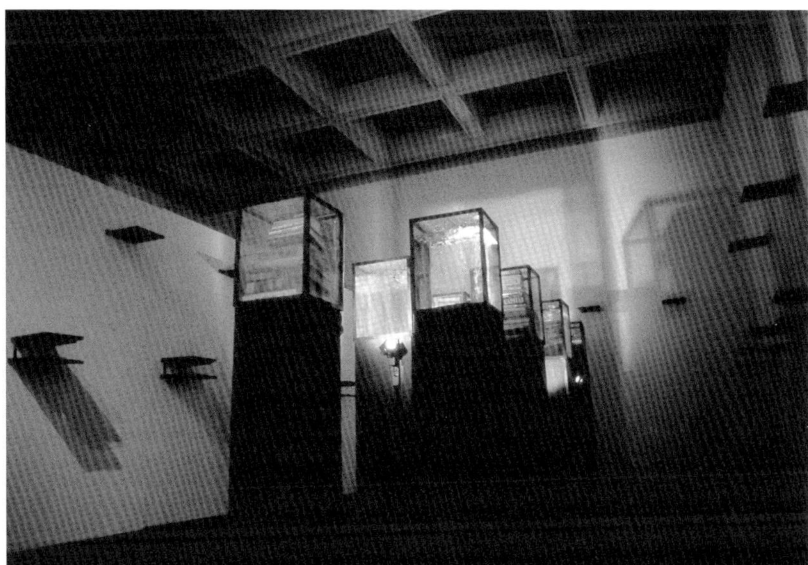

44 Choi Yan-chi, *Drowned II*, 1992, temporary site-specific mixed-media installation, Hong Kong Museum of Art.

and-white still-life photographs) gradually deteriorated inside a cabinet.

Although most of the more explicit, legible images in Tsang's installation relate to the theme of the harbour, this subject could be taken as emblematic of Hong Kong as a whole, given that the city came into being in the first place because it offered a suitable location for a deep-water harbour, and since it is primarily known as a port, a place for the coming and going of both commodities and people, rather than as a place of rooted settlement. The worries about transience and loss embedded in the work, then, are not just an environmentalist's or preservationist's protest against the effects of redevelopment and reclamation, but refer to the handover (about eighteen months away at the time the work was made) and the threat felt by a great many Hong Kong people to their way of life. In a transition beyond colonial rule to something which was not independence and which looked as if it would be remarkably similar to the existing undemocratic rule from afar, a search for identity and its fragile expression through art was to be expected. Since Leung had expressed the worry that Hong Kong's particular history may be forgotten and subsumed into Chinese history after the handover, he may also be taken as producing works which alluded obliquely to the broader issues raised by the transition of sovereignty.[5]

Several of the characteristics of *Relic/Image* were found again in the following two *Artists in Western* shows held at the first Para/Site venue (which took place in March and April 1996). In the second show (*Diving from Memory*) for instance, Lisa Cheung echoed Tsang by constructing a boat, which was again displayed above water, not in it, but right side up this time. Although it seems a dialogue with the earlier show was being initiated, Cheung was manipulating materials with associations more natural than cultural – she constructed her vessel from intertwined twigs and branches still in their raw state. Perhaps because she had lived and studied in Canada for many years, and had only returned to Hong Kong in 1992, Cheung was less concerned than Leung or Tsang with developing specific Hong Kong references in her work. Her sense of identity is perhaps more diasporic than those artists who spent all their formative years in Hong Kong, and although she retains links with Hong Kong she has been living and furthering her studies in London in recent years. Still interested in installation, she has also become more involved with photography, and has produced works which deal with being Chinese in a predominantly non-Chinese environment (for example through focusing on the ubiquitous British 'Chinese takeaways').

Leung Mee Ping, the other artist in *Diving from Memory*, also used water as an element, and like Warren Leung she carved into the floor of the improvised gallery space – in her case to create a temporary pond for a live goldfish. The floor around the goldfish was covered in curved red roof tiles of a traditional Chinese kind, and it was necessary to walk across this roof-floor to see the fish, occasionally cracking tiles in the process. Water had featured in one of her earlier installation pieces with similarities to one aspect of Tsang's *Hello! Hong Kong – Part 3*: in an untitled work of 1994 she included photographs of her family and of Hong Kong, which were submerged in metal trays filled with water, where they gradually deteriorated.

In the third show, *Site-seeing*, Sara Wong and Phoebe Man both continued the references Tsang and Warren Leung had made in their installations to the surrounding neighbourhood by using materials which indexically invoked it. Wong brought boards salvaged from nearby construction sites into the gallery (illus. 45). These hoardings, with old advertising posters sandwiched between them, were assembled into a temporary shelter form over a small pool of water (again) with contours loosely echoing those of Hong Kong. A built-in television set and fan gave a domestic or inhabited feel to the structure. Construction (or demolition, its partner) was also a theme in Man's contribution to the show (illus. 46). Whereas Wong attempted to create shelter or a provisional sense of home from the very materials of urban transformation themselves, Man foregrounded the schizophrenic sense of fragmentation caused by the rapidly changing urban environment by including construction site rubble and broken shards of mirror in her installation. An allusion back to Leung Mee Ping's work seems intended (some of the shattered roof tiles may actually have been recycled as part of the construction debris), although in Man's work the viewer was not required to become complicit in the destruction of the past. Like Tsang, Man included images of the neighbourhood as a part of her installation: fragments of projected images of the surrounding environment were picked up by the jagged shards of mirror.[6]

Sheung Wan

The first show to take place at the second Para/Site venue in Sheung Wan was Tsang's *Hello! Hong Kong – Part 7* (illus. 47–9). Held between 20 May and 20 June 1997, it was inevitably interpreted in relation to the handover of sovereignty, which occurred just ten days after it had closed. Compared to *Hello! Hong Kong – Part 3* it was a show with less legible meaning, partly because this installation made use of more objects with personal associations. Tsang had already used that strategy in an even more direct way in *Latent Space* of 1996, where he

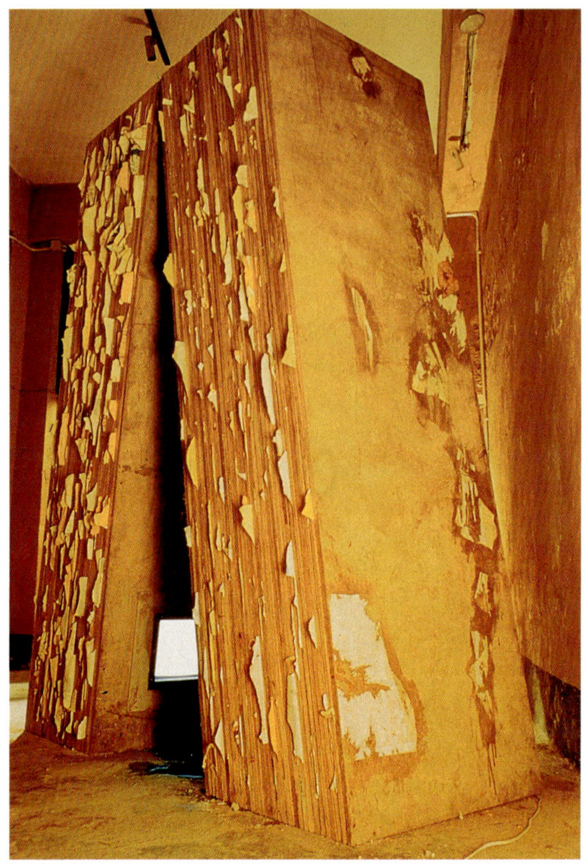

45 Sara Wong, *Site-seeing*, 1996, temporary site-specific mixed-media installation.

constructed a kind of private studio environment in the public gallery space of the invitational group exhibition *Restricted Exposure* (organized by the Hong Kong Festival Fringe at the City Hall, January to February 1996). *Latent Space* ignored the surrounding artworks and the white cube space which contained it, whereas *Hello! Hong Kong – Part 7* (although it does recreate a quasi-private, quasi-domestic environment for the viewer's appreciation of his objects through the construction of spatial compartments) was open to the quality of the space it occupied, and indeed incorporated it into the artwork. This was possible because Tsang occupied the whole of the ground-floor area of the gallery, and because as the first Para/Site artist to use the new venue he was able to decide freely what traces of the venue's previous commercial usage would be allowed to remain.

Although Tsang made use of objects with personal associations – it appeared they had a history outside their employment as art elements,

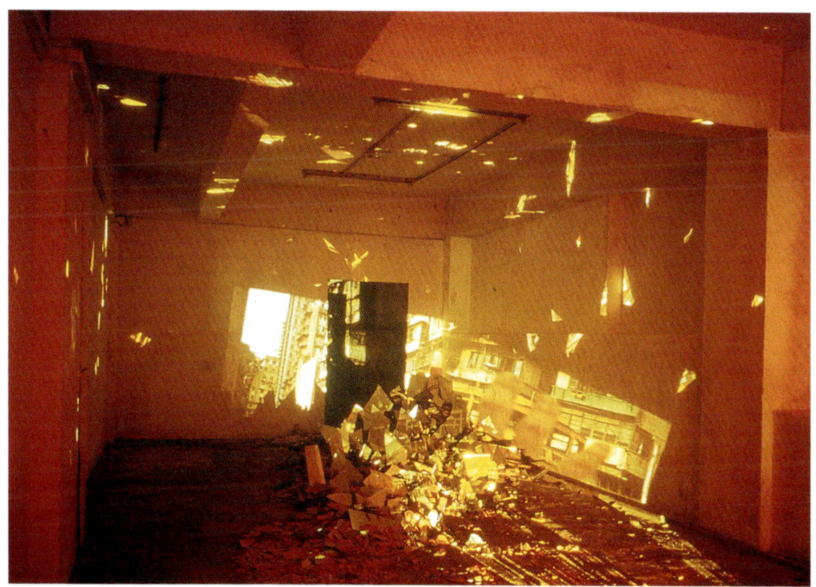

46 Phoebe Man, *Site-seeing*, 1996, temporary site-specific mixed-media installation.

and may in certain cases have played a part in his everyday life or be family heirlooms of some kind – they were not all completely unknown to regular viewers of his work since Tsang has a habit of recycling items from one installation to another, bringing them together in new (but often temporary-looking) conjunctions. As with *Hello! Hong Kong – Part 3*, Tsang chose objects with some sense of cultural history about them, and they functioned as relics or indices of an earlier time and mode of life even if we do not know all that they may mean to the artist himself.

On first entering the installation it felt like the space was rather empty, and Tsang probably went for a relatively sparse installation to help foreground the particular qualities of the space itself (a weathered wall, for instance, replaced the photographs of such walls in *Hello! Hong Kong – Part 3*). Inadvertent traces of the past were thus allowed to mingle with the more advertent ones of the objects he had brought to the site. The sparseness also worked to keep a balance between attempts to reference the past and attempts to reference the past as absent. Care was needed to avoid the pitfall of the merely nostalgic.

There was some continuation between *Hello! Hong Kong – Part 3* and *Hello! Hong Kong – Part 7*. Tsang again made use of bamboo, employing scaffolding workers to construct an inclined bamboo screen

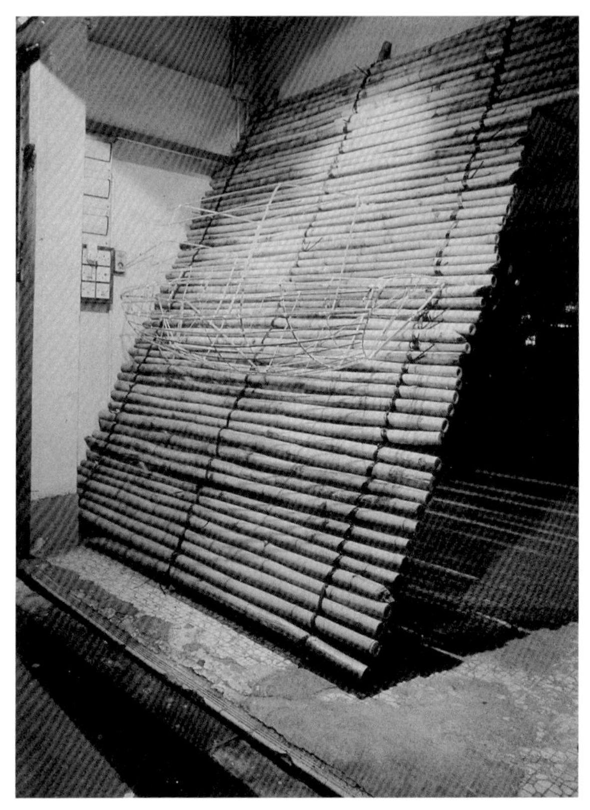

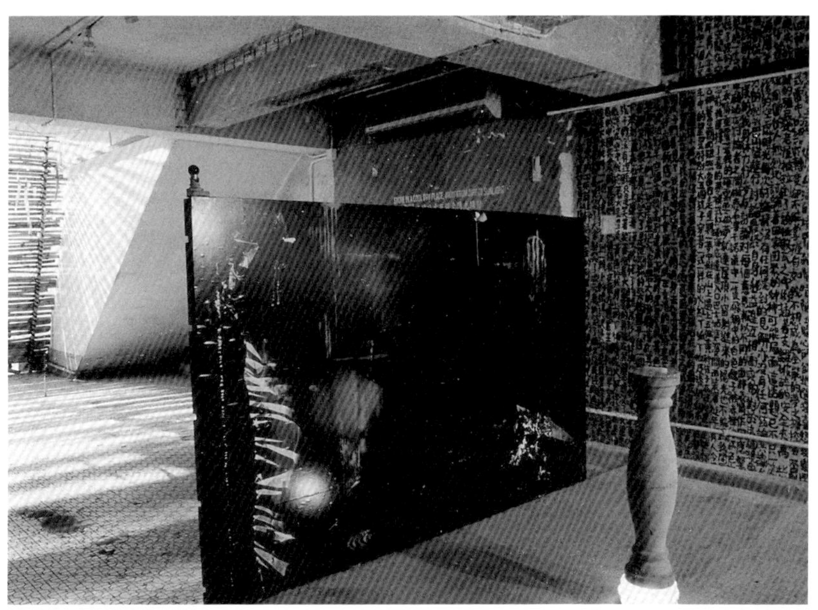

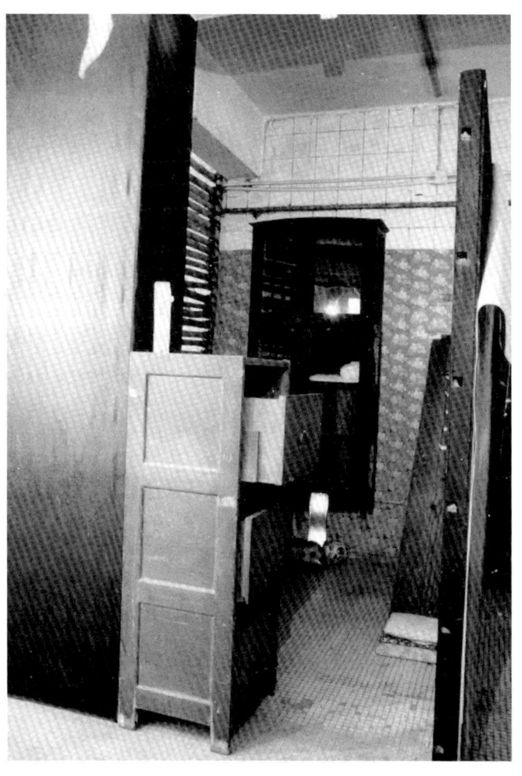

47–9 Kith Tsang,
Details from *Hello!
Hong Kong – Part 7*,
1997, temporary site-
specific mixed-media
installation.

at the front and another vertical one at the rear. The theme of the boat
was also retained – a craftsman using traditional skills was engaged to
construct two skeletal boats of bamboo strips which were installed on
these screens as if emerging from them. The boat theme also returned
in one of the more private corners of the installation, where a stack of
small paper boats was placed. These items are associated with a traditional ritual for exorcizing evil spirits – when a child has fallen ill, for
example – and were juxtaposed by Tsang with a pile of baby clothes
(perhaps an echo of the used clothes included in Lee's *Walk On*, where
they also brought associations of both presence and absence into play).

Since Tsang grew up in the neighbourhood it is not surprising that
childhood memories fed into the work. Mimicking preservationist
practice, Tsang even ventured out into the surrounding streets,
temporarily installing plaques at various points in the district on
which he etched childhood memories associated with the site in question (a map was provided to visitors). History of a more textbook kind
might also be said to haunt the installation, in part because of its close
proximity to 'Possession Point' (the spot where the British first landed

in Hong Kong, and a location now inland due to reclamation). The earlier colonial era was evoked obliquely in the installation itself by the inclusion of a blown-up photograph by Tsang of a statue of King George V taken in the Zoological and Botanical Gardens. An alienation effect was introduced by cropping the statue's head.

Even more tangential were the references to Chinese textbook history and state power. These entered the exhibition space in the form of a handwritten story describing a dream of a group of five children happily playing with stars. Since there were four smaller stars and one larger one this is a clear reference to the Communist Chinese flag, and represents an optimistic attitude towards the handover perhaps held at the time the story was originally composed. Tsang chose to preserve this lost optimism by baking the handwriting on to a series of tiles installed in the gallery space, but a more recent and less confident attitude towards communist China (and thus post-handover life) was juxtaposed with it. The phrase 'Store in a cool dry place, away from direct sunlight', taken from the label of a medicine bottle, was inscribed on a nearby wall. This instruction to preserve the fragile sums up Tsang's project in relation to Hong Kong culture and the sense of identity it sustains, of course, but given the common association of Mao Zedong with the sun in Cultural Revolution-era propaganda it also needs to be read as referring to post-handover threats from national culture. The writing was executed using prickly heat lotion, a balm widely used in sub-tropical Hong Kong against too great an exposure to the sun's power. The darkened interior of the exhibition area – for which the bamboo screen is partly responsible – encourages us to read the written warning in relation to the objects it contains.

The handover theme of *Hello! Hong Kong – Part 7* was continued in Warren Leung's *Victoria Tunnel*, held at Para/Site in January and February 1998, only a few months after the long-awaited transition of sovereignty had occurred. One item in this show (actually created before the handover like most of the art that addressed it, and previously exhibited under the title *Victory over Victoria*) was a large-scale aerial photograph. Presumably of British military origin, it shows the Central area of Hong Kong island, officially known as the city of Victoria. This surveillance image, which shows what look like military vessels in the harbour, was taken in November 1945 (according to data visible along its bottom edge), and thus belongs to the period just after the British regained control of the colony from the Japanese at the end of the Second World War. Involved then is an act of looking back to understand the present – one part of the more general pattern of retrospection as colonial rule was coming to an end which has been examined in Chapter 2. Leung looks to one moment of colonial transition not involving independence for evidence of relevance to the present one.

Word play helps complicate matters. In addition to the title there is a barely visible inscription (the word *victory*) on the protective glass in front of the framed photo itself. Is a victory over Victoria a victory over the city (symbolizing Hong Kong) or over the British (symbolized by the queen who reigned when Hong Kong was taken)? Is the word over to be taken literally or metaphorically? The panoptic viewpoint of the photograph was originally a British one, but has that position now been reoccupied, and by whom? By the Chinese state perhaps, following 1997 (because the date of the handover was fixed so many years in advance, a premature retrospection was not an uncommon phenomenon)? Hong Kong itself remains the object, not subject, of the controlling gaze no matter who owns it, but the distinctness between past and present become blurred.

Such a temporal blurring can also be found in photographs Leung has taken himself. Like Tsang and Lee, Leung is a proficient photographer, and he characteristically employs a self-made pinhole camera as his tool. This has the effect of making his images appear to belong to an earlier era. His *Opposite the Sai Ying Pun Market, Western District* (illus. 50) or *To Kwa Wan, Kowloon* (1997) are examples with this aura of age, even if the latter includes a group of modern buildings which might have given the image a contemporary feel. A series of four pinhole photos – *Fo Tan, New Territories, 1993–1996* – actually documents the construction of a number of housing tower blocks, but because of the primitive feel of these predominately dark pinhole images (in which shadow engulfs the subject) they appear to document loss rather than progress (illus. 51). These instant relics – images of the present as already lost – remind one of Eugène Atget's photographs of Paris, which show the city stripped bare of human presence.

The word play of *Victory over Victoria* is a continuation of the interest in language already displayed in *Untitled (After Dream of a Path)*, and this trend continues in other works by Leung, and indeed by Tsang and other Para/Site artists. One factor here is the way in which the Cantonese spoken language is able to function as a marker of local Hong Kong identity more effectively than the more directly visual means available to artists. All literate Chinese speakers share the same written language (albeit that mainland China uses simplified versions of many characters), and the written script thus functions as a resource for nationalist ideologies. However, the Cantonese spoken 'dialect' and the official national spoken form (Putonghua) are more mutually unin-

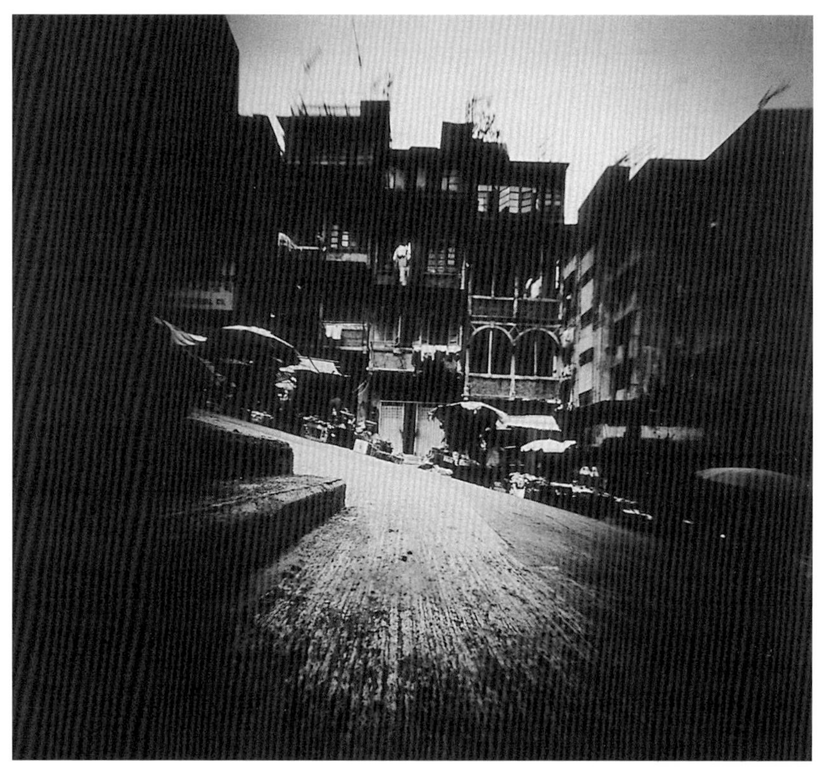

50 Warren Leung, *Opposite the Sai Ying Pun Market, Western District*, 1994, black-and-white photographic print. Collection of the artist.

telligible than some distinct 'languages'. One way in which spoken language can enter the silent world of the visual is by means of a visual/verbal pun, and such punning is common in Cantonese (where tonal difference may be the only factor that distinguishes two otherwise identical sounds of completely different meaning), for instance when fish is served at Chinese New Year because the Cantonese for fish sounds like the auspicious word meaning surplus.[7] Tsang used this approach in the case of *Guong Guen* (illus. 52), a sculptural assemblage exhibited in the Para/Site show *Art SUPERmarket* (February to March 1998) which illustrates a Cantonese slang phrase. With this work Tsang consciously attempted to continue the word play found in Antonio Mak's works (such as his previously discussed *Bible from Happy Valley*).

Simply writing down the Cantonese spoken language also allows it to enter the visual sphere, of course, but its value as a marker of local identity would generally be lost in the pan-Chinese medium of charac-

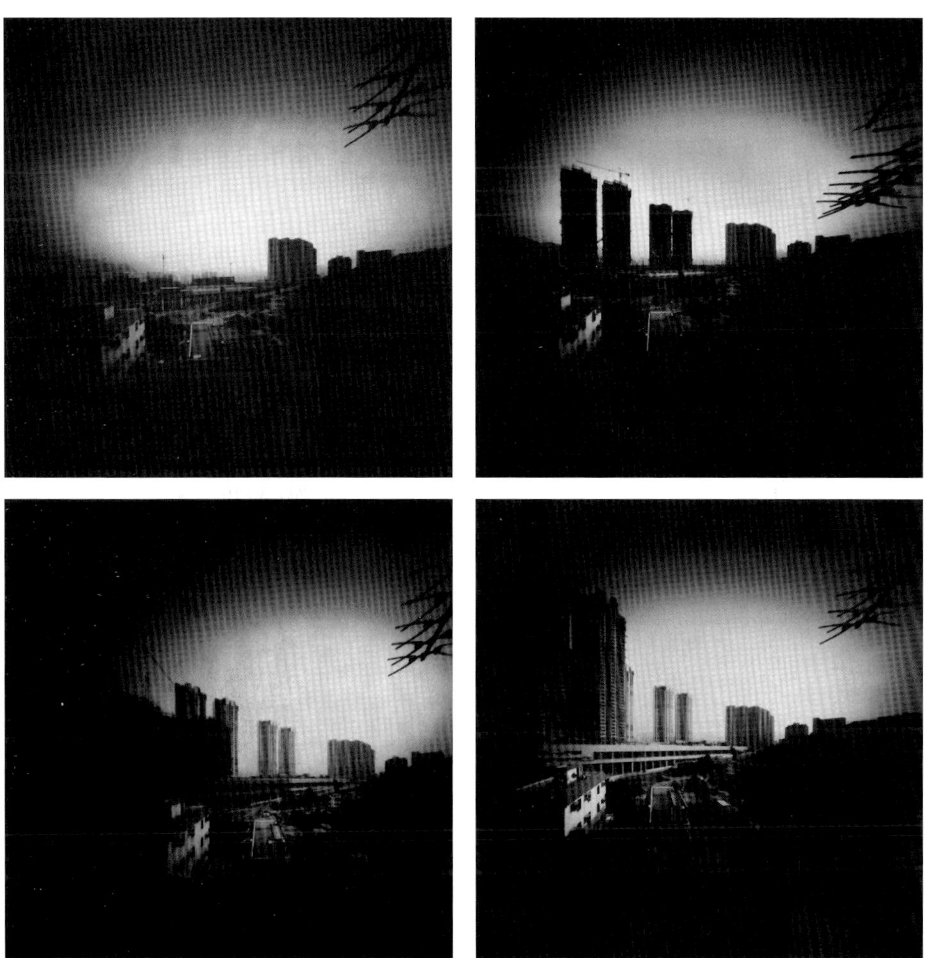

51 Warren Leung, *Fo Tan, New Territories, 1993–1996* (4 images), black-and-white photographic prints. Collection of the artist.

ter writing. Both Leung and Tsang get around this problem by using romanization (either in titles or on inscriptions within their works) as a way of preserving the sounds of Cantonese in the written form.[8] The title of *Guong Guen* is an example of this practice, preserving the opacity of the pun to English speakers (after tempting them to think they are being offered something in their own language), as well as frustrating the understanding of those literate in Chinese but unable to speak Cantonese. Just as Hong Kong artists turned towards Western art media to escape the cultural essentialism that ink painting could easily become captive to, so too they used Western linguistic resources

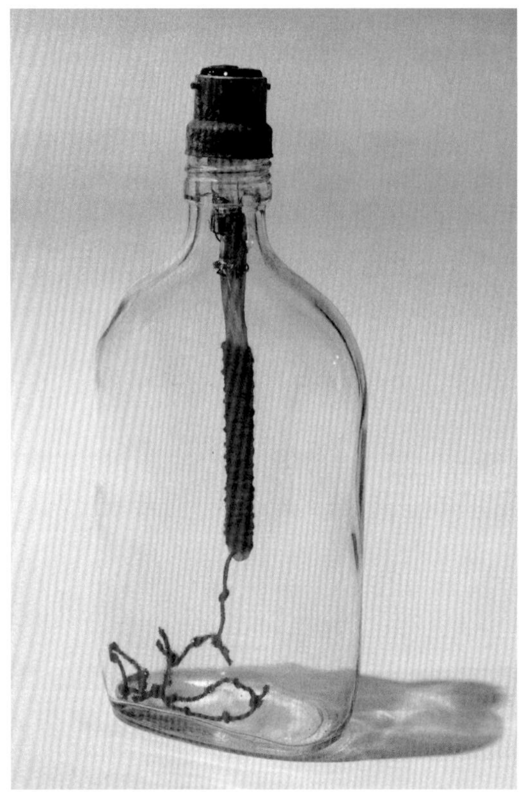

52 Kith Tsang, *Guong Guen*, 1998, mixed-media sculptural assemblage. Collection of the artist.

to escape the hegemony of written Chinese. In either case, 'Westernization' or 'cultural imperialism' are terms which completely fail to capture the active and locally orientated use of borrowed elements which has been taking place.

Leung, although not making a visual/verbal pun like Tsang, does something similar to *Guong Guen* in *Vis(i)ta* (illus. 53), the word play in the title of which signals an interest in both landscape and the tourist's gaze (the latter intrusive 'I' or 'eye' perhaps a modern variant of the imperial gaze with which *Victory over Victoria* was concerned). This conceptual assemblage consists of three sealed wooden pinhole cameras installed one above the other in an iron frame, each containing an invisible exposure taken at one of three established tourist sites in Hong Kong. The gaze of the outsider is thus simultaneously addressed and frustrated, and the verbal element of the work plays the same game. On each of the three sections is inscribed a romanization of the Cantonese name for the place the photograph was taken, as if offered by way of helpful explanation but in fact likely to compound

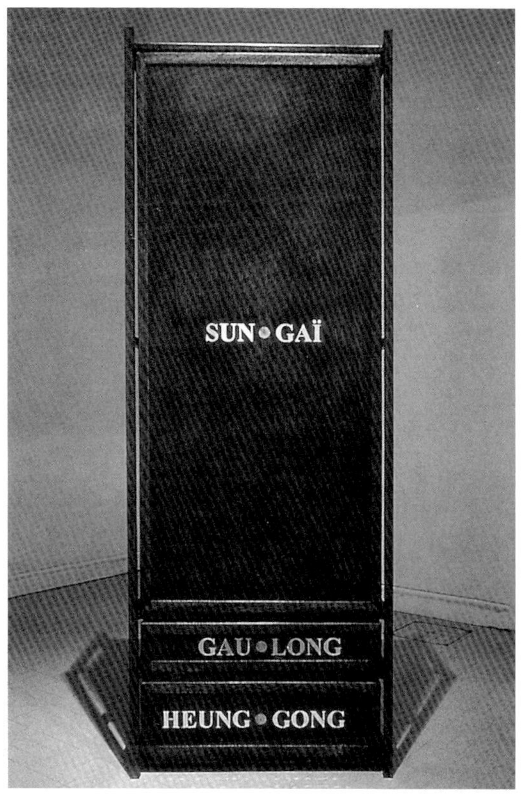

53 Warren Leung, *Vis(i)ta*, 1996–7, wood, zinc plate, mirror, iron, Liquid Light. Collection of the artist.

confusion. Since the lettering has a mirrored surface the visitor is left to contemplate his or her own reflection.

As well as using romanization Tsang and Leung have experimented with other ways of preserving Cantonese in a written form or refusing the hegemony of standard written Chinese. In the Chinese version of his series title *Hello! Hong Kong* Tsang uses a particular type of character that enables the sound of the English word Hello to be represented in Chinese, celebrating the cultural hybridity of Hong Kong, where English terms are often playfully and vividly incorporated into everyday Cantonese speech. In *Domestic Amnesia* of 1997 Leung employed a different strategy, making use of a numerical code to inscribe Chinese terms within his work. This code, developed to enable telegraphic transfer of Chinese characters, allows a distance to be opened up from the several thousand years of Chinese culture and history throughout which character writing has been used. It is nevertheless a 'Chinese written language' of sorts, both inalienably modern in association yet at the same time almost obsolete (despite its continued use in

Hong Kong on government-issued identity cards).

A concern with language has been a prominent feature of mainland Chinese contemporary art during the same period that Hong Kong artists have been exploring the possibilities of the verbal as a marker of the local. A brief consideration, however, will make clear the difference of motivation. Mainland artists tend to display a concern with the written language only, and not also with the spoken form, since they are unconcerned with marking differences within Chinese culture unlike Hong Kong artists. Their target is Chinese culture conceived of as a whole, of which the distinctive and long-established written language is a convenient symbol. Although antagonistic to this cultural heritage, their critiques can themselves be said to assume a national frame to a large degree. Xu Bing's important *A Book from the Sky* (illus. 54), for instance, consisting of the printed impressions of thousands of well-formed but meaningless Chinese characters, seems a Herculean attempt to take on the several thousand-year-old national cultural inheritance as a whole, to meet it head on and negate it in its entirety. It attempts to call into being a temporal divide, a break with the past, rather than the spatial distinction which is the main concern of Hong Kong artists.[9]

In the shows held at Para/Site's Sheung Wan venue after Tsang's and Leung's the theme of Hong Kong identity has remained of major importance. Even though the handover has begun to recede into the past, taking the most extreme worries about life under Chinese rule with it, there is a persisting concern with the local. Certain of the strategies for evoking it, such as the use of language or the employment of already culturally coded items of material culture, have continued to be used. *Kem zeg fen zeg* (a group show curated by William Cheung which took place in February and March 1999), for instance, focused on household objects. Items of everyday experience were denatured or recontextualized by the artists and designers working on the show. Its romanized name is a Cantonese saying which describes poverty through an image of someone forced to improvise cheap replacements for a bed and a pillow.

Sara Wong's video installation *Local Orientation* (March to April 1998) continued the longstanding Para/Site concern with the neighbourhood in which the gallery is sited, consisting of video recordings of various attempts to travel in a straight line out from the gallery. An exploration of the vicinity was also part of the collective working process of the artists involved in *Ghost Encounter* (curated by Chan Yuk-keung, September 1997), leading to the discovery that 'the surrounding environment was steeped in a mysterious, ghostly atmo-

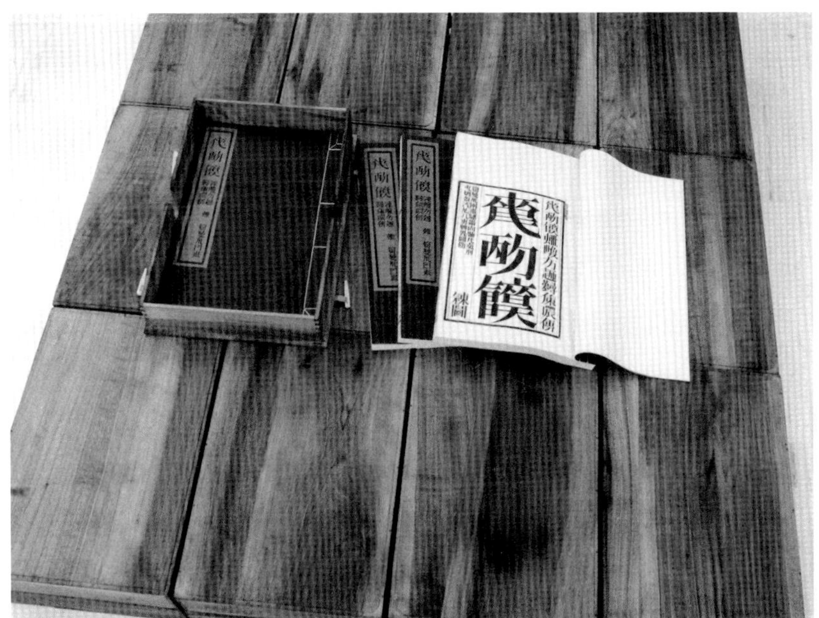

54 Xu Bing, Detail from installation of *A Book from the Sky*, 1987–91, hand-printed books.

sphere, with its shops selling paper offerings [used in funeral cere-monies and in homage to ancestors], a hospital and a mortuary house'.[10] In *Terraces Topography*, a series of exhibitions held at Para/Site and other venues during January and February 2000 and co-ordinated by Kith Tsang, the older areas of the city on the border between Sheung Wan and Central districts were again the subject of artistic investigation. Ho Siu Kee's photographic installation (shown at OP Fotogallery) contrasted the traces of older forms of life still visible in Peel Street with the gentrification and new spaces of consumerism found just one street further towards Central because of the presence there of an escalator link designed to carry commuters between the business district and the high-class residential area of Mid-levels. Tsang's own work, titled *The Storage of Amnesia* (illus. 55), was shown at the John Batten Gallery (actually located in Peel Street) and again involved the accumulation of objects with personal associations. In Para/Site itself, on the other hand, Li Wei Han displayed ceramic artworks inspired by the Hungry Ghost Festival, thus recalling the theme of *Ghost Encounter*.

Ghost Encounter had in fact taken place around the time of the Hungry Ghost Festival, an annual purification ritual conducted to

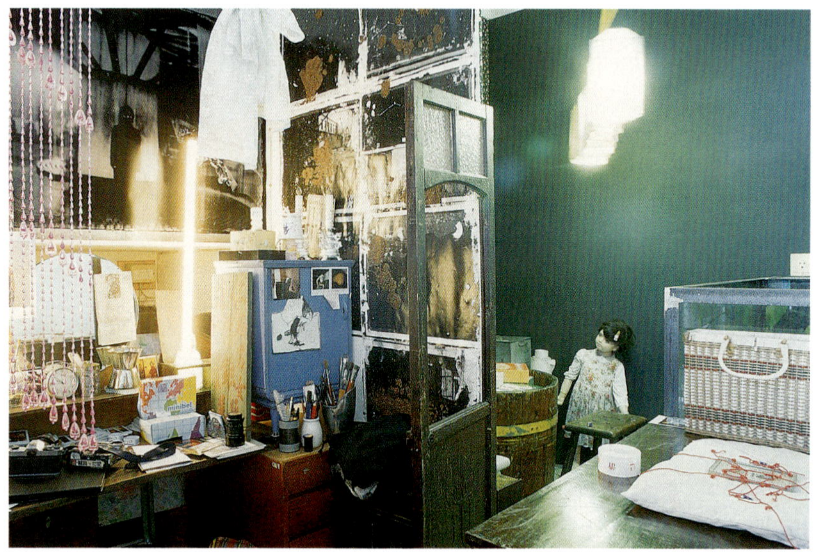

55 Kith Tsang, Detail from *The Storage of Amnesia*, 2000, temporary site-specific mixed-media installation exhibited at the John Batten Gallery as part of the *Terraces Topography* series.

appease spirits of those who have died without decendants to make offerings for them. During this time the neighbourhood of the Para/Site venue sees collective burning of offerings in temporary incinerators placed in the street, as well as outdoor opera performances. The notion of ghosts involves a consideration of the past and its traces such as Kith Tsang and Warren Leung have been more broadly concerned with, and Stanley Kwan's film *Rouge* (1988) also comes to mind in this context for its use of a ghost story as a way of commenting on the relationship (or disjunction) between Hong Kong's past and present (ghosts are a common subject of a great many more overtly commercial Hong Kong movies as well). Ghost themes also appear in several of Oscar Ho's *Stories Around Town*, and Kacey Wong (later to become a member of Para/Site) exhibited a work called *Mechanical Ghost* in *Cultural Chop Shui II* (curated by Lau Kin Wai, and held at the Fringe Club Gallery, 4–13 October 1996). Wong's work consisted of sculptural forms suspended from a ceiling fan mechanism, which was set in motion by a infra-red motion detector (as if to make the point that we create ghosts through our fears).

Tsang's attempt in *Hello! Hong Kong – Part 7* to create a private or domestic feel in the gallery was echoed in several later Para/Site shows. *Ghost Encounter*, starting from the knowledge that the gallery

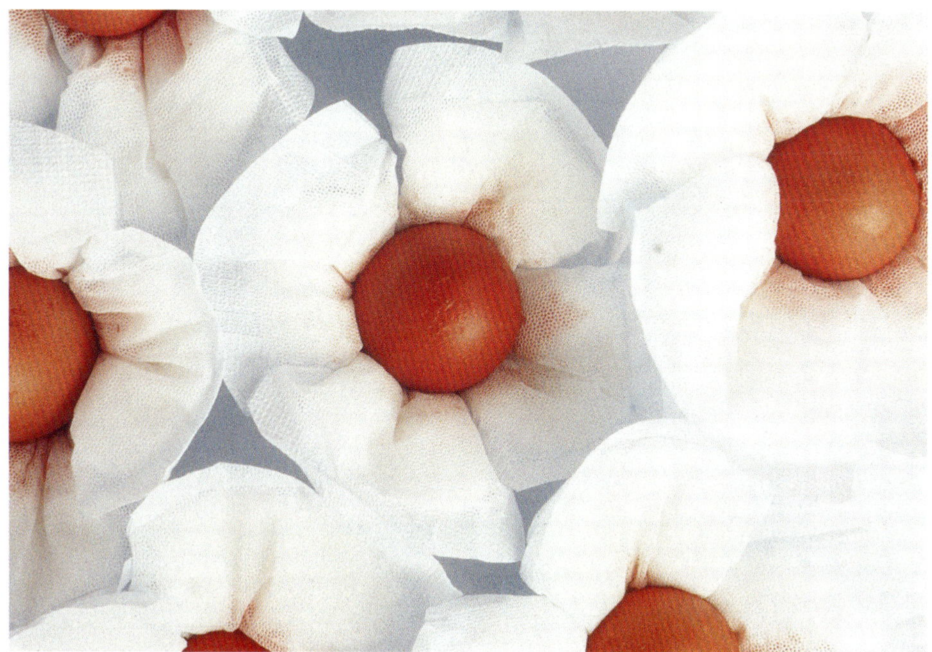

56 Phoebe Man, Detail from *A Present for her Growth 1*, 1996, temporary site-specific mixed-media installation.

had a previous history of use, divided up the exhibition space as if it were an old-style residential flat of the kind to be found in the area, placing works in the 'rooms' to which they were thematically linked. Exactly the same strategy was used by *Kem zeg fen zeg. Home* (a mixed-media show curated by the Young Architects League, January to February 1999) addressed the issue of domestic space more directly: Kacey Wong's sculptures such as *Partition* and *The Horror*, for instance, were box-like wooden structures resembling aberrant architectural models of tower blocks (perhaps inspired by Wong's undergraduate training in architecture). Cut-away views were offered of private spaces within which various human dramas were acted out with the aid of plastic figurines, the viewer placed in the role of voyeur. *Partition* and *The Horror* reappeared on display in the company of a number of other works of a similar nature in *10 Boxes*, a solo show of Wong's sculpture held at the John Batten Gallery between 12 and 30 April 2000.

Kwok Mang-ho's *Art Life at Para/Site for 72 Hours* (February 1998) was a further engagement with the theme of domesticity, literally turning the gallery into a home, albeit for only four days. An expres-

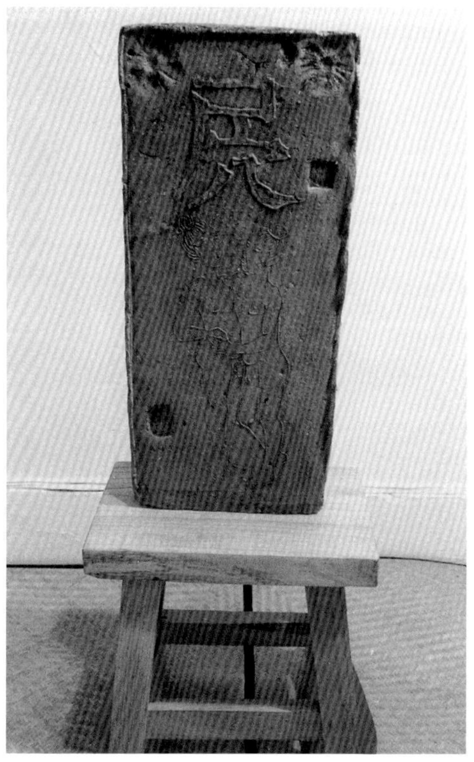 57 Leung Po-shan, Detail from *Tsao*, 1997, mixed-media installation. Collection of the artist.

sion of Kwok's desire to blur the boundaries between art and life, this performance and installation piece was one of a long series of attempts to construct temporary utopian community and banish the alienation of modern urban living.[11] Kwok was also involved in a 'Street Happening' organized in the vicinity of Para/Site on 20 January 2001 as part of the *Landscape* project (curated by Young Hay at various venues in January 2001 as part of the Fringe Club's Star Alliance City Festival). The persisting concern of Para/Site with private or domestic space was echoed in one of the other events of that outdoor art festival: Y-Space, an avant-garde dance group consisting of Victor Ma and Mandy Yim, installed in the street a 'bedspace' complete with mosquito netting as the venue for their performance.

Perhaps the work exhibited at the new Para/Site gallery that least fits the general trends already described is that by female artists with what might be taken broadly as a feminist agenda. Although they find installation a useful medium, and reference the local in their work, residual cultural traditions offer a more problematic resource for them than for many of their male counterparts on account of the dimension of gender oppression they contain. As a result there is less concern with loss in their works, and they tend to make more direct statements, even courting spectator outrage on occasion. Tradition is directly violated in Leung Po-shan's work *Tsao* (illus. 57), for example, which was included in a joint show with Man titled *P-read* (November to December 1997). The work consists of two clay 'ancestor tablets' associated with the patrilineal cult of forebears so distinctively a part of Chinese culture, but the tablets have erotic images and Chinese characters with obscene meanings inscribed on them. The tablets are placed on small stools the legs of which are inserted into female slippers (with matting below).[12]

One work by Man in *P-read* involved the employment of sanitary towels, as had several earlier related works such as *A Present for her Growth I* of 1996 (illus. 56). Strongly gender-marked, this latter piece brings together references to both pregnancy and menstruation. Light bulbs, the aforementioned sanitary towels (with traces of red paint resembling blood), and egg shells (which have also been painted red, and which thus recall the gifts given in Chinese culture on the birth of a baby) are the materials used in this piece. These elements are purposely still identifiable: the artist, as in certain earlier works, deliberately presents us with taboo objects and thus a sense of decorum breached. At the same time the materials are transformed: Man creates balls of flower forms which carry associations that are not reducible to those of their constituent parts.[13]

Because of the collective's reliance on the Arts Development Council for year by year funding of its exhibition programme, the long-term future of Para/Site's venue in Sheung Wan seems less than fully assured. Fundraising efforts, in the form of two *Art SUPERmarket* shows where Para/Site shared the income from works sold with the artists involved, raised only a relatively small amount. On the other hand the involvement of a wider circle of artists and curators with the Para/Site project during the period it has been at its second venue, as well as the opening of a small Para/Site Central spot inside the progressive commercial gallery Hanart TZ, are positive signs. Involvement in international artistic exchanges and the exhibition of work by overseas artists are other new developments. Among exchanges was the *Materia Prima* project, which saw Kith Tsang, Kacey Wong and Ching Chin Wai creating works on site at Melbourne's West Space in August 1999, and a return exhibit of Australian work in Hong Kong in December of the same year. Exhibits by overseas artists (one example was Sabina Hoertner's show in June 2000) have come about because of the growing international exposure of the Para/Site members, several of whom have spent extended periods overseas while pursuing their studies further or as a result of winning residencies or travel grants. Given all these positive signs, Para/Site surely has a role to play – in some form or another – in the development of Hong Kong's increasingly diverse artistic scene.

Oil Street

Although other artist-run spaces have not addressed local material culture and the changing urban environment in their programming in the same way as Para/Site, several groups based in one particular location did get involved more directly in debates about urban transformation which became a broader public preoccupation in the post-handover period. These groups, such as 1A Space, the Artist Commune, and Videotage (a video and new media collective), obtained temporary leases at low rent in a former Government Supplies Department depot at Oil Street, North Point in mid-1998. Because of the concentration of art spaces here, along with less audience-orientated but equally art-related tenants such as photographic and design studios (including that of Almond Chu [illus. 58]), almost by accident a geographically focused alternative cultural scene developed of a kind never before seen in Hong Kong. A model was offered for cultural planners who had so far only promoted the arts though the provision of purpose-built prestige venues, and had not considered such successful cases of artist-led urban regeneration as New York's Soho. The groups themselves, of course, had an in-built motivation to promote such a

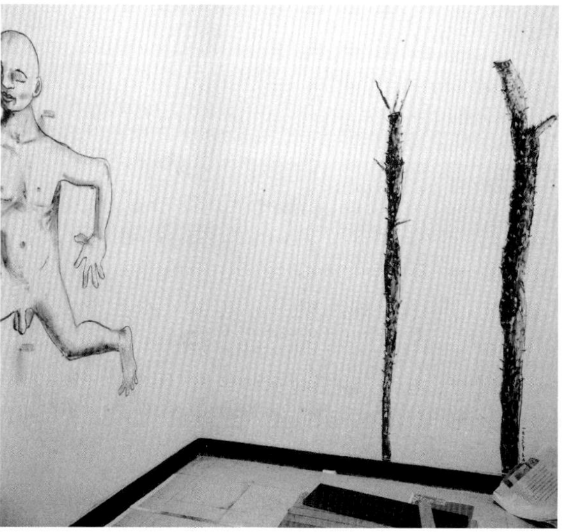

58 Almond Chu, *The Former Government Supplies Department, Oil Street*, 1999, colour photographic print. Collection of the artist.

model actively in order to save their venues from redevelopment.

With the unexpected economic downturn of the early post-handover period, triggered by the broader Asian recession, previously buoyant property values plummeted by about half, and the housing speculation boom came to an abrupt end. Criticism was rife of the government's role in sustaining high land prices through its control of freehold, and collusive relationship with large property development companies. There were many calls for a rethink of legal structures to enable renovation of older buildings and neighbourhoods for new purposes: restoration of existing structures, rather than straight clearance, was now felt by many in the community at large to offer the greatest possibilities for enhancing the quality of urban living in general and of creating the kind of cultural districts that would attract tourist income and encourage international companies to choose Hong Kong as their regional base.[14]

Although grand plans for the development of a cultural and entertainment district from scratch on reclaimed land in West Kowloon were also being considered during this period as a way of meeting these latter ends,[15] the grass-roots success of the Oil Street Art Village (as it came to be known) provided a focus for alternative visions to this top down, hardware first approach. Even though the artists' groups did eventually have to move out of Oil Street around the end of 1999 (some to a less desirable alternative venue offered by the government), an important point had been made about the value of the local and the vernacular as opposed to the supposedly modern and international. A victory of sorts had been won at the level of public consciousness, and the government's inability to support grass-root development of the arts has been again underlined. Even the Town Planning Board seems to have listened to this message: at a hearing on 29 October 1999 it voted down a plan by property developer Cheung Kong to construct a cruise ship terminal on the Oil Street site, despite the plan having been given approval in principle on an earlier occasion.[16] Clearly the issues addressed by Para/Site artists in their installations were also of concern to many people in the society at large – the amnesiac modernity of the Hong Kong cityscape was also beginning to be questioned outside of the gallery.

4 Carving Public Space

The most productive approach to Hong Kong public sculpture of the handover period is that which emphasizes what might be called the public life of artworks. Such an approach gives its primary attention to acts of display and reception (over which a particular sculpture's maker may have little or no influence). It conceives of artistic meaning as contextual in nature: subject to change over time and conditioned by an artwork's location in both physical and cultural space. Artworks should not be understood as simply passive in relation to their place and time, however, but as capable of being used in an active promulgation or contestation of social meanings by those who display or respond to them. Hong Kong in both the late colonial era and the subsequent post-handover period saw particularly intense and open contests over social meaning, with neither the colonial government nor its successor enjoying an easy hegemony, and art – especially public art – played a significant role in the ideological struggles which took place.

Although the study of other moments of post-colonial transition might lead one to imagine that the main contest of ideas would be between imposed colonial ideologies and emerging national meanings, in Hong Kong this was not in fact the case. Instead the contest was primarily one between emerging local Hong Kong meanings (allied to a struggle for democracy and local autonomy) and Chinese national meanings (as interpreted by the Chinese Communist state and those in allegiance to it). After 1984, when China and Britain signed the Joint Declaration, the colonial state was no longer a significant target in itself. Instead local concerns turned more to the post-1997 future, which offered the prospect of absorption into a larger pre-existing state entity (rather than independence, the most commonly desired and achieved sequel to colonialism). For many Hong Kong people this was not appealing – particularly after the trauma of 4 June 1989 – and a growing sense of local cultural selfhood was a consequence. Many Hong Kong artists began asserting a sense of local identity through their artworks, and even public art produced outside of the territory, proved of use to these emerging narratives of cultural autonomy.

The colonial state in its late phase lacked the will or capability to assert publicly a positive ideology of its own, in contrast to earlier and more confident phases of the imperial project. The promotion of an

'East meets West' image of Hong Kong, which relied on a conception of cultures as distinct entities without a history of previous intercourse or other opportunities for encounter, was a strategy employed for mystifying the less innocuous or mutual encounter of cultures which colonialism actually is. This ideology of a modernization that somehow retained Chineseness intact was to mutate following the signing of the Joint Declaration into the idea that material progress and prosperity would be guaranteed by the hybrid model of 'One Country, Two Systems' (again modernization and Chineseness were deemed compatible, but this time the latter was conceived in national terms). Since the Chinese state was promoting much the same thing this could be seen as a capitulation of the colonial regime to the ideology of the People's Republic. This united front was to break down catastrophically following 4 June 1989, however. Lacking any firm basis of legitimacy, the colonial regime made a strategic surrender in its last few years to the growing local demands for autonomy that might otherwise have made its position impossible. The watershed came with Governor Chris Patten's Policy Address to the Legislative Council of 7 October 1992, which announced plans for constitutional development that would meet to some extent the call for enhanced democracy. A short-lived democratic legislature was installed, with elections held on 17 September 1995. This helped buy the colonial government a modicum of approval from Hong Kong people which lasted till the end of its tenure, and incidentally made its record look more respectable for the history books at little actual cost. The post-handover regime, constitutionally subject to Beijing, renewed the active promulgation of national meanings, through public art among other means. Sovereignty in any real sense involved more than simply a raising of the national flag on Hong Kong soil, and this battle for Hong Kong people's hearts and minds was a game with high stakes and no easy foregone conclusion.

Because the transfer of sovereignty – or more accurately the foreknowledge of its certain approach – prompted the development of a strong sense of local consciousness in Hong Kong, it helped constitute a particularly distinct arena for the display and reception of public art with few direct parallels elsewhere. Physical as well as cultural factors played a part in this, the border fence for example cut Hong Kong off from its hinterland much more than most other cities, and the high population density and spatial compactness of the city enabled a large percentage of the population to have a first-hand acquaintance with many public sculptures and their environments. The amplification effect of media attention to public artworks also needs to be considered. The importance of the public arena for art in Hong Kong might also have been intensified by the absence of truly democratic political arenas in the territory either before or after the handover, resulting in a greater weight being placed on political meanings made manifest in the cultural realm. Indeed 'political' politics, and not just cultural politics, had itself been forced out into the streets in Hong Kong to a large degree: a large public demonstration on 4 June 1989 in protest at the state violence in Beijing was a defining moment in the development of Hong Kong people's sense of their own autonomy, or collective identity as political actors. Conservative estimates are that the demonstration attracted over half a million people (out of a total population at that time of less than six million), while other estimates suggest more than a million.[1]

Corporate Use of Public Sculpture

Before considering Hong Kong public sculpture during the more overtly politicized handover period it would be valuable to establish a point of reference by considering first an ensemble of sculptures created before the watershed date of 4 June 1989 for the prominent local property company Hong Kong Land. Consisting of four pieces, all by artists from outside Hong Kong, this installation can be found in front of Exchange Square, a landmark office building in the Central business district which (as the name suggests) houses the territory's stock exchange. Located in a public plaza at podium level which connects to a series of elevated walkways, the four sculptures are Henry Moore's *Oval with Points* (illus. 59), a pair of works by Elizabeth Frink, *Water Buffalo Standing* (illus. 60) and *Water Buffalo Lying* (both of 1988) and *Taichi Single Whip* by Taiwanese artist Ju Ming (illus. 61).

When completed in 1985 Exchange Square was one of the most outstanding pieces of contemporary architecture in Hong Kong, and it still commands commercial rents that reflect its prestige status. The choice of works by overseas sculptors with international reputations functions to underline and enhance profitably the building's own claims to modernity and international status (even if its form – considered in sculptural terms – is more indebted than theirs to the language of geometric abstraction). At the same time there is a note of contrast introduced at the level of subject matter which works to the same effect – the water buffaloes remind us of the old agricultural Hong Kong that trade and development have now replaced, thereby enhancing the adjacent building's sense of contemporaneity.

59 Henry Moore, *Oval with Points*, 1968/70, bronze. Collection Hong Kong Land, installed on the podium, Exchange Square.

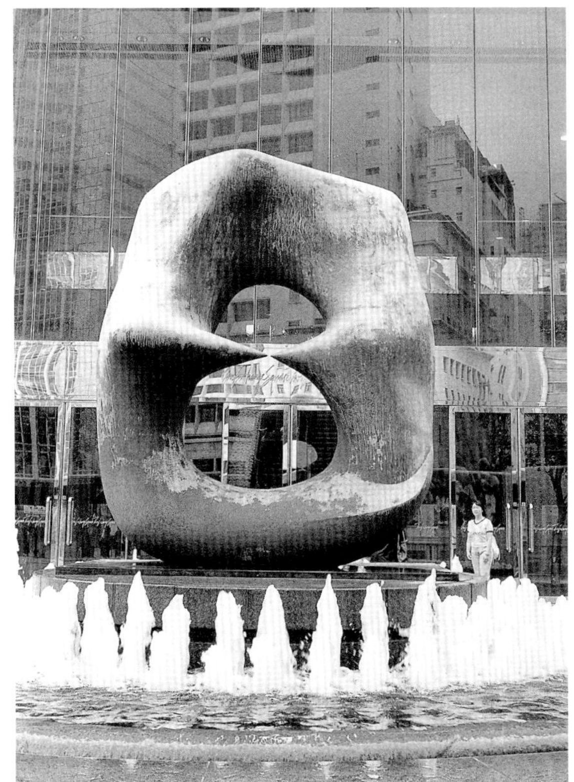

60 Elizabeth Frink, *Water Buffalo Standing*, 1988, bronze. Collection Hong Kong Land, installed on the podium, Exchange Square.

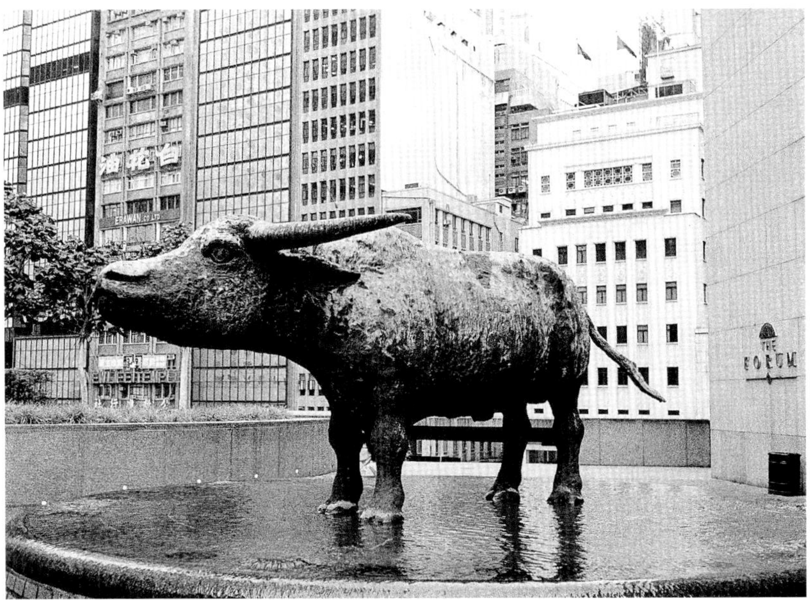

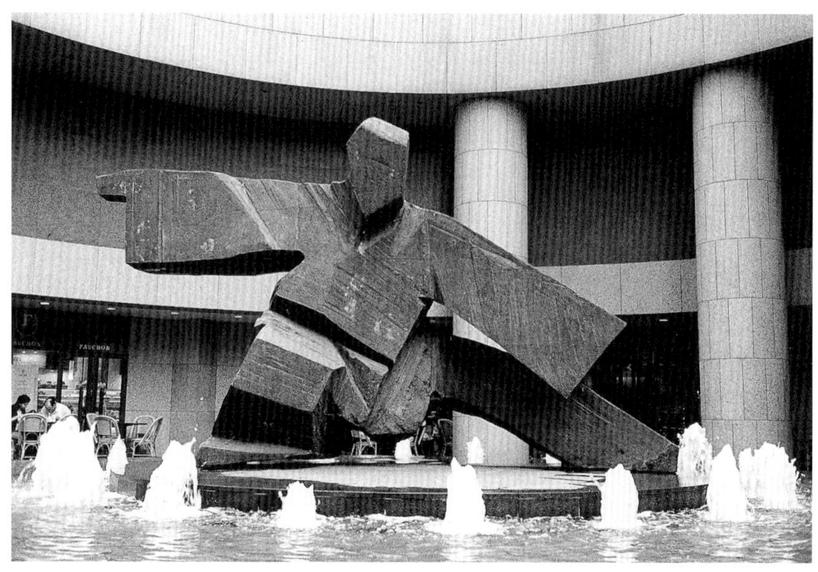

61 Ju Ming, *Taichi Single Whip*, 1985, bronze. Collection Hong Kong Land, installed on the podium, Exchange Square.

The international associations of the choice of sculptors are also appropriate to a stock exchange, a nexus of global flows of both money and information. Indeed further examination of the ensemble indicates that care has been taken to assemble works that allude to good fortune in general or even to stock market success in particular. Direct reference to the notion of a 'bull market' is surely intended in the choice of water buffalo as a subject, even if such an association would not be uppermost in a differing context of display. Since the pair of Frink sculptures were directly commissioned in 1986, it is fair to assume that local reference and auspicious connotation were intended by the artist herself and even perhaps accepted as part of her brief, but this is not the case with the other two sculptures that make up the ensemble. They were pre-existing works made without reference to this particular location and the site-specific meanings they carry are ones which have been created by the act of display itself. The Ju Ming piece (purchased from an exhibition of the artist's works held in Exchange Square's gallery, The Rotunda, to mark the building's opening) carries markedly Chinese connotations because of its subject matter. This is of course appropriate in general terms: it helps to counteract the perhaps too overtly Western language by which the building expresses its modernity, providing a balancing of cultural references that artists such as Lui Shou-kwan, Wucius Wong or Van Lau have also sought. A more specific relevance to a stock exchange and site of business, however, is provided by the resemblance between this figure with outstretched arms and splayed legs and the Chinese character meaning 'big'. Such connotations of profitability, also found in the Frink works, are echoed and reinforced in the Moore. Writing is again involved as the key to meaning: both the sculptural form of *Oval with Points* and the negative space inside it resemble a numeral eight, which is highly auspicious in Cantonese on account of a similarity between the pronunciation of the character for 'eight' and that of the character meaning 'to prosper'.

Such play with words and images to invoke auspicious meanings is prevalent within Chinese culture, and Hong Kong artists frequently use less conventional visual/verbal punning to produce distinctly local meanings only fully comprehensible to those who can speak Cantonese, the dominant dialect in the territory. In everyday colloquial speech borrowings from English into Cantonese are also common and this linguistic hybridity functions in the same way as a marker of the local. In a sense the viewer proposed by the Exchange Square display for *Oval with Points* is also linguistically hybrid (even though the work itself was relatively monocultural in its conception), since he or she must be capable of reading arabic numerals in Cantonese. This point, although important, cannot be pressed too far since such numerals are in fact as common as their Chinese character equivalents in Hong Kong, and would not be perceived as markedly foreign. Clearly though, someone ignorant of Chinese culture and language would not appreciate the way in which the Moore is participating in a game of meaning being played across the whole ensemble, and this local specificity or cultural relativity of meaning renders inadequate any attempt to explain the presence of a British sculptor's work in Hong Kong as a simple case of 'Westernization'.

A second example of corporate use of public sculpture in an architectural context where sculptures and a building interact to create an ensemble of meaning can be found in the case of the Hong Kong and Shanghai Bank building (illus. 62, 63), arguably the single most significant example of modern architecture in the city and certainly intended as such. Even more than Exchange Square, this is architecture that begs to be looked at in quasi-sculptural terms, as an ambitious structure with a public statement to make. By contrast many other buildings on the Hong Kong skyline seem only minimally concerned with addressing the passer-by, preoccupied instead with maximization of land use – the Hong Kong and Shanghai Bank building makes a point of disdaining such inwardness by elevating itself off the ground and dedi-

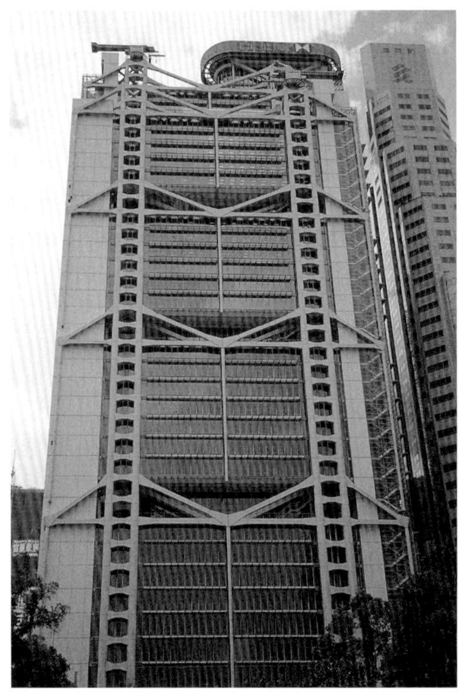

62 Foster Associates, Headquarters of the Hong Kong and Shanghai Banking Corporation, 1985 (front view).

63 Foster Associates, Headquarters of the Hong Kong and Shanghai Banking Corporation, 1985 (back view).

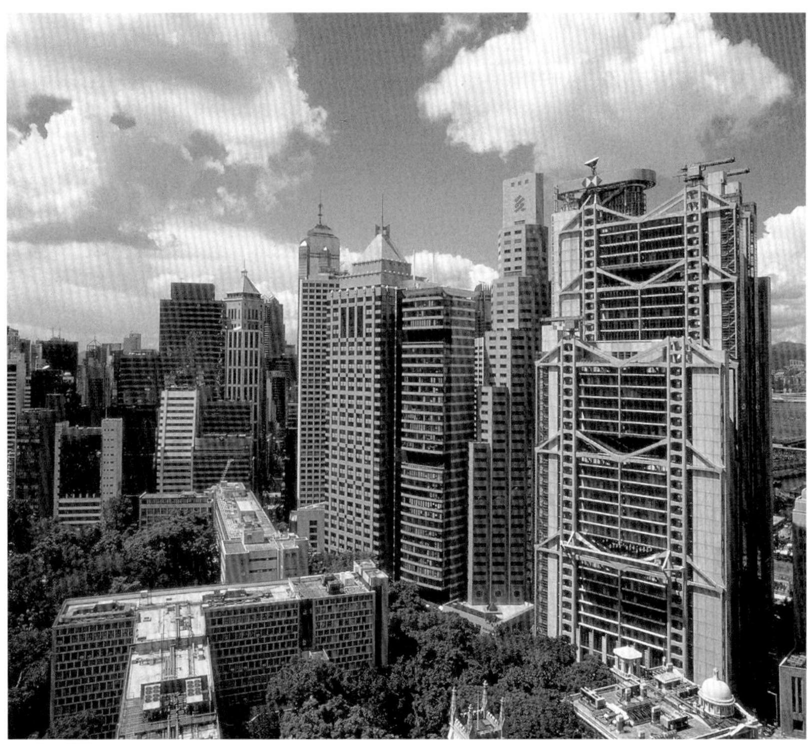

cating the vacant ground-floor area to public use as a sheltered but unglazed plaza and pedestrian short cut. As with Exchange Square, the building reflects modernity and progress, and its conspicuously high-tech externalized structure conveys these associations very well. In this case, however, there is a more specific handover-related intention as well – to convey to actual and potential customers that the bank is committed to Hong Kong beyond the transfer of sovereignty. During the handover period itself, in fact, this message of the building was given explicit expression through a sign temporarily attached to it reading 'Your Future is Our Future'.

Given the sophisticated forward-looking nature of the architecture itself, there was little place for sculpture to signify modernity and smooth progress as in the case of Exchange Square. Instead sculpture enhanced the associations of the building by means of an effect of contrast, by referring to the past (and specifically the bank's past). Whereas there is a thematic allusion to Hong Kong's past in the Frink water buffaloes, in the case of the Hong Kong and Shanghai Bank building the sculptures themselves are relics of an earlier era. A pair of bronze lions by W. W. Wagstaff (illus. 64) which stand in the quasi-public space below the building were constructed in 1935 for the previous bank headquarters building, which opened on the same site in that

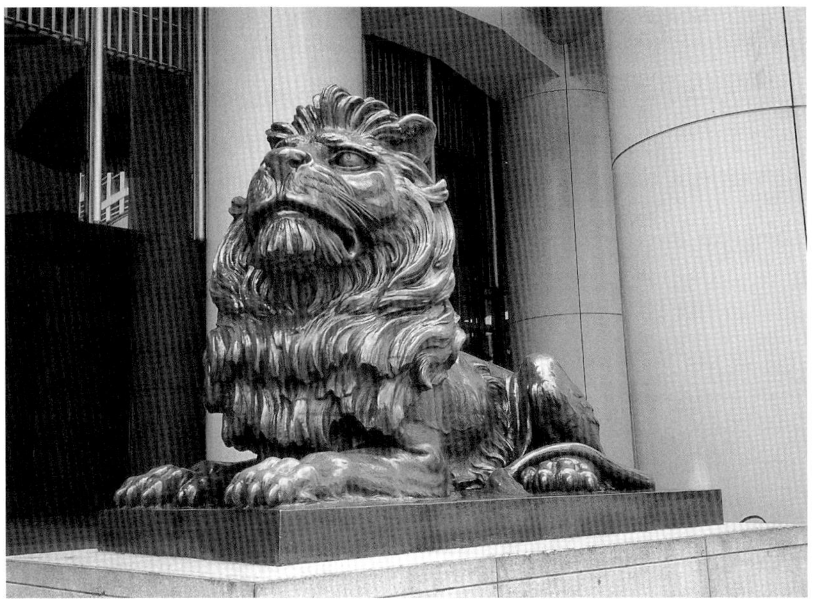

64 W. W. Wagstaff, one of a pair of bronze lions at the entrance of the Hong Kong and Shanghai Bank, 1935.

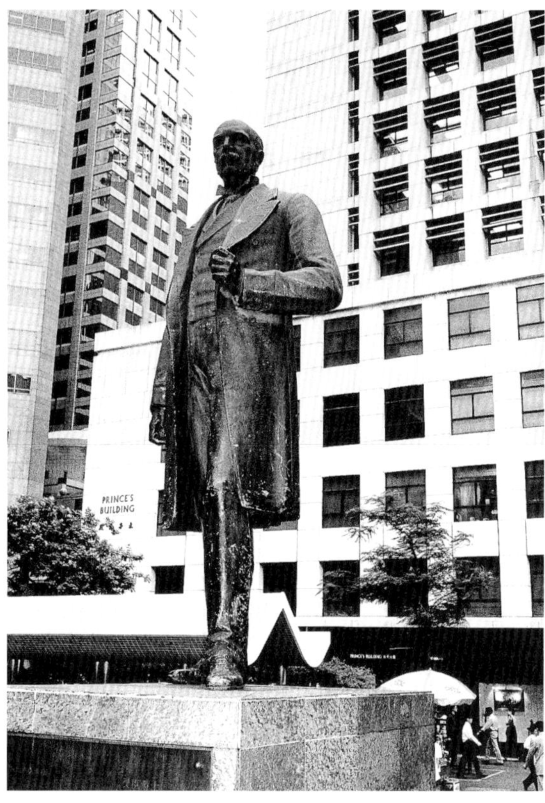

65 Raggi, *Sir Thomas Jackson*, installed 1906, bronze. Statue Square, Central, Hong Kong.

year. Their representation on notes issued by the bank (alongside an image of the building but at a much enlarged scale) underlines how important they are to it as symbols of historical continuity.[2]

Less mobilized by the bank itself for its symbolic potential in emphasizing corporate continuity is another sculpture from an even earlier period. The statue of Sir Thomas Jackson, the bank's founder, by Raggi (illus. 65), was commissioned by the shareholders and directors following his departure from Hong Kong in 1902, and unveiled on 24 September 1906. Standing in Statue Square, a park on land donated by the bank lying across the road from the headquarters building, it is less easily associated with the bank than are the lions, though the original intention was that the statue should be permanently identified with the bank by being sited close by. Partly the loss of identification is due to the general problem of historical illegibility which portrait sculptures face – many who use the square nowadays seem unaware of who it represents. Old photographs indicate that the statue originally faced the site of the bank (then occupied by an earlier head office building), thus creating a degree of connection to it. Instead of gazing towards his former company, however, Sir Thomas has now turned his attentions in the direction of the Legislative Council Building, which stands on an adjacent side of the square. Presumably his 90-degree shift of orientation occurred during a redesign of the Square. The lions, which read as guardian figures, show a much stronger allegiance to the bank itself, and have an added advantage in that they are able to bring together both Chinese and English visual associations. Stylistically they are strongly reminiscent of the Trafalgar Square lions, but they also bring to mind the guardian lions of Chinese tradition, such as can be seen in front of Tiananmen in Beijing, or indeed in front of the old Bank of China building on the adjoining plot to the Hong Kong and Shanghai Bank.

In both the case of Exchange Square and that of the Hong Kong and Shanghai Bank, harmonious ensembles of meaning have been identified linking a building and its associated sculptures. The meanings projected are upbeat statements of corporate propaganda which mesh neatly with state rhetoric about modernization and growth such as the Joint Declaration's emphasis on preserving 'stability and prosperity' in Hong Kong's future. Even corporate displays of sculpture do not always escape being contentious, however, and one of the greatest public controversies of the pre-handover period involved the display of a sculpture in the lobby of a corporate office building. The work in question was another example of Frink's art, her *New Man* of 1984 (illus. 66), and the controversy began on 19 April 1995 when this representation of a nude male figure was classified as an 'indecent article' by the Obscene Articles Tribunal. After the ruling was upheld in an appeal hearing which took place on 1 June, an intense coverage began in the local newspapers, with international news agencies also picking up the story. The issue was discussed in editorials, feature articles and guest columns (for example that of prominent pro-democracy legislator Christine Loh), and the question of possible artistic censorship following the handover was at the forefront of people's concerns. For the first time, a public sculpture had become a focus of anxieties concerning the transition of sovereignty.[3]

During the same period the Tribunal made a series of other questionable rulings. These involved a reproduction of Michelangelo's *David*, illustrations to an article warning parents about the content of certain children's comics, and a photograph showing a child from mainland China with extensive facial scarring. Clearly a new pattern of conservatism was in the process of being established and the application to the late Dame Elizabeth Frink of legislation designed to curb back-street pornographers was not simply an isolated aberration. Fear that access to public space for controversial artworks was being endangered

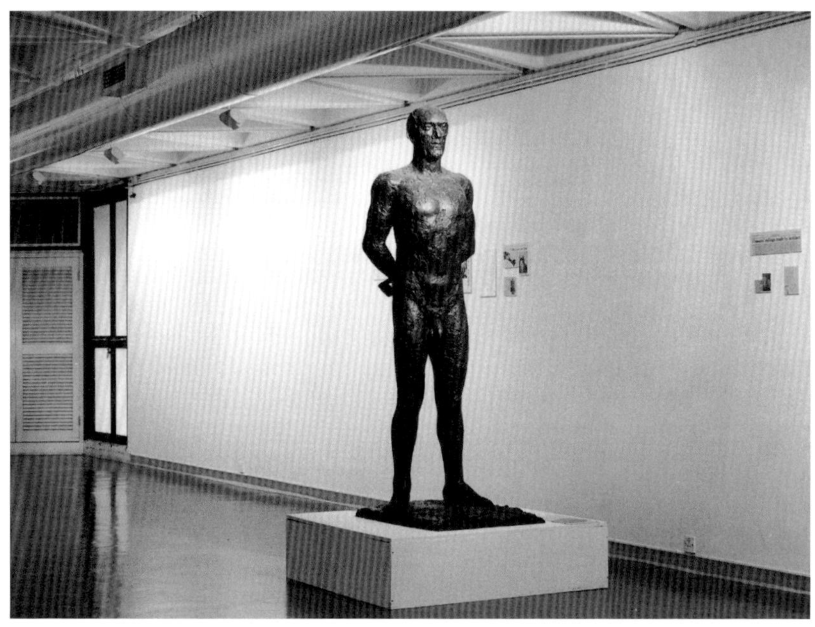

66 Elizabeth Frink, *New Man*, 1984, bronze, installed in the Pao
Galleries, Hong Kong Arts Centre, 1995. Private collection.

provoked a strong response from the local art community. This
response took many forms. An exhibition at the Fringe Club, for
instance, explored the artistic use of phallic symbolism, while a
protest rally on 24 June 1995 outside the Legislative Council Building
employed blown-up photographs of the *New Man* and other male nude
sculptures. The Hong Kong Arts Development Council, as practically
its first public act on becoming a statutory body, passed a resolution
condemning the ruling as 'a poor exercise of judgement ... tantamount
to an infringement of artistic freedom of expression'. The Hong Kong
Arts Centre, for its part, held a forum on freedom of expression with
legislators among the invited speakers. This latter event, which took
place on 9 June, was held in the presence of the sculpture itself. With
the cooperation of the owner it had been made the centrepiece of an
impromptu exhibition (the Control of Obscene and Indecent Articles
Ordinance having an exclusion for artworks displayed in museums and
galleries).

Appeal to higher judicial authority against decisions of the Obscene
Articles Tribunal can only be made on a point of law. This means that
even if there is a finding against the Tribunal the case will normally
only be returned to them for reconsideration. However, when the case

of the *New Man* was considered by the High Court on 11 August 1995 the judge quashed the ruling, deciding that the Tribunal had no right to pronounce on something that was not a publication. Although a victory for common sense the verdict did still leave open the possibility that photographic art or printed reproductions of works of art could be subject to arbitrary censorship. Worries about such policing of public cultural space remained even though small changes in the workings of the Tribunal were made by legislative amendment as a response to the public outcry concerning the *New Man* incident, and in the post-handover period the sculpture was again loaned to the Arts Centre. It went on long-term display from 10 October 1998. Whatever local public connotations it may have had before its encounter with the Tribunal, the *New Man* is now a symbol for many in Hong Kong of the struggle for freedom of expression and a pluralistic public sphere. It has become politicized in ways the artist herself could surely not have predicted.

The Public Sculpture of a (Very) Late Colonial Regime

In many ways the previously discussed examples show that corporate entities have taken the initiative in providing Hong Kong with public sculpture. One reason for the relative absence of state-sponsored public sculpture in the late colonial era was the difficulty of finding any defensible state ideology that such sculpture could actively project. How could one begin plausibly to justify an undemocratic colonial regime at such a late stage in history? This was perhaps particularly the case after 1984, when the regime's death knell had been sounded by the Joint Declaration. In such a situation it was often safer to avoid public meanings altogether, and much of the sculpture placed out of doors during the 1980s and 1990s using public funds (for example by the Urban Council in its Sculpture Walk in Kowloon Park) may be characterized as being private rather than public in its meaning. To the extent that the colonial regime could actively promote a public meaning at all following the Joint Declaration it had to be primarily economic rather than political – an echo of the business community's optimistic rhetoric of material progress or modernization. For a government so dominated by business interests this was not too difficult a step to take, and there was the added advantage that 'stability and prosperity' was a mantra that both the colonial regime and its appointed successor were happy to chant. For state bodies as well as for commercial entities, sculpture (and architecture) in an international modernist idiom was able to carry the appropriate associations.

A logic such as the one adumbrated above must have dictated the brief of the Hong Kong Cultural Centre (illus. 67), completed for the Urban Council by the Hong Kong Government's own Architectural Services Department in 1989 on a waterfront site in Tsim Sha Tsui, at the southernmost tip of the Kowloon peninsula. Clearly a landmark building was called for by both the intended function and the site (which had formerly been occupied by a railway station whose demolition in 1978 was widely opposed), and a simple abstract modernist form was chosen for the design. A curved roof shape (which introduces a distant allusion to a more flamboyant precedent for cultural architecture-as-sculpture in a waterfront setting, the Sydney Opera House) is the main feature of the building, which is otherwise minimal to the point of reticence, almost without windows and lacking a clearly expressed entrance. A major indication of the front entrance is in fact provided by a sculpture in the plaza between the building and the harbour, César's *Flying Frenchman* (illus. 68). In physical harmony with the façade, the sculpture is placed at right-angles to it opposite the lowest point of the roof's curve, a wing form which projects upward and outwards towards the harbour echoing on a smaller scale the upward sweep of the roof towards the corners of the two main auditoriums. Both modern and international, as well as an indicative sample of the world of culture to which the Centre is dedicated, the

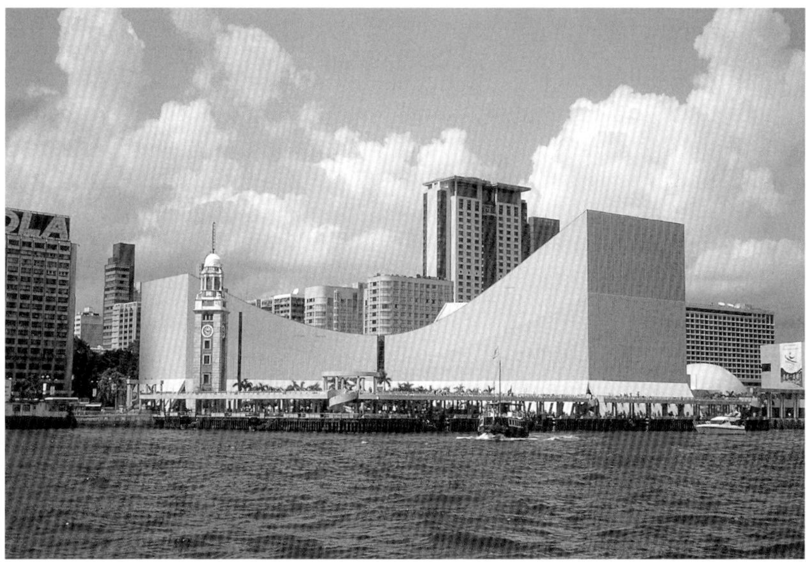

67 Architectural Services Department, Hong Kong Government, Hong Kong Cultural Centre, 1989 (general view).

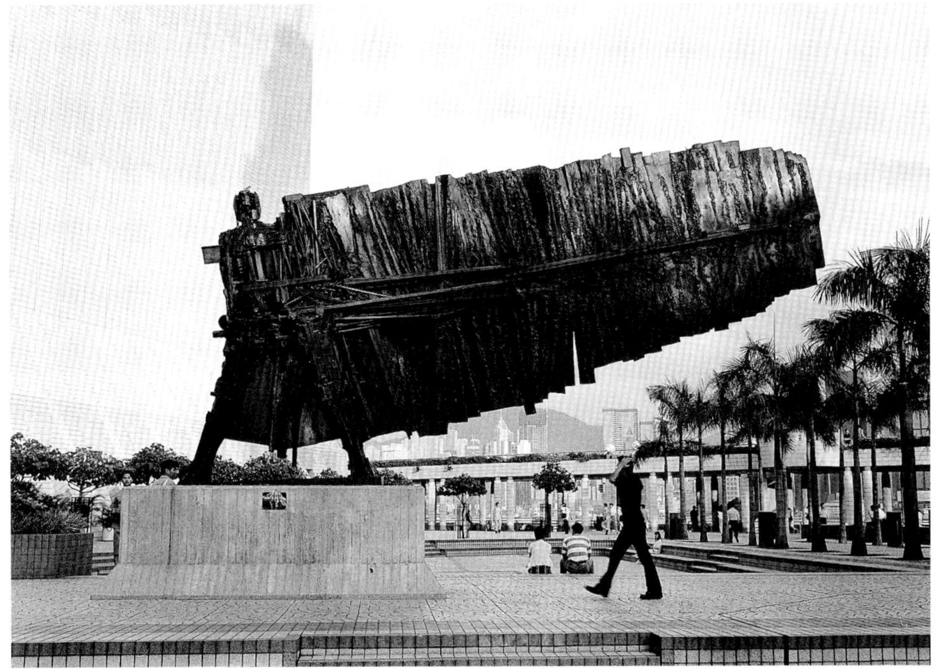

68 César, *Flying Frenchman*, 1991, bronze. Property of the Hong Kong Special Administrative Region Government, installed outside the Hong Kong Cultural Centre.

sculpture might at first sight seem dutifully to extend the building's own meaning much as the Exchange Square ensemble does. A clock-tower (all that was preserved from the old Kowloon-Canton Railway terminus) plays an analogous role to the bronze lions and water buffaloes already discussed, providing an element of historical contrast and a consequent intensification of the building's associations with modernity and progress. It stands at that end of the Cultural Centre from which the majority of visitors would approach, a spatial punctuation mark.[4]

As a civic building, the Cultural Centre was subjected to a more rigorous process of public scrutiny and criticism than corporate structures normally receive, and many felt it had failed to satisfy the expectations of the community. Its roof was ridiculed as resembling a ski jump, for instance, and its tiled walls were repeatedly likened to those of a public toilet. One correspondent to a newspaper letters page objected to the latter comparison, claiming to prefer a new neighbourhood toilet to the Cultural Centre. A similarly humorous reader's letter published in the *South China Morning Post* on 4 November

1989, while ostensibly attempting to defend the building, in fact offered a telling and not altogether erroneous 'decoding' of this structure as 'one bold, outspoken political statement not really obvious to the small minds of little people without imagination', namely the 'Joint Declaration cast in hard-setting Portland cement'. 'Undoubtedly [the letter states], the pink tiles were chosen as a subtle hint of the peculiar hybrid political and ideological system of the post-1997 Hong Kong. Although over 50 years, Hong Kong may not enjoy the delights of a full Marxist-Stalinist "red" system, some of it, overflowing from the mainland, inevitably will rub off on Hong Kong policies. The low-toned pink is thus the perfect compromise to state, perhaps to warn of the future fact of life – capitalism's ugly face caked with socialist mascara.'[5]

This less than warm public reception of the Cultural Centre was an indication of a crisis of hegemony being faced by the colonial regime. The Joint Declaration promise of continued prosperity (but no definitive guarantee about democracy and no real autonomy) was always a difficult one to sell, but following the June 1989 suppression of the Beijing democracy movement it found even fewer buyers. Conceived at an earlier time, but opening in the year of the crackdown itself, the Cultural Centre was a victim of this sharp change of local mood. For many, the 'One Country, Two Systems' model Beijing had proposed for Hong Kong's post-handover future no longer seemed viable in the face of those tanks on the television screens. A vision of happy future co-existence between Hong Kong capitalism and Chinese Communism – allegorically represented in a muted or unacknowledged kind of way by Van Lau's mural inside the Cultural Centre depicting *The Meeting of Yin and Yang* (illus. 15), the complementary cosmological principles according to Chinese understanding – no longer seemed convincing.

Although the architectural statement of the Cultural Centre was out of step with the new mood (which led to calls for the development of local grass roots art rather than the provision of prestige locations for international performances) there was – surprisingly – one part of the Cultural Centre's sculptural accompaniment that actively sought to speak to it. This was the César sculpture, which unlike the building itself was not completed in 1989 but begun around then and finished in 1991 (it was officially unveiled on 27 April 1992), and so able to respond to the events in Beijing and their Hong Kong reverberations. While the Hong Kong Urban Council had its own use for the sculpture as part of a choreographed ensemble of meaning it becomes clear that the sculptor himself had more contentious public significations in mind, even if he understood a need for some reticence in expressing them.

To understand the partially veiled meaning of the *Flying Frenchman* (the title itself being one of the veils), it is necessary to see it as a public sculpture haunted by other public sculptures. Since the work was a donation to Hong Kong from the Cartier Foundation in France (not being a paid commission gave a crucial degree of autonomy over meaning), it calls to mind another more famous French sculptural gift, the Statue of Liberty in New York. Both, after all, are positioned on waterfront sites next to busy harbours. Shared context helps suggest a shared meaning, and in a retrospective moment of frankness César did in any case identify it as a 'liberty' figure. This was not of course the first time that an allusion to the monumental New York sculpture enabled a reference to the concept of liberty in a Chinese context: the Goddess of Democracy placed in Tiananmen Square, Beijing by the 1989 democracy demonstrators also claimed the Statue of Liberty – quite openly – as an ancestor, borrowing some of her scale. The Beijing sculpture (which in turn gave rise to many progeny itself) also lies behind César's work, which may be taken as equally allegorical in nature.

The *Flying Frenchman* depicts a figure with a single intact wing. It appears to be strapped on (rather than a part of the figure's own body), and on one occasion César referred to the figure as a kind of Icarus. This flyer, however, despite suffering damage (the lost other wing) and not currently capable of flight (despite the name), is still standing and seems capable of recovery unlike its mythological counterpart. The co-existence of injury and resilience enable it to function as a symbol of wounded liberty, making it an appropriate memorial of the 4 June 1989 crackdown and its victims, and a tangible focus for hopes of greater democracy in both China and Hong Kong. When the colonial government was petitioned to allow a Hong Kong replica of the Goddess of Democracy a permanent site of display, a predictable refusal was the result. As became clear later when the text of a secret letter of appeasement written to the mainland Chinese authorities by the local government was made public, there was no wish to let a 4 June 1989 memorial be placed on Hong Kong soil, this being still the pre-Patten era when open disagreement between the two sovereign powers was yet to erupt.[6] César, an outsider employing a less confrontational strategy, was able to achieve what local Hong Kong people themselves could not. An apparently 'international' sculpture in fact had a local meaning, even if it was one created with the aid of a cosmopolitan reference to three countries on as many continents. An apparent symbol of modernity and future progress turned out to have a memory.

On account of the *Flying Frenchman*'s reticence about its memorial function it took some time before its meaning became active in local reception. Interpretations of the sculpture linking its possible address to the Beijing democracy movement did find their way into print in due course, and a rumour circulated that *Flying Frenchman* was not the original name and that it had been substituted for one which made the sculpture's subject clear (namely *Freedom Fighter*) at the request of the Urban Council. It was not until the post-handover period in fact, at a time when public memory of the crackdown faced increasing disapproval from the government, that the most active attempt to acknowledge the *Flying Frenchman*'s contentious meaning was made. On 3 June 1999, the eve of the tenth anniversary of the bloodshed, a group of artists and others led by Leung Po-shan placed flowers at the base of the sculpture in a simple ceremony or 'performance art' piece designed to attract media attention. On the same evening a memorial concert for the 1989 victims was held in front of the statue, as it had been on the same day of the year before, and this further established a link between the *Flying Frenchman* and the Chinese democracy movement.[7]

While this local use of an imported public sculpture can be described as an attempt to accentuate or exacerbate meanings already placed in the work at a formal level by the sculptor, certain other instances of active reception of public art that occurred in Hong Kong as the handover approached might be better described as semiotic subversion. Because of the difficulty of placing works with oppositional meanings in public space on a permanent basis, a strategy of appropriating existing sculptures was sometimes adopted as a means of turning a predominantly monologic public space into an arena for dialogue. With the absence even of much recent colonial sculpture, an antique bronze statue of Queen Victoria (illus. 69) became a particular focus of such attention.

Created in London by Raggi, this image of an enthroned Victoria was initially installed in 1896, thus in time for Queen Victoria's Diamond Jubilee of 1897. It was placed at a prominent location in the Central district of Hong Kong (first known as Royal and later Statue Square), facing out over the harbour and protected by an elaborate cupola. During the Japanese occupation it was removed, along with other British imperial monuments, but was discovered in Japan after the end of the war. It was eventually returned in 1952, but was never restored to its original prestigious site by the British colonial regime. In an apparent recognition of the inappropriateness of such overt imperial symbols to the new post-Second World War era of decolonization, it was instead displaced to a park built on reclaimed land in Causeway Bay (which opened in 1957). The statue was now orientated to face inland, rather than towards the harbour, of which there would not in

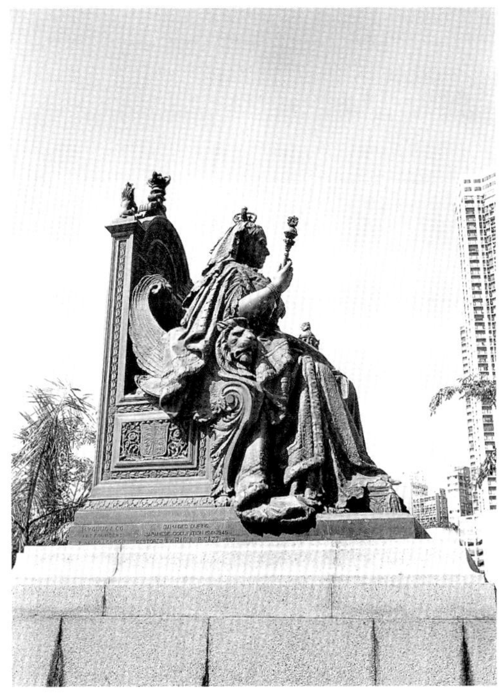

69 Raggi, *Queen Victoria*, installed 1896, bronze.

any case have been a view. Its relationship with the park was intensified by a decision to name it Victoria Park. Victoria was also the original name of the city of Hong Kong as well as of the harbour, and consequently this monarch, the early years of whose reign saw the beginning of British colonialism in Hong Kong, was in many ways its most succinct and widespread symbol.

One practice by means of which new meanings were proposed for the Victoria statue was photography. The statue appears in the images of art photographers such as Vincent Yu and Alfred Ko. Yu adopts a very low viewpoint on the statue in one photograph, and while such a viewpoint can have connotations of subservience it is so exaggerated in this instance that it works to undermine the sculpture's official rhetoric. Ko's photographs document the presence of the Victoria statue in images of the 4 June memorial rallies that are held in Victoria Park. This work is more difficult to pin down, but by being associated with the democracy rally – for example in *Victoria Park* (illus. 70) and *Victoria Park* (1996) – the statue's colonial connotations are being evacuated. Victoria somehow becomes a participant in the demonstration.

The use of the Victoria statue by art photographers is paralleled in the photographic practices of ordinary Hong Kong residents. On the

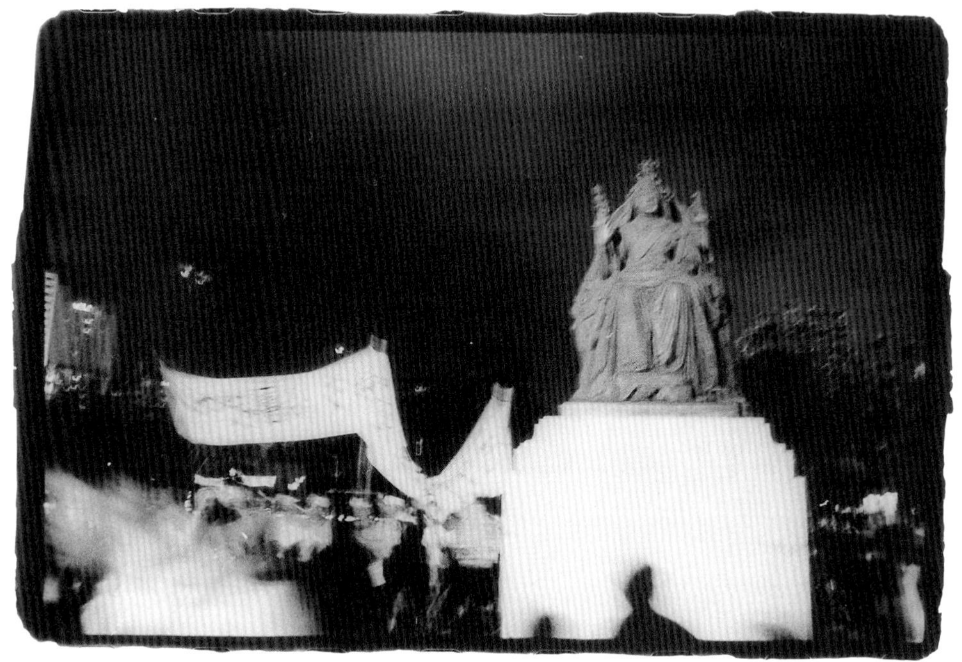

70 Alfred Ko, *Victoria Park*, 1989, black-and-white photographic print. Collection of the artist.

day of the 4 June memorial rallies it is not uncommon to find people taking photographs of the statue, tying it in somehow to the event that takes place there, and in the period directly before the 1997 handover the statue was the object of more generalized photographic attention. Rather than seeing this as a nostalgic fondness of Hong Kong people for colonial rule one should interpret it as an attempt to assert a sense of identity in the face of post-handover uncertainty. In the absence of other public props for the narration of local selfhood even colonial artefacts were subject to appropriation for this fragile project.

One engagement with the Victoria statue that differs quite radically from those so far described is that of Pun Sing Lui, a mainland-trained artist who arrived in Hong Kong in 1992. In 1995 (as part of a larger project mentioned in Chapter 2) he created a photograph of himself wearing a jacket with the design of the Communist Chinese flag on the back, standing in front of the statue. This work, a playful pre-envisioning of life after the handover, turned out to be a forewarning of a much less humorous performance art piece executed on 16 September 1996. In an act that gained this relatively unknown artist instant local notoriety he covered the statue itself in a layer of red paint, and attacked its nose with a hammer. The sculptor, himself covered in red paint, stayed at the site to take the consequences of his action, and arrest and a brief period of imprisonment inexorably followed. Local reaction, fed by numerous press reports, did not at first identify this iconoclastic gesture as a consciously intended art event, and questions concerning the perpetrator's sanity were widely raised (indeed he was initially taken to Eastern Hospital for psychiatric observation). To the extent that the meaning of Pun's act was interrogated, however, it was viewed in a very unfavourable light. This seems particularly to have been the case within the local art community. Damage to a work of art (even a not particularly outstanding one) was seen as a dangerous precedent by a people worried about the possibility of future artistic censorship, memories of the *New Man* incident still being fresh. Equally disturbing was the implication that Hong Kong culture could be equated with colonial culture, and seen as something 'un-Chinese' that needed to be cleared away. Pun's attack on this antique colonial symbol, whose political potency had long since been lost in the eyes of Hong Kong's people, seemed too easy a gesture, and one which worked against the affirmation of local identity.[8]

Oppositional Meanings in Public Space

On 31 May 1997, the handover year, a sculptural gift arrived in Hong Kong. Unlike the *Flying Frenchman*, this was not a gift to the state but to the Hong Kong Alliance in Support of the Patriotic Democracy Movement in China, an independent political umbrella organization that campaigns for democracy in China and organizes the annual 4 June memorial rallies. Titled the *Pillar of Shame* (illus. 71, 72), it was the gift of its maker, Danish sculptor Jens Galschiot. A vertically orientated array of some 50 figures displaying tortured facial expressions, this not particularly outstanding artwork made no specific reference to any particular historical event. Indeed it was deliberately generic in nature, the artist hoping to place copies of the work at sites around the world where acts of violence and oppression had occurred, as part of a performance or happening (both terms being used in the publicity material). In Hong Kong, however, it was intended as referring to the Tiananmen crackdown and the deaths associated with it, as a plaque attached to its base indicated. The plaque read 'The Tiananmen Massacre, June 4th 1989' and 'The old cannot kill the young forever'. Another plaque on the base gave the sculpture a more context-specific Chinese name, which might be translated as the *Pillar of the Nation's Wound*, although in English it continued to be referred

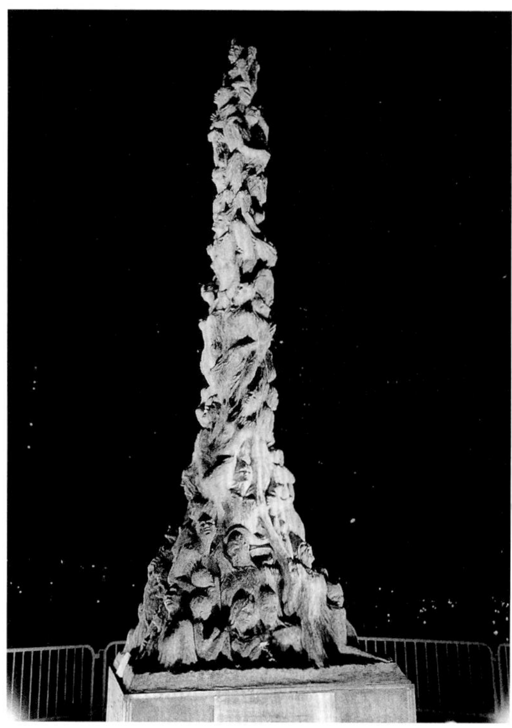

71 Jens Galschiot, *Pillar of Shame*, concrete armoured with fibres, on display in Victoria Park during the memorial rally, 4 June 1997.

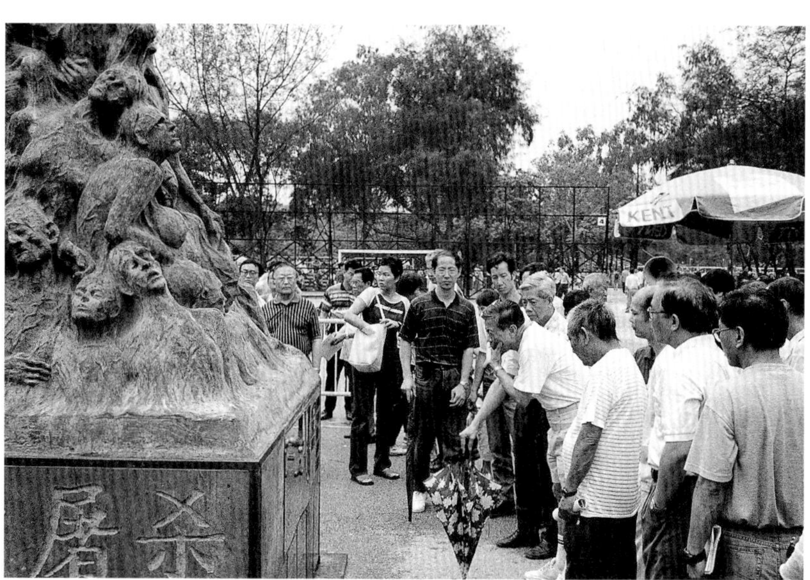

72 Jens Galschiot, Detail from *Pillar of Shame*, on display in Victoria Park, 31 May 1998, with crowds gathering for the start of a memorial march.

to as the *Pillar of Shame*. Whereas public monuments characteristically commemorate supposedly heroic events, in the case of this sculpture the intention was to remember a shameful act. According to the sculptor's own publicity, he considered the *Pillar of Shame* as a kind of 'Nobel Prize of Injustice'.[9]

The unusual willingness of this sculpture to have its meaning specified and developed by acts of display beyond the artist's own control made it a useful tool for the Alliance. They gave it a privileged site during that year's 4 June rally (a crucial one since it was the last to be held before the return of Hong Kong to Chinese sovereignty) and it was assigned the role of prompting memories of the bloodshed. Eight metres tall and dramatically spotlighted, the obelisk-like form of the *Pillar of Shame* was clearly visible from all points of the rally. Attempts were also made to find a more long-term site for display, and both the Urban Council and the Regional Council (the two municipal bodies with responsibility for parks and other such public spaces) were approached by the Alliance with requests. The response was negative in both cases, but the opportunity to test publicly the political position of the two councils was no doubt considered of value in itself. The Urban Council's Recreation Committee had on 14 May voted down a request to display the sculpture in Kowloon Park and Chater Garden (a prominent site near the Legislative Council Building) from June till September, claiming the period was too long, and that regular park users would be inconvenienced. Appeal was made to the full Council, which also voted down the request by eighteen votes to thirteen on 20 May, leading to a walkout by eleven Urban Councillors, who donned masks with 'political censorship' written on them before leaving. Full press coverage was given to the issue, and to Alliance chairman Szeto Wah's denunciation of the decision as politically motivated. The Legislative Council's panel on Recreation, Culture and Sports met to consider the issue later in the same week, and passed a resolution to write to the Chief Secretary urging her to investigate whether Urban Service Department officials had failed to maintain political neutrality in handling the Alliance's application.[10]

Following the rally, with the end of the Alliance's hire period, the *Pillar of Shame* needed to be removed from Victoria Park, and its chosen destination – no Municipal Council venue being forthcoming – was the campus of the University of Hong Kong. The student union was entrusted with its care and arranged its display on the podium in front of the student union building, but only after a very public altercation with campus security guards and police who initially attempted to prevent it being taken on to University property without permission.

Once installed, it was to remain through the handover period, becoming the first explicit sculptural commemoration of the June 1989 killings to be displayed on the soil of the People's Republic of China. Later it travelled to other universities, testing out the possibilities for freedom of expression on the campuses in the new era. It reappeared in Victoria Park for the 1998 and 1999 4 June rallies (on 4 June 1999 it was splashed with red paint mixed with blood by a performance artist, in a farcical echo of Pun's defacement of the Victoria statue), and another attempt was made in 1998 to obtain a site of exhibition on public land, this time on a permanent basis. On this occasion the Urban Services Department took advice from consultants on the artistic merit of the sculpture (13 out of 21 opposed the application), and the relevant Provisional Urban Council select committee subsequently voted against accepting the work by a majority of six to four, with three abstentions. A few months later (on 24 and 25 September) students at the University of Hong Kong held a campus poll which produced a majority in favour of a permanent home at the University for the sculpture, and it did return to the campus for further display there. It was erected by the student union on 5 June 1999 without permission being sought from the University authorities, who reacted by issuing a press statement disclaiming any liability for the consequences (Typhoon Maggie was in the vicinity at the time, and fears were expressed about the stability of the structure). At the end of 2000 it was still on display near the student union building, and was showing no sign of impending departure. It had failed to make a visit to Victoria Park for the 4 June 2000 rally, perhaps because of space restrictions caused by renovations at that site.

Even when forced out of public space into storage the *Pillar of Shame* has proved a newsworthy item. Its migrations in search of a place of permanent residence had become symbolic of the difficulty of keeping recognition of the crackdown alive in the face of government disapproval. Whereas the meaning of other public sculptures was enhanced by their relationship to a particular architectural setting, the *Pillar of Shame*'s very homelessness proved significant. Even prior to its first exhibition in Hong Kong it was understood that the reaction of the authorities would have a symbolic value. Negative treatment would read as an insult to the victims of the crackdown, whose representative the sculpture claimed to be, and even destruction – as the pre-publicity material stated – would be a kind of repetition of the original atrocity. Although created in Europe, like the *Flying Frenchman* the *Pillar of Shame* seems to owe a debt to the 1989 Beijing Goddess of Democracy, which was also constructed with an understanding of the meaningful-

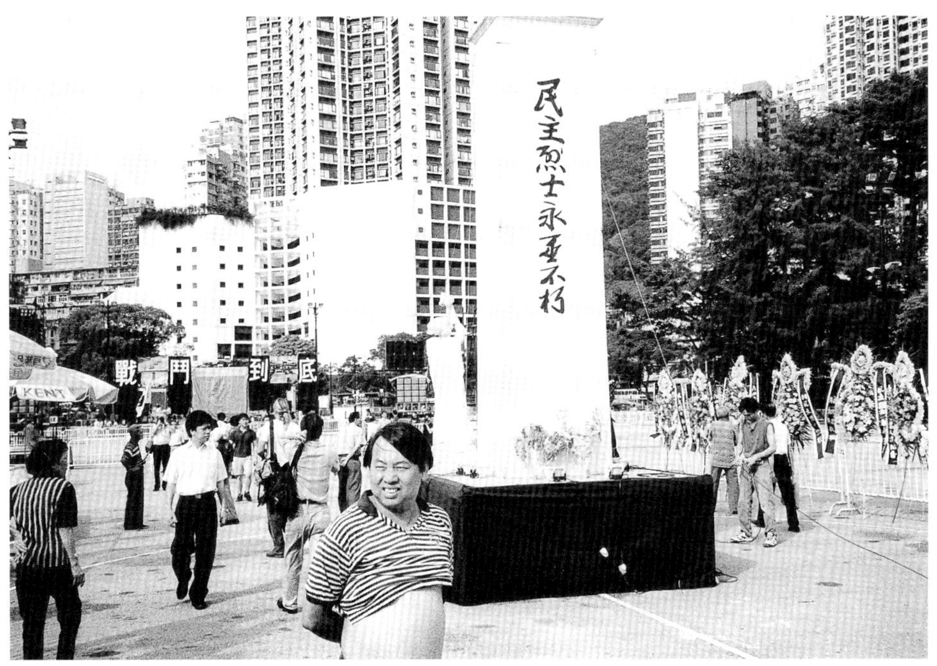

73 Replica of the Monument to the People's Heroes, Victoria Park, 4 June 1997, painted wood.

ness of its possible destruction.[11]

Although its status as an overseas gift gave the *Pillar of Shame* certain advantages, arguably of greater importance to the 4 June rallies themselves was a quite simple locally produced sculptural prop. This item was also more than purely local, however, since it was a reduced scale copy of the Monument to the People's Heroes in Beijing's Tiananmen Square (illus. 73). Its original, completed in 1958 as a memorial to the dead of the Communist revolution and hence a key carrier of state ideology in the nation's most important public space, had become through events in March and April 1976 and again in May and June 1997, a more equivocal signifier. A wreath had been laid on it on 23 March 1976, to commemorate the death of Zhou Enlai that January, and a mass demonstration ensued on 4 April (the festival of Qingming when the dead are remembered). Although bloodily suppressed on 5 April, this marked the beginning of the end of the Cultural Revolution. When demonstrators placed wreaths to Hu Yaobang on the monument on 15 April 1989 they were consciously recalling these earlier events, and throughout the occupation of the square the monument was the focus of speeches and other activities.[12]

This structure, bearing a further layer of memorial connotations following 4 June, was a powerful signifier for the Hong Kong demonstrators to appropriate, concerned as they were with the remembrance of history.[13] The formal laying of a wreath on the replica Monument during the Victoria Park rallies helps highlight the function of the original, and activates memories of its role on earlier occasions of protest. The inscription on the original monument ('eternal glory to the people's heroes') had also been subtly rewritten so that it now referred to the heroes or martyrs of *democracy* rather than the heroes of the *people* (*minzhu* rather than *renmin*).

Rather than simply seeing the use of the replica Monument to the People's Heroes as enabling a reference to another time and place of significance, however, one can view it as enabling an act of empathic identification. Although a temporary presence in Victoria Park for the duration of the rally, this sculptural object does create an ensemble of meaning with its surrounding environment. Unlike at Exchange Square, however, it is the sculpture that plays a dominant role, turning the rather nondescript space of Victoria Park into Tiananmen Square for a short while so that a very specific kind of imagined community could come into being. Here public sculpture plays a crucial role in shaping political practice, the theatrical nature of which mainstream political science seems ill equipped to comprehend. Evidence of the degree of identification between the Victoria Park demonstrators and their Beijing predecessors can be seen by the way they carry lighted candles, which are collectively raised in the air at certain points of the ceremony (illus. 74). Again public sculpture is involved, but this time as a model: in their actions the demonstrators are mimicking the raised torch gesture of the Beijing Goddess of Democracy, embodying her or bringing her back to life.[14]

The Goddess of Democracy also appears in effigy during the rallies. In 1997, for instance, a large banner depicting her was hung (illus. 75), and a relatively small-scale replica was placed on the replica Monument (as if to help identify which 'vintage' of the original Monument was being referred to). Even smaller portable copies were also sold to participants of the rally as a way of raising funds, this proliferation of replicas effectively symbolizing an irrepressible spread of the democratic spirit despite the Chinese state's physical destruction of the original. Democrat Cheung Man-kwong placed one of these miniatures in a time capsule containing contributions from members of the pre-handover Legislative Council (which was sealed just as that fully elected legislature was coming to the end of its prematurely truncated life). Artist Kith Tsang displayed a mobile artwork titled *6+4=10* in Victoria Park

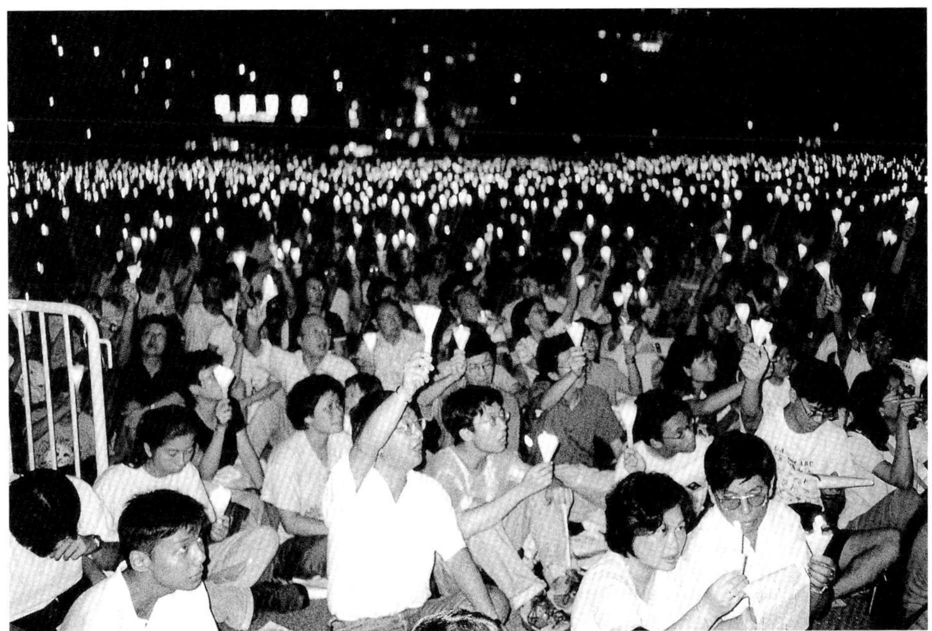

74 Participants in the 4 June 1997 memorial rally raising candles aloft in imitation of the gesture of the Beijing Goddess of Democracy.

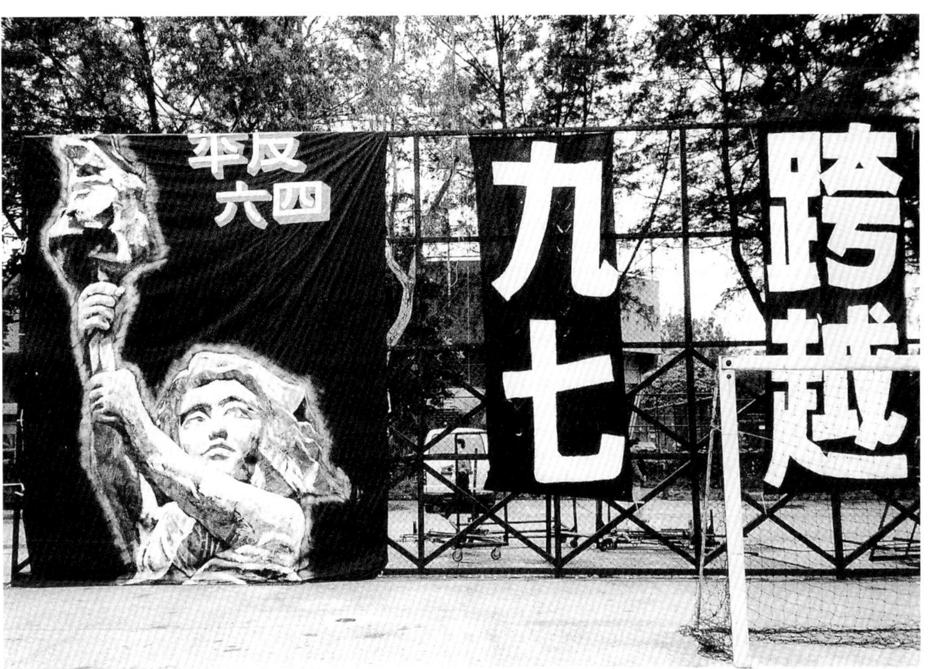

75 Banner showing the Goddess of Democracy, Victoria Park, 4 June 1997.

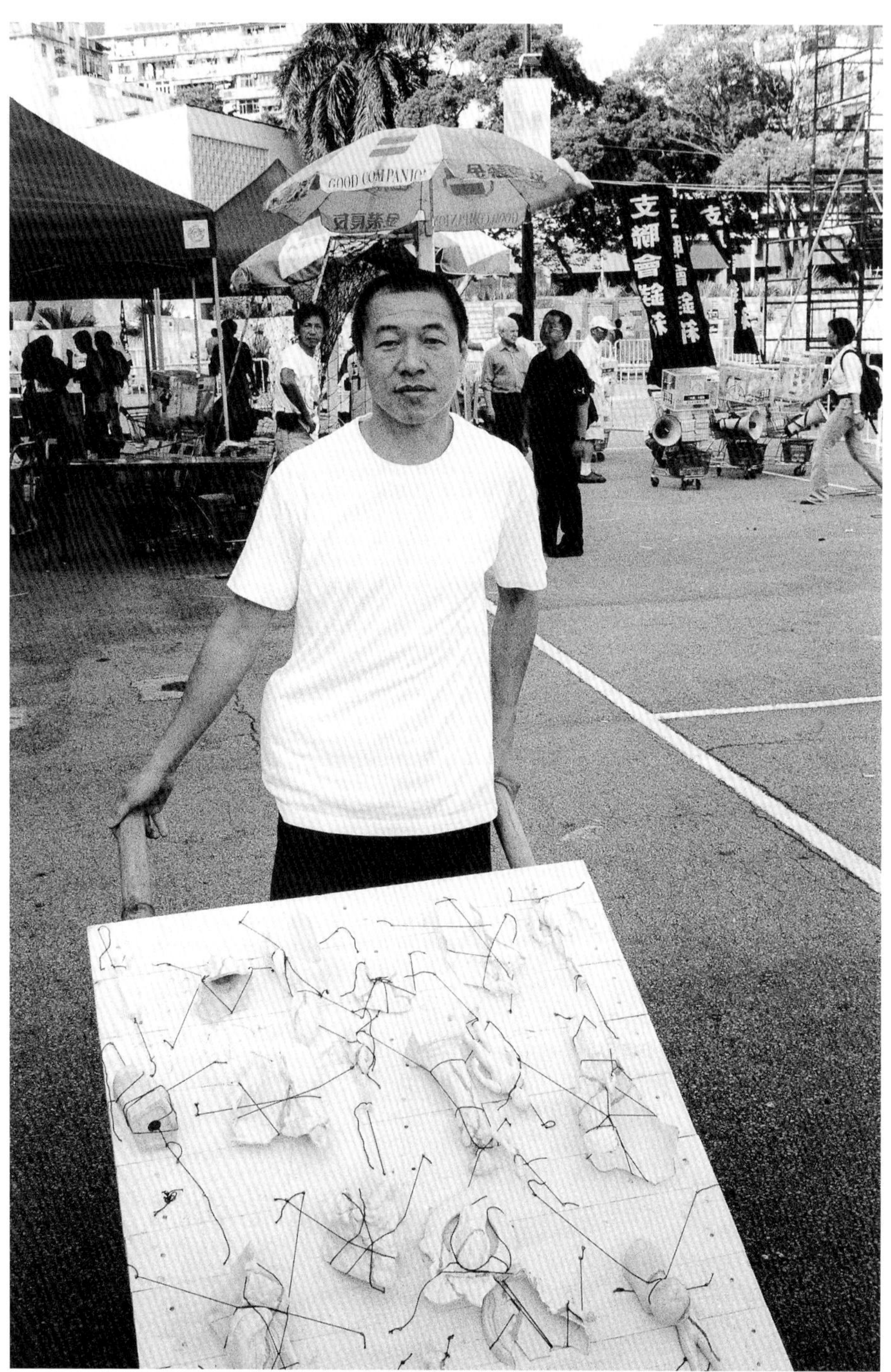

76 Artist Kith Tsang with his mixed-media mobile work *6+4=10*, Victoria Park, 4 June 1999.

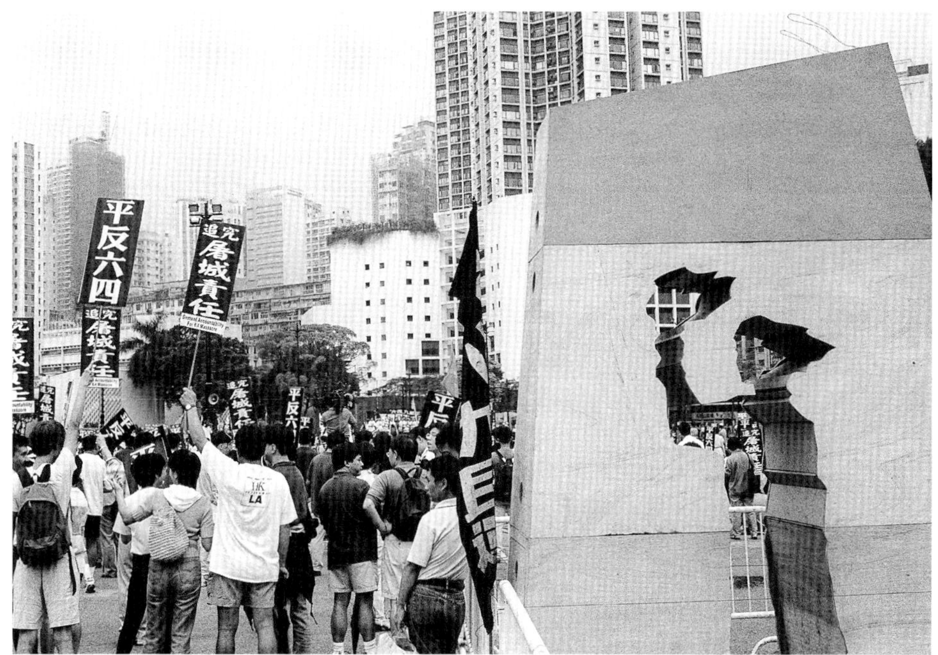

77 The painted wood *Goddess of Democracy Stone Wall* (still in the process of completion), on display in Victoria Park, 31 May 1998, with crowds gathering for the start of a memorial march.

and other locations during the day of 4 June 1999 (illus. 76) which contained, in addition to fragments of other statues and dolls, all painted white, a miniature replica Goddess of Democracy statue.

In 1998 a further sculptural prop appeared at the Victoria Park rally for the first time. This was a wall-like painted wooden structure with an empty space in the middle taking the form of the Goddess's silhouette (illus. 77). It had been created by artist and movie art director Yank Wong (with the collaboration of others) at the invitation of the Hong Kong Alliance in Support of the Patriotic Democratic Movement in China, and was named the *Goddess of Democracy Stone Wall*. Associations of presence and absence were being played with: a negative image would invoke or give new life to the Goddess, but at the same time symbolize the absence of democracy in China. Since a view of Hong Kong now made up the body of the Goddess she was, as it were, being made present in or by Hong Kong. She could also be read as having broken through the wall: imprisonment is evoked, but also liberation.

Like the original statue, this negative image of the Goddess was clearly designed as a sculpture for the era of mechanical (and electronic) reproduction – the rallies attracting intense media attention which offered the possibility of an extended remote audience. In an interview published in the *Ming Pao* newspaper on June 4 1998 Yank Wong told the interviewer that he hoped photographs of the sculpture would appear in the following day's newspapers, and expressed the wish that such photographs would be seen by the Beijing authorities. His experience managing props and arranging film sets would have sensitized him to the needs of the camera lens, making it easier to produce an object capable of photographic relay. The rally organizers played their part in encouraging such dissemination by helpfully placing a stepladder at an appropriate spot for the use of the many photographers wishing to get an image, and Cheung Man-kwong, speaking as a member of the Alliance's Standing Committee, stated in an interview that he expected people would stand in the hollow silhouette to take pictures. Again the theme of bodily identification arises: Cheung interpreted the meaning of such a gesture as a blending of bodies with the Goddess of Democracy, a uniting of democracy and the people of Hong Kong.[15]

There were many successful photographs in the press of the *Goddess of Democracy Stone Wall*, including several day-time shots which attempted to catch images of the demonstrators through the silhouette. Among the most outstanding of the press photographs, however, was an Agence France-Presse image taken during the 1999 rally (illus. 78), which appeared in the *Apple Daily* (5 June 1999, p. A2) and also, differently cropped, in the *South China Morning Post* (5 June 1999, p. 1). This image was particularly successful in creating an impression of a ghostly luminescent Goddess standing among the crowds of demonstrators (who were also reduced to silhouettes). As the Goddess raised her torch, so they raised their candles.

Artists, and not just members of the press, brought their cameras to the 4 June rallies: photography's stubbornly persistent memory made it a particularly valuable tool in aiding recall of this crucial but suppressed episode of China's national history. Among the strongest images of the Victoria Park rallies and of the Hong Kong movement for democracy in China are those of Alfred Ko, who eschews the legibility of photojournalism in search of a more subjective viewpoint on this emotive topic. One photograph of 1993, for instance, shows the replica Monument to the People's Heroes, but only by means of a partial reflection in a rain puddle (illus. 79). The structure itself is outside the frame, as is the head of the only human figure in the image (all we see is a pair of legs, silhouetted against the light, and blurred by motion). An attentive

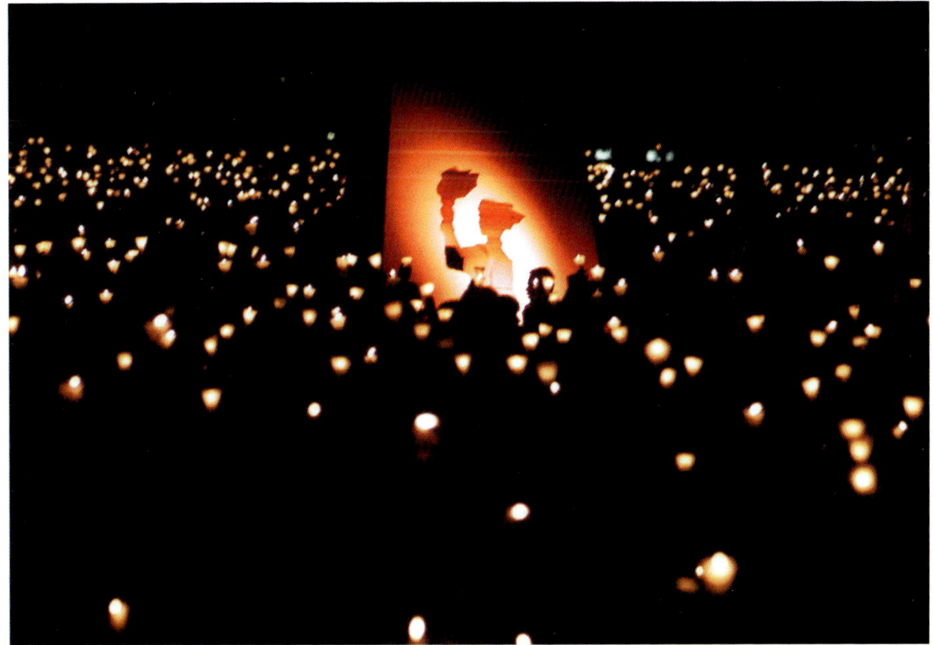

78 The *Goddess of Democracy Stone Wall* during the 4 June 1999 memorial rally, Victoria Park.

viewer would be able to tell that the image was taken in Hong Kong and not Beijing because of the lights of a tower block reflected in the puddle (and because the inscription differs on the replica), but Ko has deliberately blurred distinctions between Tiananmen Square and Victoria Park (or between past and present) because of a desire for empathic identification.

Equally personal in feel to Ko's photographs are those of Wong Kan Tai. Images of local democracy rallies by him and Karl Chiu are included in a published album *Beijing Story* (Hong Kong, 1999), where they are interwoven with photographs of Beijing taken by Wong in 1989, as well as photographs he and Chiu took on a visit to that city during the winter of 1998–9. Among the most impressive of these latter is a 1999 image by Wong titled *Tiananmen* (illus. 133). In what seems like a search for traces of an event from nearly a decade earlier, he encounters a Tiananmen Square buried in snow, as if frozen in mourning still. Working in a more objective, documentary register Wong also photographed the graves of some of the crackdown's victims (illus. 80). As with Ko's photograph of the replica Monument to the People's Heroes, these are memorial images of what are already memorial structures.[16]

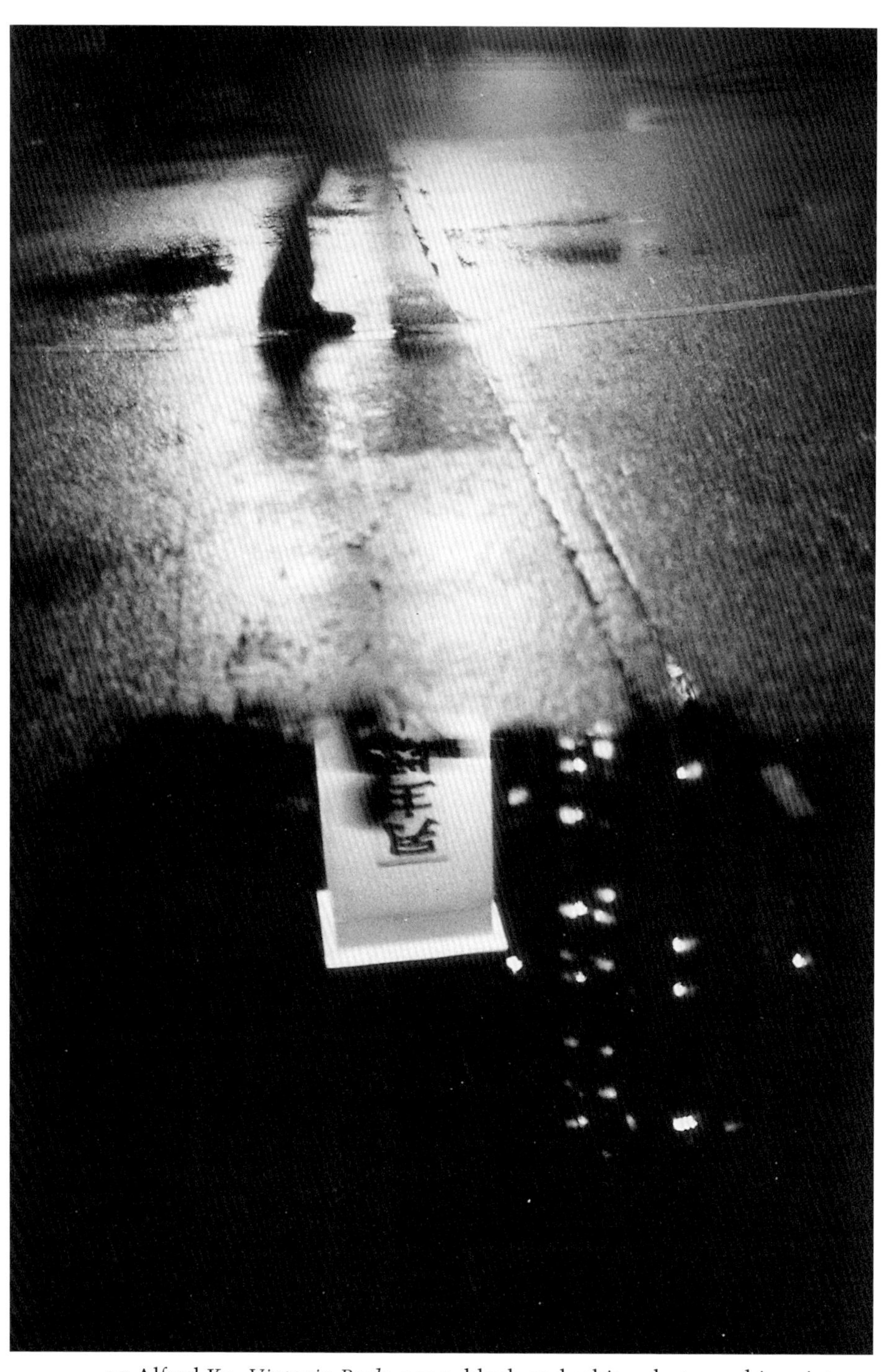

79 Alfred Ko, *Victoria Park*, 1993, black-and-white photographic print. Collection the artist.

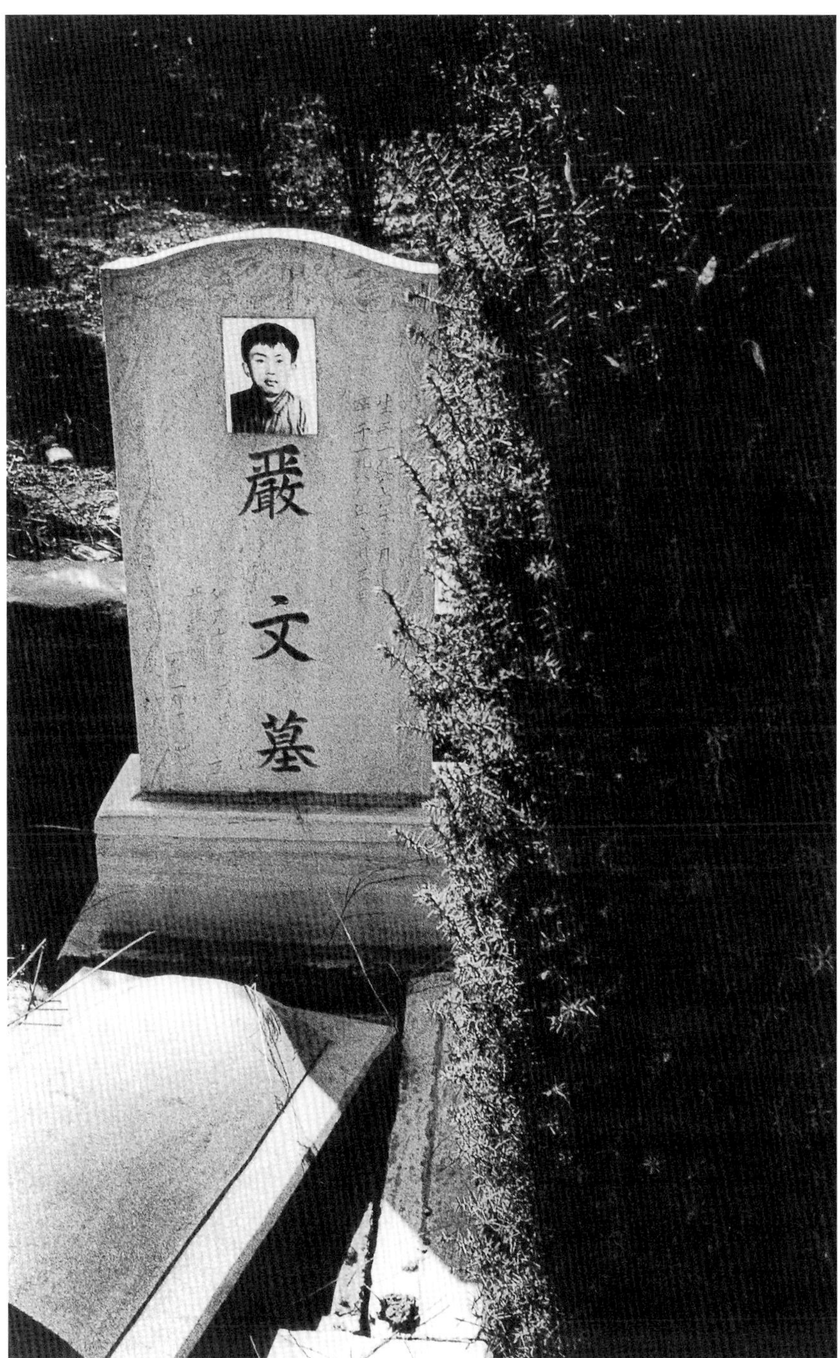

80 Wong Kan Tai, *Untitled* (grave of Yan Wen, student aged 22, killed by bullets, Beijing, June 4 1989), 1999, black-and-white photographic print. Collection the artist.

Public Sculpture and Chinese National Identity

Oppositional public sculpture in the very last phase of British colonial rule and during the early post-handover period showed a strong concern, through acts of identification with Tiananmen Square, with Chinese national concerns. It played a part in contesting the official national ideology of the Chinese Communist party by its insistence on remembering the trauma of 4 June 1989 and its promotion of the cause of democracy. This address to national concerns (which after the handover was actually taking place within the People's Republic itself) was not of course at the expense of local issues: by constructing their rallies and marches as a continuation of the Beijing protest the demonstrators were also using its momentum and authority for their own project of greater democracy in Hong Kong, they were reading the lessons of Tiananmen Square on to their own situation (as many Hong Kong people had done since the crackdown).

During the handover period and beyond, the return of Hong Kong to Chinese sovereignty was used by the Chinese leadership as a way of enhancing patriotic fervour in the country as a whole (nationalism being the only viable unifying ideology left to the state after the widespread collapse of belief in Communism). In an ironic symmetry, while Hong Kong people were in early June 1997 asserting a sense of autonomy in Victoria Park by an identification with Tiananmen Square, in the Square itself, at the end of the same month, the government was encouraging a sense of national unity through attention to Hong Kong, with celebrations focused on a digital clock attached to the façade of the Museum of History which counted down to the moment of return.

Although the meaning that could be attached to the return of Hong Kong for a mainland audience was a primary concern, there was also of course an ideological address by the Chinese government to Hong Kong residents themselves following the handover, in an attempt to interpellate them as national citizens. This was not an easy task, given the strong sense of local cultural identity that had developed in the territory and the fact that Hong Kong's population largely consisted of refugees from Communist China or their locally born children. For this audience Communist ideology had little appeal, and patriotic rhetoric was – even more than in the mainland itself – the only possible common currency. Whereas oppositional public sculpture gained a strength from the specificity of its references, such patriotic meanings gained benefit from a certain vagueness or obliqueness of expression that helped mask possible differences of understanding.

One common form such obliqueness took was the invocation of 'tradition', an essentialized conception of Chinese cultural history mobilized in a disguised way for contemporary political ends. Shortly after the handover, for instance, the Urban Council's Museum of Art held a major show of artefacts dating from the Neolithic period to the Qing dynasty, *National Treasures – Gems of China's Cultural Relics* (16 December 1997 to 1 March 1998). This show, explicitly framed as being in celebration of the handover, included pieces from both Tibet and Hong Kong, even though the latter were hardly of 'national treasure' quality – as certain reviewers in fact pointed out. Clearly the items were included to emphasize a point about territorial boundaries of the contemporary Chinese state, as well as to encourage audience identification. According to the Museum's chief curator, Gerard Tsang, 'self-confidence and respect can only be founded on our understanding and identification with our own cultural heritage'.[17]

An attempt to invoke traditional Chinese culture can also be seen in the case of a piece of public sculpture which went on what turned out to be temporary display in Victoria Park from 6 July 1997 (a purportedly 'auspicious' date in the first week after the handover). This was an enormous 5-tonne bronze *ding* (or antique Chinese tripod vessel) cast in Nanchang, Jiangxi province. It was designed by veteran local sculptor and long-time pro-Communist Van Lau, who submerged his signature style (a geometricized modernist idiom) to create this homage to tradition. The tripod was decorated with a stylized Bauhinia flower (the official symbol of the post-handover Hong Kong Special Administrative Region), and had extracts from the text of the Basic Law of the SAR inscribed within it. In addition to the political references thus introduced there are those which adhere to the form by historical association, it being symbolic of dynastic power and legitimacy.

On 16 June 1997, after a 33-hour journey from China, the giant tripod arrived at the China Merchants' Godown in Kennedy Town. This warehouse was intended as its temporary home until going on display but almost immediately after arrival, while being lifted back on to a truck, an accident occurred. The tripod fell to the ground, breaking one of its legs. As a consequence it had to make a hurried return to China for repair. The intended auspicious symbolism of the sculpture was undermined by this mishap, as press reports quickly pointed out. Although the *I Ching* associates the *Ding* hexagram with 'great progress and success', the 'cauldron with its feet broken' has a very negative omen: 'its contents, designed for the ruler's use, overturned and spilt. Its subject will be made to blush for shame. There will be evil.' Clearly, tradition is not an unproblematic resource for the

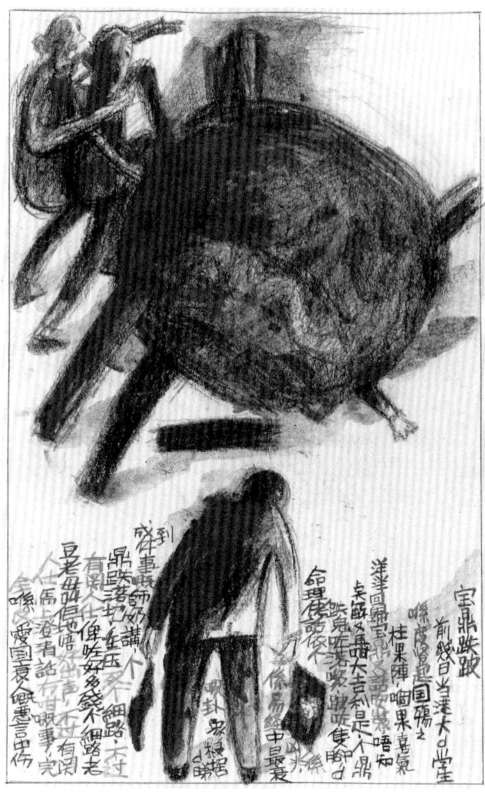

81 Oscar Ho, *The Crippled Ding*, 1997, mixed graphic media on paper. Collection of the artist.

promotion of nationalist meanings, and signification can in any case be altered by events in the physical life of the signifier.

Local artist Oscar Ho was quick to exploit the tripod's accident, producing a graphic image as part of his *Stories Around Town* series, titled *The Crippled Ding* (illus. 81). This work was reproduced in a local newspaper, *The Hong Kong Economic Journal*, during the handover period itself. Other artists attempted to undermine the effectiveness of the work after it eventually went on public display, like Ho employing humour as a deflationary tool. Pitting tradition against a work that invoked tradition, or using what might be characterized as subversive obedience, a group of artists burnt joss sticks and knelt in front of the tripod in a performance piece executed on the day of the sculpture's unveiling. The event was documented for a wider audience by a press report the next day.

Although the organization responsible for putting the tripod on display, the Association for All Sectors on Hong Kong Island for the Celebration of the Handover, had announced that it wished to donate the work to the Urban Council for permanent display in Victoria Park,

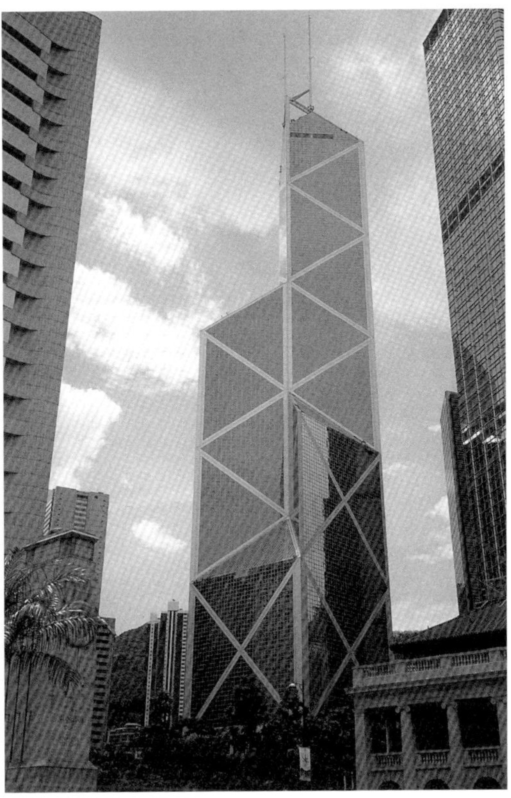

82 I. M. Pei and Partners/Kung & Lee Architects Designers Ltd, Bank of China building, 1989 (front view).

in fact the work disappeared after a short showing and has not been seen since. Perhaps the negative reception prevented a more permanent display from occurring, or comparisons with the then recent decision not to allow long-term display of the *Pillar of Shame* were too embarrassing.[18] Another monster tripod (this time weighing 6 tonnes) was among the various official gifts from China to the post-handover government, and was put on display in the Convention and Exhibition Centre Extension during the handover. The tripod was sponsored by Yiu's Holdings, and was designed and built by craftsmen in Shanghai.

The attempt to introduce Chinese national meanings into Hong Kong public space began some time before the handover itself, but had its first major expression in an architectural rather than a sculptural structure, I. M. Pei's Bank of China building, completed in 1989 (illus. 82). Like the Hong Kong and Shanghai Bank building this was intended as a major architectural statement, and although a commercial building it carried political associations as well on account of it being the new local headquarters of the Chinese state bank (the former Bank building

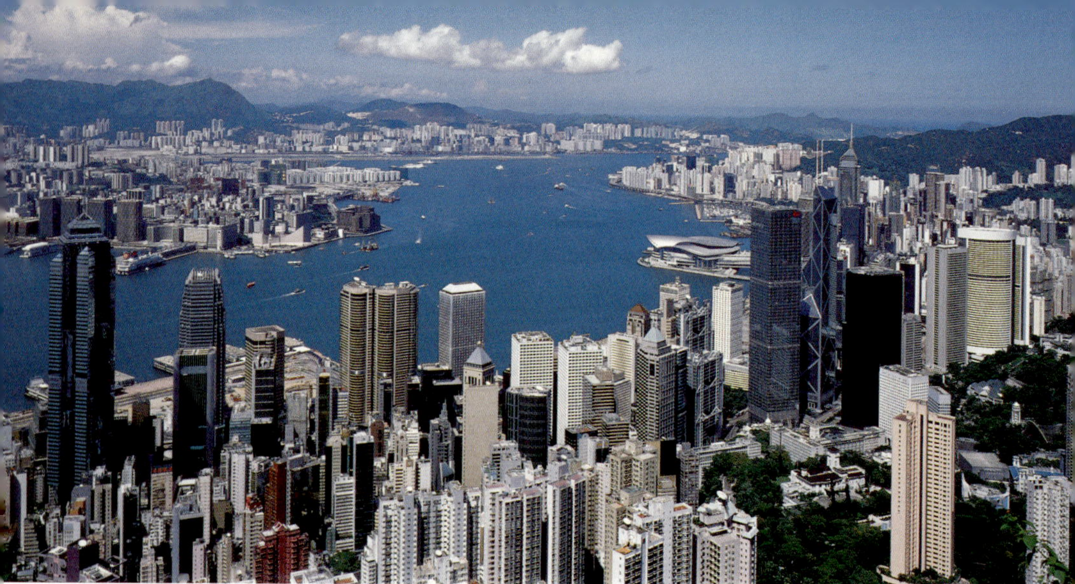

83 Panorama of the Hong Kong skyline showing the spatial relationship of major buildings in the Central district, including the Bank of China and the Hong Kong and Shanghai Bank building. The tall building between these is the Cheung Kong Centre; the Convention and Exhibition Centre Extension in Wanchai can be seen behind it, jutting out into the harbour. Government House is directly below the Bank of China, while the Cultural Centre can be seen across the harbour towards the left. The runway of the former airport at Kai Tak can be seen in the centre background.

still stands, and older residents can remember it being used as a site for Maoist propaganda during the Cultural Revolution period). Unveiled in 1984, Pei's design carries associations of growth that are both politically and commercially appropriate, supposedly recalling the form of the bamboo (a particularly fast-growing plant) in its segmented vertical structure.[19] Bamboo is of course emphatically Chinese in its associations, and since the minimal and geometric international modernism of the building's style does little to evoke Chineseness the presence of a Ju Ming *Taichi* sculpture at its base is also helpful in introducing a counterbalancing emphasis. The sculpture is aided in its task by extensive landscaping with stones and water (flowing northwards and thus, according to the architect, in accordance with the geomantic principles of *fengshui*. The traditions of Chinese landscape gardening are recalled, and Chineseness is further invoked by the use of granite, rather than glass and aluminium, at the base of the building. The fortifications of Beijing's ancient city gates are said to be referenced by this stone base, which features a crenellation motif.

Although a highly sophisticated piece of architecture, the Bank of China building nevertheless signifies through a logic less subtle than

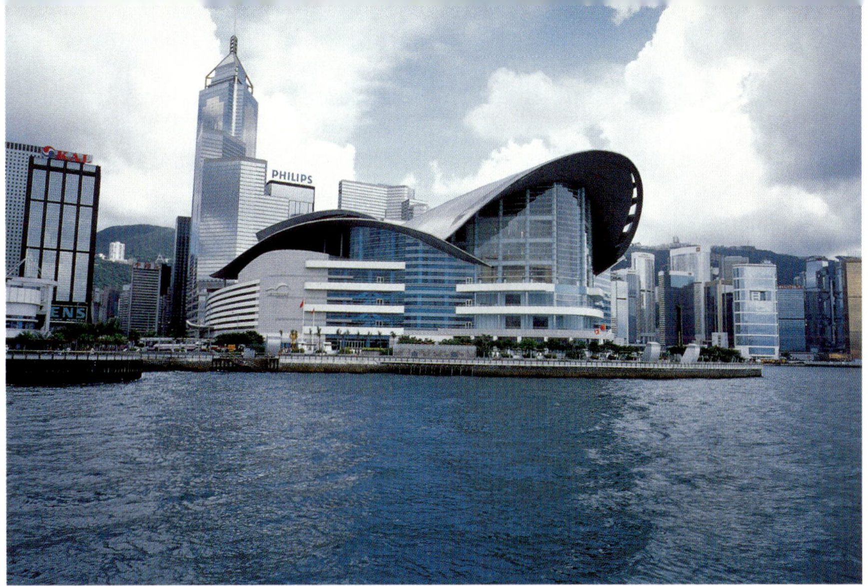

84 Convention and Exhibition Centre Extension (front view).

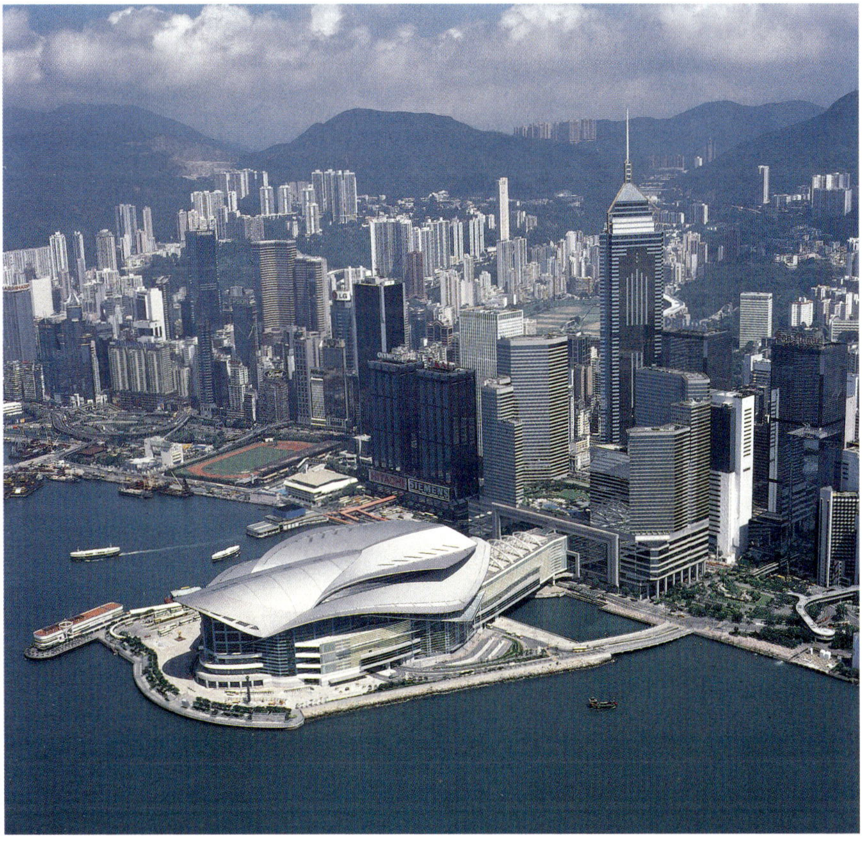

85 Convention and Exhibition Centre Extension (view from above).

the Hong Kong and Shanghai Bank building, namely that of scale. On
its completion it was (at 315 metres) the tallest building in Hong Kong,
and although this is no longer the case no building in its vicinity (such
as the recently finished Cheung Kong Centre) has dared to over-top it
(illus. 83). Clearly architectural scale has strong associations with
progress and modernity, in Hong Kong and elsewhere in East Asia
perhaps more so even than in Manhattan, but one senses that the Bank
of China building was also particularly concerned to overshadow the
nearby Hong Kong and Shanghai Bank building, the *de facto* central
bank of the colonial era. When first finished the building read as a
message to Hong Kong people about the post-handover era and coming
Chinese authority, its sheer size evoking the vastness of China when
compared to Hong Kong.

Like the Cultural Centre, the Bank of China building was to come to
completion in 1989 (it was officially opened in May 1990), and thus
faced problems of reception as a consequence of the changed political
circumstances that followed the Beijing crackdown of that year. Its
scale now appeared threatening rather than symbolic of progress (or
just comfortingly vast and therefore reliable). A negative popular reception can be documented through rumours that spread concerning its
bad *fengshui* properties. The twin mast structure which tops the roof
was said to resemble a pair of empty chopsticks, for instance, and thus
connote bad fortune. The angular forms of the building were interpreted as 'knives' threatening the surroundings, and in particular it
was noted that one 'blade' projected towards Government House, the
residence of the colonial governors. Even prior to the building's
completion worries were expressed about the building's *fengshui*, and
they can be interpreted as a form of disguised or unconscious semiotic
critique. In a May 1987 newspaper interview, *fengshui* expert Sung Siu-
kwong stated that the new bank was a bad omen in geomantic terms.
Sung critiqued the triangular basis of the design, in part because of the
inauspicious association between the Chinese term for pyramid and
that for the urn in which remains of the dead are stored.[20]

Strong national associations were also developed by the Extension to
the Convention and Exhibition Centre in Wanchai (illus. 84, 85), built
by Wong and Ouyang (HK) Ltd (with Skidmore, Owings and Merrill Inc
associated during conceptual design). Even more than the Bank of
China, the connotations of this building are orientated to the future.
Although oppositional public sculpture in Hong Kong had been deeply
concerned with remembering recent history, after 4 June 1989 it
became increasingly imperative for buildings and sculptures that
hoped to project a Chinese national ideology to develop amnesia.

There was also a particular reason why the Extension needed to erase history: it was to be the location of the 1997 handover ceremony, and thus a nationally (and indeed globally) crucial site for nationalist discourse.[21] The ceremony had to take place in a structure (and on a site) totally untainted by colonial associations or any memories of the past that could disrupt the carefully choreographed symbolism of 'the resumption of the exercise of sovereignty'. The ceremony had to take place in Hong Kong, but Chinese national ideology had no secure locus in the territory. Consequently the ceremony occurred in this newly constructed building (completed just in time for the handover and thus in a 'virgin' state), built on land reclaimed from the harbour for the purpose. Symbolism of a new beginning was possible in this site without memory, and the architectural structure (most notably the wing-like roof forms) made this meaning explicit. The aluminium-clad roof has been described as portraying a seabird taking off over water, and since the Extension juts out into the harbour the implied movement is (significantly) northwards, as well as upwards.[22] Much more than simply a functional structure, this building begs to be read as a quasi-sculptural monument pointing to an upbeat nationalist future.

Since the handover itself the nationalist associations of the Extension have been further underlined and strengthened, and a site has been created for Chinese national meanings which, despite the constitutional fact of the transfer of sovereignty, have (as yet) no easy place elsewhere in Hong Kong. A major role in extending the Extention's patriotic meanings has been played by two public sculptures that are to be found in the open space to the northern or harbour side of the building. In fact there are three sculptures associated with the Extension altogether, but the third, another Ju Ming piece (*Unbroken Taichi Flow*, 1991), can be taken as simply extending associations of modernity in a way already documented in the case of other architecture/sculpture ensembles of meaning such as Exchange Square, and as attempting to provide an antidote for the lack of explicit Chineseness in the building's architectural language.

The first of the two patriotic sculptures to be placed in association with the Extension is an abstracted representation of a Bauhinia flower, titled the *Forever Blooming Bauhinia* (illus. 86). The Bauhinia had been designated as the official emblem of the post-handover Hong Kong Special Administrative Region and a stylized image of it is used on both the seal and flag. The sculpture is constructed of bronze, but with a gold plating and gold leaf finish. Six metres high, it stands on a base of red Sichuan granite. Like the *Flying Frenchman* and the *Pillar of Shame*, the *Forever Blooming Bauhinia* was a gift from outside of

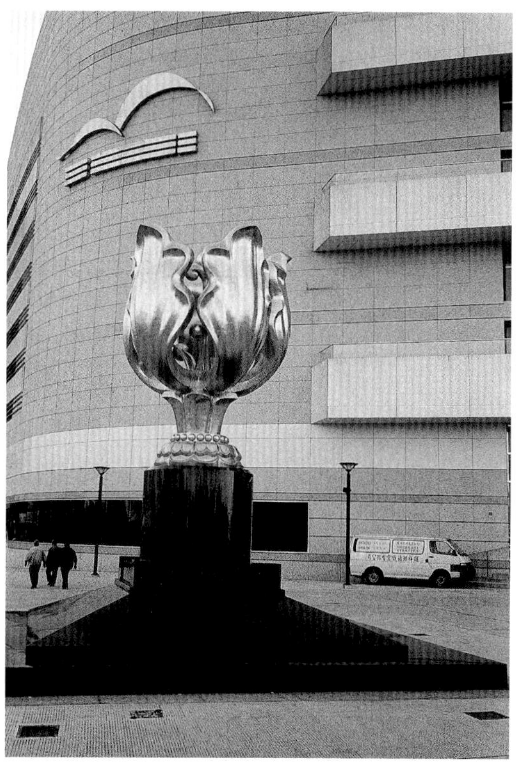

86 *Forever Blooming Bauhinia*, 1997, bronze, gold and red Sichuan granite, installed in 1997 next to the Convention and Exhibition Centre Extension. Property of the Hong Kong Special Administrative Region Government.

Hong Kong, in this case from the Central People's Government. It was thus the foremost in status of a great number of such handover celebration presents from the mainland – some 31 provinces and regions had also sent gifts – and the only one to go on outdoor public display. It would hardly have been possible for the Hong Kong Government to avoid installing it in a prominent location, and although the unveiling ceremony planned for 1 July 1997 (the first day of Chinese sovereignty) was postponed due to bad weather a symbolic presentation to the newly appointed Chief Executive, Tung Chee Hwa, was made by Chinese foreign minister Qian Qichen.

Other donated artworks from China were displayed inside the Extension itself during the handover period. A selection have since also been shown at the new Hong Kong Museum of History building in Kowloon and (by the Provisional Regional Council) in an exhibition at Shatin Town Hall which opened on 13 June 1998 titled *More than Gifts*. At one point there was a plan to convert Government House (the former colonial Governor's mansion) into a museum in which the gifts could all be displayed, but this was abandoned. Perhaps the variable aesthetic

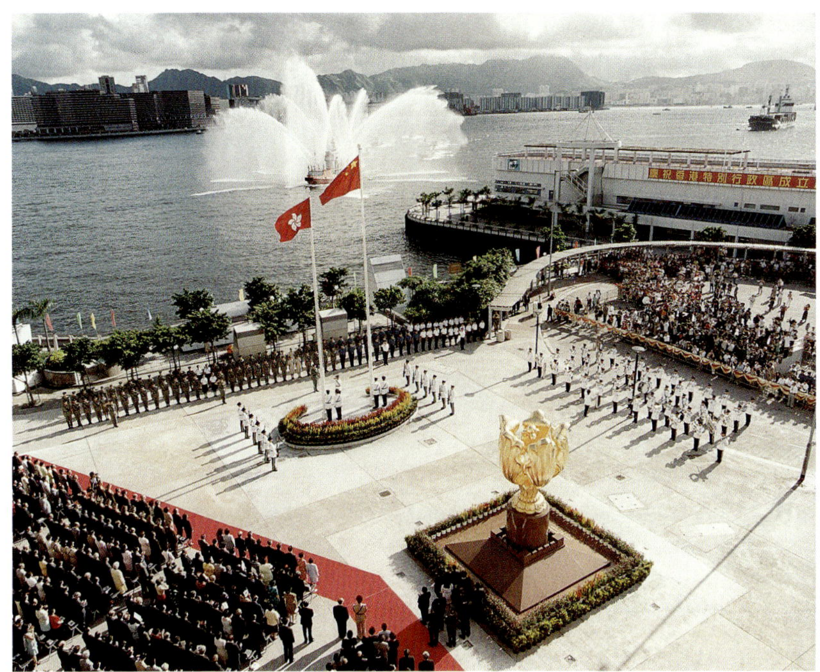

87 Flag-raising ceremony on 'Establishment Day' 1998 (1 July, the anniversary of Hong Kong's return to Chinese sovereignty), held in the open space next to the Convention and Exhibition Centre Extension before an invited audience. *Forever Blooming Bauhinia* (see illus. 86) can be seen in the foreground.

quality of the artworks was a factor in this decision: like the *Forever Blooming Bauhinia*, many of the gifts had a kitsch flavour. Heilongjiang province, for instance, presented a 1,997-millimetre-high vase made entirely of walnut, except for its marble bauhinia-flower handles. Hubei province gave a golden statue of dragons leaping out of the sea with a crystal bottle inside decorated with a Hong Kong harbour view.[23]

Although from mainland China, the *Forever Blooming Bauhinia* did not take China or Chineseness in general as its subject. Nor did it make reference to British imperialism, unlike the enormous public sculpture of a pair of hands snapping an opium pipe in half (*A Test of Strength – for Hong Kong's Return* by Pan He and others) which can be found a little way over the border in Humen (where the Opium War began). Perhaps hoping to be more acceptable to a Hong Kong audience by avoiding an overtly patriotic message, it instead made its subject a local symbol. Issues of power were still embedded in the work, of course, despite its apparently innocuous botanical subject, since it affirmed a definition of the local that was subservient to the national, and not in competition with it as many Hong Kong cultural expressions of autonomy have been. If anyone failed to understand this then they would only have to look from the sculpture to the ceremonial flagpoles which were installed right next to it. From one the Communist Chinese national flag is hung, and from the other, at a symbolically lower height, the SAR flag, again with a Bauhinia emblem (illus. 87). The base of the sculpture also makes clear the new official understanding of the relationship between Hong Kong and China: it makes a reference to the architectural form of the Great Wall, thereby symbolizing that the blossoming of Hong Kong is dependent upon its rootedness in Chinese soil or on the protection of the mother country.

The Bauhinia sculpture and the pair of free-standing flagpoles help to give focus to a public space that has been created at the foot of the Extension. Regularly visited by busloads of mainland tourists because of its national connotations, this harbour-side area comes into its own on 1 October, China's national day. The daily flag-raising ceremony gains a special significance on this occasion as the focus for a celebratory gathering attended by senior government officials and other important figures. Anson Chan, head of the civil service and deputy to Hong Kong's first post-handover Chief Executive, Tung Chee Hwa, claimed in a much-publicized statement to have experienced a rediscovery of her Chinese identity while watching the first of these national day flag-raisings. In this space free from colonial memories even someone as closely associated with the previous colonial government as her could experience existential rebirth, apparently.[24]

The second of the two patriotic sculptural accompaniments to the Convention and Exhibition Centre Extension is a monument dealing explicitly with the handover itself. Installed, like the *Forever Blooming Bauhinia*, in public space between the Extension and the harbour (but at the other end of its façade), it was completed in time for the second anniversary of the handover in 1999 (Chinese Vice-President Hu Jintao officiated at the unveiling ceremony). The monument had its beginnings in a decision of the Preparatory Committee of the Hong Kong Special Administrative Region at its third plenary session on 25 May 1996 that a commemorative monument be erected and that the HKSAR Government be entrusted with the task. The SAR's Chief Executive set up a Working Group on Reunification Monument and Government House Renaming on 1 July 1998, and they in turn announced an open invitation for a design for the Reunification

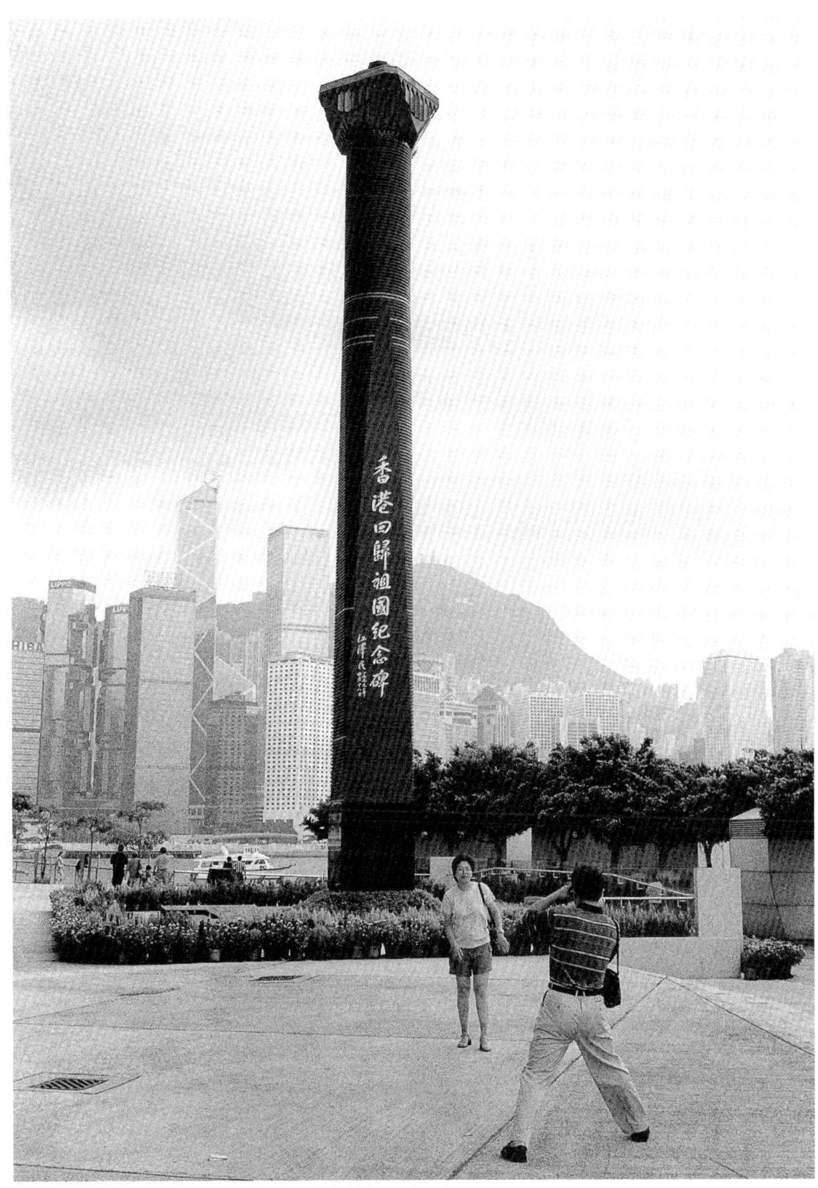

88 *Monument Commemorating Hong Kong's Reunification with China,*
installed 1999, granite and bronze, with tourists from Mainland China
taking a photo, 24 July 1999. Property of the Hong Kong Special
Administrative Region Government.

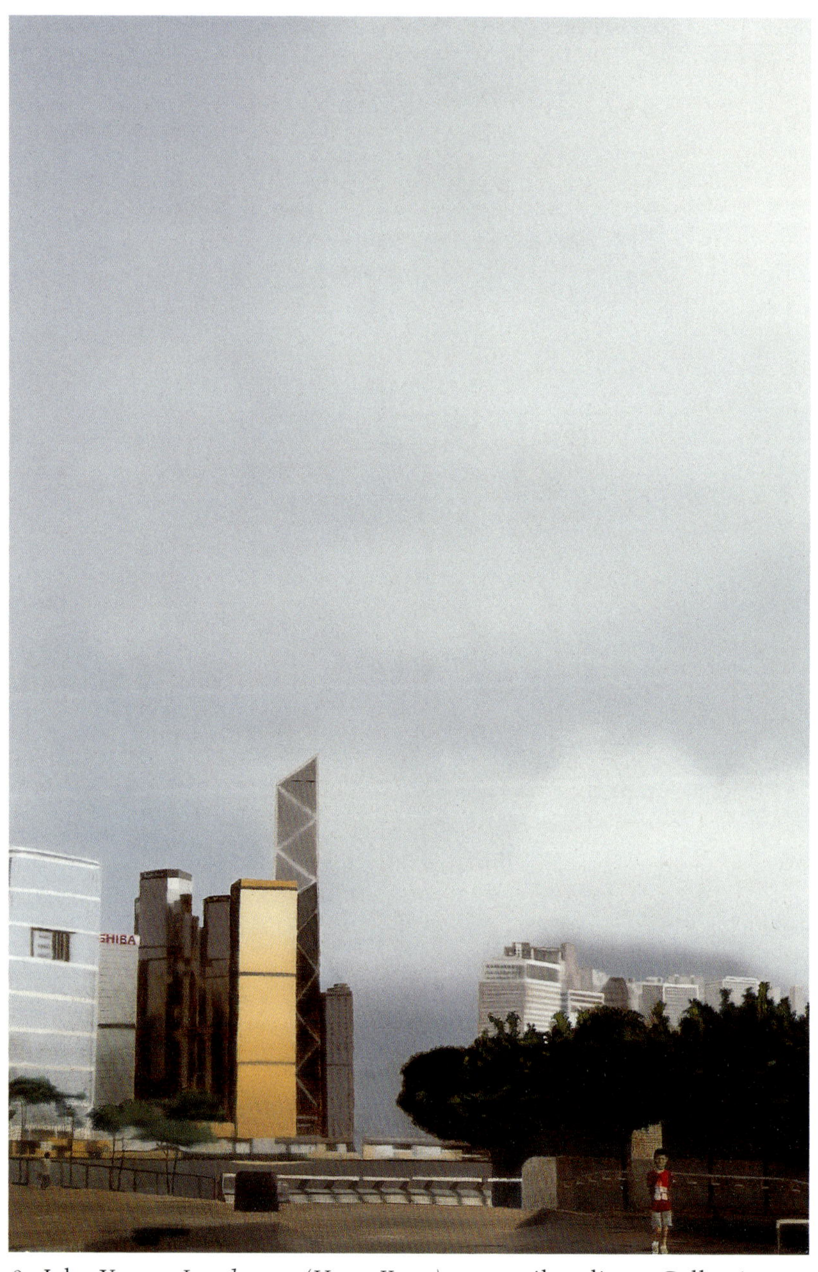

89 John Young, *Landscape (Hong Kong)*, 2000, oil on linen. Collection John Batten Gallery.

Monument with a closing date of 14 November. The final design (announced at a press conference on 20 April 1999) was adapted from one of the submissions by members of the working group (including the sculptor Van Lau). With a total height of about 20 metres and a width of 1.6 metres, it is an abstract form made of granite topped with bronze (illus. 88). Such an idiom is not entirely unexpected, since Van Lau had announced even before the Working Group's first meeting that he felt the structure 'should avoid the style of mainland monuments, which usually show soldiers and people participating in the revolution'.[25]

The reunification monument's primary models are more architectural than sculptural, since it resembles a free-standing column with capital and base. It has some associations with the Chinese traditions of *hua biao* (columnar structures) and *bei* (stele). The association with the stele, a surface for preserving carved versions of important pieces of handwriting, is enhanced by the presence of a vertically orientated carved inscription on the surface of the monument, in the handwriting of President Jiang Zemin. The inscription simply gives the object its name: the *Monument Commemorating Hong Kong's Reunification with China*. Inscription by a political leader in this way in order to convey endorsement and project personal political power is an established public use of the ancient Chinese calligraphic art in the People's Republic, and is the most direct way in which the monument conveys a message about China's newly re-established sovereignty over Hong Kong.[26]

As befits a monument attempting to commemorate an event about which local people had complex feelings, however, in other respects it displays a certain obliqueness in the expression of patriotic meaning. Whereas such obliqueness in the instance of Van Lau's tripod took the form of a reference to tradition, and in the case of the *Forever Blooming Bauhinia* the form of a strategic foregrounding of the local, with the reunification monument it took the form of a minimalist reticence. Like Maya Lin's *Vietnam Veterans Memorial* in Washington, DC (which dealt with an equally contentious event) it has a reductive abstract structure and no figurative subject. A knowledge of earlier Hong Kong artistic concerns can help us decode the work, however. Like many earlier sculptures and paintings it seems concerned with the reconciliation of opposites, with representing in formal terms the harmonious meeting of East and West. While such concerns sometimes sprang from a generalized sense of being caught between two cultures, in this specific case one can read a political allegory of the handover process. The cross section of the columnar body of the monument changes from a square at the base to a circle at the top, and thus provides a metaphor for smooth and untraumatic transition between opposites (rather than the accommodation of differences within the same space). A common Chinese association would equate squareness with earth and circular forms with heaven, but this polarity also begs to be read as referring to the change from British to Chinese sovereignty. Chinese sovereignty, of course, would be associated with the top of the column, and thus with progress and the future. This reading of the vertical dimension of the sculpture as representing the passage of time is made more explicit by a series of rings around the pillar created by the overlapping granite slabs. There are 206 of these, one to represent each year from 1842 to 2047 (when the promised 50-year period of Hong Kong's partial autonomy from China under the 'One Country, Two Systems' principle comes to an end). Lighter coloured granite is used for the six circular slabs representing 1842, 1860, 1898, 1982, 1984 (the year of the Joint Declaration) and 1990. 1997 is picked out by a glass ring with built-in lighting. Upward movement, already thematized in the Extension itself through the bird commencing flight theme, and in the *Forever Blooming Bauhinia* by the organic metaphor of growth, is further emphasized in the monument at night by a floodlight beam which projects up from its top. This is said to symbolize that 'Hong Kong will continue to flourish 50 years after returning to the motherland'.[27] Again the refrain about stability and prosperity is repeated.

As soon as it was completed the reunification monument was added to the itinerary of the mainland tourists already visiting the *Forever Blooming Bauhinia* sculpture, and it became the object of their photographic attention, clearly enjoying some success with that audience as a signifier of national reunification. The monument's local reception, however, was less unequivocally positive, as one might expect given the degree of local scepticism concerning Beijing-defined conceptions of national identity and the fragile legitimacy of the undemocratic post-handover government. *Next Magazine*, for instance, had an irreverent article likening the monument and its floodlight beam to an ejaculating penis, a somewhat predictable but nevertheless successfully deflationary reference to its power symbolism. A cartoon by prominent local political cartoonist Zunzi elsewhere in the same issue of *Next Magazine* makes use of a photograph of the monument's inauguration ceremony, and by means of an added speech bubble turns the event into a naming ceremony in which Tung Chee Hwa is made to christen the structure 'Stand-up Comedy' as a comment on the first two years of the SAR's existence.[28] John Young, Hong Kong-born

Australian artist, produced a work in oil on linen titled *Landscape (Hong Kong)* (illus. 89) which offers a view of the Hong Kong skyline from the podium of the Convention and Exhibition Centre Extension, based on a photograph which depicted the monument. In his painted version, which otherwise follows its source in meticulous detail, the monument is missing. A kind of iconoclasm is effected, but of a more subtle kind than Pun Sing Lui's attack on the Victoria statue. Such an erasure begs to be likened to a favoured strategy of authoritarian regimes (including China), namely airbrushing out or otherwise eliminating from images figures no longer in political favour.[29]

Such a critical reception in the mass media and in artworks would be hard to prevent without a wholesale crackdown on press and artistic freedom, but the Extension and its surrounding public space and monuments can be said to have learnt some lessons from the 1989 occupation of Tiananmen Square and taken defensive measures against any attempt at physical contestation or appropriation. Although the widespread use of glass in the walls of the Extension helps create associations of openness, it could be read against the grain as a disguised fortress. It is separated from the Convention and Exhibition Centre itself by a water-filled moat, and can be reached only by two road entrances (at either side) or by a footbridge to the main building (a sort of 'drawbridge' which could symbolize the disconnectedness of this place of national meanings from the rest of Hong Kong). The site for patriotic gatherings (and home of the *Forever Blooming Bauhinia*), despite reading as a public space, is actually for carefully controlled crowds only. When an event of political import takes place in the building or around the flagpole the roads to the Extension are sealed off, and demonstrators who might otherwise take disruptive possession of the space are left to protest behind police barriers on the other side of the protective moat.

References to history, so rigorously excluded from the Extension, tend to figure prominently in the activists' theatre of protest, and as in the Victoria Park 4 June rallies, Tiananmen Square and its problematic weight of memories is continually being recalled. On the first anniversary of the handover, for instance, when Chinese president Jiang Zemin attended a ceremony in the Extension, protestors demanded an official admission of guilt for the 1989 deaths. One carried a placard with an image of a tank, depicted as driven by Jiang Zemin and inscribed with the date of the massacre, and shown crushing a human figure (illus. 90). Others carried a mock coffin with an inscription calling for redress of the verdict on 4 June. They attempted to carry this obvious symbol of the Beijing killings through the police lines in the

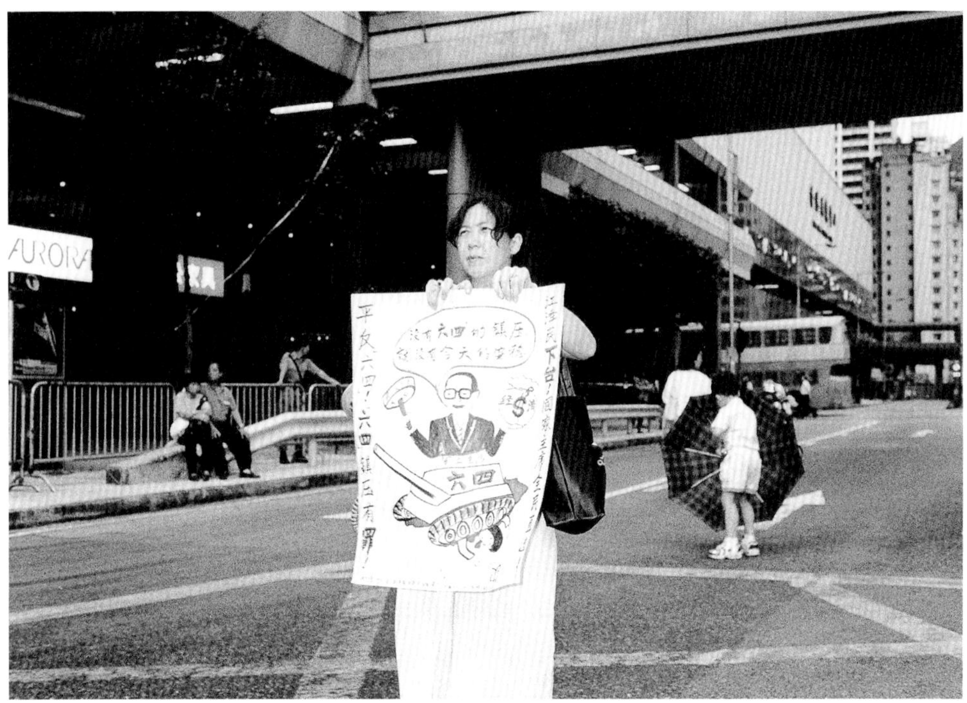

90 Demonstrator with a placard, adjacent to the Convention and Exhibition Centre Extension, 1 July 1998 (the first anniversary of the handover).

direction of the Extension, in what was always going to be no more than a symbolic attempt at overcoming their exclusion from that space of national meanings. After a predictable failure to penetrate the police barrier they instead burnt the coffin in the street.

Sound of course is able to penetrate a physical barrier such as a police line, and chanted slogans (often enhanced in power with the aid of megaphones) were habitually employed by demonstrators making the Convention and Exhibition Centre Extension their focus. On the second anniversary of the handover, during the unveiling ceremony for the handover monument, protestors had unexpectedly managed to break through the police barricades on the road bridges into the Extension to occupy a closer position about 300 metres from the ceremony. From there they were able to make their anti-government chants heard by the guests, until their megaphones were temporarily confiscated. On the occasion of the handover ceremony itself police had attempted to counter such attempts at sonic penetration of the building by drowning it out with music: Beethoven's *Fifth Symphony* was played over loudspeakers outside the handover venue. At the time Police Senior Assistant Commissioner Dick Lee Ming-kwai implausibly claimed that he had ordered the amplified music to be played to 'relieve the atmosphere, and for the enjoyment of the police and public', although later a letter from Police Commissioner Eddie Hui Ki-on to the chairman of the Independent Police Complaints Council admitted that the tactic was aimed at preventing mainland leaders including President Jiang Zemin and then-Premier Li Peng (widely held as responsible for the 1989 Tiananmen crackdown) from hearing chanted slogans such as 'down with butcher Li Peng'.[30]

In recent decades, art history has become more aware of the historical specificity of artistic meaning, with T. J. Clark's study of the critical reception of Manet's *Olympia* at the moment of its public debut in the 1865 Salon being a paradigmatic example.[31] The present investigation follows in the footsteps of that pioneering analysis by attempting to demonstrate the subtle changes which can occur in the environment for reception of art works over even quite short periods of time. Although conceived as a historical study it concerns itself with a contemporary example capable of being studied in real time, and attempts to extend the art historical literature by its deliberate focus on a non-Western instance. Since the period of time covered by the study includes a colonial transition, it is able to make a contribution to the field of post-colonial studies, and treats a case which may contradict simplistic conceptions of how art functions at such times.

As well as being concerned with the temporal specificity of artistic meaning this study of Hong Kong public sculpture has also been at pains to emphasize the importance of the spatial relativity of meaning, a question that has been less fully addressed so far in the discipline of art history. In a more narrow sense it has been concerned to demonstrate the way particular contexts of display and use, especially those created by or in concert with a sculpture's architectural setting, influence the meaning it is able to carry. In a broader sense it has been concerned to show the cultural relativity of artistic meaning. Although an understanding that artistic meaning is conditioned by cultural context is not lacking in art history, such an understanding tends to be applied more to objects created within such a cultural context. The orientation towards display and reception of the present study enables consideration on an equal basis of art objects created outside a cultural context, discovering cultural relativity of meaning to Western artworks, for instance. The possibility is raised that a heterogeneity of geographical perspectives exist from which art history needs to be written, none of which may claim any necessary centrality. Less compartmentalized in its conception than many studies, it takes a globalized perspective in which movement of objects across cultural space is considered, and in which cultural boundaries are not assumed to exist only at national frontiers. Local meanings are given a priority, even if those local meanings are of the national or the international, or are understood as making use of culturally hybrid knowledge bases, or as employing a globalized intertextuality.

The picture that emerges is of public art's active employment in the creation and contest of public meanings of an often highly politicized nature. Sculpture in Hong Kong between 1984 and 2000 has been involved in a central way in conflicting attempts to constitute publics. And this process continues, without the possibility of a stable state ideological hegemony being anywhere yet in sight.

5 The Visual Production of a Transition

So far this study has focused primarily on visual art more narrowly defined, except where some discussion of architecture has been required to indicate fully the context within which public sculpture's meanings were made. Now aspects of the field of visual production as a whole will be considered, exploring how the transition of sovereignty was mediated in the broader visual realm.

The response of artists to the handover was often quite critical. Issues of local identity came to the forefront during a period when neither the colonial government nor its appointed (and later actual) successor enjoyed widespread public confidence. Artists in Hong Kong enjoyed a particularly high degree of autonomy because of the absence of a developed commercial market for local avant-garde art, and because of the relative lack of institutional opportunities to display their work. Condemned either to artist-run spaces such as Para/Site, or to the Hong Kong Arts Centre (the largest local independent arts programming institution), or (increasingly in recent years) to prestigious overseas shows,[1] there were few external constraints on the content of their work. Naturally the degree of relative autonomy enjoyed by artists was not shared by most other types of visual producers. Although graffiti (considered below) had an even greater degree of freedom, with most other kinds of visual production there was a fettering of producers by the requirements of commercial or state employers, clients or markets. The way in which architecture has serviced (often remarkably consonant) commercial and state ideologies has already been noted, and commercial designers of all kinds worked with similar constraints.

A degree of concern with the expression of local identity could nevertheless be seen in a variety of design work produced within the constraints of the marketplace. Since many in the population at large shared identity concerns, there was a sizable constituency to whom appropriate commodities could profitably be marketed. When no meaning disruptive of business as usual seems intended, however, anxieties provoked by the transition can still sometimes be seen to have left their mark on a design. Even in cases where an official viewpoint is more securely embodied, there remains nevertheless the possibility that public reception will see a contestation of meaning. Such contestation in respect of architecture and public sculpture (and the role of artists in it) has already been noted, as has artists' engagement with PRC and SAR emblems. Here the engagement of artists with other types of visual production will again be discussed, resulting in a clearer picture of the differences of social function that exist within the field of visual production. While the abandonment of a reified notion of art, and the subsequent expansion of the field of study of art history is a wholly beneficial tendency of recent years, it is important to retain a sense of the different critical potential of the various types of visual productivity. A dethronement of art should not necessarily lead to a kind of levelling out that ignores its socially produced distinctness.

Architecture

Several key examples of recent Hong Kong architecture have already been discussed, namely the Hong Kong Bank, the Cultural Centre, the Bank of China and the Convention and Exhibition Centre Extension. All of these buildings, considered as more than simply functional structures, have been shown to be bearers of handover-related connotations. Commercial or governmental messages of optimism concerning the post-handover future were being projected, and patriotic meanings can also be divined. Because of this alignment of architecture with official ideology the reception of these buildings, particularly the last three, was mixed. A similar pattern has occurred in other cases too: buildings have been created or co-opted to carry handover-related meanings, and those meanings have been contested in turn. Structures built using money from the public purse have been among the most controversial: both the new building of the Hong Kong Museum of History in Kowloon and the new Central Library in Causeway Bay, for instance, have provoked debate, as have the new Hong Kong Stadium and a proposed Museum of Contemporary Art.

In the case of the new building for the Hong Kong Museum of History there was an extensive dialogue in the press concerning the kind of historical narrative the museum would be offering. Fears were expressed that there would not be enough of a local emphasis in the displays, and that contentious issues such as the response of Hong Kong people to the 4 June 1989 Beijing crackdown would be glossed over.[2] In the case of the Central Library, however, the building itself proved particularly controversial, with many expressing the view that the chosen design was not ambitious and cosmopolitan enough (even though it was consciously 'post-modern' in style, having a classical temple façade as if embedded at the top of its front face [illus. 91]). Protests against the design came from architectural professionals as

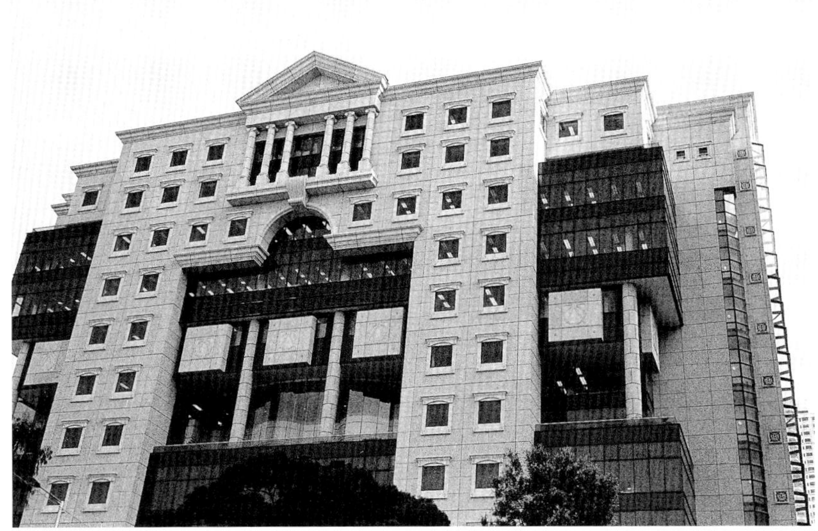

91 Central Library, Causeway Bay (detail of façade).

well as from the broader community: Institute of Architects president Tao Ho, for instance, described the design (by Government Architectural Services Department chief architect Ho Chiu-fan) as 'vulgar' in a television programme. Arguments broke out even within the commissioning body itself: there was a public clash over the design between Provisional Urban Council chairman Ronald Leung Ding-bong and Director of Urban Services Elaine Chung Lai-kwok on 24 July 1997, with the latter being accused of attempting to introduce a new design without the Council's permission. This alternative design, prepared by architect Rocco Yim Sen-kee, was rejected by a Provisional Urban Council joint committee on 29 July, which went on to censure Chung. Democratic Party members of the Provisional Urban Council (as well as some independents) had attempted in a special Standing Committee meeting to get agreement to seek independent professional opinion on the design. The Democrats also called for an end to the Architectural Services Department's monopoly on public building provision, and for the adoption of a system of open competition in the case of large-scale projects. In autumn 1999 a new row broke out over alterations to the façade made without approval of the Urban Councillors.[3]

Such active public and media interest in civic architecture is best seen as a dimension of the broader local struggle for greater democratic participation. While the battle for political enfranchisement has of course been the central expression of this desire, contests in relation to architecture and public space have proved important as well, partly because of frustrations in the political arena. Those contests can be viewed as a displacement of blocked political energies into other channels, but on occasion they do actually spill over into the arena of politics as narrowly understood. The previously noted attempts by demonstrators to enter the Convention and Exhibition Centre Extension or its adjoining plaza on politically significant occasions would be a case in point. Those attempts to gain access to an architectural structure, or to make seemingly public space more truly public as a site of politicized dialogue had a parallel in actions focused on the Legislative Council Building in the Central district of Hong Kong Island. This early colonial era structure, completed in 1912 as a Supreme Court building following plans prepared by the London architectural firm of Webb and Bell, was the site that leaders of the Democratic Party and other prominent pro-democracy legislators from the short-lived wholly democratically elected legislature of the late colonial era chose to mount their first protest of the post-colonial era. Soon after the transfer of sovereignty at midnight, 30 June 1997, they entered the building and took up positions on an exterior balcony overlooking crowds below. From here they gave speeches concerning their hopes for the re-establishment of democracy. Since their tenure as legislators had been abruptly terminated with the handover they had become symbolic intruders and were exposing themselves to the possibility of prosecution. This invasion by democrats of a building which had just become less public (with the replacement of elected representatives by appointed successors) made the architectural structure itself a site for a spatialized metaphor of disenfranchisement and its resistance.[4]

Such meanings were also proposed by protestors who placed stickers on the columns of the Legislative Council Building on the handover day which read (in Chinese) 'Pillar of Shame' (illus. 92). This inventive borrowing of associations from the by-then well-known public sculpture of that name made a link between the Tiananmen Square demonstrations and the handover period protests, although the 'shame' now being referred to was the elimination of the limited and short-lived local democracy rather than the 1989 loss of life. Still on public display at that time at the University of Hong Kong, the *Pillar of Shame* was metaphorically cloned through the stickers, and given a more prominent location than it otherwise could have expected.[5] In the post-handover period, when the democratic legislature had been replaced by

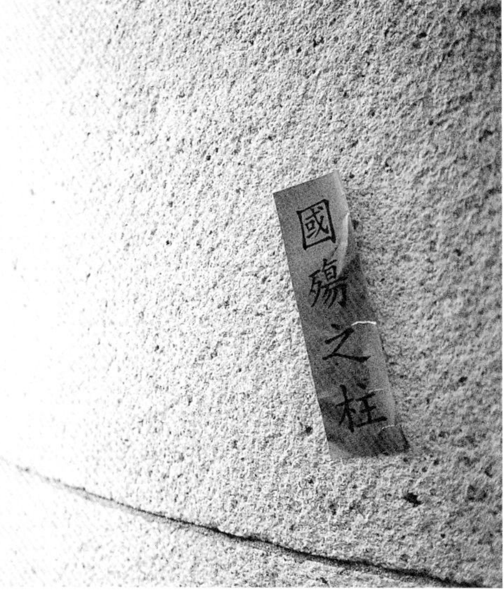

92 'Pillar of Shame' sticker on a pillar of the Legislative Council Building, 30 June 1997.

a compliant appointed successor (a 'Provisional Legislative Council' that lasted until elections of a less fully democratic kind could be held), April 5th Action Group member Leung Kwok-hung, together with two other activists, echoed the action of the democrats on the handover night. On 16 July 1997 they made use of the public gallery inside the Council chamber to protest against the activities of the Provisional Legislature, which was debating a government move to freeze certain laws passed by the pre-handover legislature. By their actions they were turning the chamber into a space for political theatre of a particularly physical sort: to restore order these members of the public had to be forcibly ejected from the public gallery, in full view of the press gallery at the chamber's opposite end. On 7 November of the same year Leung and three others again made a protest in the public gallery before walking out. They had been demonstrating outside and had eventually managed to gain entry to the public gallery. Leung also succeeded in using the public gallery to shout slogans on 7 October 1998 while the Chief Executive was answering questions about his policy speech to the Legislative Council of the previous day. A similar protest on 7 October 1999 led to Leung being given a two-week prison sentence starting on 26 May 2000, but on 12 October 2000 he again managed to gain admission to the Council chamber's public gallery and (accompanied by three other April 5th Action Group members) once more disrupted the Chief

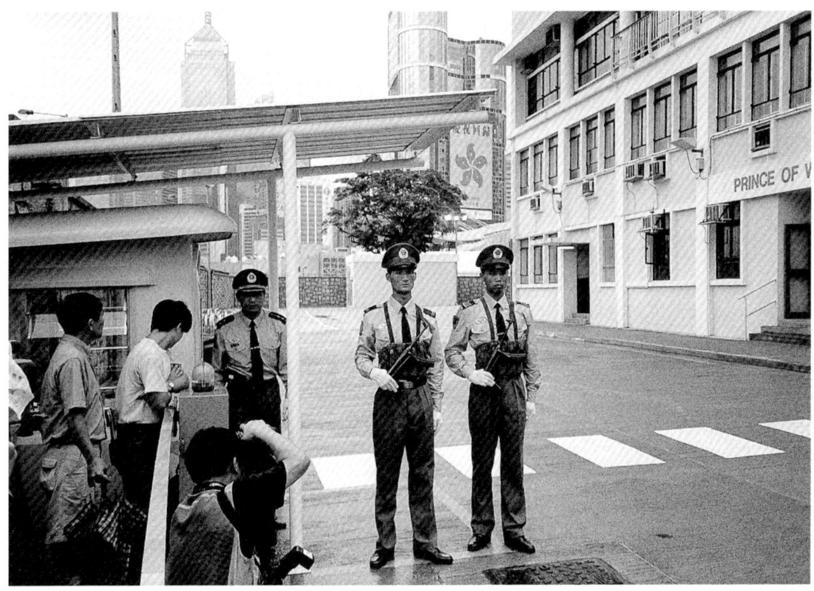

93 Soldiers of the People's Liberation Army at the former Prince of
Wales Barracks, Central, with onlookers, 1 July 1997.

Executive's question and answer session.[6]

While symbolic occupation of buildings was in this way used to
register protest against a perceived privatization of government in the
post-handover era, the symbolism of occupation was also used as a
prime means of demonstrating the transfer of sovereignty itself. The
most potent symbol that Hong Kong was now under Communist
Chinese rule was the convoy of People's Liberation Army troops that
crossed the border in the early hours of 1 July 1997, an event witnessed
by many residents on their television screens, at least on news reports
later in the day. These troops occupied the various facilities left behind
by the departing British garrison, the most prominent of which, since
it is to be found on a waterfront site in the Central area of Hong Kong
Island, was the Prince of Wales Barracks (illus. 93). While a suitably
patriotic message capable of nocturnal illumination was soon attached
to the side of the military base's main high-rise building, exhorting the
reader to love Hong Kong and to love China, it is interesting that for a
long time the highly visible lettering indicating the distinctly colonial
name of the barracks was not taken down. It was finally removed
towards the end of 1998, and even after that time the name could still
be read from the traces left behind by the now-absent lettering (illus.
94). It was as if the full symbolic meaning of the PLA's occupation of

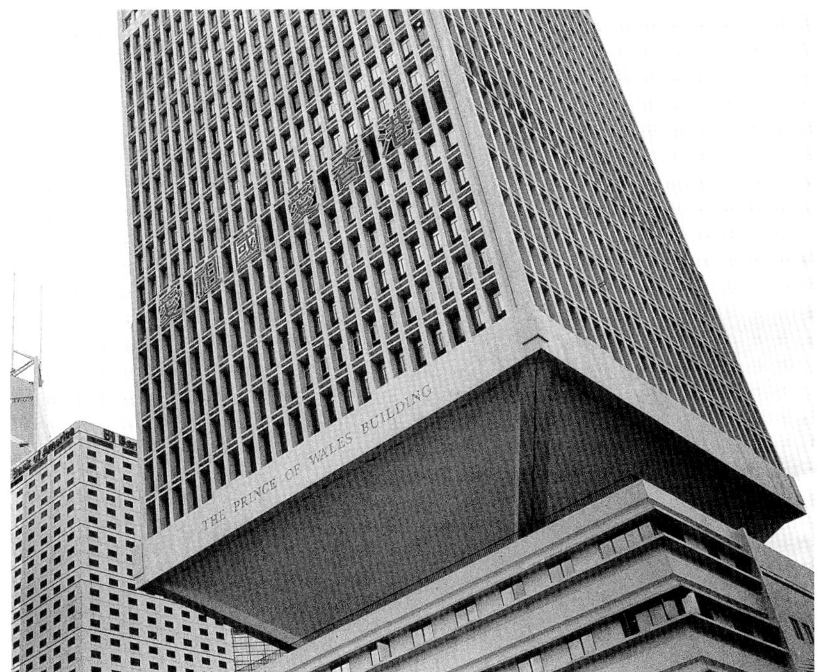

94 Detail of the former Prince of Wales Building, now occupied by a People's Liberation Army garrison, 16 December 1998. The structure has been decorated with a patriotic slogan ('Love the mother country, love Hong Kong'), and although its colonial-era name had been removed not long before the photograph was taken, traces of the letters were still clearly visible.

the site could not be understood unless one was able to see what had been replaced, as well as who was doing the replacement. Only on 25 May 2000 did the PLA announce an official renaming of this and the seven other barracks it had taken over from the British forces. Neutral names were chosen, with the Prince of Wales Barracks becoming Central Barracks.[7]

While the Prince of Wales Barracks was the most visible military symbol of the colonial era, Government House (illus. 95), the colonial governor's residence, was the most prominent civil symbol. Here the post-handover strategy was not one of reoccupation, but of abandonment. Tung Chee Hwa, Hong Kong's first Chief Executive, decided not to make it his official residence (apparently partly on *fengshui* grounds), preferring to carry on living in the same private flat in Grenville House that he had occupied before his appointment. His decision was challenged, in part because it read as a privatization of

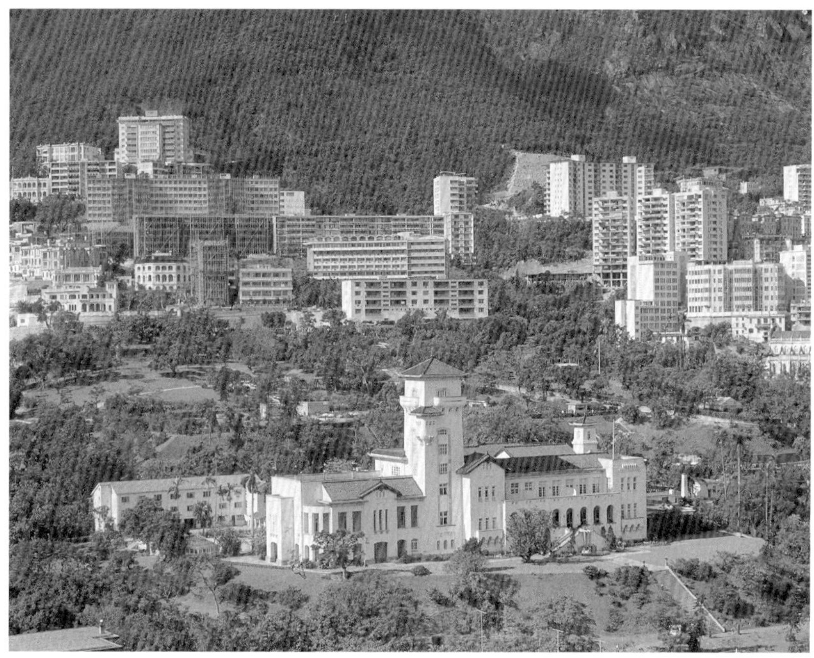

95 Government House in 1962.

government, coinciding as it did with the abolition of the democratically elected legislature. The future use of the now-vacant Government House also became a matter of public debate. The government at first suggested that it might be turned into a museum to house the many handover gifts from China, but then decided against the idea and suggested it might be used as a guest house or for entertaining visiting VIPs (Clinton dined there on one occasion, and there was some controversy when Tung considered holding an 80th birthday party there for Sze-yuen Chung). With no firm picture of its future use decided a year after the handover, the Government was accused of vacillation and waste of resources. Democrat Cheung Man-kwong, for instance, speaking on 26 June 1998, accused Tung Chee Hwa of being indecisive over even minor matters. He claimed that it was a waste to use Government House in the manner the Government had been doing, and that Tung should move into the building, if only for the sake of his successors. In December 1997 Cheung had also urged the Director of Audit to investigate whether public money had been wasted on Government House since 1 July of that year, because of Tung's decision not to live there.[8]

The government (acting on the advice of a Working Group on

Reunification Monument and Government House Renaming appointed on 1 July 1998) proposed a renaming of the building to erase colonial associations. The favoured replacement name was *Chi Lo*, which has been translated as 'The purple air from the East cottage', with *Chi* also referring to the Bauhinia, which appears on the SAR emblem. This suggestion met with widespread opposition from the general public, as well as from entities such as the Hong Kong Tourist Association. Tung Chee Hwa was grilled on the issue by legislators during a formal Legislative Council question and answer session on 6 May 1999, where he attempted to defend the renaming decision, and rejected claims that he wished to erase colonial history. The Legislative Council debated the proposed name change on 2 June 1999, with tourism functional constituency representative and Liberal Party legislator Howard Young sponsoring a motion urging that the building be called *Chin Kong Duk Fu* ('Former Government House'). The Working Group bowed to the gathering public pressure and invited further suggestions of names, thus creating an opportunity for Hong Kong people in general to voice their discontent with the plan. Providing well-known buildings with nicknames or humorous descriptions is one way in which Hong Kong people have attempted to come to terms with the architectural environment that has been imposed on them, and the list of proposed new names for Government House (duly displayed on the government's own website) included some less than fully serious suggestions. Although hardly showing a reverence for the colonial era, a great many of the suggestions did not want to forget it either. In the end the government capitulated to community wishes to some degree, and the simple name *Heung Kong Lai Bun Fu* ('Government Guest House') was adopted as the official Chinese language name, although the English version of the name was not changed.[9]

Of all the architectural projects that can be said to be handover-related, the most extensive (and expensive) was the construction of a new airport and its associated transport infrastructure. Replacing Kai Tak International Airport, which occupied an inner-city waterfront site not capable of expansion to deal with the increasing traffic, the new airport was constructed on Chek Lap Kok Island, just beyond Lantau Island. Chek Lap Kok was completely cleared and levelled, then extended by reclamation and connected via road and rail links to the city. Both road and railway line pass along the side of Lantau Island, then cross the specially constructed Tsing Ma Bridge, apparently the longest road/rail bridge in existence (with a span of 1,377 metres). The airport terminal building, claimed as the largest in the world, was designed by Norman Foster. Altogether the project was to cost HK$155 billion.

The decision to make Chek Lap Kok the site of the new Hong Kong airport was announced by Governor David Wilson in his policy address to the Legislative Council on 11 October 1989, and it was the most significant aspect of the confidence-building initiative of the colonial government in the post-4 June 1989 era (which also included measures such as the expansion of higher education, designed in part to counter the effects of new high levels of emigration). Plans for a new airport had been mooted during the era of Governor MacLehose, but had been shelved by Governor Youde because of cost considerations. Clearly they had been hurriedly dusted down and revised following the 4 June crackdown by a government faced with a significant crisis of legitimacy because of declining local confidence in the post-handover future, but which did not feel able to alienate China by acceding to demands for greater local democracy. Intended both to symbolize continued progress and prosperity and to help create it (on account of the sheer scale of this infrastructural project) the airport plan nevertheless proved controversial and ran into opposition from China. For some time the project was a bone of contention between the two sovereign powers, whose Joint Declaration era united front was unravelling in the wake of the Beijing crackdown. The Chinese government exhibited worry over the potential drain on the territory's reserves in the period before it was to regain sovereignty, and since the popularity of the airport project was not high in Hong Kong (as opinion polls of that time consistently showed) it had a rare opportunity to make common cause with local people. In an attempt to gain some measure of influence over events in Hong Kong during the pre-handover period, China called for (and in due course gained) the establishment of an Airport Consultative Committee. A united front between the two sovereign powers was restored when British Prime Minister John Major made a trip to Beijing to sign a Memorandum of Understanding on the new airport project with Li Peng, his Chinese counterpart, on 3 September 1991. Clearly Britain was making a big concession in agreeing to Major's visit to the Chinese capital so soon after the 1989 crackdown, and the agreement over the airport was touted as a major reconciliation between the two powers. Although it was originally planned to hold the signing ceremony in the Fujian Hall of the Great Hall of the People, a decision was later taken to move the ceremony to the West Hall, where the signing of the 1984 Joint Declaration had occurred. Major likened the two agreements when he remarked that 'the Joint Declaration sets our course, the Memorandum of Understanding helps us on our way'.[10]

Although this great show of solidarity was accompanied by agreements on a variety of other issues no concessions were offered by China concerning the pace of democratic development, the issue of most concern to local people. As a consequence the precariously re-established united front did not last long, and collapsed when the new Governor, Patten, attempted to gain a measure of legitimacy by offering enhanced participation in the electoral process rather than more promises of prosperity and progress in his 7 October 1992 policy address. Even before that time new disagreements with China had occurred: negative comments about the soaring budget estimates for the airport made on 6 March 1992 by Lu Ping, the head of China's Hong Kong and Macau Affairs Office, had caused the local stock market to fall by 50 points. A final agreement on the financing of the airport was only eventually signed in the Airport Committee of the Sino-British Joint Liaison Group on 4 November 1994. Because of the delays caused by the protracted dispute between the sovereign powers, the initially projected opening date of the airport was to become unrealistic, and its inauguration was inevitably postponed till after the end of British sovereignty. According to the initial plan, the airport was due to open in early 1997 and thus become a symbol of the colonial government's achievement. Indeed, one factor influencing the choice of location had been this possibility of a pre-handover completion date, despite Chek Lap Kok being less suitable in terms of both aeronautic considerations and passenger convenience.[11] In the event, only the Tsing Ma Bridge was completed in time to serve as a colonial symbol. The Lantau Link, of which it was the centrepiece, was officially opened by former British Prime Minister Baroness Thatcher to some fanfare on 27 April 1997. The bridge was lit up by a large-scale firework display that evening (illus. 96). A commemorative $10 coin was issued, showing an image of a bridge on one side, and a $5 stamp showing the bridge was issued as part of a 'Modern Landmarks' series of commemoratives.

The airport itself, opening after the handover on 6 July 1998, was unashamedly appropriated by the incoming regime as a symbol of its own success. President Jiang Zemin was the guest of honour at the opening ceremony, flying out on the first international passenger flight to use the runway, while President Clinton, fresh from a summit in Beijing, became the first world leader to fly in and out of the new airport. Even the already-opened bridge became a ready-made three-dimensional national reunification symbol, as witnessed in its use as the main feature on a float representing Hong Kong in the 1 October 1999 Tiananmen Square celebrations for the 50th anniversary of the founding of the People's Republic.[12] A salon-style photograph of the

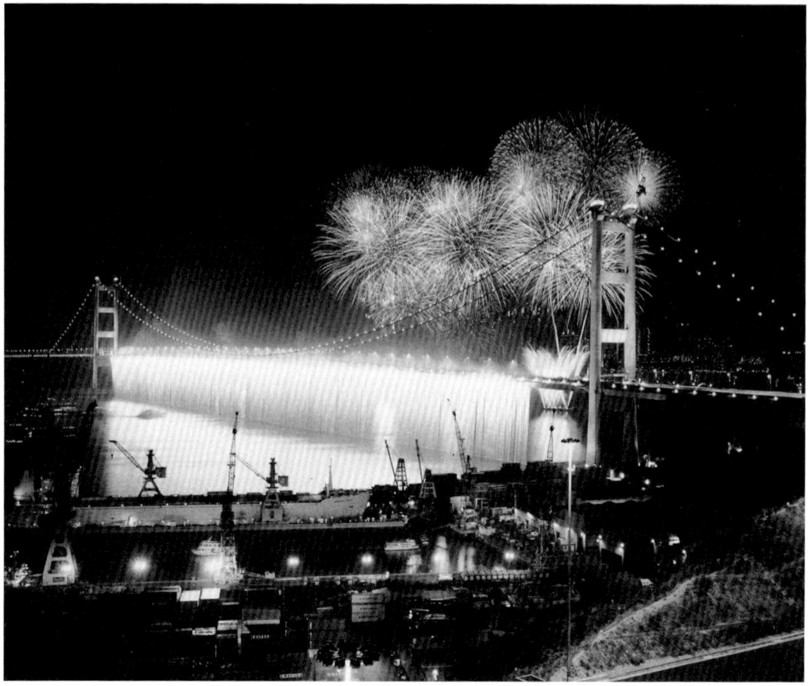

96 The opening ceremony of the Tsing Ma Bridge and the Lantau Link,
27 April 1997.

bridge's opening ceremony, included in a patriotic outdoor photographic exhibition organized by the Hong Kong Creart Photographic
Association in Chater Garden near the Legislative Council Building
around the time of the handover, turned the fireworks for the opening
into a celebration of reunification by context and titling. A sculptural
model of a bridge as a symbol of the reunification of Hong Kong with
China (the *Bridge of Unity*) was the gift of the Guangxi Zhuang
Autonomous Region to Hong Kong SAR government. This 2.5-metre-
long and 2-metre-high wooden carving was on display in the new Hong
Kong Museum of History during June 1999.

Unfortunately, almost as soon as the new airport opened for business
there were teething problems of a quite extensive kind. Primarily
caused by computer glitches, and the rush to open the airport in time
for the first anniversary of the handover, the subsequent tarnishing of
the airport's image was all the more extreme because of the symbolic
weight it had been required to bear. Subsequent inquiries only
extended the agony and recrimination well beyond the point where the
airport itself had attained the efficiency of operation it was designed

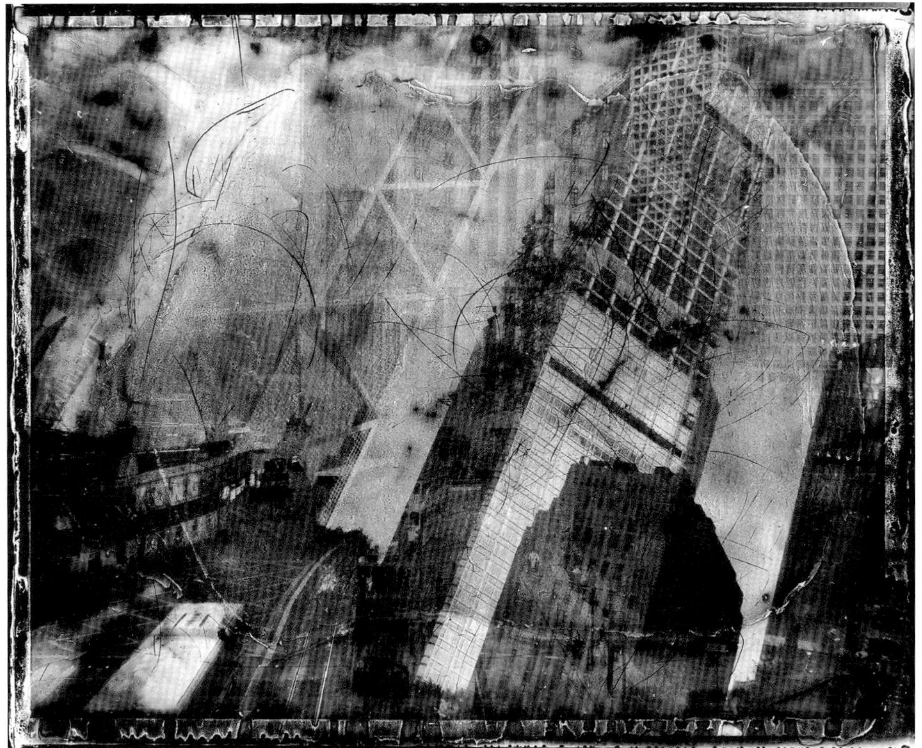

97 So Hing Keung, *Central, Hong Kong*, 1999, photographic print.
Collection of the artist.

for. A symbol of all that was new, so valuable to a political order that was itself new, was ignominiously compared to the old and less grand but apparently more user-friendly Kai Tak airport, the subject in any case of a great deal of nostalgic attention prior to its closure.[13]

Just as patriotic or optimistic meanings for the Tsing Ma Bridge were created and propagated in images of it, so too images could play a role in contesting a building's ideological freight. Both artists and film-makers can be said to have engaged with Hong Kong architecture in this way, sometimes displaying a degree of rage towards specific structures. In the 1997-themed and special effects-packed movie *The Wicked City* (1992), directed by Peter Mak Tai-kit and produced by Tsui Hark, for instance, an airliner crashes into the Bank of China Building, while in Benny Chan's *Gen-X Cops* (1999) the Convention and Exhibition Centre Extension is blown up at the climax of the movie. The Hong Kong skyline as a whole is the target of several photographs by So Hing Keung. *Central, Hong Kong* (illus. 97) shows the Bank of China Building

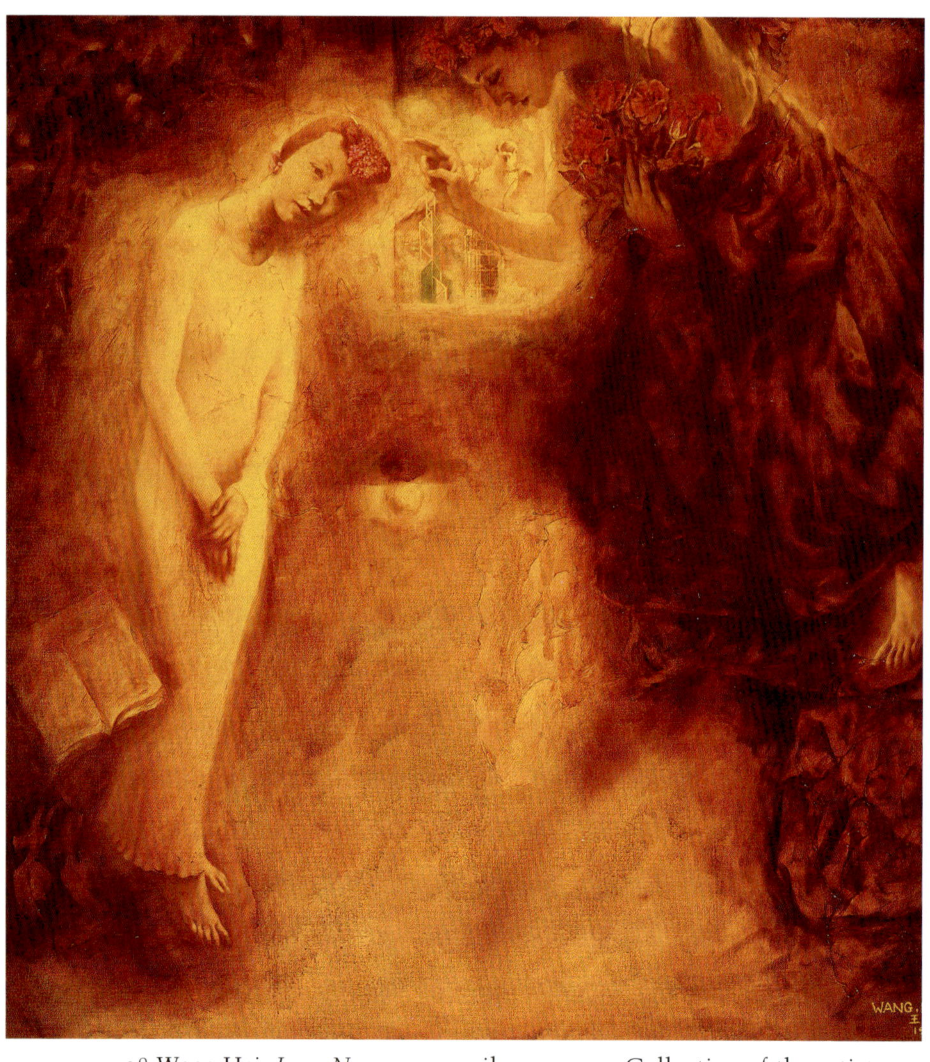

98 Wang Hai, *Icon No. 2*, 1993, oil on canvas. Collection of the artist.

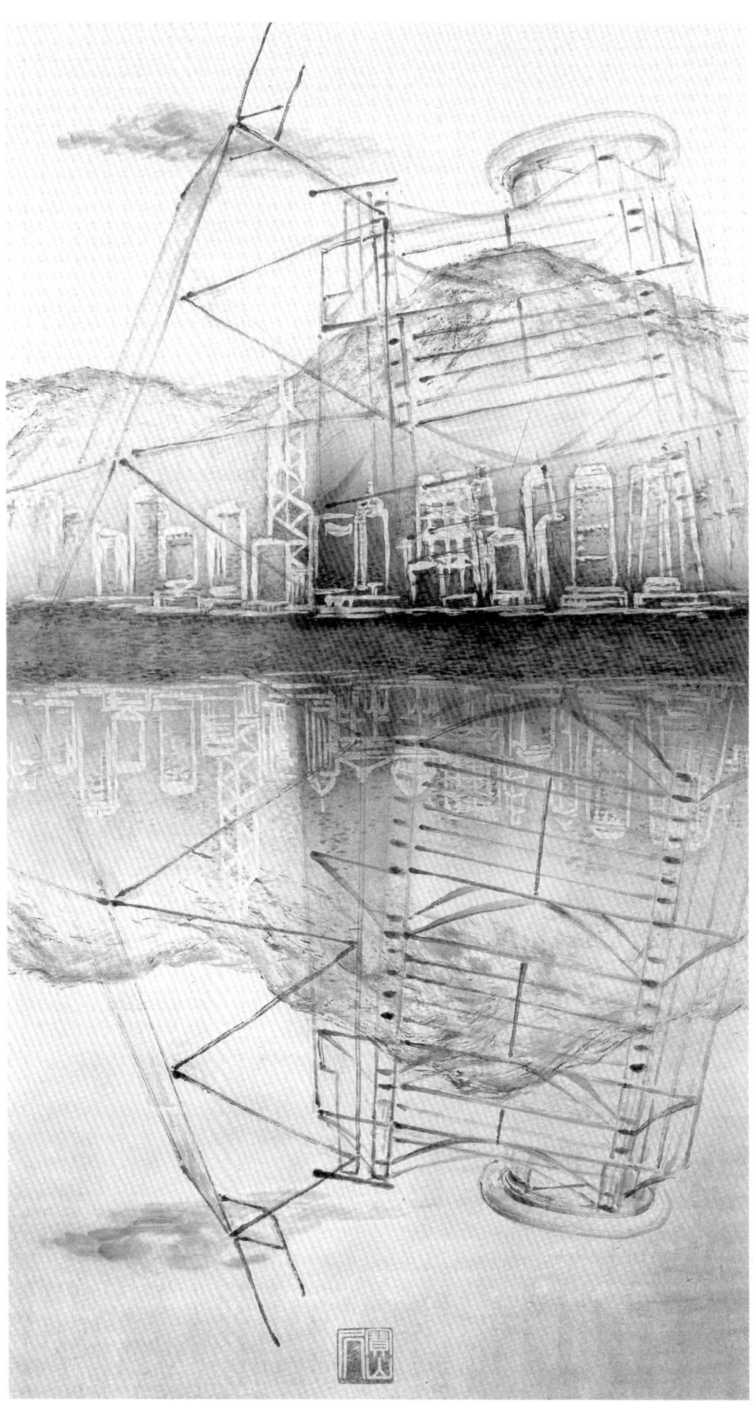

99 Lucia Cheung, *Invisible City*, 1997, ink and colour on rice paper.
Collection of the artist.

as well as the Cheung Kong Centre (then still under construction), both
from a very low viewpoint. As with other works in the same series, So
has manipulated the image by a variety of means, so that (as with
Warren Leung's previously discussed pinhole images) the modern city
under construction seems old and worn. Scratching of the negative's
surface, one of the means of manipulation employed, reads as an attack
on the structures shown. Their own rhetoric is cancelled in his alienated vision of the urban landscape.[14]

Both Wang Hai and Lucia Cheung have produced painted images in
which the political connotations of certain Hong Kong buildings are
accentuated, even if there is no direct attack involved as in the case of
So. Wang Hai for instance produced a curious image *Icon No. 2* (illus.
98), which seems to represent the Joint Declaration as a modern-day
Annunciation. The Hong Kong Bank and the Bank of China are visible
in the background, functioning as attributes of Britain and China
respectively.[15] Lucia Cheung also uses the two bank buildings as signifiers of the two sovereign powers in an equally odd image, *Invisible
City* (illus. 99). Skeletal outline representations of the two banks overlap and interpenetrate. Behind them we can make out the Hong Kong
Island skyline (with the two banks again shown, in their appropriate
locations, but at a smaller scale). A colour coding helps underline the
political associations: the right-hand side of the painting, which
contains both versions of the Hong Kong Bank, is a British blue, while

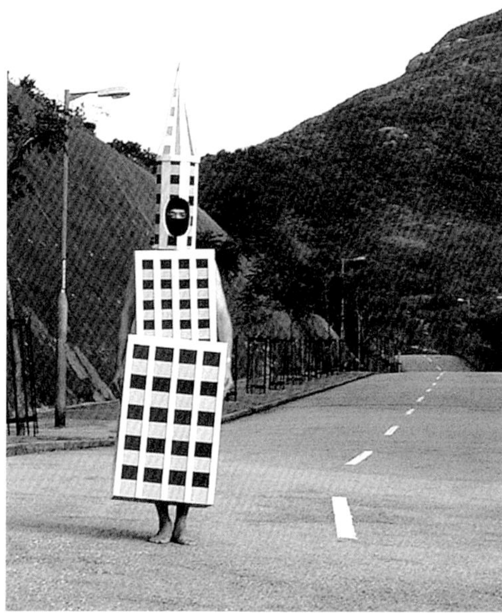

100 Kacey Wong,
Personal Skyscraper,
2000, black-and-white
photographic print.
Collection of the artist.

the left side which appropriately contains the two China banks, is a Communist red. In the area of the skyline behind the interpenetrating sections of the two foreground bank buildings a purple is used, to indicate mingling in a colouristic way.[16]

One curatorial response to the alienating nature of the Hong Kong architectural environment that occurred in the post-handover period was the *Personal Skyscraper* show organized by Kacey Wong at Para/Site (9 to 29 October 2000). Reacting to a sense of powerlessness in relation to the built environment, Wong invited the participants in his group show (who included both artists and architects) to imagine that they had unlimited resources to construct a building for themselves. In fantasy they were being given power to reinvent a cityscape which projected public meanings of governmental or corporate entities, and invest it with their own private associations. Wong himself created a skyscraper costume which he wore to the exhibition opening, and which featured in a series of photographs taken at different Hong Kong locations (illus. 100).

Fashion Design

In the case of architecture, oppositional meanings associated with attempts to assert the local or to claim a stake in relation to public space have been created by actions taken against built structures, or proposed in publicly circulated or displayed texts or images which engage with them. The structures themselves have tended to be subservient to commercial and governmental ideology, which has generally emphasized material progress and modernization. In the post-handover era such meanings have often been given a nationalist colour, and colonial associations (as might have been expected) have been erased or overlaid. Fashion designers (particularly when working independently under their own label) have more room to manoeuvre than architects, if not permitted quite so much freedom as artists have enjoyed, and there has therefore been some attempt to reference the local in Hong Kong fashion design of the period around the handover.

Like various artists previously discussed, certain fashion designers turned to distinctly local material and popular culture in search of Hong Kong references, but a problem they faced was that such references were not likely to be legible to their main audience. Whereas Hong Kong artists were producing first and foremost for a local audience, fashion designers were producing primarily for the international market. In a sense their situation is the opposite to that of architects: even overseas architects, if building in Hong Kong, are addressing their work primarily to the local situation, but in fashion the local is served up for the passing diversion of the international buyer. Local references tend to be signifiers of the ethnic or exotic borne by objects for sale in whatever international spaces of consumption they can reach. In such spaces they can clearly have no local Hong Kong critical function, and references which specify Hong Kong-ness will in any case be less distinct than those which specify Chineseness. The national frame for identity is stronger than any which Hong Kong-ness can mobilize, but Chinese motifs are just as likely to be used in the international fashion market by non-Chinese designers such as John Galliano or Jean Paul Gaultier for whom there is no personal identity issue involved.

On occasion Hong Kong designers have been concerned to make a specific address to the local audience of a kind comparable with that of visual artists, but the work in which they do so tends to be to one side of their main commercial practice, and is often presented in art world contexts. Prominent Hong Kong fashion designer William Tang, for instance, was one of the creators of fake archaeological objects for the Hong Kong Arts Centre's handover exhibit *The Prehistoric Hong Kong Museum*, while fashion designer and academic Miranda Tsui was a participant in *Kem zeg fen zeg* (1999) and *Ma'am's Box* (1999), two group shows at Para/Site Art Space. Tsui also presented a video piece *Shoe-Stories* at the Cultural Centre Exhibition Gallery as part of the *Landscape* project (curated by Young Hay for the Fringe Club's Star Alliance City Festival, January 2001). Wessie Ling chose the Visual Arts Centre in Hong Kong Park as the venue for her *Clothink* event (17 January 1998), apparently hoping that a visual arts context would allow a greater space for critical thinking about the nature of fashion than is possible in a commercial catwalk show. Non-professional teenage models were used (illus. 101), which produced an alienation effect in itself, and the glamour of fashion – although present at times – was also questioned (for example, through the employment of sacking or tarpaulin instead of fabrics). These unconventional materials also allowed local references to be introduced. Tsui's *Shoe-Stories* also had a local focus, as if attempting to map Hong Kong through the shoes of its residents. A series of 'portraits' of Hong Kong people's shoes was presented on one part of a split-screen projection, and another part offered a shoe-level vantage point on a busy urban location.

One could argue that there are more opportunities for non-producers to participate actively in the creation of meaning through dress than through architecture. In architecture the commissioning party and the end user may be widely different, and only invasive or confrontational strategies may be left to the general public to express their views about

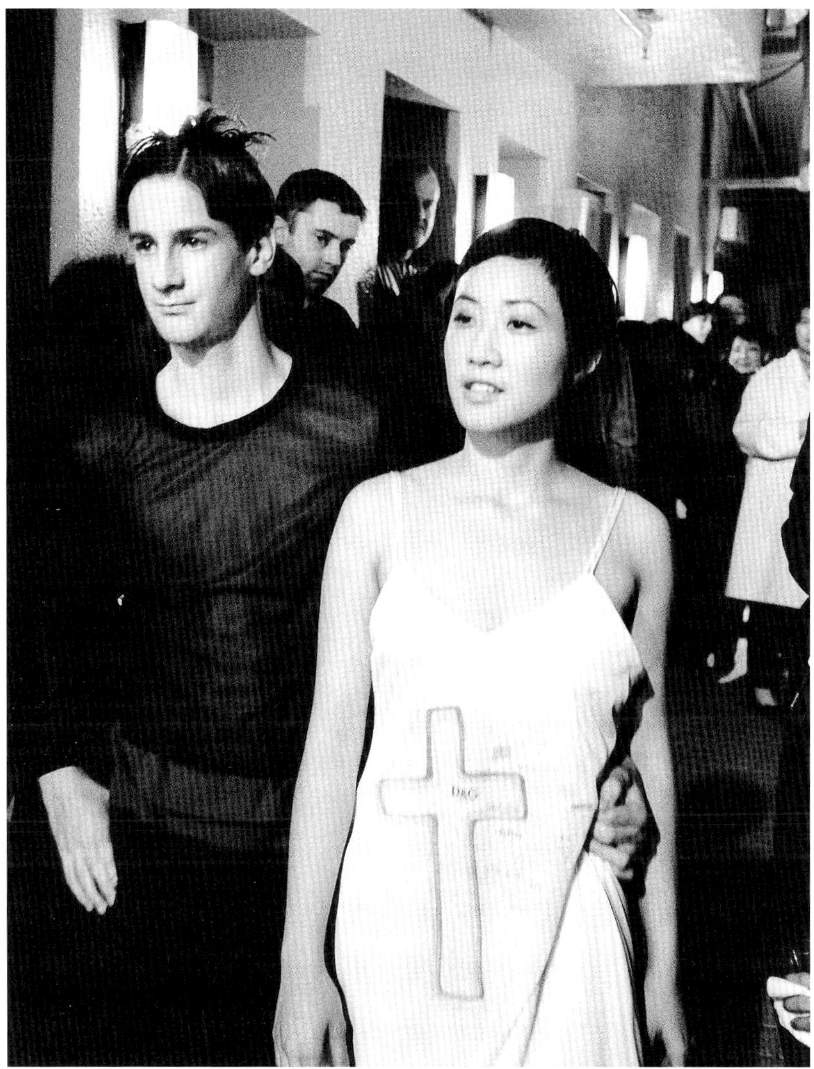

101 Wessie Ling's *Clothink* fashion event in progress at the Visual Arts Centre, Hong Kong Park, 17 January 1998.

architectural meaning (as we have seen). With dress however the unit cost is much lower and the purchaser and end user will characteristically be the same person. Although monetary considerations do of course play a part in determining size and nature of wardrobe, everyone is an owner of clothing and makes decisions about how to dress in public spaces. One can think of fashion as analogous to the performing arts in that items of dress are not fully complete till worn, and thus

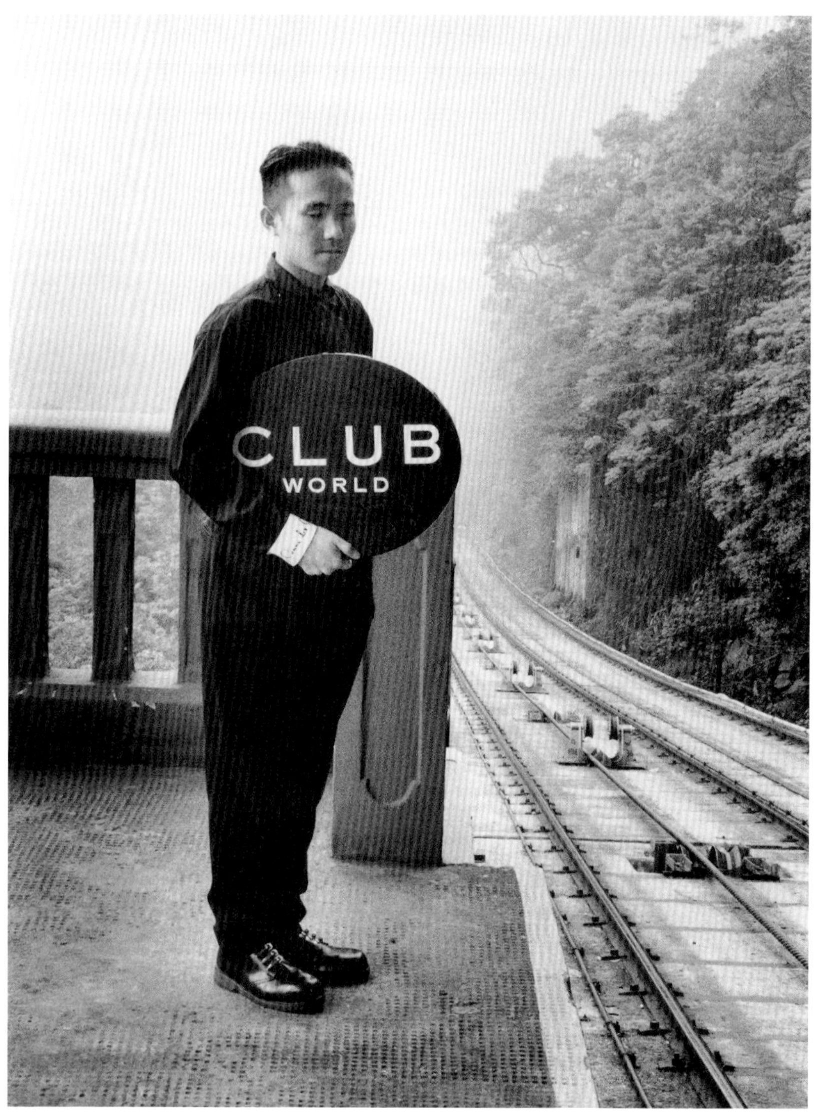

102 Hiram To, *Casual Victim*, 1990/91, photographic print. Collection of the artist.

dependent on the bodies of consumers-as-performers to have a life in public space.

Despite this opportunity to create meanings through consumption and dressing decisions, no strong local tendencies in dress could be discerned during the handover period. The difficulty of referencing the local which fashion designers (and artists) have faced was also present for the public in general, and the sense of being excluded from decisions over public matters may in any case have been less in relation to clothing (where one's consumption and dressing decisions gave one a sense of participation, of being able to vote for one's preferences). The dominant mode of dress among Hong Kong's urban population throughout the pre- and post-handover period therefore remained 'Western-style' and 'modern' in its connotations.[17] Although depoliticized ideologies of material progress were challenged in the field of architecture nothing equivalent occurred with dress. The love affair with modern fashion that had begun in the 1960s when the Federation of Hong Kong Industries decided quite consciously to promote Hong Kong as a centre of garment production (for example by funding the Hong Kong Festival of Fashions, later renamed the Hong Kong Fashion Week) was to continue largely unchallenged.[18] This Hong Kong brand name fascination appears to be the target of Hiram To's *Casual Victim* (illus. 102), a photographic work in which the artist himself plays the role of fashion model. In dialogue with the genre of fashion photography (a 'scenic backdrop' is provided by the Peak Tram), To undermines from within both commodity fetishism and the seductive images that help produce it. Certain works by Antonio Mak also adopt a questioning attitude towards the world of fashion. His *Best Suited* (1988) is a bronze male figure whose upper torso is represented only by a jacket. The absence of a head (as well as of any body inside the jacket) implies the metaphorical hollowness of those who trust too much to their clothes for their identity. *Bound to Win*, a 1991 bronze that engages in dialogue with the visual/verbal play of Bruce Nauman, shows a pair of racehorses dressed up in suits, shirts and bow ties. Although such formal wear might normally be associated with someone dressed for success in the business world, here it render the horses a very bad bet indeed.

In the early days smart or fashionable Westernized dress would have been perceived in Hong Kong as an option in contrast to more 'traditional Chinese' dress options (still visible today on certain older women of the rural New Territories or Outlying Islands as a generational counterpoint to more cosmopolitan urban styles), but also in contrast to the drab uniformity of Cultural Revolution-era mainland dress. A joke at the expense of the latter seems intended by the name of a boutique chain that appeared in Hong Kong as the handover was approaching – *People* [sic] *Republic of Chic*. Although there may have been a few unconscious worries that Hong Kong's post-handover life might share something of China's Cultural Revolution past even in fashion terms (one young woman told me of a dream in which the handover had already happened and she was forced to have her hair cut in the deeply unfashionable style of Jiang Qing, Mao's widow), in fact by the 1990s Chinese rulers were also liable to wear Western suits on public occasions. Unusually, President Jiang Zemin did wear a Mao suit during the parade celebrating the 50th anniversary of the founding of the People's Republic (on 1 October 1999), but since all other members of the Politburo wore Western-style suits by contrast this was clearly intended to signal his status as analogous to that of Mao or Deng. Indeed the whole parade was widely noted as 'retro' in its styling.[19] Signifiers of depoliticized modernization proved as valuable to Chinese national discourse as to its British colonial equivalent (and provided a common currency during the immediate post-Joint Declaration era).

From time to time, signifiers of Chineseness could be introduced into what were primarily Western-style items of dress to give an 'East/West' feel or to temper a sense of cultural deracination. Using silk or a high 'mandarin' collar, for instance, would be the fashion equivalents of employing Chinese ink to make abstract paintings or taking bamboo as the subject of a bronze sculpture. For cosmopolitan city dwellers, however, more overtly 'Chinese' dress had become something reserved for special occasions only, a form of ritual costume. At Chinese New Year, for example, children will often be dressed in brightly coloured satin jackets and other such 'traditional' clothing items. Anson Chan, head of the civil service both before and after the handover, would often wear a cheungsam (a 'Chinese style' dress) on formal occasions, as do many other mature women of social standing.[20]

Since the handover was itself a kind of special ritual occasion, albeit one not found in the customary calendar, sales of Chinese-style clothing did apparently see an upsurge during that time. A link between Chinese dress and patriotic feeling was even explicitly promoted during the transition period by local store Shanghai Tang, which was involved in organizing a 'Dress Chinese Day' on 3 July 1997, the first day back to work after the handover holidays. Designed to raise money for charity in an analogous way to earlier 'Dress Casual Day' campaigns, it was also described in the announcement pamphlet as 'a unique opportunity for you to demonstrate an important aspect of Chinese culture'. Participation in this event did not appear to be widespread, however, and Oscar Ho was to satirize it in one of his *Stories Around Town* images, titled *Anecdote About Chinese Dress* (illus. 103).

Although local entrepreneur David Tang Wing-cheung, the founder of Shanghai Tang, is an advocate of Chinese dress,[21] that store's range of clothing actually signals a degree of ironic distance from Chinese tailoring practice rather than a simple revival of it. Jackets, for

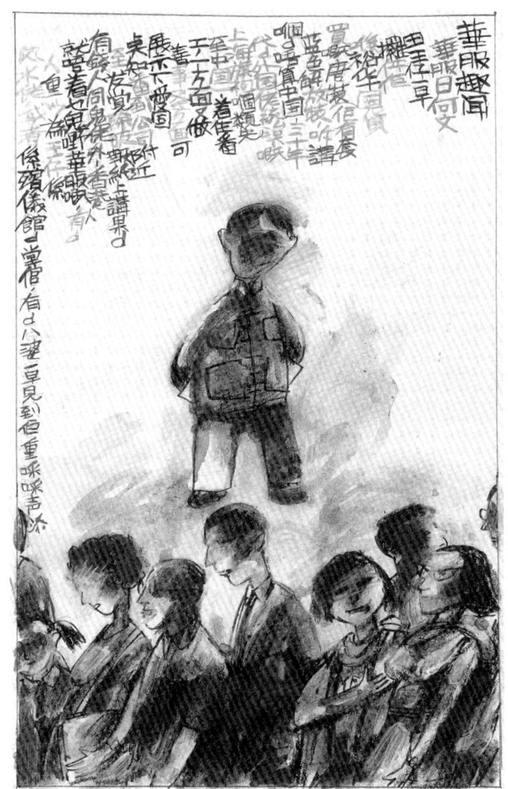

103 Oscar Ho, *Anecdote About Chinese Dress*, 1997, mixed graphic media on paper. Collection of the artist.

instance, although traditional in cut, have often been marketed in a variety of lurid post-modern colours which seem to make more impact on the tourist market than on local taste. Adverts for the store often encourage a less than serious approach to the products being promoted because of their reliance on humour. If tradition returns, then, it is only as a masquerade costume.

Shanghai Tang clothes may have been worn at high-class handover parties, but in the street more inexpensive carnival costumes prevailed, with T-shirts and accessories such as hats being the main items by which people signalled to each other an awareness of the moment they were living through (illus. 104, 105). T-shirts of, course are a well-established means of expressing allegiance to identities of various kinds, or of protesting against topical events, and many handover-themed items were produced, commercially or otherwise. Most common were those which featured British and/or Chinese flags, emblems of the two sovereign powers that were deciding Hong Kong's fate. One T-shirt that was widely sold during the pre-handover years

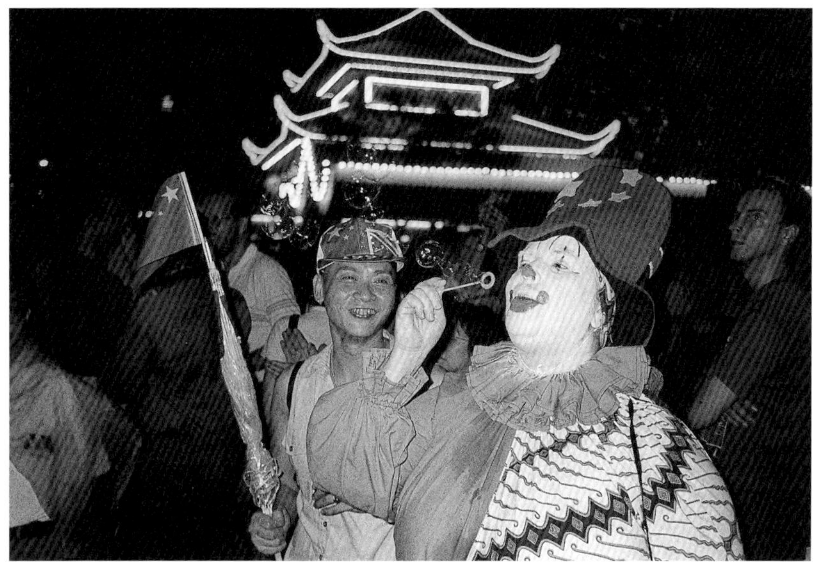

104 Crowd member at a rally held by the Democratic Party in front of the Legislative Council Building on handover night, 1 July 1997, blowing bubbles and wearing a clown costume with a flag hat.

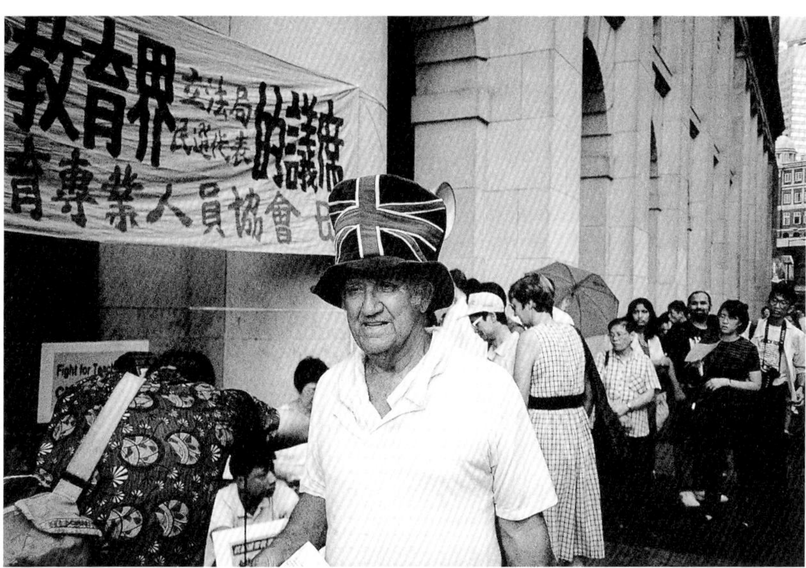

105 Participant at a demonstration in front of the Legislative Council Building on the last day of British colonial rule (30 June 1997), wearing a commercially produced handover-theme hat.

(thus functioning as a reminder of the handover's approach rather than as a souvenir) showed a workman over-painting a Union Jack with a Communist Chinese flag. While such a use of national flags on items of clothing might be taken as displaying a degree of irreverence towards them, one senses that (in this case and others) the handover is being treated as little more than a marketing opportunity, with overseas as well as local buyers in mind.

Given the difficulty of specifying Hong Kong-ness in fashion, even professional fashion designers who wished to reference the handover in their work tended to manipulate British and Chinese state symbols. In one dress by Pacino Wan displayed in his Spring/Summer '96/'97 collection, for instance, a simple binary logic dominates which recalls the T-shirt discussed above (although of course the garment is an altogether more sophisticated product which cannot be compared in other respects). A British flag, the main design on the dress, is partially overlaid with a (Communist) red towards both neck and hemline.[22] Elsewhere in the same collection national symbols again provide design motifs: one dress takes the forms and colours of the British Union Jack and plays with them deconstructively (illus. 106). The British Queen and Queen Mother both appear on a further dress in the collection, by means of a photo-print image. The Chinese model presenting the dress in the parade sported a green headscarf similar to that the Queen is herself shown as wearing. Such a play of identification and disjunction is not too dissimilar to that employed by photographic artist Holly Lee when she reworked a formal portrait of the British Queen (such as would be commonly seen in government offices during the colonial era), digitally replacing the royal visage with the features of an ethnically Chinese friend (*The Great Pageant Show, circa 1997*).

Graffiti

While it is common to hear complaints in Hong Kong that the population takes no pride in the appearance of the city, and television public service announcements frequently exhort viewers to stop dropping litter, graffiti is relatively rare. A defacement of the flagpole next to the *Forever Flowering Bauhinia* by a graffiti tag on 16 January 2000 merited television and press coverage, in part because it was an attack on a symbol with strong national associations, but also because of the novelty of such an event. This scarcity of graffiti makes the case of Tsang Tsou Choi particularly unusual, and affords the results of his efforts a high degree of public visibility. Since he has apparently been

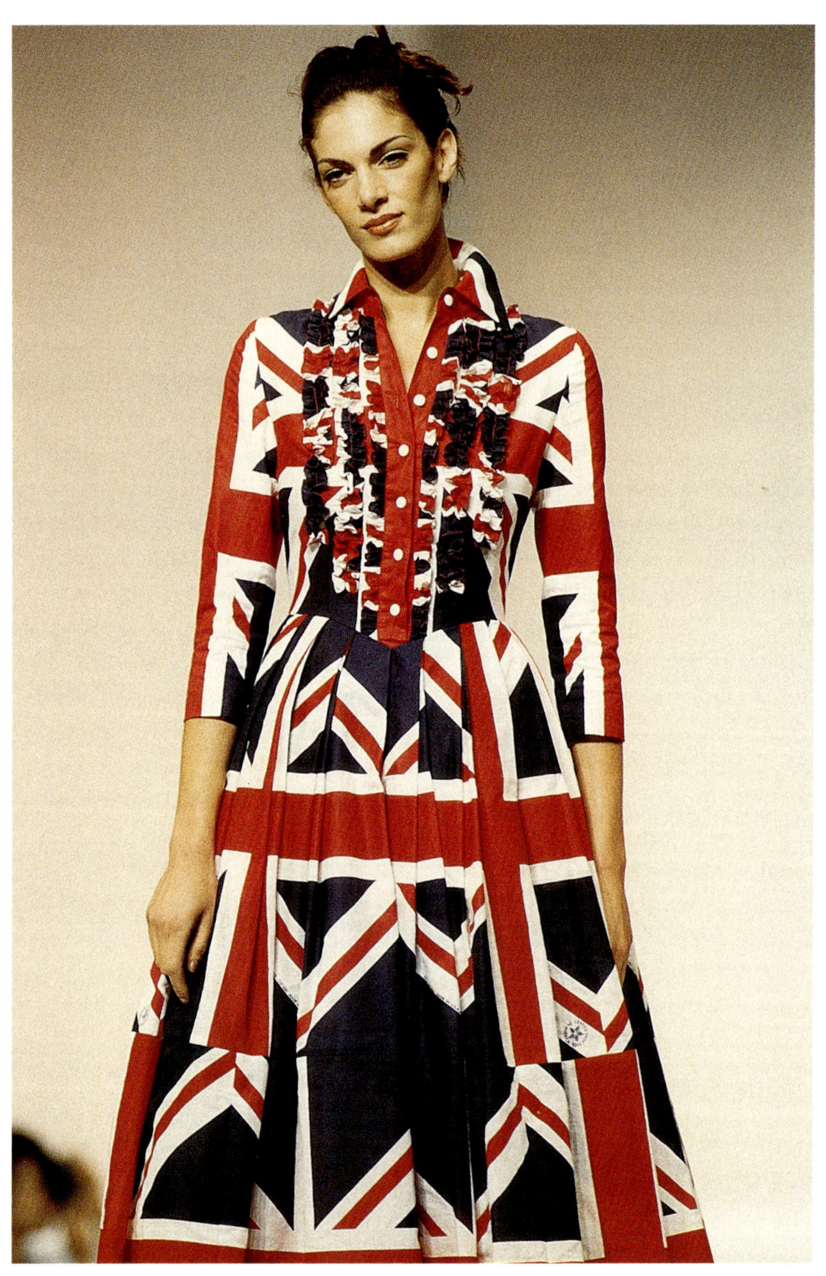

106 Pacino Wan, Union Jack dress from the Spring/Summer 1996/7 Collection.

writing in public places for several decades (starting before the New York graffiti art phenomenon began, for instance) his handiwork has become very well known to Hong Kong residents, who are liable to encounter it anywhere in the city's public spaces. Tsang, who was 76 years old by the time the handover arrived, declares that he is the emperor of Kowloon. He inscribes his claim on walls or on lamp-posts and other street furniture using brush and ink, those traditional Chinese writing means (illus. 107–10). Although the Chinese imperial age is long gone, Hong Kong during most of the period in which Tsang has been making his mark has remained an imperial possession, albeit of a foreign crown, and it is this usurpation of territory that he bemoans in his writings.

With an acute sense of the topography of power, the 'King of Kowloon' (as Tsang is usually referred to in English) often placed his calligraphic inscriptions of the colonial era so that they were direct challenges to the signifiers of British crown authority. They could be found on a wall near the entrance to the Central Government Offices (illus. 111), for instance, next to the path which leads up to Government House, or around the perimeter of Victoria Park (and on the bus stop by the entrance towards which the statue of Queen Victoria faces). Given the absence of a public arena for the expression of dissent, Tsang invades or defiles existing sites of power, or at least occupies their margins. Usually he places his writing in sites with high pedestrian traffic, where it will have a ready visibility, but he is normally careful not to choose surfaces which are too sensitive, and from which his inscriptions would be immediately cleared. Since his calligraphy can be found all over the territory it becomes a trace of its author's wanderings, like the track left by an animal. Perpetually in motion, apparently, he seems to enact the sense of displacement his texts speak of: the ruler wanders in exile.

When the residents of the island of Chek Lap Kok were displaced to provide a site for the new Hong Kong airport, they left behind on their abandoned homes calligraphic protests against their forced removal and the destruction of their community (illus. 112). In contrast to those statements, which were written by a hand familiar with established calligraphic practice, Tsang's analogous but more generalized protests against dispossession – he claims family land was stolen by the British crown – are executed in a raw manner, without clear precedent in calligraphic tradition and all the more vivid for this. Lacking any alternative medium of his own, Tsang has been forced to mimic that of the powerful in his own rough way, adapting it to the vertical and awkwardly shaped surfaces he borrows for his work. Dispossessed

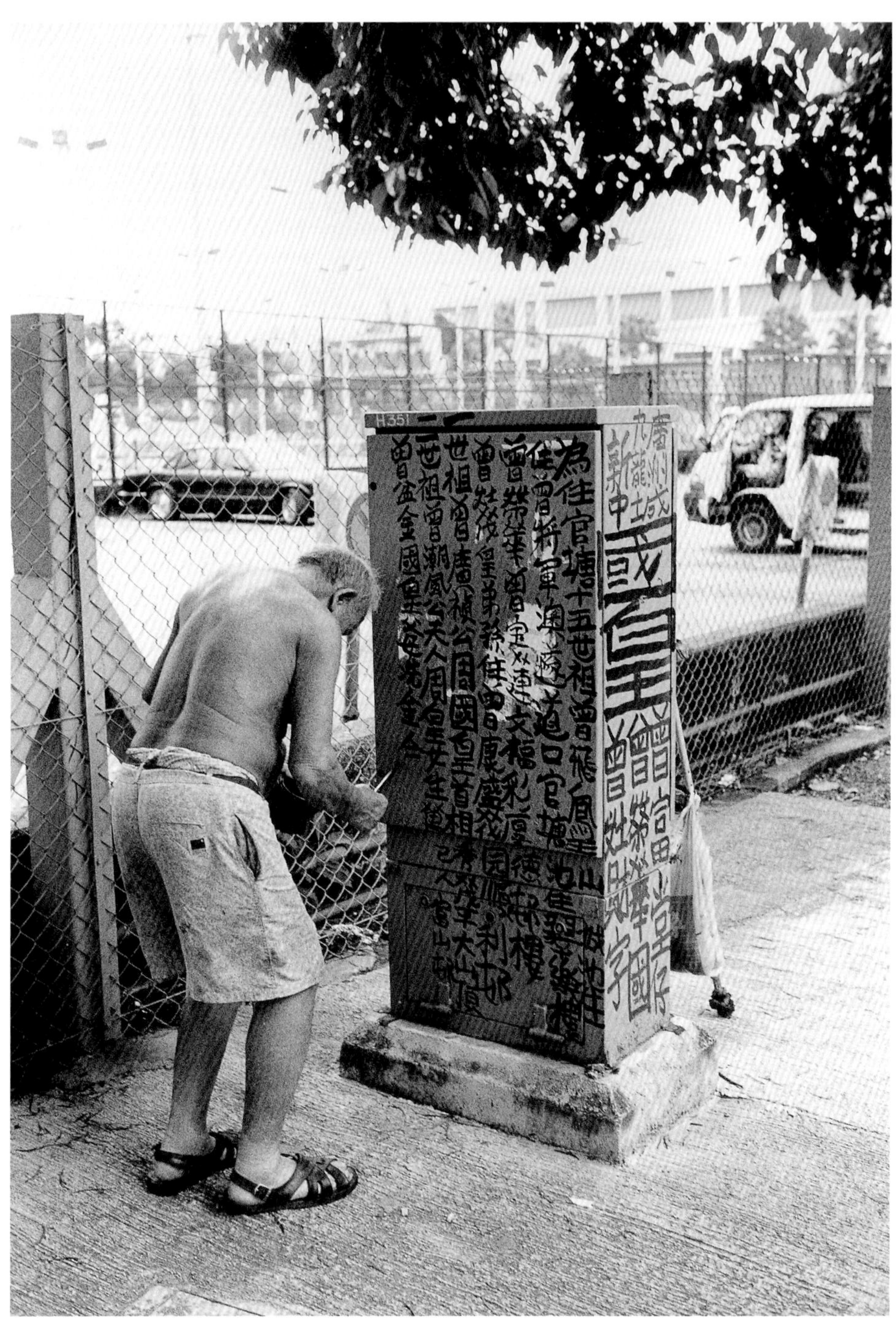

107 Tsang Tsou Choi (the 'King of Kowloon') adding a calligraphic inscription to an item of street furniture on the border of Victoria Park, Causeway Bay, 27 September 1996.

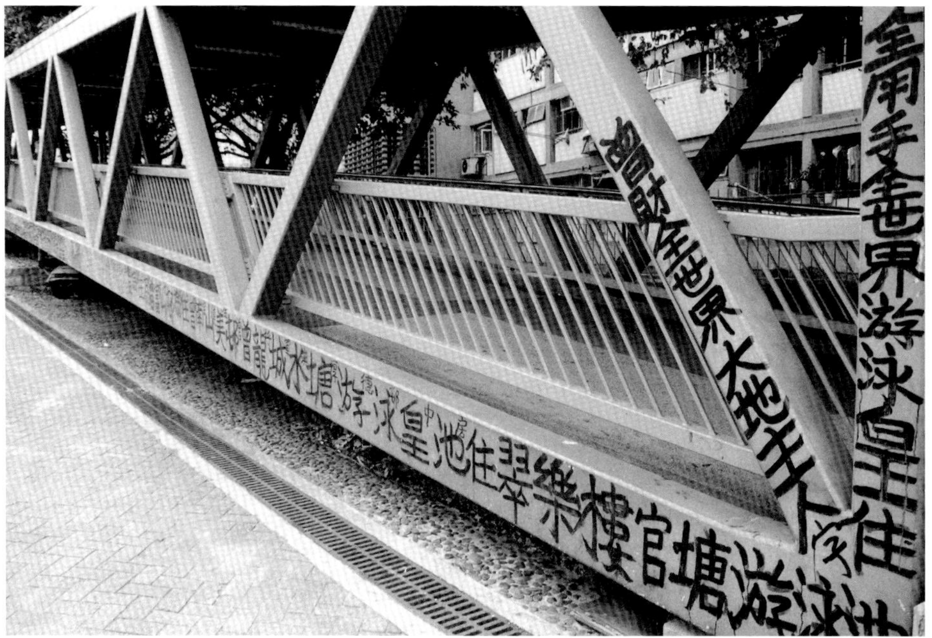

108 Calligraphic inscription by Tsang Tsou Choi on the side of an overpass ramp in Choi Hung.

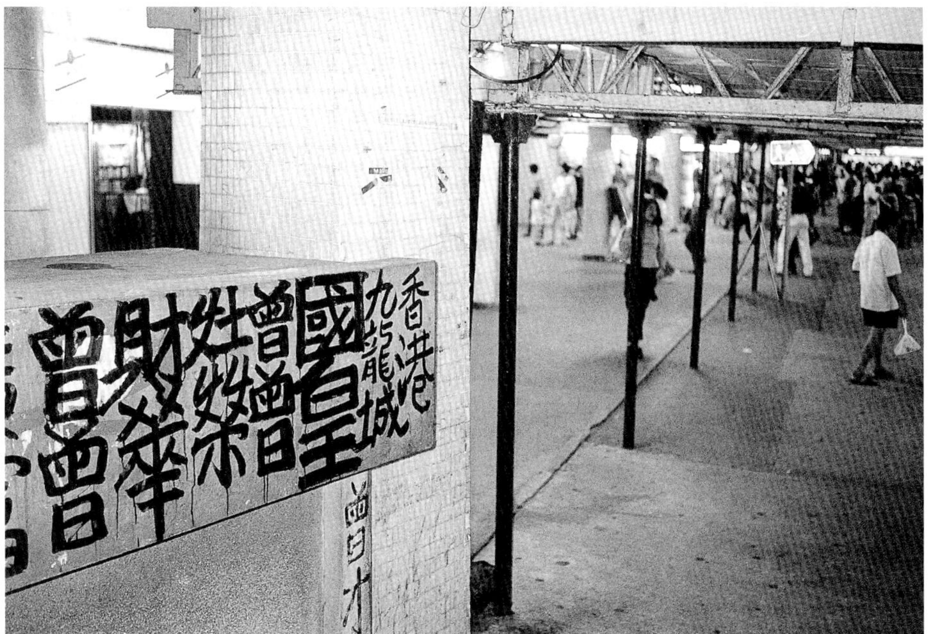

109 Calligraphic inscription by Tsang Tsou Choi adjacent to the Hong Kong Island Star Ferry concourse, 22 September 1996.

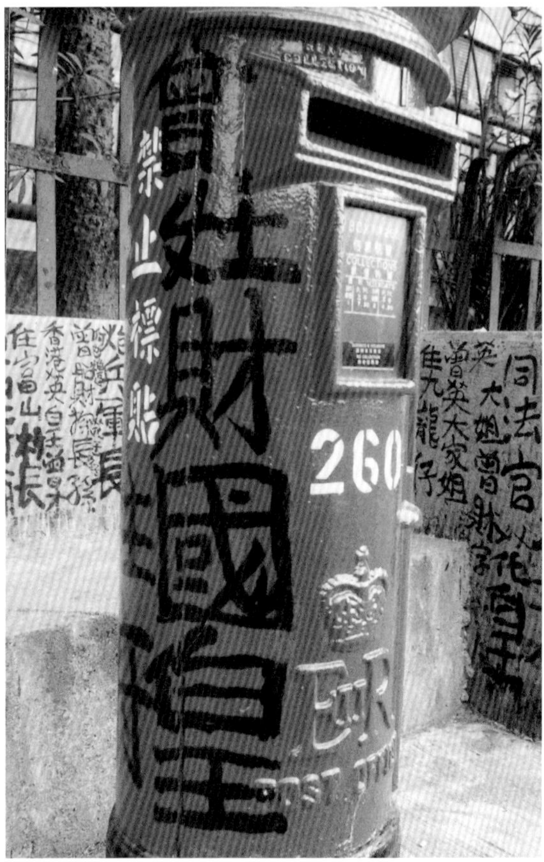

110 Calligraphic inscription by Tsang Tsou Choi on a colonial-era postbox in Sau Mau Ping.

of even a language of resistance, he has articulated his sense of power-lessness by making an imperial claim, by mimicking the rhetoric of those whose power he has so publicly contested.

Tsang made the British crown the focus of his crusade, often includ-ing unflattering references to the British Queen in his inscriptions. Even on the very last day of colonial rule, 30 June 1997, he was hard at work: art critic Gérard Henry spotted Tsang defiling with his writing a surface in the vicinity of Government House which had recently been painted white because of the handover. Apparently Tsang was inscrib-ing his anti-colonial graffiti even as Governor Patten's car was passing (following his final departure from the official residence). Tsang's zeal for protest was not diminished by the demise of the colonial regime, however, despite a pre-handover indication (given in response to an interviewer's question) that he might adopt a lower profile under Chinese rule. Instead Tsang made some subtle shifts in his choice of

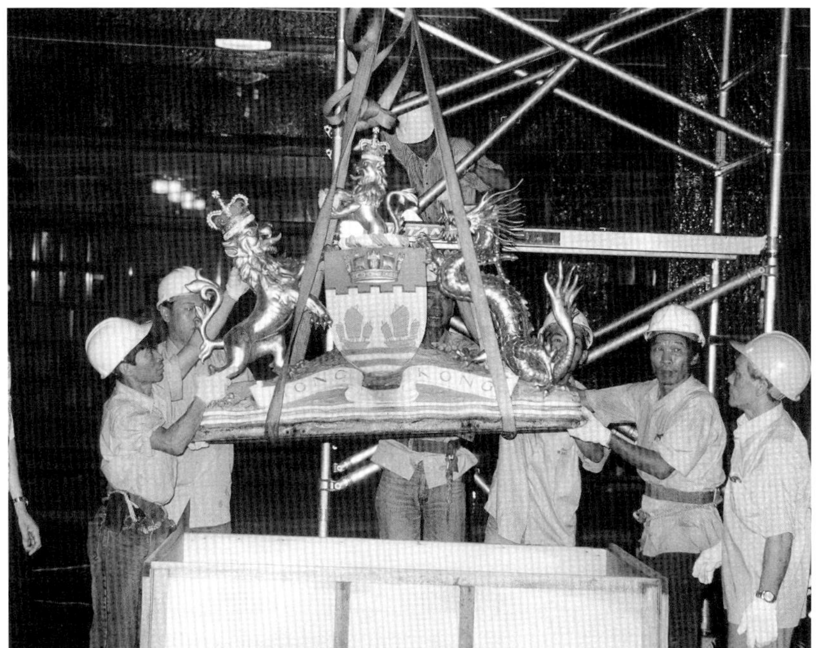

III British coat-of-arms coming down from the exterior of the Central Government Offices as colonial rule came to an end.

site, demonstrating an awareness of the changes that were occurring in the topography of power. Soon after the handover, for instance, a large piece of his calligraphic graffiti was placed on the support of a flyover directly opposite the front entrance of the Bank of China, that symbol of Chinese state authority.

This shifting of targets aside, it would be hard to see Tsang's project as handover-related in intention because of the long time-scale over which it has been pursued. There is however a handover-related dimension to the reception of his activities, since in the years leading up to the transfer of sovereignty his work gained more active attention, becoming a much-circulated symbol of the local. This process of valorization began among cultural workers, later involving the media and through them a wider public. Local press attention was intense, and even overseas publications such as the *International Herald Tribune* were attracted to the issue when art critic Lau Kin Wai (one of the first from the cultural sphere to make personal contact with Tsang) arranged an exhibition of his work in the art gallery of the Goethe Institut in the run-up to the handover (*The Street Calligraphy of 'King of Kowloon' Tsang Tsou Choi*, Agfa Gallery, Goethe Institut, 24 April

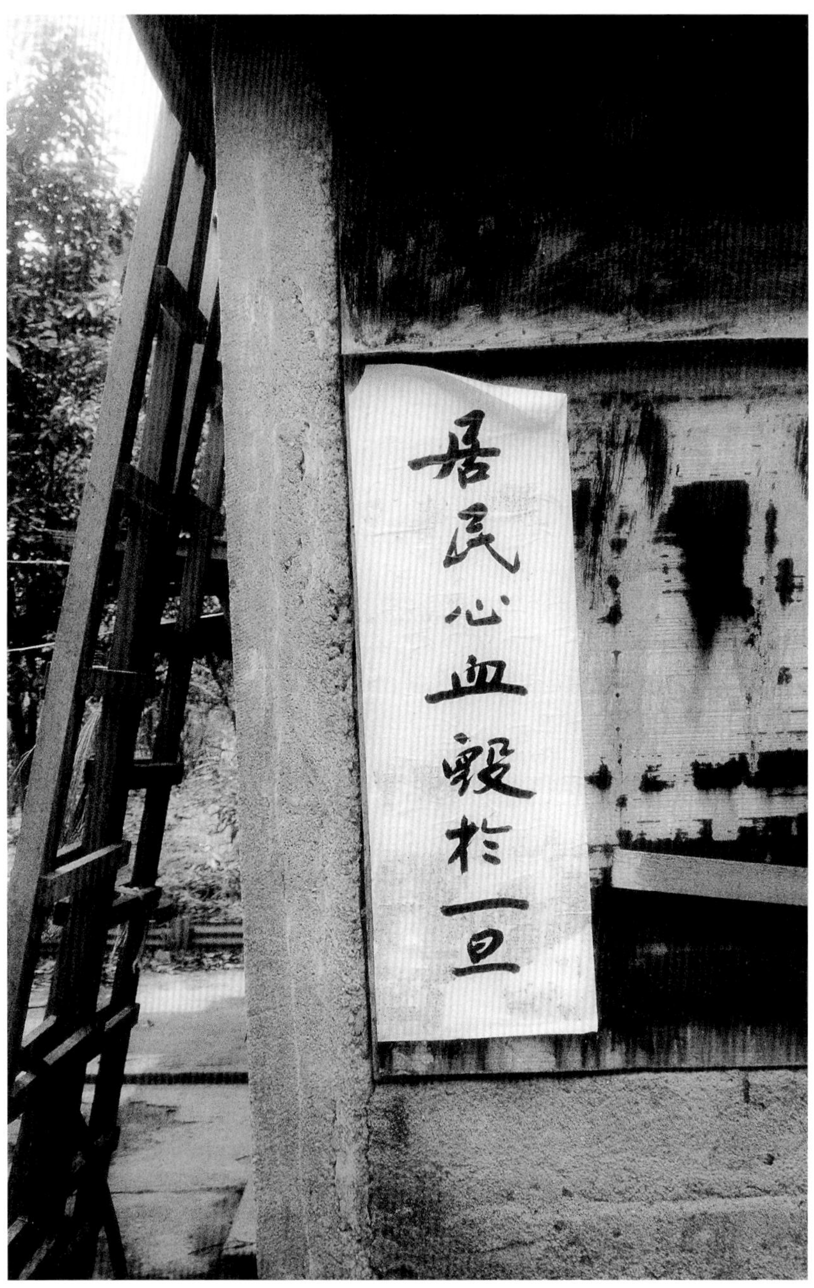

112 Calligraphic protest left behind by people displaced from the
island of Chek Lap Kok prior to the construction of the new airport,
24 March 1991.

to 17 May 1997). Objects and surfaces previously inscribed (some on the direct suggestion of Lau) were brought into the exhibition space, and the gallery walls themselves were soon also covered in calligraphy by the tireless Tsang. Needless to say there was a great deal of controversy over the decision to treat a defacer of public property as an artist in this way. Although Tsang himself appeared to be enjoying the attention – his photogenic grin in the many press images revealing the man behind the graffiti suggests as much – Lau was nevertheless accused by some of manipulation. His claim that Tsang's calligraphy was of aesthetic (and not merely sociological) interest also predictably incensed defenders of artistic tradition.[23]

As well as this direct promotion of Tsang, his transformation into a signifier of the local was aided by the engagement with his work of a number of artists and designers during the pre-handover period. Photographer Simon Go, who was among the first to make contact with Tsang, documented his work and life (as he has that of many poor and marginalized members of Hong Kong's population) offering a reminder that not everyone shared in the widely vaunted story of prosperity and modernization. In another exhibit organized by Lau Kin Wai (*Cultural Chop Shui I*, Fringe Club Gallery, 4–18 October 1995), where artists were assigned cultural partners of an earlier Hong Kong generation to

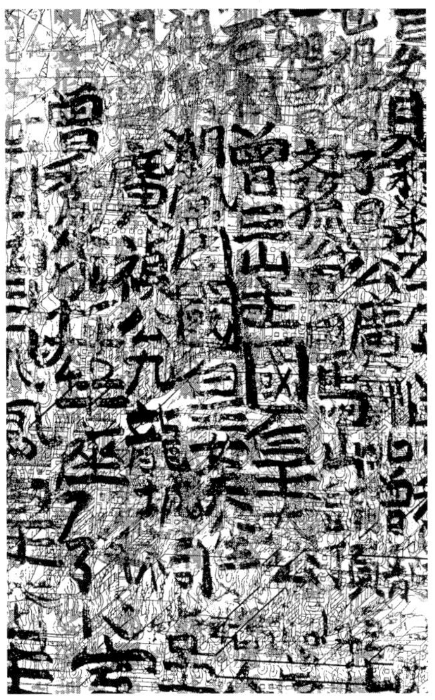

113 Lee Ka-sing, Untitled limited-edition photocopy print produced for the *Cultural Chop Shui I* exhibition, 1995. Private collection.

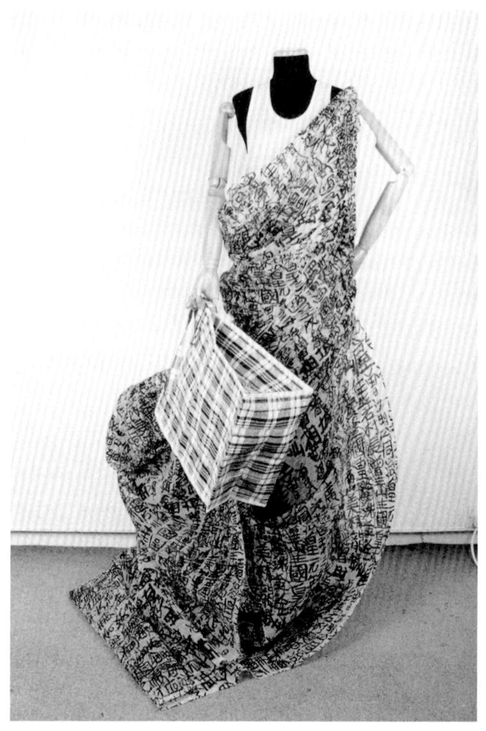

114 William Tang, Dress made using fabric with a 'King of Kowloon' graffiti motif, as displayed in the Hong Kong Arts Centre, Summer 2000.

engage with, Lee Ka-sing took Tsang's calligraphy as source material for his own work. Tsang's distinctive handwriting was combined by Lee with images and printed Chinese characters appropriated from other sources in a series of black and white photocopy prints (illus. 113). These were produced in large but limited signed editions, and visitors to the exhibition were invited to help themselves to copies without charge. Oscar Ho was also to imitate Tsang's distinctive writing style in the inscriptions on certain of his own *Stories Around Town*, such as *Anecdote About Chinese Dress*. Among designers who used this street calligraphy as a motif to enable local associations is William Tang. His Autumn/Winter '97/'98 collection included a silk organza dress decorated with motifs borrowed from Tsang's calligraphy (illus. 114). Local furniture and fittings store G.O.D. also referenced it on a line of bed-linen, which was featured in its adverts towards the end of 1996.

Graphic Design

The use of Tsang's calligraphy as a local signifier by artists and design-ers may be taken as parallel to the already mentioned use of local popular and material culture by installation artists. Certain items of distinctively local material culture were also picked up by graphic designers in cases where an assertion of the local was needed. One advertising campaign on behalf of the Hong Kong Arts Centre, which made the promotion of local cultural expressions its hallmark throughout the 1990s, featured both Tsang's calligraphy and a certain type of striped plastic bag widely found in Hong Kong (illus. 115, 116). A similar plastic bag was used by William Tang as a handbag-like 'fashion accessory' when one of his Tsang Tsou Choi dresses was displayed on a mannequin in an Arts Centre exhibition during the summer of 2000, and for a time Cantopop diva Faye Wong – who has always had a flair for self-fashioning – made a point of employing such bags as airport luggage instead of the designer labels other celebrities tend to be seen using.

Despite being in common use such plastic bags have the association of being survivals from the past and are normally found in a space of economic circulation below that occupied by alluring contemporary

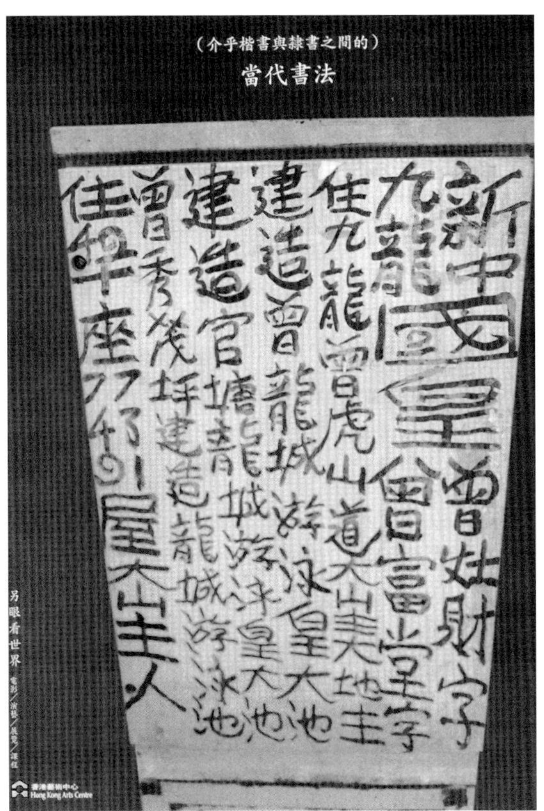

115 Image from an advertising campaign for the Hong Kong Arts Centre employing graffiti by Tsang Tsou Choi and used in its *Artslink* publication during 1998.

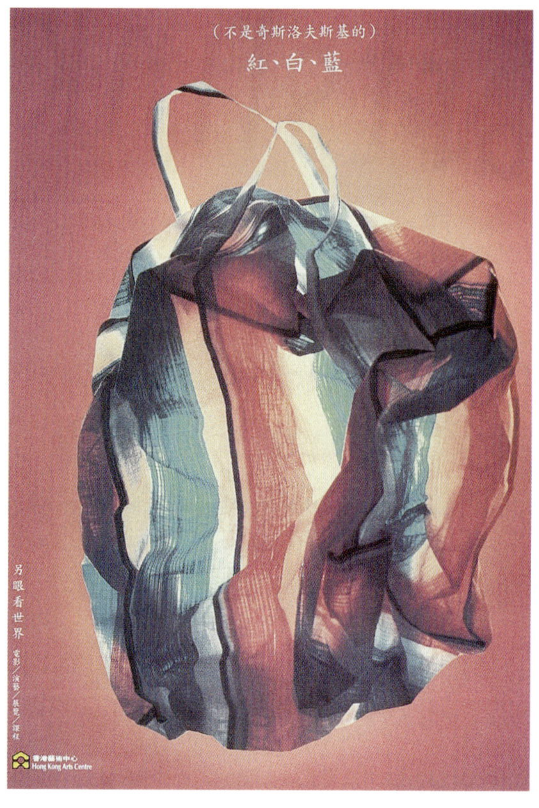

116 Image from an advertising campaign for the Hong Kong Arts Centre used in its *Artslink* publication during 1998.

commodities, existing almost as a reproach to them. Since encouragement to buy is often the aim of graphic design a rejection of the fetishistic magic of commodities such as that found in the Arts Centre campaign is not all that common, and references to local material or popular culture in design often tend towards the seductively nostalgic. Here art and design part company since artists referencing the past of memory and lived experience to evoke the local have generally consciously avoided the nostalgic tone found in, say, designs produced by Alan Chan for items as varied as coasters, tea caddies and shopping bags. The allure of Chan's designs is reinforced by his frequent recourse to representations of the female body. Images culled from promotional calendar and poster art of a bygone era, and which in their time signified a specifically Chinese contemporaneity, now refer to a past with a feminized and modern flavour.

Investigation of the nostalgic tendency in Hong Kong mass culture is a complex matter. A phenomenon of the pre-handover period and its previously identified mood of premature retrospection, it included

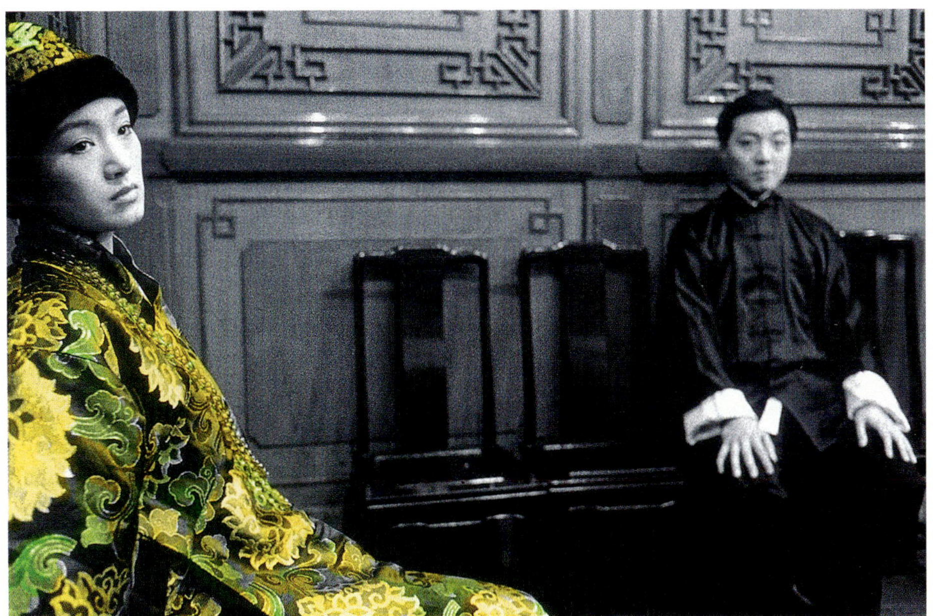

117 Image used in Shanghai Tang's 1997 advertising campaign, with actress Gong Li (left) as model.

such phenomena as food outlets that revived items from the menus of bygone street stalls and a movie '92 *The Legendary La Rose Noire* (Joseph Chan, 1992) which made ironic references to an earlier more naïve era of Hong Kong film and television. There was a nostalgia for Shanghai during these years, equally handover-related in that it showed a fascination with a city whose past might prefigure Hong Kong's future: Shanghai was also a modern Chinese capitalist city that had been taken over by the Communist regime. Shanghai Tang, already mentioned for its fashion line, was the store which made the most of this particular thread of nostalgic interest, as its name suggests. All sorts of products that recalled earlier Chinese modern design were sold, such as leather-bound photograph albums (even the function here suggesting nostalgia). Film mediated the image of old Shanghai, and in particular mainland Chinese Fifth Generation film-maker Zhang Yimou's *Shanghai Triad* (1995), which featured Gong Li in the female lead as a cabaret singer and mistress of a 1930s gangster named Tang. Gong Li later appeared in adverts for Shanghai Tang, acting for a time as the company's 'muse' (illus. 117). *Ye Shanghai* ('Shanghai at Night') was the most popular of the 1930s Shanghai cabaret songs being revived and marketed during this period:

it even gave its name to a Hong Kong restaurant (whose cards and publicity material paid homage to Shanghai Art Deco style). In early 2001 the song was being used as the soundtrack for the animated sequence which played when the Shanghai Tang website (www.shang-haitang.com) was accessed. Old Shanghai cabaret songs were performed to diners at Ye Shanghai, as well as at the China Club (founded, like Shanghai Tang, by entrepreneur David Tang). The China Club, one of the first Hong Kong expressions of Shanghai nostalgia (it opened in 1991, three years before Shanghai Tang), evoked the former grandeur of that metropolis in aspects of its interior design. Stanley Kwan's film *Centre Stage* (1991), which stars Hong Kong actress Maggie Cheung as 1930s Shanghai actress Ruan Lingyu, involves a conscious juxtaposition between Shanghai of that time and Hong Kong of the 1990s. The use of a combination of fictional and documentary modes, however, prevents a simple nostalgic identification with the past even as its fascinations are explored.[24]

Perhaps the most inventive reference to the handover in images produced with a marketing role was an advertising campaign for mobile phone company Sunday using television commercials as well as posters, newspaper adverts and postcards. Taking place after the handover itself, the images promoted the imminent arrival of a day from which mobile phone users would be given the freedom to keep the same number when transferring between providers. The day was labelled 'Independence Day', and the images used in the campaign adopted the rhetoric of political liberation, even giving a specifically Chinese flavour by employing the face of Sun Yat-sen, the founder of the Chinese republic (illus. 118). Given the then-recent countdown to an end of colonialism which did not lead to independence, this count-down to a fake day of liberation had deeply ironic implications. Whereas real political rhetoric was unable to make the achievement of independent statehood a goal, and had to imagine its politics other-wise, an advertising campaign attempting to give an underdog brand a feisty, playful and local image was able – in passing – to dramatize the situation of post-handover Hong Kong by alluding to what could not be allowed to happen.[25]

Of all the locally produced pieces of graphic design the most centrally important to the handover was the design for the emblem of the Hong Kong Special Administrative Region, variants of which appear on the seal and on the flag. Looking more like a commercial logo than a governmental emblem, this design was the work of Tao Ho, a prominent local architect, and – as previously noted – it represents a stylized Bauhinia flower. Bauhinias are commonly found in Hong

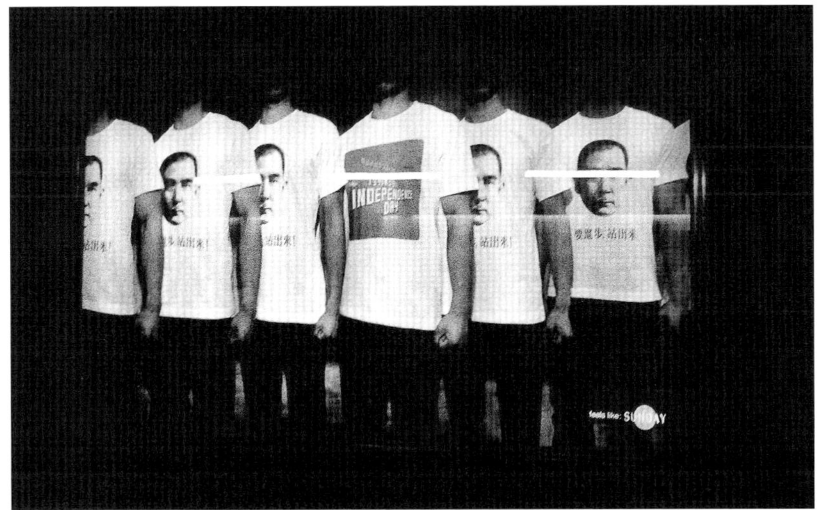

118 Illuminated poster on display in Shau Kei Wan Mass Transit Railway station showing images of Sun Yat-sen on T-shirts. A part of the mobile phone company Sunday's post-handover 'Independence Day' advertising campaign, 7 February 1999.

Kong, and Bauhinia blakeana, the particular species on which the SAR emblem is based, was discovered locally and declared in 1908 to be a distinct species unique to Hong Kong. It was named for one of Hong Kong's most oppressive colonial governors, Sir Henry Blake, who held office from 1898 to 1903, making its choice as a post-colonial emblem somewhat unusual. The Bauhinia was adopted by the colonial government in 1965 as the official floral emblem of Hong Kong, and served (in a slightly different design) as the emblem of the Urban Council. It appeared on stamps of the colonial era issued in 1968, 1985 and 1988.

In both the flag and seal versions of the SAR emblem, the Bauhinia flower itself is represented in white against a red background. The red (the same as that of the national flag) represents China, symbolically surrounding the white flower representing Hong Kong to indicate that Hong Kong is an inseparable part of China. The stamens of the flower are a group of five small red five-pointed stars (the same number and type as are found on the national flag of the People's Republic). These small stars are described as representing the love of Hong Kong people for the motherland and can thus be said to incorporate into the design for all time a specific pre-handover worry that Hong Kong people might not in fact harbour strong patriotic feelings. The stars of the national flag are also referred to by the emblem in a further, veiled way: the five-pointed star, the most well-established emblem of the Communist state, is an invisible structuring principle of the emblem.[26] The yin/yang symbol, so beloved by Hong Kong artists of an earlier generation as a way of symbolizing the reconciliation of opposites is also a structuring principle of the design. Ho used it again, more overtly this time, in a candleholder he created for the Austrian crystalware company Swarovski, which was publicized in 1999.

Because a supposedly local symbol is actually saturated with references to national sovereignty over Hong Kong, local artist Wong Shunkit did not need to make any particular effort to deconstruct it when he made it the focus of his oil painting *Idea* (illus. 119). Instead, in the spirit of Pop artworks which appropriate other types of visual imagery without declaring an attitude towards their sources, he simply represented the diagrams produced to indicate the evolution of the design. More overtly disrespectful was Leung Po-shan's 'Love the fucking country' T-shirt design, featuring a purple Bauhinia (as well as a Chinese character with a taboo meaning). The design was launched at an opening reception held at Para/Site Central on the first anniversary of the handover, and one suspects that being able to send invitations with the design printed on them (as well as the phrase 'sponsored by Hong Kong Arts Development Council') was part of the pleasure for the artist.

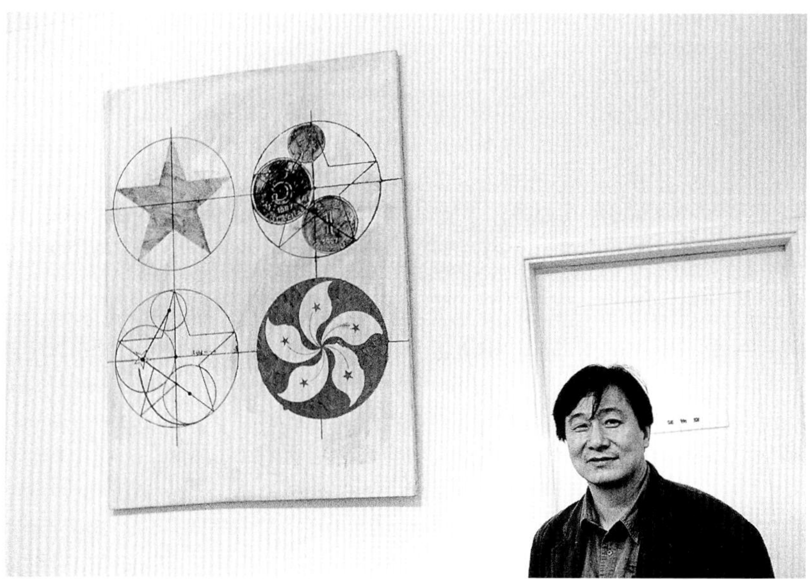

119 Wong Shun-kit with his painting *Idea* (1996, oil on canvas, collection of the artist), on display at the Artist Commune, Oil Street, 12 March 1999.

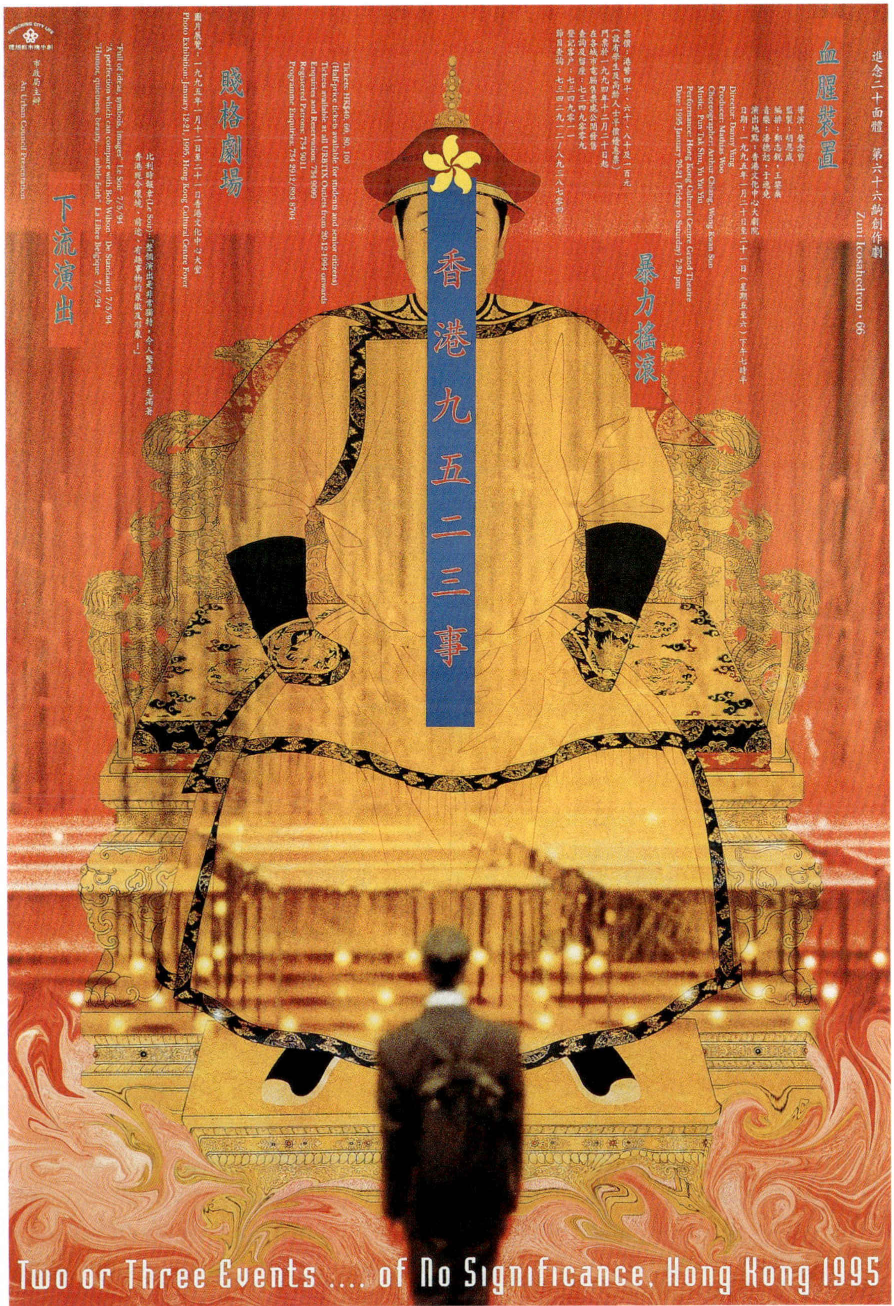

120 Freeman Lau, Poster for *Two or Three Events ... of No Significance, Hong Kong 1995*, a Zuni Icosahedron performance, 1995.

Such active artistic reception of the Bauhinia emblem as Wong's or Leung's serves to undermine the design's power to some extent, and steps were taken after the handover to protect state emblems from some types of semiotic play. Even prior to the handover, artist and graphic designer Freeman Lau had been pressured by cultural bureaucrats to remove the Bauhinia emblem from a poster (he did so, but replaced it with something very similar [illus. 120]),[27] but the introduction of a National Flag and Emblem Ordinance on 1 July 1997 made actual desecration of local and national state emblems punishable by fine and imprisonment. A black version of the Communist flag or an original flag with the large star cut out – both of which had been carried in pre-handover demonstrations – were now illegal. Before long this new legislation was tested out by two activists who, in the course of a 1 January 1998 demonstration, crossed out the Bauhinia emblem on an SAR flag with black ink and cut a hole in the middle of a national flag. They were convicted in May 1998, but that conviction was overruled by the Court of Appeal on 22 March 1999. The judgement stated that the post-handover flag law was unconstitutional and an unnecessary restriction on freedom of expression. In a judgement dated 15 December 1999, however, the Court of Final Appeal restored the convictions, upholding the new laws.

One attempt to get around the post-handover law against desecration of Chinese national emblems involved locating such desecration on the internet, using an overseas website which people in Hong Kong were invited to interact with.[28] Finding an alternative space beyond Hong Kong legal jurisdiction for engagement with the national flag was also the strategy of Leung Po-shan. In a 1998 performance (again titled *Love the Fucking Country*) which took place at the Singapore Art Museum during the opening of an ARX regional art exchange exhibition she attacked with an axe a block of ice onto which an image of the Chinese national flag had been projected (illus. 121). A related installation involved projection of a video image of the flag onto a red carpet over which the audience needed to walk. The event was given added meaning in that it took place on the Chinese National Day. The main reason Leung was able to get away with these acts in Singapore public space seems to be that the Museum staff were preoccupied at that time with removing from display (and destroying) a work by another Hong Kong artist, Zunzi, which made satirical comments about Singapore's political leaders.

As well as the adoption of new laws to protect the national flag itself, there was also a utilization of existing legislation to prevent the display of competing emblems. It had been a common sight in pre-handover years to see Taiwanese flags placed in public locations on 10 October, the Taiwan national day, but flags placed in celebration of the 'Double Tenth' in 1997 were quickly removed by police. Some 22 flags and four banners were removed, most of which had been placed at roadsides or on public footbridges (where they could be seen by motorists passing beneath). The Crown Lands Ordinance (the name had not yet been changed) was invoked to justify their removal, since it required permission to be sought for anything to be erected on government land. At an outdoor exhibition in Tsim Sha Tsui police required a man to stop waving a Taiwanese flag, and this was justified under the Public Order Ordinance, which gives any police officer of the rank of inspector or above the power to prohibit the display of any flag, banner or emblem at any public gathering, and seize the offending item if they deem necessary.[29]

Fashion designer Peter Lau, who had produced a line of clothing that featured the Chinese national flag in the year or so prior to the handover, was to become one of the first cultural sector victims of the changed legal environment. The Trade Development Council sent designers a memo warning them not to break the new flag law during Hong Kong Fashion Week, which opened at the Convention and Exhibition Centre (site of the recent handover ceremony) on 16 July

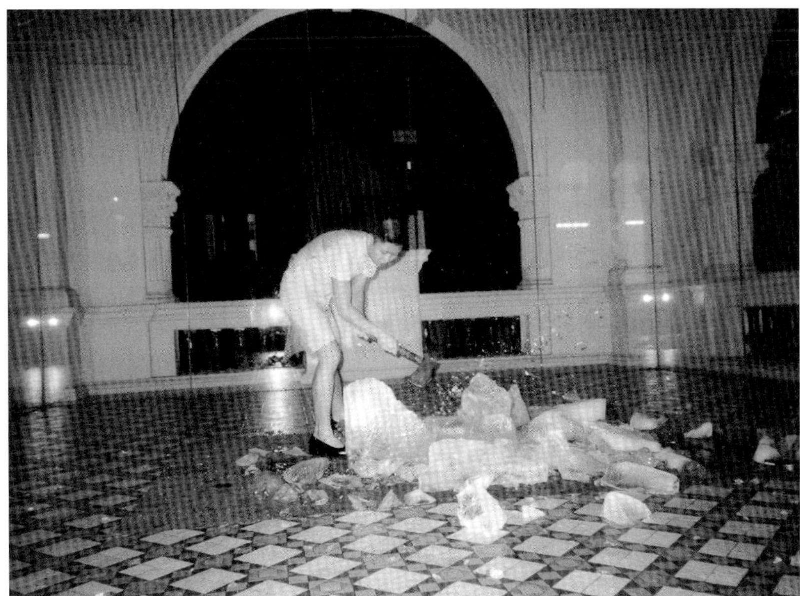

121 Leung Po-shan, *Love the Fucking Country*, performance at the Singapore Art Museum, 1 October 1998.

1997, and according to Lau, edited his Chinese flag designs out of its publicity material. As a consequence of the TDC memo Lau's partners withdrew two of his flag jackets from the show. The China Doll label had already removed his flag designs from their Tsim Sha Tsui shop four days prior to the handover. Lau ran into trouble again on 8 October of the same year: during rehearsals for a charity show on the following day (to celebrate the eleventh anniversary of the Hong Kong Fashion Designers Association), two of his pieces were removed by organizers. One had the Chinese flag on it, and another made use of its Taiwanese equivalent. Commenting on the earlier episode Lau said: 'I used the flag because I wanted to take an image people regard as very serious and powerful, turn it 180 degrees and make it into something soft, feminine and seductive. It's nothing to do with insulting the flag. Of course some people might think its disrespectful to make it into ladies' knickers, but that's up to them.'[30]

Photographs produced in association with Lau's Autumn/Winter '97 Collection (illus. 122) show models with red veils over their eyes – one with a yellow star to suggest the Chinese flag. The veils have the look of blindfolds, and one model also has her hands 'bound' in front of her with a similar red cloth to compound negative political associations. Several models carry candles, thus recalling democracy rallies, which Lau has himself attended.

After the handover the national and SAR flags appeared over the Legislative Council Building, next to the Central Government Offices (which also had a national badge over its entrance in a location similar to that occupied by a royal crest in the colonial period [illus. 123]), and on many public buildings. Schools were provided with flagpoles, universities without them hurried to remedy their situation prior to the 1 October national day, and the Committee on the Promotion of Civic Education, as part of its 1998 'Ideal Citizen' campaign, began disseminating information about national songs, flags and emblems. Although the government said that its priority was to increase national awareness through civic education, and had no plans to make flag-raising at schools compulsory, it did give notice that laws might be introduced in the future to punish behaviour disrespectful to the national anthem or national flag. 'When the national flag is raised [said Secretary for Constitutional Affairs Michael Suen Ming-yeung], those who are present should stand up and regard the national flag in solemn silence.'[31]

In addition to the official SAR flag and seal, the Bauhinia also began to feature in other contexts of significance. Standard Chartered Bank-issued banknotes with a slightly different Bauhinia symbol on them (in

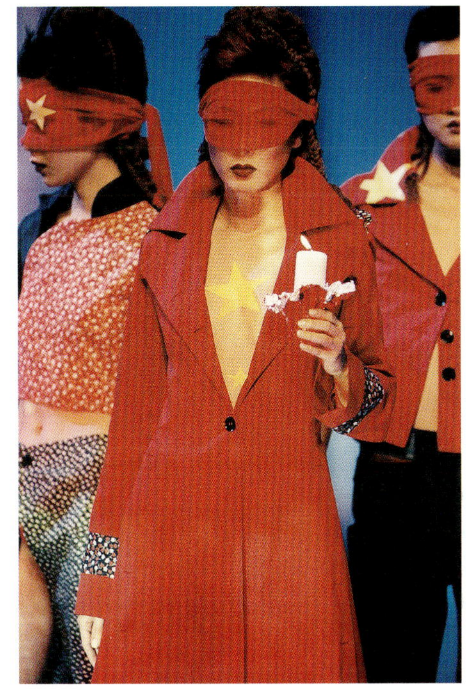

122 Peter Lau, Designs from the Autumn/Winter '97 Collection ('Winter under the red flag') presented during the fashion parade.

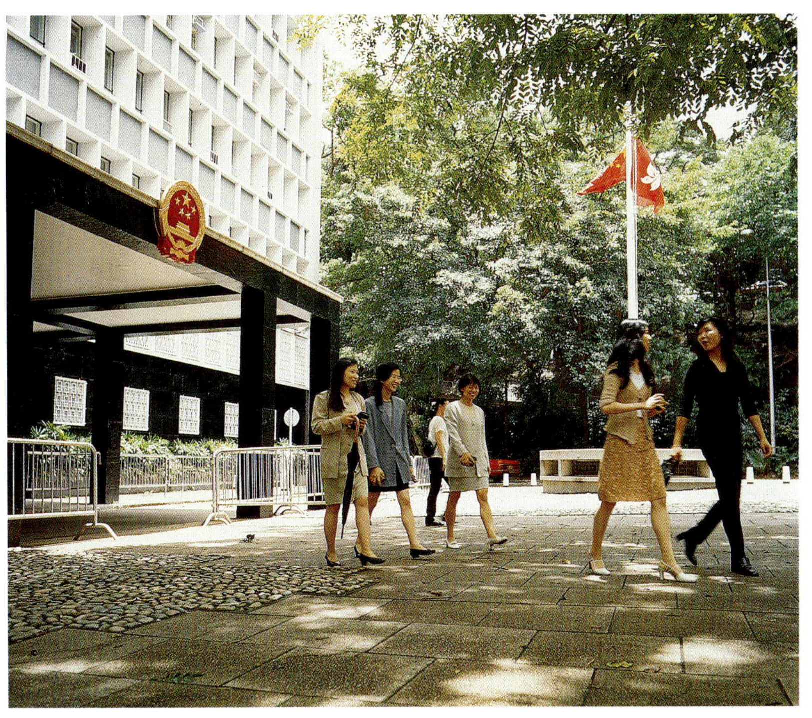

123 Chinese national emblem above the entrance to the Central Government Offices, with national and Hong Kong Special Administrative Region flags on an adjacent flagpole.

the place formerly occupied by the royal coat of arms) had already begun circulating from 1 January 1993. Coins featuring yet a further Bauhinia design gradually started circulating from January 1993 (the last coin of the new series was issued in November 1994). The coins they were designed to replace – those with the Queen's head – were allowed to continue in circulation after the handover, being gradually withdrawn, but stamps bearing the royal emblem could not be used from 1 July 1997 (if old coins or banknotes had been declared invalid overnight in this way there would of course have been an unacceptable risk of undermining confidence in the currency). The new stamps bore no graphic emblem at all, but Chinese sovereignty was acknowledged on commemorative issues by a written inscription: 'Hong Kong, China.' The first set of post-handover definitive stamps (designed by Kan Tai-keung) showed the architecture of the Hong Kong skyline instead of the Queen's head.

Government-issued identity cards, which could not be replaced in a short time-scale or without considerable expenditure of manpower, had been redesigned some time prior to the handover so that they could pass through the transition period without needing alteration. Curiously, they have no written reference to sovereignty or governmental issuing authority at all, and their only graphic symbol is a watermark depicting an antique sailing junk, one of the most venerable apolitical symbols of Hong Kong (found for instance on the Hong Kong Tourist Association logo). Emblems which began circulating before the handover itself had to be acceptable to both the sovereign powers, hence also the relatively innocuous nature of the Bauhinia flower emblem found on coins, which made no reference to Chinese national symbolism (unlike the SAR badge version). The new coin designs were not the work of a professional designer, unlike the banknotes, but were personally devised by Joseph Yam, later the Chief Executive of the Hong Kong Monetary Authority. Yam gave a retrospective explanation of the process in an informal article published on the website of the Hong Kong Monetary Authority on 18 November 1999: 'The ... task was to come up with the politically neutral design. But the confidential nature of this matter did not allow the appointment of an artist, and so the task was given to yours truly. I obtained a number of photographs of the Bauhinia from the Information Services Department [of the Hong Kong Government] on the pretence that I was designing the logo for the HKMA soon to be established then. For the Chinese characters, I copied the relevant ones myself from a piece of calligraphy I commissioned on a passage containing those characters. It was a simple scissors and paste job that a primary school child

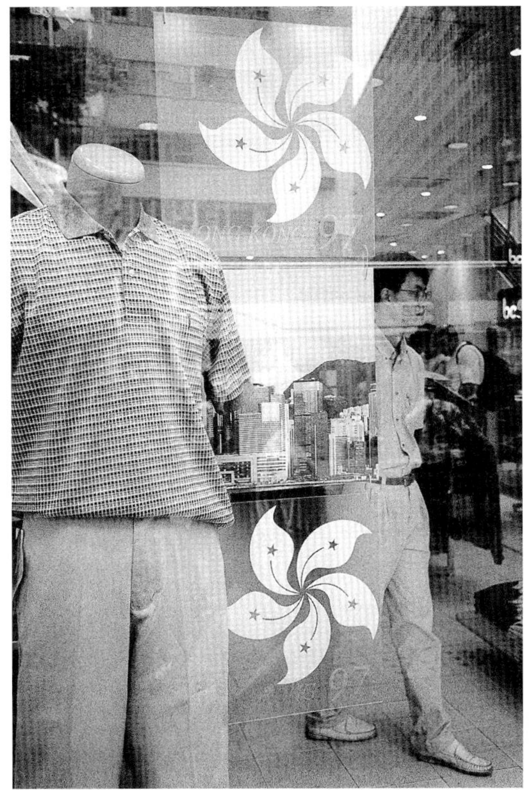

124 Window display during the handover period in a shop of the clothing retailer Bossini, Nathan Road, Tsim Sha Tsui. Bauhinia symbols and images of the Hong Kong skyline make up the design.

would find easy.' Yam's design does indeed follow closely the photographic source he used: it takes its angle of view on the flower from that adopted by the photographer, and faithfully reproduces the accidental curl of the petals found in that photograph's particular subject.

In addition to official or quasi-official circulation of emblems of sovereignty, there were also of course expressions of patriotism by private individuals and neighbourhood and other community or political organizations. Within the commercial realm too the display of flags was common: many taxis flew miniature national and SAR flags in the days immediately following the handover, and the official SAR Bauhinia emblem (perhaps because its political connotations were less up front than the Communist five-star flag) featured heavily in many designs for shop window displays over the handover period. A variant of it even appeared on handover-themed Tiffany jewellery. Images of the Hong Kong skyline were also popular in shop window displays – clothing chain store Bossini combined Bauhinia emblems with skyline images, for instance (illus. 124). Giordano, another clothing chain, actually went as far as handing out pamphlets about the Opium War and produced window displays with similar historical content (illus. 125). Other stores tended to avoid reference to the details of colonial history, preferring a more upbeat mood as better for business, and Giordano's action can be understood as a conscious attempt to dissociate itself from the company's previous owner, Jimmy Lai. Lai is an outspoken critic of the Chinese government, and he had put T-shirts with anti-government slogans on sale in his stores in 1989, damaging Giordano's commercial prospects on the mainland as a result.

If even the Bauhinia symbol proved too heavily laden with political meaning to be good for business, a lighter alternative was available in the form of the official handover mascot, a cartoon image of a smiling Chinese White Dolphin leaping from the water. Designed by Hon Bing-wah, the mascot was chosen from amongst a number of submissions by the Preparatory Committee's celebration sub-group. The leaping movement, according to the sub-group's convenor, Raymond Wu Wai-yung, symbolized the vibrance of Hong Kong society, although the fact that the local dolphin population is threatened with extinction due to environmental pollution did not go without mention.[32] The mascot appeared on mugs, T-shirts (illus. 126) and all kinds of touristic

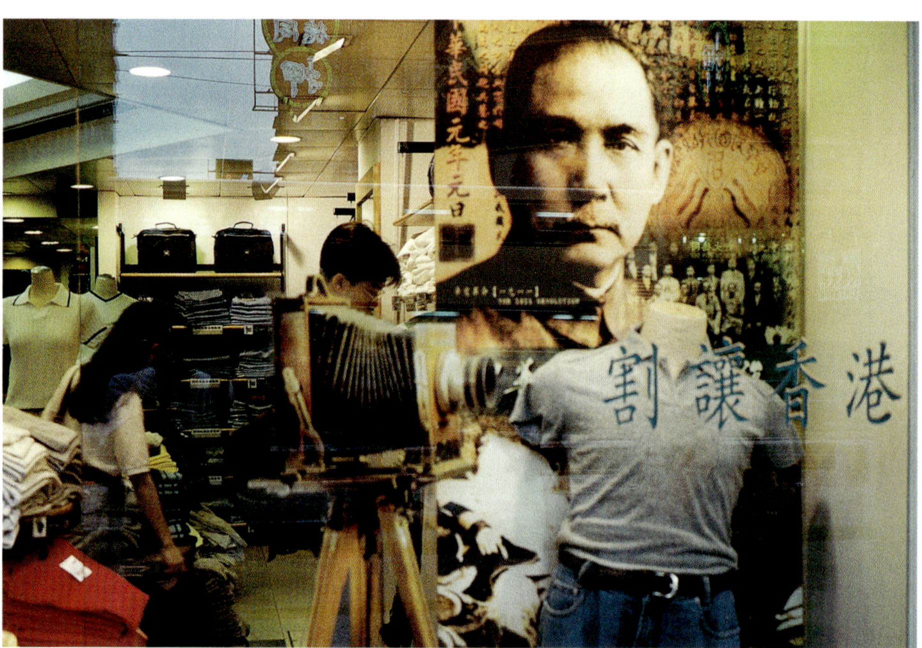

125 Handover-theme window display of the clothing retailer Giordano, with an image of Sun Yat-sen, Hennessy Road, Wanchai, 4 May 1997.

souvenirs, and also provided the subject matter for illuminated decorations draped over the façades of buildings (illus. 127). Many buses in handover livery also sported its likeness. In addition several white fibreglass dolphins were to be found during the handover period leaping for joy in an artificial pond in front of the Hong Kong Space Museum in Tsim Sha Tsui (illus. 128).

If the Communist five-star flag proved too problematic a symbol of Chineseness there were animal equivalents available for it too: decorative panda lanterns helped defuse possible tensions in the vicinity of the Legislative Council Building (illus. 129), while across the harbour a collection of large dragon lanterns were gathered on the waterfront near the Cultural Centre (illus. 130). On the evening of 1 July 1997 a flotilla of barges carrying illuminated representations of dragons, pandas and assorted auspicious images circulated around the harbour prior to a celebratory firework display. On the same day there was a symbolic release of ten thousand mainland homing pigeons in Shatin, but most decided to stay in Hong Kong, perhaps because of the heavy rain being experienced at the time. Just one pigeon was reported to have completed the journey home successfully, and then only after 35 days.

As well as considering the manipulation of emblems of sovereignty

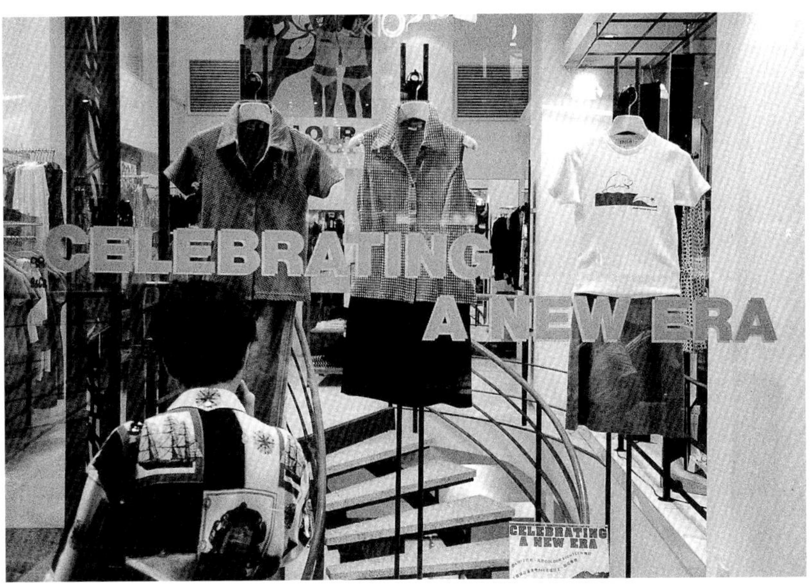

126 Handover-period window display of the clothes shop Colour Eighteen, Queen's Road, Central. Note the official leaping-dolphin handover symbol on the T-shirt displayed in the window.

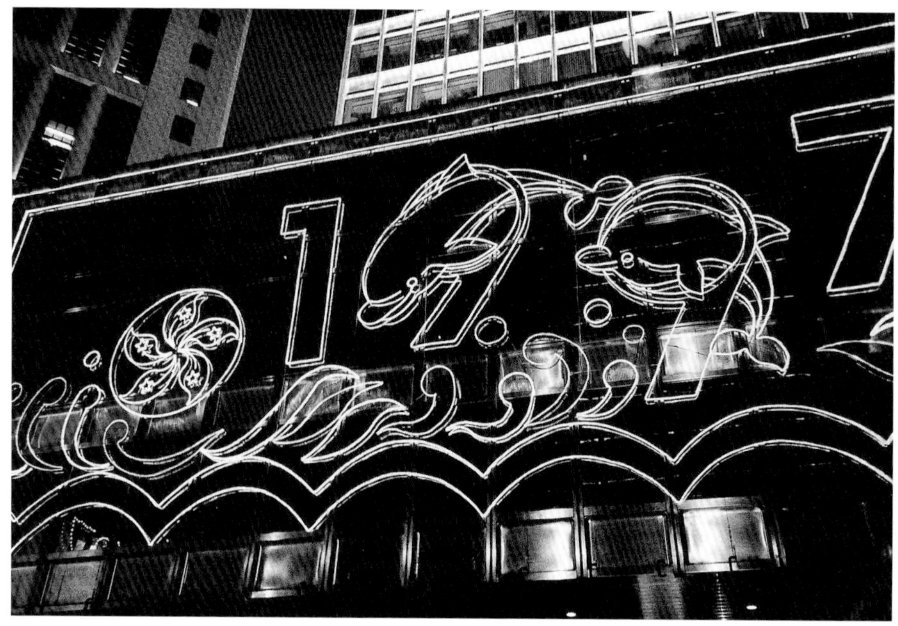

127 Illuminated decoration on a façade, Central, showing the official handover mascot, June 1997.

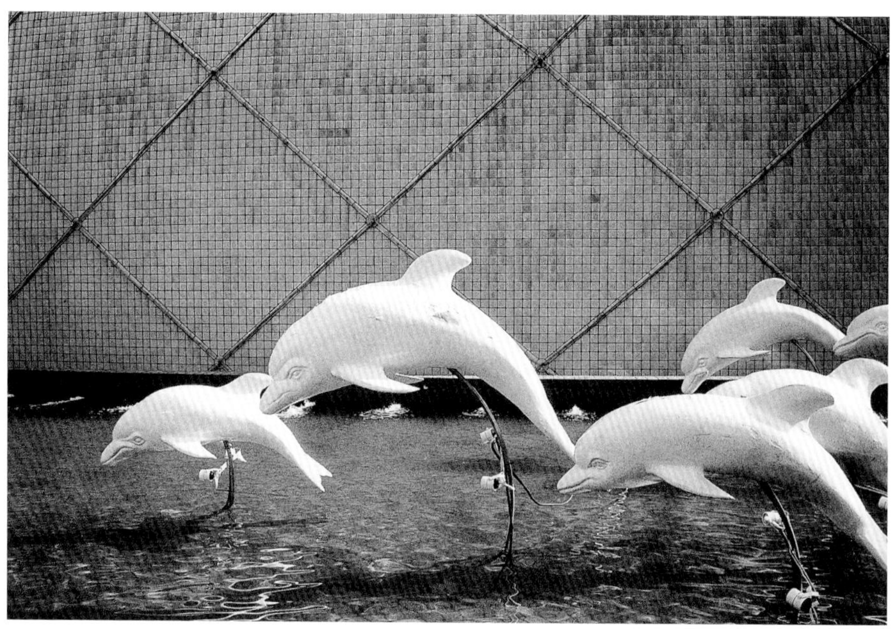

128 Leaping dolphins installed outside the Space Museum, Tsim Sha Tsui, Kowloon, during the handover period, July 1997.

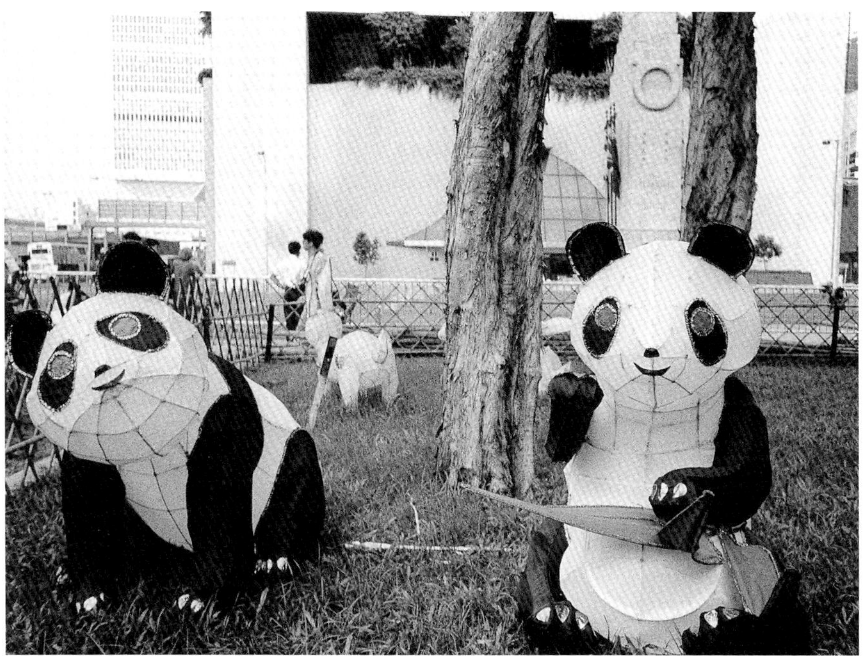

129 Panda-shaped lanterns installed near the Legislative Council
Building during the handover period, 28 June 1997.

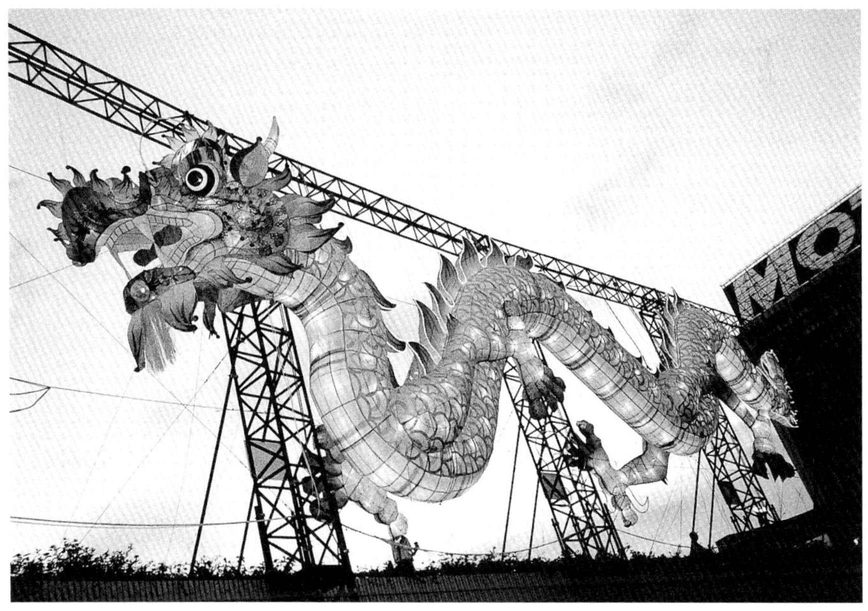

130 Dragon-shaped lantern installed on the waterfront at Tsim Sha Tsui,
Kowloon, during the handover period, 19 June 1997.

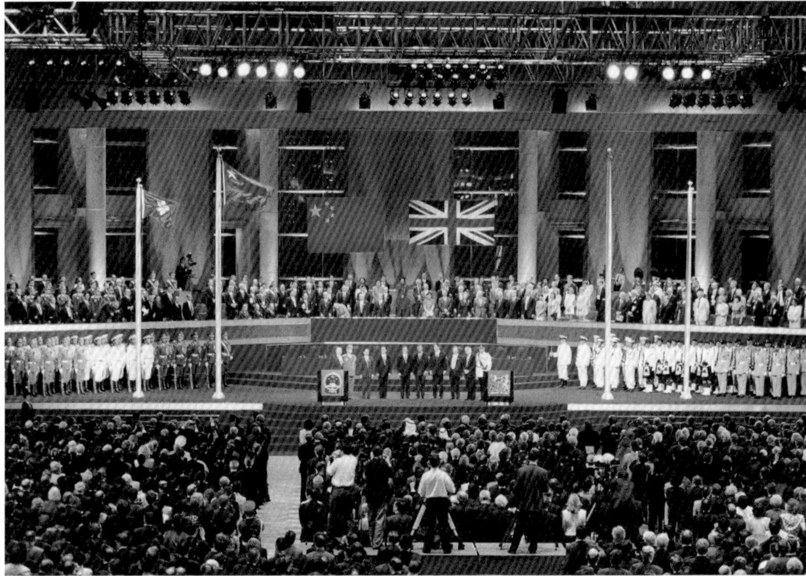

131 The handover ceremony taking place in the Convention and Exhibition Centre Extension, Wanchai. The Chinese and Hong Kong Special Administrative Region flags flying from flagpoles to the left in an artificial breeze were raised after midnight. British and colonial Hong Kong flags had been lowered from the right-hand flagpoles immediately before.

before and after the handover, one can also argue that the handover ceremony itself consisted of little more than a movement of flags down and up poles. Indeed, since for most people – in Hong Kong and elsewhere – the ceremony was only something they could view on their television screens, in a real sense this moment of history was a media spectacle, a series of images of visual symbols in motion being fed to a global public (illus. 131). The visual symbols being moved were British and Chinese national flags (nations being the privileged subjects of historical narratives), with no place for Hong Kong itself to be represented except via the emblems provided for it by its colonial and national sovereigns. While such a visual pageant might appeal to a mainland audience as symbolizing national wholeness being recovered, for Hong Kong viewers, excluded from physical or even symbolic participation, a degree of alienation might be excusable. Indeed the very symmetry of the event, with everything British being doubled by its Chinese equivalent, might even have been read as promising a future which would resemble the colonial past.[33]

Epilogue

In conceiving of the handover ceremony as an image made up of carefully juxtaposed Chinese and British symbols we are in a sense coming full circle, back to the images of Wucius Wong and Lui Shou-kwan discussed in Chapter 1, with their anxious desire to juxtapose the Chinese and the Western. A binary logic in which the local makes no appearance is found in both cases, albeit that the earlier instance wishes to keep both narratives in play within the same space, whereas the later case presents one as superceding the other in temporal sequence (the duality retained in the notion of 'two systems' was not visible in the handover ceremony, with its focus on sovereignty). Between these two moments, however, there have been enormous changes in Hong Kong cultural space that amount to what was earlier characterized as a psychic decolonization. Artists have both shared in and to some degree helped further this process. Albeit fragile, and ungrounded in any illusion of essence or foundation, a sense of local identity has emerged which makes the 'East/West' discourse of a few decades ago seem dated, let alone any monolithic, Beijing-propagated sense of national identity. Only mainland tourists decanted from tour buses and guests at official ceremonies pay any attention to the reunification monument, and the patriotic political rhetoric of Hong Kong's Chief Executive Tung Chee Hwa has an almost antique quality to the Hong Kong ear. Paternalistic in tone, it has little appeal to a people who have tasted democratic politics, even in the heavily diluted form Patten provided.

The sense of local selfhood which had developed in the pre-handover years meant that Tung's incoming regime was faced with a crisis of legitimacy. Already restricted in its freedom of manoeuvre because it derived its authority from Beijing and needed to roll back the political freedoms given by the Patten government, its ability to appeal to Hong Kong people was further damaged by a series of unexpected post-handover events over which it had no direct control. Most significant of course was the massive economic downturn which Hong Kong experienced as a result of the pan-Asian economic crisis. Although it was not as badly hit as Indonesia or a number of other countries – the Hong Kong dollar remained pegged to the US dollar – nevertheless wages fell and unemployment grew. For as long as many people could remember the economy had been growing, often at a prodigious annual rate, but now it was actually contracting.

The single most dramatic effect of the downturn was a sharp drop in property prices to about half their previous value, and with architecture figuring so prominently in Hong Kong narratives of progress or modernization, this was a symbolic as well as an economic blow. When an attempt was made to revive the belief in progress by the funding of a massive 'Cyber-Port' on reclaimed land at Telegraph Bay in Pokfulam, popular reaction was largely sceptical. Apparently a belated attempt to mimic Silicon Valley, it was quickly unmasked as a property development scheme in disguise, and since one particular developer was being favoured over others without tenders being openly invited, even billionaires were showing a degree of dissatisfaction with the new political status quo.

In addition to the property market collapse, other traumatic events with a significant symbolic importance included the red tides of spring 1998 that came down from the direction of China killing fish farm stocks and making the ingestion of sea fish dangerous, and the late 1997 outbreak in the city of a new and potentially lethal H5N1 flu strain, dubbed the 'bird flu' (illus. 132). The strain claimed victims, but was not able to establish human to human transmission and thus failed to develop into the feared epidemic. Nevertheless it added to the developing sense of crisis, and although no firm scientific evidence for this was forthcoming, it was widely felt to have come to Hong Kong from China.[1] As well as the termination of the elected Legislative Council on the first day of Chinese sovereignty, the post-handover period also saw the erosion of Hong Kong's judicial autonomy when a Court of Final Appeal judgement on right of abode was overruled after the government appealed to the National People's Congress Standing Committee in Beijing for a 'reinterpretation' of the Basic Law. There were many demonstrations on this issue, and the Legislative Council Building and the Central Government Offices (with the new national seal above the entrance) were particular targets. A further erosion of democratic structures occurred with the abolition of the two municipal councils (the Urban Council and the Regional Council) around the end of 1999. The government took back control over the services which these two councils had previously provided, in a massive centralization of power which left Hong Kong without a secondary tier of government and enhanced the general sense that things were moving backwards instead of forwards. Since the municipal councils had been responsible for much of Hong Kong's cultural provision this meant a far greater direct say for the government over the infrastructure by which local art was supported than had been the case in the

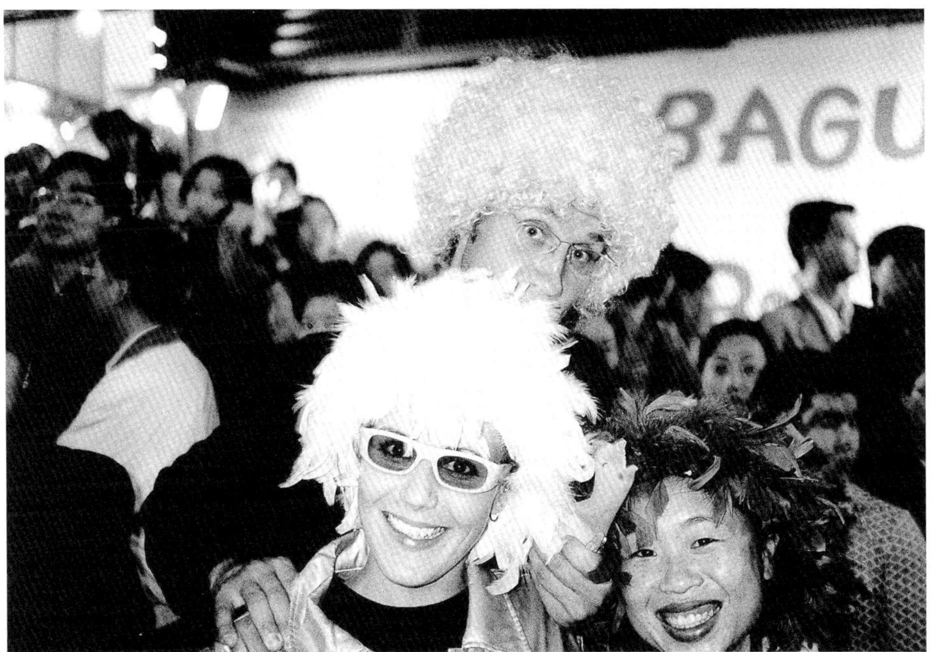

132 New Year's Eve revellers in the Lan Kwai Fong nightlife area with
chicken-feather wigs and a plastic chicken (recalling the slaughter of all
commercially farmed chickens in Hong Kong as a preventative measure
against the so-called 'bird flu' virus), 31 December 1997.

pre-handover phase.

In mainland China as a whole the appeal of nationalist rhetoric is a
lot stronger than in Hong Kong, and it has proved a reasonably effective tool for building national unity. Indeed patriotic feeling, fed by a
sense of economic progress and by the recovery of territorial integrity
with the return of Hong Kong and Macau, may be the main rhetorical
tool available to the Chinese state, given the demise of Communist
ideals and the unwillingness to envisage significant growth towards
democracy and the end of one party rule. Nevertheless, even in the
mainland, nationalist rhetoric's appeal is likely to have limits.
Nationalism always needs to look to the future, and there is no guarantee that the economic growth which has fuelled China's transformation so far will continue without serious setbacks and thus provide
fuel for a depoliticized state story of progress. Even if it does continue
smoothly, increasing economic globalization itself – together with the
freer flow of information it requires – may serve to undermine the
power of the state, as it has elsewhere in the world. With Hong Kong

and Macau back under Chinese sovereignty, only Taiwan can now provide a significant focus for nationalist concerns over territorial integrity, but it is a much more problematic case. State rhetoric has foregrounded the issue of Taiwan's return to Chinese sovereignty in the period since the Macau countdown clock in Tiananmen Square reached zero at midnight on 19 December 1999, but the absence of any agreement with Taipei means that no new clock is yet running to replace it. Indeed, the birth of the new millennium has seen the prospects of peaceful reunification get even more distant, with democratic presidential elections in Taiwan bringing separatist Chen Shui-bian to power, definitively ending one-party rule on that side of the Taiwan Strait. With Taiwan enjoying democracy and an independence in all but name, Beijing has little to offer by way of positive inducements, and military threats towards the island have been renewed.[2] Clearly such a strategy is a high risk one, offering plenty of opportunities for the Beijing regime to damage rather than enhance its ideological appeal to the Chinese people.

Hong Kong and Taiwan, in different ways, both offer challenges to the notion of nationhood being propagated by the Chinese state, but the fragility of national narratives can be sensed even in their most prominent site of expression, Beijing's Tiananmen Square. Since 1989 this most centrally important of Chinese public spaces has become deeply vulnerable: a consciously created Communist theatre of memory has become overburdened with too heavy and problematic a weight of historical association. Wong Kan Tai evoked this troubling burden of the past in his images of Tiananmen Square produced during his 1998–9 visit to Beijing along with Karl Chiu (illus. 133). Even a simple black-and-white image by Chiu of a bicycle half-buried in the snow inevitably conjures up memories of the trauma of June 1989 (illus. 134).

A direct testing of the vulnerability of Tiananmen Square by a Hong Kong artist was to occur in March 2000 when Young Hay went there during the Beijing section of his performance art piece *Bonjour, Young Hay (After Courbet)* (illus. 135). This performance consisted of the artist walking around with an empty white 1.5-metre by 1.2-metre canvas strapped to his back. Documentation by a collaborating photographer was an integral part of the project, resulting in images that show the white rectangle as a spatial void in a variety of urban environments. *Bonjour, Young Hay (After Courbet)* first took place in Hong Kong in 1995, New York and Berlin performances occurred in 1998, with the Beijing performance completing the piece. Because Young had deliberately chosen to use a blank canvas his work was completely

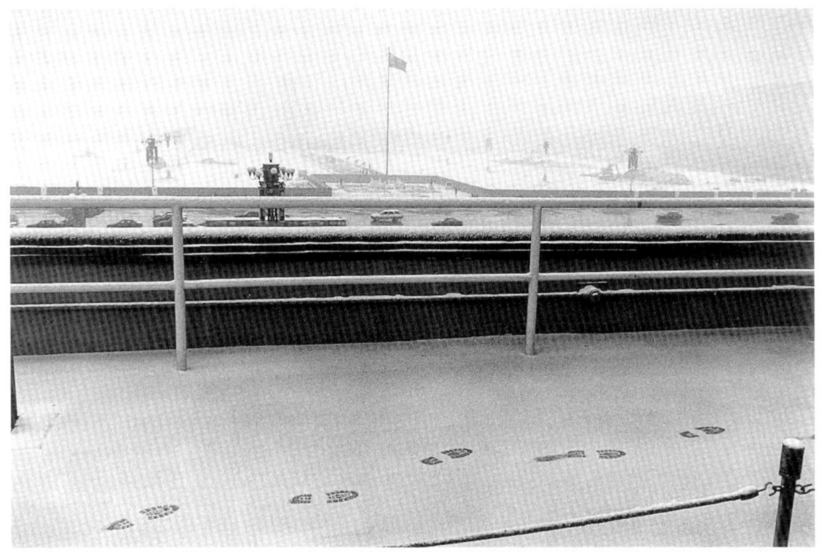

133 Wong Kan Tai, *Tiananmen*, 1999, black-and-white photographic print. Collection of the artist.

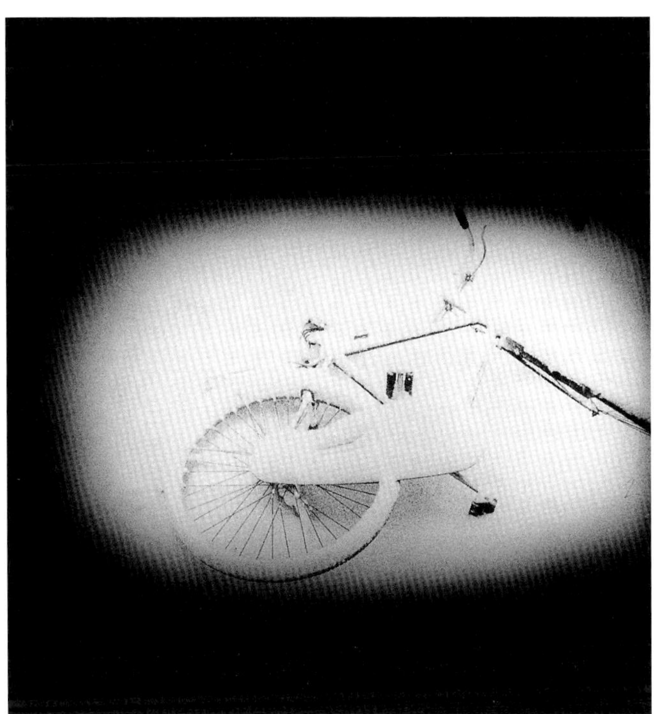

134 Karl Chiu, *Beijing 1998*, black-and-white photographic print. Collection of the artist.

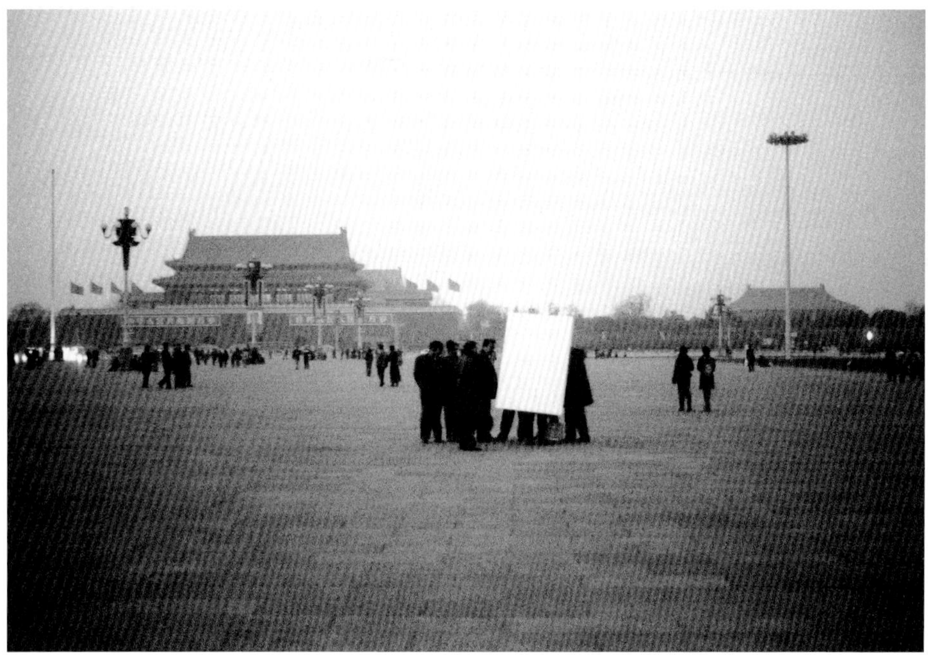

135 Young Hay, *Bonjour, Young Hay (After Courbet)*, 2000, black-and white-photographic print by Fang Fang documenting a performance. Collection of the artist.

lacking in any literal content and so could hardly be described as politically subversive in the ordinary sense. Nevertheless the whole time he was in the Tiananmen Square area he was subjected to police attention. Guards drove him away from Tiananmen saying that his white canvas was 'too eye-catching'[3] and he was subjected to an interrogation by a plain clothes police officer when he attempted to gain access to the Square itself via an underpass. Only with difficulty was Young eventually able to enter the Square from another direction and (despite further questioning by guards) stay long enough to both complete his performance and enable photographer Fang Fang's surreptitious documentation of his presence there.

Because of the weight of problematic historical associations which Tiananmen Square has acquired, and the vulnerability this has given it, the Chinese state has chosen to downplay the Square's references to a Communist past and has instead attempted to make it a site for anticipation of a nationalist future. A renovation of the Square and its surrounding buildings, including a repaving which conveniently kept it out of bounds to the public during the tenth anniversary of 4 June

1989,[4] can be read as an attempt at a symbolic new beginning. A key event, however, was the placement of a digital clock on the façade of the Museum of History on 30 June 1994 which counted down the days and seconds left till the moment of Hong Kong's handover.[5] Not only did this provide a clear focus for nationalist anticipation, but it also created a new east–west axis in the Square. This contrasted, conveniently, with the existing north–south orientation marked by the Mao Memorial Hall, the Monument to the People's Heroes and Mao's portrait on Tiananmen itself (from where the founding of the People's Republic was declared) – an orientation that had been accentuated during the protests of May and June 1989 because the Goddess of Democracy statue had been placed facing Mao.

The beginning of the new millennium provided a further golden opportunity to look to the future, and it was not surprising that the celebrations at midnight on 31 December 1999 were more extensive in Beijing than in Hong Kong. The focus was displaced from Tiananmen Square to a new China Millennium Monument in West Beijing, which purportedly cost some 200 million yuan to construct. Jiang Zemin lit an eternal flame at this future-themed structure of (symbolically) yellow stone as the new century began. Tiananmen Square, although relegated to second place, was not left out of the picture altogether: a specially constructed giant bronze 'harmony bell', weighing 50 tonnes, was rung there at the same moment. The consciously modernistic architecture that has been springing up elsewhere in Beijing seems set to transform the flavour of Tiananmen Square too: 1999 saw the announcement of plans to build a futuristic National Theatre in its vicinity. The contract was awarded to French architect Paul Andreu, perhaps because a cosmopolitan feel was intended and it was felt that the selection of an overseas architect would help contribute that.[6]

Despite such official displays of optimism, the future of China remains open, and alternative ways of imagining identity to those propagated by the state have now become widespread. The popularity of the Falun Gong religious movement in China is a further symptom of the ideological vacuum left by the erosion of belief in Communist dogma, and it is unsurprising that the Chinese government moved to ban the organization as subversive. A demonstration by ten thousand Falun Gong practitioners on 25 April 1999 at Zhongnanhai, the seat of government power, showed the strong basis of support the organization enjoys, and protests continue in Tiananmen Square itself on a regular basis, by Falun Gong supporters and sometimes by others. On 11 May 2000, and again on National Day (1 October 2000), for instance, large groups of Falun Gong members were forcibly removed from the Square by police. Sect followers also raised banners and scattered leaflets on 26 October 2000, and the northern portion of the Square was closed for about twenty minutes (it had been temporarily closed on 1 October as well). On 1 January 2001 hundreds of protestors were again violently removed from the Square.[7] The authorities know that any event that takes place in that arena is of special symbolic significance, hence their vigilant watch over it, but they are unable to prevent their own violence there from itself being symbolic. While the state makes use of naked force to preserve the status quo, it cannot rely on it solely: coercion cannot substitute completely for consent. State hegemony must also be fought for in the symbolic or ideological realm, and here, as evidence from Hong Kong and elsewhere clearly shows, the odds are less stacked in its favour, and the long-term outcome is by no means fully assured.

References

Introduction

1 The inadequacy of Clement Greenberg's formalist account of modern art's development is discussed in David Clarke, 'The All-Over Image: Meaning in Abstract Art', *Journal of American Studies*, XXVII/3 (1993), pp. 355–75.

2 No adequate survey exists of Hong Kong art as a whole. The present author's *Art and Place: Essays on Art from a Hong Kong Perspective* (Hong Kong, 1996) attempts to give a picture of the Hong Kong art world in the period immediately prior to the one covered by this text, and includes some discussion of art from earlier periods as well. Petra Hinterthür's *Modern Art in Hong Kong* (Hong Kong, 1985) attempts a brief survey, but is of course unable to throw light on more recent developments. A chronology of Hong Kong art development from 1922 to 1994 is given in *Hong Kong Artists. Volume I* (Hong Kong, 1995), pp. 21–32. A rather patchy and sometimes imprecise chronology of Hong Kong artistic events from 1967 to 1998 is given in Gao Minglu, ed., *Inside Out: New Chinese Art* (Berkeley, 1998), pp. 207–11. The latter chronology also covers political and other broader historical events of the period. A valuable resource (in Chinese) for research on the early period of Hong Kong art is provided by Edwin Lai and Jack Lee, 'A Chronology of Visual Arts Activities in Hong Kong, 1900–1930', in *Besides: A Journal of Art History and Criticism*, I (1997), pp. 135–230.

3 For more on the New Ink Painting movement see *Art and Place*, Chapter 12. Nigel Cameron's 'Hong Kong: The Development of Modern Art', in Oscar Ho and Eric Wear, eds, *Hong Kong Art Review* (Hong Kong, 1999), pp. 60–65, is a personal reminiscence by an art critic of that period when modernism came to Hong Kong. Wucius Wong's 'Chinese Painting in Hong Kong', in Kao Mayching, ed., *Twentieth-Century Chinese Painting* (Hong Kong, 1988), pp. 210–23, is an account of it by one of the main artists involved. Artists associated with New Ink Painting (but who are not featured in the present study) include Cheng Wei-kwok, Irene Chou, Chui Tze-hung, Leung Kui-ting, Ng Yiu-chung and Lawrence Tam. Prominent ink painters in Hong Kong who were not a part of the New Ink Painting trend include Fang Zhaoling, Ding Yanyong and Zhao Shao'ang. Certain painters favouring Western media (such as Hon Chi-fun) shared New Ink Painting's goal of balancing references to the Chinese brushwork tradition with references to then-current Western modernism.

4 For more on this phase of modern Chinese art history, see David Clarke, *Modern Chinese Art* (Oxford/New York/Hong Kong, 2000), Chapter 4.

5 See *Modern Chinese Art*, Chapters 1 and 2, for a discussion of Chinese modernism of the 1920s and 1930s.

1 Varieties of Cultural Hybridity

1 The literature on hybridity is now quite extensive, as Nikos Papastergiadis demonstrates in 'Restless Hybrids', *Third Text*, XXXII (Autumn 1995), pp. 9–18), and I do not intend to summarize it here. I refer readers in search of an analytical account of the term's use in critical theory to Papastergiadis's valuable essay. Clearly Homi Bhabha has played a crucial role in developing a non-essentialist understanding of hybridity (see *The Location of Culture*

[London, 1994], and elsewhere), and his work is a precondition for what I am attempting here. I am also endebted to Stuart Hall who, like Bhabha, operates with a conception of hybridity informed by Derrida's notion of *différence*. His 'Cultural Identity and Diaspora', in Jonathan Rutherford, ed., *Identity: Community, Culture, Difference*, (London, 1990) is particularly useful, offering an explicit placement of his work in relation to Derrida. Judy Purdom, in 'Mapping Difference', *Third Text*, XXXII (Autumn 1995), pp. 19–32 gives an account of Bhabha's conception of hybridity, showing how Derrida's notion of *différence* underpins it. Unfortunately not all usage of the notion of hybridity in relation to international visual art has the theoretical sophistication of Bhabha and Hall, and my essay may be taken as a critique of some of the shortcomings of this discourse (in which pre-Derridarian conceptions of hybridity can return), or as offering suggestions as to how Bhabha and Hall's ideas can be applied (and thus developed) in one specific context. Some of my reservations concerning the notion of hybridity are shared by Jean Fisher, see her editorial in *Third Text*, XXXII (Autumn 1995), pp. 3–7; Sarat Maharaj '"Perfidious Fidelity": The Untranslatability of the Other', *Global Visions: Towards a New Internationalism in the Visual Arts* (London, 1994), pp. 28–35; and Michael Hardt and Antonio Negri, *Empire* (Cambridge, MA and London, 2000), pp. 138 and 156.

2   The practice of allowing all immigrants from China to become Hong Kong residents ended in 1974, and the 'reached-base' policy (which allowed illegal immigrants who had managed to settle in the urban areas to become legal residents) ended in 1980. From that year all residents were required to carry identity documents.

3   For a discussion of Abstract Expressionist interest in East Asian brushwork, see David Clarke, 'The Calligraphic Spirit and Modern American Art', in *Eloquent Line* (Washington, DC, 1993), pp. 19–27 and David Clarke, *The Influence of Oriental Thought on Postwar American Painting and Sculpture* (New York, 1988).

4   For an analysis of Hong Kong art from this period, see Jack Lee Sai Chong, *Painting in Western Media in Early Twentieth Century Hong Kong*, M.Phil. thesis, Hong Kong University, 1996.

5   Wong studied in the USA during the early 1960s. Mak studied in London in the early to middle 1970s.

6   The article was 'The Hong Kong Artists' Group', *The Studio*, CXLVIII (July 1954), pp. 84–7. Chan was to publish another article, 'Fundamental Principles of Chinese Painting', in volume CL (1955). Chan was a prolific author, writing a great many books on art in Chinese.

7   Chan adds ('In conversation [with Chang Tsong-zung]', in *Luis Chan at Eighty* (Hong Kong, 1985) 'if you see one on which I've put my name-chop, it is a Chinese painting, otherwise it is not!' The following two quotations from Chan in the text are from the same book, the first from Chang Tsong-zung's introduction, the second from the above-mentioned interview.

8   For an example of a complex Cantonese pun using the similarity of sound between the words for book and lose see Hugh Baker, 'The English Sandwich: Obscenity, Punning and Bilingualism in Hong Kong Cantonese', in Roger Ames *et al.*, eds, *Interpreting Culture Through Translation. A Festschrift for D. C. Lau* (Hong Kong, 1991), pp. 43–4. For avoidance of the word for book as inauspicious see p. 40 of the same essay.

9   The two short quotes from Mak are from an interview conducted by the author on 1 October 1993.

10 Although Van Lau exploits bamboo's associations with literati brushwork, other Hong Kong artists explore its craft or everyday associations. Ha Bik-chuen, for example, uses bamboo as a sculptural material as opposed to a

subject in works such as *Poet* (1979), while Kith Tsang references its local use as a scaffolding material in his installations (see Chapter 3).

11 E. Hobsbawm and T. Ranger, eds, *The Invention of Tradition* (Cambridge, 1983).

12 Continuity may even be at the level of the art object, rather than just at the level of the signifier. Museum displays can make classical Chinese artworks signify as elements in an entirely modern narrative of national tradition. I discuss museums as propagators of cultural narratives in Chapter 2 of my *Art and Place: Essays on Art from a Hong Kong Perspective* (Hong Kong, 1996).

13 In an introduction to the catalogue of a 1981 exhibition of Hong Kong art at the Museum, Lawrence Tam (an ex-student of Lui Shou-kwan and formerly the Museum's Chief Curator) talks of the exhibit as containing 'happy evidence of the blending of aspects of two streams of world culture, the East and the West', *Hong Kong Art, 1970–1980* (Hong Kong, 1981), p. 12. The art of Lui probably fits this ideological frame rather more easily than that of Wong, which refuses to simply 'blend' East and West. Wong's paintings seem more aware than Tam's statement of the problems of the 'East meets West' project.

14 I discuss the pressure group activities of artists in Hong Kong at various points in *Art and Place*, especially in the first two sections. See particularly pages 47, 52, and 58.

15 The exhibition was *The Grand Opening Exhibition – A Tribute to Antonio Mak*, held by the China Oil Painting Gallery Ltd at the Rotunda, Exchange Square, 5–10 July 1996. The political implications of Mak's work were discussed by Lau Kin-wai in his column for *Ming Pao*, 8 July 1996, p. D2. This account is most likely to be responsible for the non-appearance of the New China News Agency official, since it mentions him by name. Zhang was due to be the guest of honour at a cocktail reception in the exhibition on that day.

2 Living in the Shadow of the Future

1 The more-or-less democratic Legislative Council election which took place on 17 September 1995 did not employ a simple 'one person one vote' principle. A percentage of the seats were elected in accordance with geographic constituencies in this way, but a second set of votes became available to just about anyone who wished to register as an elector in so-called 'functional constituencies'. These functional constituencies had originally been created to give an anti-democratic extra power to certain small-circle business and professional groupings, but under Patten's reforms they were greatly enlarged to enable mass participation. It should be noted that the election of a democratic legislature had no direct effect on the executive branch of government, as it would in – say – the British parliamentary system where the largest party in the House of Commons normally forms the government. In effect the Legislative Council elections were being held to elect an opposition to the government.

2 I date the crisis of legitimacy to the period after 4 June 1989, but Ian Scott, in *Political Change and the Crisis of Legitimacy in Hong Kong* (Hong Kong, 1989) prefers to think of the crisis as beginning in the time when the British and Chinese governments decided to negotiate over Hong Kong's future. Scott's study offers a valuable close reading of the political situation in Hong Kong during the post-Joint Declaration era (as well as a detailed study of earlier periods), but does not consider artistic and cultural factors either in the government's attempts to gain legitimacy, or in challenges to it.

3 Deng Xiaoping had expressed the hope that he might live long enough to travel to Hong Kong after it had again become Chinese sovereign territory.

Liu Yuyi's *Liangchen* was reproduced in the *Hong Kong Economic Journal*, 25 June 1997, p. 36. A colour reproduction accompanies a more recent article about Liu's work ('Move over Michelangelo', *Sunday Morning Post*, 22 October 2000, Agenda section, pp. 1–2).

4 For a discussion of the use of Cultural Revolution-era iconography by mainland Chinese artists, see David Clarke, *Art and Place: Essays on Art from a Hong Kong Perspective* (Hong Kong, 1996), pp. 236–49. Yung later changed the name of *The Star* to *The Wishing Star* (e-mail communication, 17 March 2000). Five smaller versions of *The Star* (each about the height of an adult) were also created. These were mobile versions on wheels and were used as props during a parade performance along the Tsim Sha Tsui East waterfront which took place on 19 and 20 February 1994, and ended in the vicinity of the large star. Since the parade began from the new Kowloon-Canton Railway terminus at Hung Hom and ended at the Cultural Centre (the site of the previous KCR terminus) it referenced the history of the latter location. Taking red star forms from the terminus of trains from Beijing to the Cultural Centre was metaphorically a taking of Beijing things to Hong Kong, a completion of a journey south.

5 A red five-pointed star also appears in Lee's *Hello, Hong Kong* (1989). A visually fragmented Chinese national flag, its yellow stars clearly identifiable, is the subject of *June Forth* (1989), clearly a response to the Beijing crackdown. In this work the red and yellow of the flag is visually interrupted by black. Two artists whose work is reproduced in *Tiananmen Memorial Art Exhibition*, Washington, DC, Congressional Human Rights Foundation, 1990 also use the Chinese flag as a way of commenting on the 4 June 1989 crackdown. Vito Acconci's *China Doll Flag* has a mannequin as if shrouded or smothered by a Chinese flag, and Bing Lee (a New York-based Chinese artist) employs a black version of the flag with stars in red. The four smaller stars on the flag are represented as if melting.

6 Not all artists arriving in Hong Kong from the mainland adopt 'Mainlander' personas. The sense of Hong Kong cultural identity is not indigenist in nature (unlike, perhaps, the sense of local identity which has developed in Taiwan), since so many Hong Kong people have come from the mainland.

7 The 'birdcage democracy' metaphor can be found, for instance, in Samantha Wong and Cynthia Wan, 'Law now in a bird cage, says democrat', *Sunday Morning Post*, 27 June 1999, p. 3, and Chris Yeung, 'A Bird-cage Democracy', *South China Morning Post*, Saturday, 10 July 1999, p. 15. Kum and Pun, together with a number of other artists, put together a group exhibition in 1995 called *Pre '97 Special Arts Zone*, the works in which seemed primarily concerned with responding to the rapid approach of the handover.

8 Painter Annie Chan has also shown an interest both in old buildings and construction sites, see Clarke, *Art and Place*, pp. 109–13. Among other Hong Kong artists to show an interest in Lai Chi Kok is Lee Ka-sing (see his *Dinosaur in the City, Near Laichikok*, 1998, which is illustrated in his book *Forty Poems: Photographs 1985–1998* (Hong Kong, 1998).

9 Chan Yiu Hung's photographs were shown in *Spirit in Rennie's Mill* (Agfa Gallery, Goethe Institut Hong Kong, 17–31 May 1996). Images of Rennie's Mill by both So Hing Keung and Raymond Chan can be found in Sylvia S. Y. Ng (ed.), *The Metropolis – Visual Research into Contemporary Hong Kong (1990–1996)*, (Hong Kong, 1996), which contains documentary work by a number of other Hong Kong photographers as well. Raymond Chan's images are also collected in *Hong Kong. 1986–1997.1.1. The Works of Raymond Chan* (Hong Kong, 1997). Rennie's Mill was not only of interest to photographers: Kith Tsang made an installation piece there in 1996. Titled *Hello! Hong Kong – Part 4*, it was sited in the courtyard of Tiu Keng Leng

Middle School. A further Hong Kong landmark to be cleared of its inhabitants and erased in the run up to the handover was the Kowloon Walled City. Japanese photographer Ryuji Miyamoto's documentation of it was featured in a Hong Kong Arts Centre exhibit (*Kowloon Walled City: The Lost City*, 10 October to 18 November 1998), as part of *Invisible Cities* (Festival Now '98) which had as its theme memory, erasure and the Hong Kong public sphere (see *Invisible Cities*, Hong Kong, 1998) for documentation. Local photographic artists who documented the Kowloon Walled City or its destruction include Victor Chiu Chung Hoi (see *The Metropolis – Visual Research into Contemporary Hong Kong [1990–1996]*), Vincent Yu (see *HKG*, Hong Kong, 1998) and Raymond Chan (see *Hong Kong. 1986–1997.1.1.*). The clearance of the Walled City was completed on 1 July 1992.

10 Warren Leung describes Kith Tsang's work as having a sense of 'cyclical time' as opposed to 'linear time' in 'The Native Sense of History', in *Hello! Hong Kong – Part 7* (Hong Kong, 1997), pp. 32–5.

11 Around the time of the handover there was a debate about the way in which the Hong Kong Museum of History's displays represented local history, occasioned in part by the fact that a new museum building was then under construction. See Chapter 5 for further detail on this controversy. For Oscar Ho's curatorial perspective on *The Prehistoric Hong Kong Museum* see his 'Inventing History', in Oscar Ho and Eric Wear (eds), *Hong Kong Art Review* (Hong Kong, 1999), pp. 46–53.

12 See Grant Evans, 'Ghosts and the New Governor', in Grant Evans and Maria Tam Siu-mi, eds, *Hong Kong: The Anthropology of a Chinese Metropolis* (Richmond, Surrey, 1997), pp. 267–96, for an academic analysis of one of the most flagrantly handover-related urban myths of this period. A model for Ho's *Stories Around Town* are late Qing illustrations such as those found in *The Dianshizhai Pictorial*, a lithographic supplement to the Shanghai newspaper *Shen Pao* (see Don J. Cohn, ed., *Vignettes from the Chinese* [Hong Kong, 1987] for examples). Like Ho's works these are often based on topical events, have a fantastic element and have text inscribed on the images themselves. Dung Kai Cheung's *The Atlas: Archaeology of an Imaginary City* (Taipei, 1997) offers something of a literary equivalent to Ho's *Stories Around Town*. It purports to offer a history of urban Hong Kong in the colonial era, but has the same fantastical quality as Ho's work. Like Holly Lee's *Bauhinia, in front of Hong Kong Harbour, circa 1997*, *The Atlas* takes a retrospective look as if from some time far in the future (it is set in a different century in which the city has already changed beyond recognition). Excerpts of the book have been translated into English in Martha Cheung, ed., *Hong Kong Collage. Contemporary Stories and Writing* (Hong Kong, 1998).

13 One important attempt to theorize political subjecthood in a non-essentialist manner is that of Ernesto Laclau. Although he does not address at all closely the role of the arts in the political process, his non-reductive post-structuralist conception of political agency (as developed in *Hegemony and Socialist Strategy* [with Chantal Mouffe] (London, 1985), and *New Reflections on the Revolution of Our Time* (London, 1990) has been of influence on the present study.

3 Para/Site Art Space

1 On Chinese artistic modernism, see David Clarke, *Modern Chinese Art* (Oxford/New York/Hong Kong, 2000). A modernist painting had existed in mainland China during the 1920s and 1930s, but unlike its later counterpart in the art of Hong Kong and Taiwan it had little international ambition, and was altogether more tentative and experimental in nature.

2 Oscar Ho, in 'The Long Road Back Home', *Art AsiaPacific*, no. 15 (1997), pp. 48–53, discusses this trend towards the private in Hong Kong art. In January and February of 1996, the Hong Kong Fringe Festival organized an exhibition titled *Restricted Exposure*, which showcased local artists whose work was in some sense 'private'. A related book, *Private Content: Public View* (edited by Eric Wear and Lisa Cheung) was published by the Hong Kong Festival Fringe in 1997.

3 Tsang's analysis of his own art (which is drawn upon in the present discussion) can be found in his MA thesis, *Hello! Hong Kong*, De Montfort University, England, 1997.

4 Tsang's installation also makes an allusion to museum display: the Hong Kong history display of the Hong Kong Museum of History (at its former site) had a fishing junk installed indoors as a major element of the display. As with Tsang's boat, you could walk around it and there was a sound recording being played. A more direct mimicry of the museum mode, of course, occurred with the Hong Kong Arts Centre's *The Prehistoric Hong Kong Museum* (discussed in Chapter 2). The museum display mode was even adopted by a resident of the Lantau Island fishing village Tai O in an attempt to preserve and represent the village's history. Between 18 and 20 June 1999 a temporary 'museum' was opened in a room of Wing Chor School at Tai O displaying artefacts of that distinctive settlement, gathered over the years by homemaker Wong Wai-king. For an account see Clarence Tsui, 'Tai O history in the making', *Sunday Morning Post*, 20 June 1999, p. 3.

5 Leung's remarks are quoted by Robert Hobbs in *Hong Kong Now!* (Seattle, 1997), p. 32. See also Leung's essay 'The Native Sense of History' in *Hello! Hong Kong - Part 7* (Hong Kong, 1997), pp. 32–5.

6 There are parallels to the concern of Man, Wong and other Para/Site artists with the changing urban environment in the work of mainland Chinese artists. Zhan Wang, for instance, carefully restored a section of a half-demolished house in *Ruin Cleaning Project* of 1994 (see Wu Hung, 'Ruins, Fragmentation, and the Chinese Modern/Postmodern', in Gao Minglu, ed., *Inside Out: New Chinese Art* [Berkeley, 1998], p. 64). Rong Rong has produced photographs of half-destroyed houses on Beijing demolition sites showing traces of their former occupancy in the form of posters still on interior walls now exposed to view, while Song Dong and Yin Xiuzhen have both produced installations making use of items scavenged from demolition sites which are presented as relics (see Wu Hung, *Transience: Chinese Experimental Art at the End of the Twentieth Century* [Chicago, 1999], pp. 114–26). Both the Hong Kong and Beijing work can be read as critical of the modernization process and its erasure of the past, but the way references to urban transformation become elevated into symbols for Hong Kong itself at a moment of transition is particular to the territory's art.

7 Such visual/verbal punning can work with objects or with images of objects. Visual/verbal punning also occurs in Putonghua, an unconventional example being the small bottles (*xiao ping*) which students threw from their dormitory windows after the suppression of the 1989 Democracy Movement as a way of venting their frustration with the Chinese patriarch Deng Xiaoping, whose given name was being recalled. In the run-up to the crackdown's second anniversary Beijing University authorities invited pedlars onto campus to collect empty bottles, and higher prices were being offered than usual. See S. I. Law and Agencies, 'Campus bottle drive to stop silent protests', *The Hongkong Standard*, 3 June 1991, p. 1.

8 Whereas written English represents the sound of spoken English (one can approximate the pronunciation of a written word one has never heard before), a given Chinese character can be interpreted through the sounds of a variety

of dialects, much as the same Arabic numeral could be interpreted in different spoken languages ('2' becoming either 'two' or 'deux', etc). Romanization can sometimes creep into informal Cantonese writing as an aid to transcribing speech which would be written with a different grammatical structure and with different characters in formal written Chinese (an example would be the use of a letter 'D' to represent the second part of the compound 'nidi', meaning 'these'). Oscar Ho's *The Crippled Ding* (illus. 81) uses a lowercase 'd' in this way in an inscription on the image. On word play in Hong Kong Cantonese that assumes awareness of English, see Hugh Baker, 'The English Sandwich: Obscenity, Punning and Bilingualism in Hong Kong Cantonese', in Roger Ames *et al.*, *Interpreting Culture Through Translation. A Festschrift for D. C. Lan* (Hong Kong, 1991), pp. 37–58.

9 In an interview with the author on 2 June 1992, Xu Bing spoke of his sense of liberation on arriving in the United States, a 'young' country without the weight of thousands of years of tradition. Other examples of mainland art in which the Chinese written language has been confronted are Gu Wenda's *Pseudo-Character Series: Contemplation of the World* (1984) and Qiu Zhijie's *Writing the 'Orchid Pavilion Preface' One Thousand Times* (1986/1997). For discussion of the use of written language in mainland art see Simon Leung with Janet A. Kaplan, 'Pseudo-Languages: A Conversation with Wenda Gu, Xu Bing and Jonathan Hay', *Art Journal*, LVIII/3 (Fall 1999), pp. 86–99. For a detailed examination of visual/verbal issues in Hong Kong art see Eliza Lai Mei-lin, *Words and Images in Contemporary Hong Kong Art: 1984–1997*, M.Phil. thesis, Hong Kong University, 2000.

10 Quoted from 'About "Ghost Encounter"' by Chan Yuk-keung, in *Ghost Encounter* (Hong Kong, 1998) (unpaginated).

11 Kwok is somewhat older than the Para/Site members, and was perhaps Hong Kong's first installation artist. Unlike almost all the younger installation artists he does make use of Chinese ink as a medium, but juxtaposes his calligraphy or ink painting with photographs and objects of local material culture in his installations in a way that would be unthinkable to other ink painters of his generation. Other pioneering installation artists particularly worthy of mention are Choi Yan-chi (who began working with the medium from an early date, but who was living in Canada between 1993 and 1997) and Chan Yuk-keung (who has been quite influential on young installation artists through his teaching at the Chinese University of Hong Kong).

12 Ancestor tablets have also been referenced in two artworks by Danny Yung. His *Deep Structure of Chinese (Hong Kong) Culture, no. 4* (1991) made use of a series of oversized tablet forms with mirrored surfaces. Mirrors, since they return the gaze to its origin, perhaps symbolize a break with the past – just where connection with it is sought. *Deep Structure of Chinese Culture, no. 5* (1996) had tablet forms made of transparent acrylic, filled with ice cubes. A time dimension was introduced into the work though the gradual melting of the ice, which enabled previously inserted wooden sticks to float upwards. The sticks had inscriptions referring to Article 23 of the post-handover Basic Law of the Hong Kong Special Administrative Region, a controversial provision which requires the SAR to enact laws against acts of 'subversion against the Central People's Government'. The writing on the sticks is mirror-reversed.

13 Feminist themes were also foregrounded in *Women Who Dare*, curated by Irene Ngan and featuring the work of Lo Yin Shan, Lily Lau and May Fung (March to April 1999). Sanitary towels were also used as a material by mainland Chinese artist Gu Wenda in *Oedipus Refound no. 1: 2000 Natural Deaths*, first made in 1990, and with a version produced in Hong Kong in 1993. Phoebe Man's more recent work has continued to show an interest in

taboo subjects, but these are being explored through new media such as video and the internet. Her video *Rati* (2000) stars a walking vagina, observed going about daily life activities.

14 A critique of government land policy is found in Simon Pritchard, 'A barrier to a better future', *South China Morning Post*, 28 August 1999, p. 15.

15 See Kong Lai-fan, '$31m wasted on arts centre site', *South China Morning Post*, 19 November 1999, internet edition. The lack of public consultation in the development of a plan for a cultural and entertainment district in West Kowloon was criticized in an editorial in *Xpressions*, 18 (6 May 1999). The plans were detailed elsewhere in the issue.

16 See Richard Woo, 'Planning blow to tycoon Li's cruise ship terminal', *South China Morning Post*, 30 October 1999, p. 1. Press articles on Oil Street include: Clarence Tsui, 'No place for art to call home', *South China Morning Post*, 7 March 1999, p. 5; Clarence Tsui, 'Homing in on the problems', *South China Morning Post*, 12 March 2000, p. 6. A final farewell exhibition (*Big Act in Oil Street: Towards a Cultural Metropolitan City*) was held collaboratively by all the Oil Street venues between 27 November and 28 December 1999. An exhibition of photos by Stanley Wong documenting the closure of the Oil Street Art Village (*Before and Ever After. 522 Days of Oil Street*) was held at OP Fotogallery, 3–31 March 2000. Almond Chu also produced a series of photographs about the Oil Street artists' village, which were shown at the Würth Gallery, Goethe-Institut Hong Kong, 5–24 October 2000 in an exhibition entitled *Traces*. Chu's images (illus. 58) show traces of the artistic use of the Oil Street site as well as traces of its previous function – two layers of ruination or abandonment are represented. Although it does not show Oil Street itself, much of the material used in Ellen Pau's video *Recycling Cinema* (1999) was shot from the vantage point provided by the Videotage office at that location, looking out at the adjacent elevated highway (the Island Eastern Corridor).

4 Carving Public Space

1 Large-scale demonstrations in support of the democracy movement in China had also taken place prior to the 4 June military crackdown, from 18 May onwards.

2 The banknotes referred to here are the set issued on 1 January 1993, which continued in use into the post-handover period. A similar image of the two lions (at enlarged scale) beside the new bank headquarters building also appeared on the previous set of banknotes. A large-scale lion head also appears on the other side of all denominations of the 1993 set of notes, replacing the bank's crest containing royal emblems which featured on the previous set. The $500 and $1,000 notes of an even earlier set featured similar large lion heads, with the bank's previous headquarters building visible behind. A lion's head also appears as the watermark of the 1993 set of notes.

3 Press coverage of the *New Man* incident was extensive, see for example: Jane Moir, 'Naked truth too much to bare', *South China Morning Post*, 6 June 1995, p. 1; 'Editorial: Tribunal's poor judgement', *South China Morning Post*, 6 June 1995, p. 18; Mariana Wan, 'A case of too much exposure', *South China Morning Post*, 6 June 1995, p. 17; 'Decent or indecent: you decide', *Eastern Express*, 7 June 1995, p. 3; Liam Fitzpatrick, 'Pitiful case of censorship hits the statute books', *Eastern Express*, 7 June 1995, p. 18; Ruth Mathewson and Jane Moir, 'Censor's rulings made by instinct', *South China Morning Post*, 7 June 1995, p. 6; 'Editorial: This obscene charade must go', *Eastern Express*, 8 June 1995, p. 14; Michelle Murphy, 'You say we are right to show photos', *Eastern Express*, 8 June 1995, p. 4; Alex Lo, '*New Man* becomes

exhibitionist', *Eastern Express*, 8 June 1995, p. 4; Ella Lee, 'Call to end "ignorance"', *Eastern Express*, 10 June 1995, p. 4; Jane Moir, 'Arts body raps obscenity law', *South China Morning Post*, 22 June 1995, p. 4; Emma Batha, '*New Man* to go on show in all his glory', *South China Morning Post*, 12 August 1995, p. 3; Darren Goodsir and Michelle Chin, 'Photos still exposed to the censors', *South China Morning Post*, 12 August 1995, p. 3; Jane Moir, 'Censor lays blame for failure to woo women', *South China Morning Post*, 1 September 1995, p. 5; an example of overseas news coverage is 'Bronze too brazen for Hong Kong', *Daily Telegraph* (UK), 7 June 1995, p. 16; see also *International Herald Tribune*, 8 June 1995, p. 24. On the post-handover re-exhibition of the *New Man* see: Anne-Marie Evans, '*New Man* strips off for Arts Centre show', *South China Morning Post*, 14 September 1998, internet edition.

4 The role played by the clocktower in providing historical contrast for the adjacent modern building is undertaken for the whole Hong Kong skyline by a sailing junk which the Hong Kong Tourist Association regularly hires to ply the waters of the harbour, the *Duk Ling*. It appears, juxtaposed with the skyscrapers behind, in numerous tourist postcards and publicity images. Sailing junks are not otherwise seen in Hong Kong waters nowadays, and even this one has an engine in addition to sails, making it a pure signifier of 'tradition'. In 1998 plans were announced by Henderson Land for three towers in the shape of a junk's sails on the northern edge of the Central Reclamation, near the ferry piers. Dennis Lau and Ng Chun Man were mentioned as the architects (see Keith Wallis, 'Henderson to set sail on tower project', *Sunday Morning Post*, 19 July 1998, *Money* section, p. 1).

5 Sammy Lee, 'Cultural Centre a symbol of Joint Declaration' [letter to the editor], *South China Morning Post*, 4 November 1989, p. 14.

6 The letter, dated 23 October 1989, was published in its entirety on the front page of the 26 October *South China Morning Post*. The text states that the 'Hong Kong government has no intention of allowing Hong Kong to be used as a base for subversive activities against the People's Republic of China', and points out by way of evidence that 'the Hong Kong government has recently rejected a proposal for a permanent site for a replica statue of democracy'. 'No group in Hong Kong has any more tolerance than the law allows', it adds.

7 An interview by Regis Kawecki with César ('César, Le Français Volant', *Paroles*, no. 14 [April 1993], pp. 7–9) contained what is perhaps the first published suggestion that the sculpture might be commenting on the Chinese democracy movement. During this interview César stated that the work is a symbol of liberty. The iconography of the *Flying Frenchman* was discussed by the present author during a lecture at the Hong Kong Museum of Art on 15 May 1993, and as an aside in 'Rodin and Modern Art: A Fragment about Fragments', *Hong Kong Economic Journal*, 1 June 1993, p. 36 (reprinted in an English version in *Art and Place: Essays on Art from a Hong Kong Perspective* [Hong Kong, 1996]). On the rumour concerning a name change, see articles on p. A4 of *Ming Pao*, 3 June 1999. For a report of the flower ceremony (and a photo) see Gérard Henry, 'César: "C'est un Symbole de liberté, un Icare en quelque sorte"', *Paroles*, no. 167 (July–August 1999), p. 35. Press articles about the *Flying Frenchman* include 'Artistic gift from France', *South China Morning Post*, 7 February 1992, p. 4. The winged man theme appears in earlier works by the artist, such as *The Man of Saint-Denis* (1958), which was apparently inspired in part by Leo Valentin, the French 'bird man'.

8 For press coverage of Pun's action, see Clifford Lo, 'Red menace puts Her Majesty's nose out of joint', *South China Morning Post*, 17 September 1996, p. 1; Norma Connolly, 'Royal "artist" gets caught red-handed', *Hong Kong Standard*, 17 September 1996, p. 1. More informed discussion is found in two

articles on the cultural page of the *Hong Kong Economic Journal* (16 September 1996, p. 30), including a report of an discussion meeting held by artists and critics. Pun himself is interviewed about the incident in Joanne Shen, 'Why does this man see red?', *HK Magazine*, issue 158, vol. 6, no. 35 (14 February 1997), pp. 6–11.

9 Galschiot describes his intentions in a pamphlet entitled *Pillar of Shame – a Happening of Remembrance* dated 24 May 1997, and distributed at that year's memorial rally. The pamphlet notes that the first time a *Pillar of Shame* was exhibited in public was at the NGO Forum of the UN's Food and Agriculture Organization summit in Rome, 13–17 November 1996. According to Galschiot, the display of the sculpture in Hong Kong was intended to mark 'the initiation of an art happening that will spread over the planet over the next ten years. Once or twice a year, a Pillar of Shame will be mounted around the world as a memorial of a severe infringement against humanity.' Further information about the sculpture was also posted on websites prior to the sculpture's first Hong Kong display.

10 Press reports concerning the *Pillar of Shame* were numerous. A selection of reports dealing directly with it in just one newspaper, the *South China Morning Post*, is given here to demonstrate the scale of coverage (reports in the associated Sunday paper, *Sunday Morning Post* are also mentioned, and identified by the paper's name): Joice Pang, 'Sculpture to feature in June 4th vigil' (3 May 1997, p. 6); Quinton Chan, 'Memorial to Tiananmen cold-shouldered by Council' (15 May 1997, p. 3); Angela Li, 'Request for permission to display *Pillar of Shame* statue denied' (21 May 1997, p. 3); Angela Li, 'Anger at sculpture rejection' (23 May 1997, p. 10); Angela Li, 'Bid to exhibit sculpture in Sha Tin Park voted down' (30 May 1997, p. 6); Joice Pang, 'Fear of Beijing behind sculpture ban, says artist' (31 May 1997, p. 6); 'Banned *Pillar of Shame* arrives in Hong Kong' (1 June 1997, p. 4); Genevieve Ku, 'Stand off over *Pillar of Shame*' (5 June 1997, p. 3); Joice Pang and Genevieve Ku, 'The *Pillar of Shame* on campus after scuffles' (6 June 1997, p. 6); Genevieve Ku, 'College to exhibit *Pillar of Shame*' (7 June 1997); 'No action over statue' (8 June 1997, p. 4); May Sin-mi Hon, 'Campuses may share memorial' (11 June 1997, p. 6); Quinton Chan, 'Sculpture backed by university chiefs' (25 June 1997, p. 6); Genevieve Ku, 'Statue goes from pillar to post, then nowhere' (1 November 1997, p. 6); Genevieve Ku, 'Fresh bid to find site for statue' (4 April 1998, internet edition); Kevin Kwong, 'Pillar props up politics ... but is it art?', *Sunday Morning Post*, 10 May 1998, p. 5; Genevieve Ku, 'Sparks fly over statue site' (13 May 1998, p. 2); Genevieve Ku, 'Councillors put off decision on *Pillar of Shame* site' (14 May 1998, p. 2); No Kwai-yan, '*Pillar of Shame* still homeless as Kowloon Park plan scuppered' (28 May 1998, p. 3); No Kwai-yan and Felix Chan, '*Pillar of Shame* left in limbo' (6 June 1998, p. 1); 'The shame of it' (20 August 1998, internet edition); Lau Han-tao and Helen Luk, 'The *Pillar of Shame* faces a test of opinion' (23 September 1998, internet edition); Angela Li, 'Students vote for permanent pillar display' (26 September 1998, internet edition); Audrey Parwani, '*Pillar of Shame* to be moved' (2 December 1998, internet edition); Alex Lo, '*Pillar of Shame* splits campus', *Sunday Morning Post*, 6 June 1999, p. 2. Among other press discussions of the *Pillar of Shame* are Danny Yung's 'The public art and public space that we need', *Hong Kong Economic Journal*, 29 May 1998, p. 32. A photo of the *Pillar of Shame* being splashed with red paint is to be found in *Apple Daily*, 5 June 1999, p. A2.

11 The creation by Governor Chris Patten of a wholly elected legislature during the last years of colonial rule can also perhaps be seen as influenced by the Goddess of Democracy statue: a symbolic democratic structure was in both cases created in the knowledge that it would likely be knocked down by the

Chinese government in front of a world audience. Perhaps the same precedent also influenced Hong Kong cartoonist and artist Zunzi when in 1998 he created a satirical image of Singapore senior statesman Lee Kuan Yew for display in the Singapore Art Museum as part of the ARX5 artists' regional exchange project. Museum staff took the image down from the walls and destroyed it shortly before the opening of the exhibition, thereby demonstrating the limits of artistic freedom in Singapore.

12 On the 1989 Tiananmen Square rallies see David Clarke, *Art and Place*, pp. 236–49, and McKenzie Wark, 'Vectors of Memory ... Seeds of Fire. The Western Media and the Beijing Demonstrations', *New Formations*, X (Spring 1990), pp. 1–11. For a detailed reading of the iconography of Tiananmen Square, including the Monument to the People's Heroes, see Wu Hung, 'Tiananmen Square: A Political History of Monuments', *Representations*, XXXV (Summer 1991), pp. 84–117. Demonstrators in Hong Kong occupied the memorial's nearest local equivalent, the Cenotaph in Central (erected to commemorate the dead of the two world wars). This occupation was documented in a photo by Bobby Yip, exhibited in *Those Days in 1989. A Contemplation after 10 Years* (Hong Kong Arts Centre, 4–20 June 1999). A photograph in the *South China Morning Post* (5 June 1990, p. 6) shows wreaths and banners placed on the Cenotaph during the first anniversary of the killings.

13 This concern for memory persisted in the face of governmental opposition. On Hong Kong Chief Executive Tung's warning to Democrats to stop holding 4 June vigils, see Angela Li, 'Stop June 4 vigil, warns Tung', *South China Morning Post*, 8 October 1999, internet edition. On Tung's 1997 call for Hong Kong people to 'put the baggage of June 4' behind them see C. K. Lau, 'A test of Tung's tolerance', *South China Morning Post*, 4 June 1998, p. 17. On the occasion of the tenth anniversary of 4 June in 1999, Chinese Premier Zhu Rongji claimed in response to questions that he had forgotten about the anniversary until reminded by his interlocutor. Memory is the content of one of the most popular rally and demonstration chants (which translates as the injunction 'don't forget June 4'). See Angela Li, 'Tiananmen date encoded in memory', *South China Morning Post*, 31 May 1999, internet edition, for a discussion of people using numbers associated with 4 June 1989 as their mobile phone and pager numbers, or bank account pin codes. A bar in the Lan Kwai Fong nightlife area is called 'Club 64'.

14 The identification of Hong Kong people with the Tiananmen demonstrators was not merely retrospective to the crackdown. Because donations from Hong Kong played a very significant role in sustaining the 1989 Tiananmen Square demonstrations at a time when they were beginning to lose their momentum, one can even talk of the importance of Hong Kong identification with the demonstrators in creating the protest itself. Victoria Park was not the only location to became Tiananmen Square in imagination: despite Chinese government protests, the Swiss city of Lausanne renamed its Place de la Louvre 'Tiananmen Square' for the day on 4 June 1999, to commemorate the tenth anniversary of the Beijing crackdown.

15 The interview with Cheung Man-kwong is in Li Wai-ling, 'The Goddess of Democracy Stone Wall greets June 4th', *Ming Pao*, 28 May 1998, p. A6. A photograph of Cheung putting a miniature Goddess of Democracy in the time-capsule can be found in *Ming Pao*, 29 May 1997. Various Hong Kong artists, including Wong Shun-kit and Lau Kin Wai, created artworks which were displayed in Victoria Park during the handover year rally. Coverage of their works (which were placed near the western entrance of the Park and not integrated into the symbolic theatre of the rally itself) can be found in Victoria Finlay, 'Show of support for those who died', *Sunday Morning Post*, 1

June 1997, p. 6.

16 Photographing graves as a way of documenting the violence of the 1989 crackdown is an extremely sensitive matter. A Hong Kong newspaper report (Jonathan Mirsky, 'Trying to bury the past', *Eastern Express*, 11 April 1994, p. 6) records the case of a reporter who had been photographing graves of young victims of the 1989 crackdown in Beijing's Wan An cemetery. He was detained for allegedly 'taking photographs in a graveyard without having gone through the necessary procedures'. June 4-related photographs by Ko, Wong, Chiu and other Hong Kong artists were exhibited in *Those Days in 1989. A Contemplation after 10 years* (Hong Kong Arts Centre, 4–20 June 1999). Many of Ko's images of Victoria Park and of the Democracy movement can be found in *The Blues. Photographs by Alfred Ko* (Hong Kong, 1997), an album of his Hong Kong work of the pre-handover period (1989–1997).

17 Tsang's remarks are quoted from the catalogue preface (*National Treasures – Gems of China's Cultural Relics* (Hong Kong, 1997), p. 29. The inclusion of Hong Kong artefacts in a 'National Treasure' exhibition was questioned by Xiao Li, 'Well water changed into river water: local cultural relics turned into national treasures', *Hong Kong Economic Journal*, 28 February 1998, p. 3. Leung Man-to returned to the issue in the same publication on 4 March ('Treasures belong to the nation, but eyes are ours', p. 28). The traditional does not of course automatically belong to Communist notions of the national, and could even be quite antipathetic to it: on the use of the National Palace Museum in Taiwan by the Guomindang, for instance, see *Art and Place*, pp. 12–18.

18 Press references to the tripod include: Ng Kang-chung, 'Monster pot adds to storage problems', *South China Morning Post*, 25 June 1997, internet edition; Angela Li, 'Bid to leave tripod in park permanently', *South China Morning Post*, 7 July 1997, p. 4. The *Hong Kong Economic Journal* has a photo of the tripod (7 July 1997, p. 5). The performance piece directed at it is shown in a photo on page 24 of the same issue. For a discussion of the traditional political associations of the tripod, see Wu Hung, *Monumentality in Early Chinese Art and Architecture* (Stanford, 1995), pp. 1–15. It should be noted that large scale was an attribute of mythic tripods. *I Ching* quotations are from the edition edited and introduced by Raymond Van Over (*I Ching* [New York, 1971], pp. 253, 254).

19 The bamboo metaphor is discussed in an I. M. Pei and Partners press release of 18 August 1984: 'The inspiration for this design is rooted in classical Chinese philosophy and iconography. There is a Chinese proverb, using bamboo as a symbol: its sectioned trunk, propelled ever higher by each new growth, metaphorically describes the measured steps in the quest for strength and excellence. In this sense, the architecture of the new Bank of China Building is symbolic of the modernization efforts now undertaken by China.' Pei emphasized the theme of modernization in interview ('A shining vision', *Asiaweek*, 31 August 1984), stating that although the Bank gave him no preconditions for the design, 'the architect cannot be totally oblivious to the fact that this building is for an important Chinese institution ... and should reflect the country's strong modernization drive'.

20 For Sung's remarks on the Bank of China's *fengshui* see Charles Lewis, 'New bank's fung shui is a sharp worry to locals', *South China Morning Post*, 20 May 1987, p. 1. See also Christina Cheng Miu Bing, 'Resurgent Chinese Power in Postmodern Disguise: The New Bank of China Buildings in Hong Kong and Macau', in Evans and Tam, eds, *Hong Kong: The Anthropology of a Chinese Metropolis* (Richmond, Surrey, 1997), pp. 102–23. The final positioning of the Hong Kong and Shanghai Bank's bronze lions outside the new headquarters building was determined by the bank's *fengshui* expert

Lung King Chuen, who also chose an auspicious time for the lions' move from their temporary home in Statue Square (5 am on 1 June 1985).

21 The architects did not know for certain that the Extension would be used for the handover ceremony till November 1996, although there had been speculation about this earlier, and a significant aspect of the project was a non-negotiable mid-1997 completion deadline. See interview with Wong and Ouyang's Lam Wo Hei in Steven Rose, 'Hong Kong Convention and Exhibition Centre Extension: A Herculean Task', in *Hong Kong Convention and Exhibition Centre Extension: Poised for Flight (HKCECE Project Review)* (Hong Kong, 1997), p. 13. Lam adds 'Of course it was the natural choice. It is designed for exactly such purposes. It has a huge capacity and, being a virtual island, it is easy to manage from a security point of view.' The Macau handover ceremony of 19 December 1999 was similarly held in a new (but this time temporary) structure, on recently reclaimed land between the Macau Cultural Centre and the Mandarin Oriental Hotel.

22 The bird metaphor came from the architects, but Choong Voon Yow, one of Wong and Ouyang's designers on the project, noted that the Trade Development Council 'were looking for something soaring and uplifting as part of the designs' (Huw Morgan Griffiths, 'Pride of Place', *Asian Architect and Contractor*, April 1996, p. 18). The building has also been likened to a turtle going down into the water (see Oscar Ho, 'City of Make Believe', *Art AsiaPacific*, no. 25 [2000], pp. 46–9).

23 Press coverage of the *Forever Blooming Bauhinia* and other handover gifts is found in Ng Kang-chung, 'China gifts "for Government House show"', *South China Morning Post*, 24 June 1997, internet edition, and Suzie Weldon, 'Special gifts laden with symbolism', *South China Morning Post*, 2 July 1997, internet edition. See also 'Monster pot adds to storage problems', *South China Morning Post*, 25 June 1997, internet edition.

24 Chris Yeung, 'Anson tells of her spiritual return to China', *South China Morning Post*, 13 June 1998, p. 1, explains how Anson Chan, speaking at an Asia Society Dinner in Washington, DC, recounted a patriotic epiphany that occurred on 1 October 1997 at the National Day ceremony next to the *Forever Blooming Bauhinia*. Chan stated that the 'real transition is about identity, not sovereignty'. 'As I watched the flag unfurl in the early morning breeze [Chan is quoted as saying], I was suddenly filled with emotion.' 'The ceremony, the sight of the flag and the sound of the anthem touched something deep inside and moved me in a way that is difficult to describe'. 'I think for the first time, I began to appreciate the spiritual propriety of Hong Kong's return to the Mainland.' Chan's comments are also discussed in Felix Chan, 'Civil service chief "feels" for Anson', *Sunday Morning Post*, 21 June 1998, p. 4. Since the handover, the Chinese National Day has become a public holiday.

25 Van Lau's statement is quoted in 'Government House Museum rejected', *South China Morning Post*, 27 June 1998, p. 1. The chosen site for the reunification monument is perhaps a provisional one. Even at the time when designs for the monument were being invited, it was suggested that the monument might eventually be moved to a public square at a possible future Central Government office complex on the waterfront between Central and Wanchai, a site formerly occupied by the British HMS Tamar naval base.

26 On the political use of calligraphy in the People's Republic see Richard Curt Kraus, *Brushes With Power: Modern Politics and the Chinese Art of Calligraphy* (Berkeley, 1991).

27 The quotation is from a press release titled 'Reunification Monument and Government House Renaming', dated 20 April 1999 and placed on the Hong Kong Government website.

28 The irreverent article referred to is 'Phallic reunification monument defended against attack' ('Yangju huiguibei fang xi'), *Next Magazine*, no. 487 (9 July 1999), p. 117. Zunzi's cartoon is on page 119 of the same issue, and there is also a cartoon about the monument (p. 8). An anonymous but informed architectural critique of the monument ('A Hong Kong invention *in absentia*') is to be found in *Xpressions*, no. 18 (6 May 1999), p. 5.

29 The photo Young used had accompanied an article on Hong Kong public art by Oscar Ho ('City of Make Believe', the photo is on page 48). Young's work was displayed in his one-person show at the John Batten Gallery, 'Works for a Considered Tourist', 14 March to 9 April 2000. I owe this information about the original photographic source to John Batten.

30 See Stella Lee, 'Police chiefs accused of lies on protest role', *South China Morning Post*, 6 June 1998, p. 1. On the same day an editorial ('Policing the police', p. 16) called for the Independent Police Complaints Council to be given greater authority and a statutory status, after it had upheld a complaint against Assistant Police Commissioner Dick Lee Ming-kwai over the playing of loud music on the evening of the handover. The complaint had earlier been rejected by the Police's own in-house complaints body. Police confiscated demonstrators' loudhailers on the occasion of a protest during the national day flag-raising ceremony, 1 October 1999 (see Jo Bowman, 'Officers hurt in scuffle with activists', *South China Morning Post*, 2 October 1999, p. 4). On the protests at the Convention Centre Extension on the second anniversary of the handover (1 July 1999) see Ng Kang-chung, 'Protestors' slogans interrupt celebration', *South China Morning Post*, 2 July 1999, internet edition.

31 See T. J. Clark, 'Preliminaries to a Possible Treatment of Olympia in 1865', *Screen*, XXI/1 (Spring 1980), pp. 18–41.

5 The Visual Production of a Transition

1 Overseas shows to feature contemporary Hong Kong art include *Hong Kong Now!* (Anderson Gallery, School of the Arts, Virginia Commonwealth University, 1997); *Inside Out: New Chinese Art* (a travelling show organized by the Asia Society, New York and the San Francisco Museum of Modern Art, which opened in New York in 1998 at the Asia Society and P.S. 1 Contemporary Art Center); and the First and Second Asia-Pacific Triennial of Contemporary Art, held at the Queensland Art Gallery, Brisbane, in 1993 and 1996 respectively (the third show, held in 1999, did include Hong Kong artist Wilson Shieh amongst the Chinese representatives, but there was no separate representation for Hong Kong in this post-reunification exhibition).

2 Press debates about the new Hong Kong Museum of History can be found in: Angela Li, 'June 4 crackdown will not be ignored, promises chief curator', *South China Morning Post*, 10 January 1998, internet edition; Kevin Kwong, 'Handling of history taxes the curators', *South China Morning Post*, 13 January 1998, p. 9; Angela Li, 'Do they want Tiananmen tank on show, asks curator', *South China Morning Post*, 16 January 1998, internet edition; Victoria Findlay, 'A poor reflection of history', *South China Morning Post*, 13 March 1998, internet edition; Joseph Ting, 'Letter: Adopting lively presentation approach', *South China Morning Post*, 2 April 1998, internet edition. Following the opening of the new Hong Kong Museum of History building a patriotic twentieth-century Chinese history show was held – a co-presentation with the National Museum of Modern Chinese History, Beijing. Titled *Rise of Modern China* (16 September 1999 to 21 November 1999), it included such relics as wreckage from Lin Biao's plane crash. A statue of Lin Zexu (Imperial Commissioner during the Opium War period) was put on display in the new museum in 1999. Displayed as part of an exhibit about Lin

and the Opium War (characteristically treated in Chinese historical narratives
as the beginning of the colonial injustice which the recovery of Hong Kong
ends) it was a sponsored gift to the Museum. Press reports concerning a
proposed Museum of Contemporary Art include: Rodger Lee, 'Row over
approval of art museum design', *South China Morning Post*, 23 September
1997, internet edition; Rodger Lee, 'Museum design contest vetoed', *South
China Morning Post*, 8 October 1997, internet edition; Gren Manuel, 'Row
looms over $196m museum. Leading architect denies supporting design for
Kowloon Park project', *South China Morning Post*, 12 October 1997, internet
edition. Press reports on the controversy over the Hong Kong Stadium
include: So Lai-fun, 'Departments trade blows over stadium', *South China
Morning Post*, 15 April 1994, internet edition; So Lai-fun, 'Cover-up alleged
over stadium', *South China Morning Post*, 30 April 1997, internet edition.

3　On the Central Library controversy see: Rodger Lee, 'Architect defends design
of neo-classical library', *South China Morning Post*, 30 July 1997, p. 4; Rodger
Lee, 'New row as library cost soars to $800 million', *South China Morning
Post*, 2 August 1997, internet edition; Angela Li, 'Call for revamp of vetting
process', *South China Morning Post*, 2 August 1997, internet edition; Wendy
Lim Wan-yee, 'Go back to drawing board, say architects', *South China
Morning Post*, 4 August 1997, internet edition; Rodger Lee, 'Working group
mooted for library', *South China Morning Post*, 5 August 1997, internet
edition; Rodger Lee, 'Working group bid rejected', *South China Morning Post*,
6 August 1997, internet edition; Elisabeth Tacey and Rodger Lee, 'Library row
anger on rise', *South China Morning Post*, 11 August 1997, p. 1; Linda Choy,
'Urbco leader faces grilling on library row accusation of "improper
procedures"', *South China Morning Post*, 14 August 1997, internet edition;
Ng Kang-chung, 'Council hits roof over library façade fiasco', *South China
Morning Post*, 30 September 1999, p. 6; Ng Kang-chung, 'Architects deny
fault over library change', *South China Morning Post*, 6 October 1999,
internet edition.

4　For press reports on the controversy surrounding the Democratic Party's
Legco balcony protest see: Linda Choy, 'Democrats barred from balcony',
South China Morning Post, 27 June 1997, internet edition; 'Balcony row goes
on', *South China Morning Post*, 29 June 1997, internet edition; Angela Li,
'Balcony protest on agenda', *South China Morning Post*, 3 July 1997, internet
edition; Angela Li and No Kwai-yan, 'Democrats' balcony protest
condemned', *South China Morning Post*, 4 July 1997, internet edition; Linda
Choy and Wendy Lim Wan-yee, 'Success part of symbolic gesture', *South
China Morning Post*, 1 August 1997, internet edition.

5　Another borrowing of the *Pillar of Shame* for a new theme occurred in a *Far
Eastern Economic Review* cartoon (11 June 1998, p. 33). A group of
demonstrators gathered around the *Pillar of Shame* are placed next to a group
of people who have lost money due to the post-handover downturn in the
property market. This latter group are gathered round a 'Pillar of Grief'
sculpture.

6　For press coverage of the protests in the Legco public gallery see: Angela Li,
Sharon Cheung and Linda Choy, 'Pre-July 1 laws frozen', *South China
Morning Post*, 17 July 1997, internet edition; Angela Li and Genevieve Ku,
'Gallery protestors may face legal action', *South China Morning Post*, 18 July
1997, internet edition; Angela Li and Sharon Cheung, 'Three face charges
over protest in Legco chamber', *South China Morning Post*, 31 October 1997,
internet edition; Sharon Cheung, 'Activists force way into chamber', *South
China Morning Post*, 8 November 1997, internet edition; Angel Lau, 'Activist
told no politics in court', *South China Morning Post*, 16 November 1997,
internet edition; Michael Wong, 'Unwanted cut in prison sentence', *South*

China Morning Post, 27 May 2000, internet edition; Vicki Kwong, 'Unwanted cut leaves "short hair" defiant', *South China Morning Post*, 9 June 2000, internet edition; Ambrose Leung and Annette Chiu, '"Long Hair" arrested again', *South China Morning Post*, 13 October 2000, p. 4.

7   On the name change see Felix Chan, 'PLA name change for ex-British barracks', *South China Morning Post*, 26 May 2000, internet edition.

8   Cheung Man-kwong's remarks are quoted in Linda Choy, 'Government House funds call', *South China Morning Post*, 8 December 1997, internet edition and May Sin-mi Hon, 'Government House museum rejected', *South China Morning Post*, 27 June 1998, p. 1. Tung's decision not to live in Government House was criticized as early as May 1997, on the grounds that his successors may not have the same private resources as him (see John Flint, 'Government House ideas sought', *South China Morning Post*, 8 May 1997, internet edition). On Tung's decision not to move into Government House see also: Rachel Clarke, 'Military residence may house Tung', *South China Morning Post*, 20 March 1997, internet edition; No Kwai-yan, 'Decision on Government House soon', *South China Morning Post*, 22 March 1997, internet edition; Chris Yeung, 'Post-handover office for Tung selected', *South China Morning Post*, 1 April 1997, internet edition.

9   Even in the colonial era there was often a disparity between the meaning of British and Chinese versions of a road name, with the Chinese names not always carrying colonial associations. On the survival of colonial signifiers after the handover see Arthur Hacker, 'Colonial heritage lives on', *South China Morning Post*, 1 July 1999, p. 15 (which notes suggestions that Victoria Park may be renamed 'Central Park'). See also Simon Buerk, 'Blasts from the past: colonial symbols or cultural icons?', *Sunday Morning Post*, 27 April 1997, Agenda section, p. 3, which discusses the difficulty of deciding whether something is a sign of colonial authority or not, and mentions the government's procedures for dealing with British symbols on public buildings. Similar issues are treated in Bruce Gilley, 'Effacing empire', *Far Eastern Economic Review*, 12 June 1997, pp. 28–9. On the placement in museums of items removed from use because they bore connotations of British sovereignty, see John Flint, 'Colonial corner for museums', *South China Morning Post*, 16 July 1997, internet edition. On the proposal that Government House might become a museum, see Ng Kang-chung, 'China Gifts "for Government House show"', *South China Morning Post*, 24 June 1997, internet edition; 'Editorial: Government House', *South China Morning Post*, 10 November 1997, internet edition; Wanda Szeto, 'Public "should be given access to colonial HQ"', *South China Morning Post*, 10 November 1997, internet edition. On the renaming issue see 'SAR to play the name game again', *Hong Kong Standard*, 7 May 1999, p. 4; No Kwai-yan, '"Impartial Grandpa Tung" lost for words in the name game', *South China Morning Post*, 7 May 1999, p. 6; Angela Li, 'Pressure on not to demote governors' house to a cottage', *South China Morning Post*, 8 May 1999, p. 6; Angela Li, 'Don't rename Government House says tourist industry', *South China Morning Post*, 29 May 1999, p. 3; Angela Li, 'Touch of Purple urged for Government House', *South China Morning Post*, 2 June 1999, p. 6; Samantha Wong and Angela Li, 'Government House to be "Guest House"', *South China Morning Post*, 25 June 1999, internet edition.

10   John Major, quoted in Chris Yeung, 'Major and Li seal HK airport deal', *South China Morning Post*, 4 September 1991, p. 3.

11   Secretary for Land and Works, Graham Barnes, admitted the importance of the time factor in selecting the site for the airport in Fanny Wong, 'Lantau site tipped for new airport', *South China Morning Post*, 22 August 1989, p. 3.

12   The float also featured a model of the Bank of China. For pictures see No

Kwai-yan, 'Float leaves sinking feeling', *South China Morning Post*, 2 October 1999, p. 4 and *Hong Kong 1999* (Hong Kong, 2000), colour photo section following page vi.

13 The airport opening fiasco is discussed in numerous newspaper reports, including Norma Connoly, Mukul Munish and Lauretta Wong, 'Anatomy of a disaster', *Hong Kong Standard*, 12 July 1998, p. 1.

14 So Hing Keung's manipulated cityscape images are documented in *This Mortal Coil: So Hing Keung's Alienated Urban Landscape Photographs* (Hong Kong, 1999). A sense of alienation is found in many other nocturnal cityscape images by So, although this series is the first in which he has directly manipulated the images to such an extent.

15 A pairing of the Hong Kong Bank and the Bank of China on HK$1.60 stamps issued to celebrate the establishment of the Hong Kong Special Administrative Region also seems predicated on an understanding of them as political symbols of Britain and China respectively.

16 Colour is also used to introduce political associations in Shen Ping's *Skyscrapers* (1996), a work included in the patriotic show *Reunion and Vision: Contemporary Hong Kong Art*, held at the Hong Kong Museum of Art just after the handover (11 July to 17 August 1997). Here the Hong Kong skyline is represented schematically by a group of buildings, in which the Bank of China features prominently. All the buildings have turned red as if out of patriotic fervor, symbolizing the return of Hong Kong to Chinese Communist rule. A red Bank of China also features in Ricky Yeung's *Danger* of 1992, although here a very different political perspective is being taken. This installation work features a red sign reading 'danger' (such as might be found where roadworks are taking place) and a photographic image showing a red-tinged Bank of China looming over the Legislative Council Building. Recent Hong Kong architecture also features in other works by Lucia Cheung: see for example *Golden Section* (1997), a painting largely executed in a 'traditional' Chinese ink landscape style that appears to depict the Tsing Ma Bridge. This work is illustrated in *Exhibition 6.30* (Hong Kong, 1997), the unpaginated catalogue of a handover-related exhibition held at the gallery between 20 and 30 June 1997. Hong Kong-born Australian artist John Young depicts Chek Lap Kok airport in three canvases dating from 2000 which were exhibited at the John Batten Gallery between 14 March and 9 April 2000 (in the one-person show *Works for a Considered Tourist*). In each of these paintings the terminal building itself is relegated to the background, rather than being celebrated as an architectural masterwork, and atmospheric effects dominate because of the low horizons. The pall of smog which hangs in the air clearly evokes the post-handover mood of malaise.

17 Perhaps some clarification of terms is warranted: the dress is 'Western-style' rather than 'Western' since the actual origin of the specific design and the place of manufacture of the items themselves are not particularly important – it is the signification carried which is being referred to. Even if the clothing is locally produced, or sold by a local company whose name (unlike, say, that of local clothing chain Giordano) does not have any specific Western associations, it will still be perceived as 'Western' dress (even by local Chinese consumers who never wear anything else). Almost by definition 'Western' dress is 'modern' in the Hong Kong context, since 'Chinese' dress occupies the position of being 'traditional'. While some clothing items may engage with contemporary Western-led fashion trends, even an item of dress that would bear few modern associations in London or New York – say a classic business suit – partakes of modernity in Hong Kong. Indeed even a 'traditional' white wedding dress would be in some sense modern in Hong Kong.

18 For an analysis of the beginnings of Hong Kong modern design in fashion as well as other areas see Matthew Turner, '60s/90s: Dissolving the People' and 'The Festival of Fashions 1967: Designing a Hong Kong Identity', both in Matthew Turner and Irene Ngan, eds, *Hong Kong Sixties: Designing Identity* (Hong Kong, 1995), pp. 13–34 and pp. 104–5 respectively. For an anthropological study of the Hong Kong fashion world in the late 1990s see Lise Skov, *Stories of World Fashion and the Hong Kong Fashion World*, PhD thesis, University of Hong Kong, 2000.

19 A photo of Jiang in his Mao suit appeared in *South China Morning Post*, 2 October 1999, p. 3. For a critique of the 50th anniversary parade see Jasper Becker, 'Jarring Throwback to naïve, disgraced era', *South China Morning Post*, 2 October 1999, p. 5. For an account of the event see Jasper Becker, 'Jiang elevated to Mao status', *South China Morning Post*, 2 October 1999, p. 1.

20 The cheungsam, although nowadays usually 'traditionally Chinese' in its associations, is a dress of twentieth-century creation. See Naomi Yin-yin Szeto, 'Cheungsam: Fashion, Culture and Gender' and Hazel Clark and Agnes Wong, 'Who Still Wears the Cheungsam?', both in Claire Roberts, ed., *Evolution & Revolution: Chinese Dress 1700s–1990s* (Sydney, 1997), pp. 54–64 and pp. 65–73 respectively, and Hazel Clark, *The Cheongsam* (Oxford/New York/Hong Kong, 2000). In Wong Kar-wai's movie *In the Mood for Love* (2000) a series of stylish cheungsams worn by actress Maggie Cheung are foregrounded very strongly to the viewer's attention, and made to function by context more as signifiers of a certain lost era of modern Hong Kong history than as signifiers of a generalized 'Chineseness'.

21 Turner, '60s/90s: Dissolving the People', p. 26, quotes fashion designers Ragence Lam and Eddie Lau expressing a patriotic sense of belonging at some point between the Joint Declaration and 4 June 1989.

22 A Chinese flag juxtaposed with a British one (and meant to be read as in the process of overlapping it) is also found in a T-shirt design by New York-based artist Zhang Hongtu (see *Public Culture*, IX/3 (Spring 1997), p. 420). Pacino Wan's handover-related work is discussed and illustrated (along with that of Peter Lau) in Claire Roberts, 'Fashion Cultures: Contemporary Chinese Dress', in Roberts, ed., *Evolution & Revolution*, pp. 88–102.

23 Tsang's graffiti was again featured in an art context when photographs of it were included in the travelling exhibition *Cities on the Move*, curated by Hou Hanru and Hans-Ulrich Obrist, which was at London's Hayward Gallery 13 May to 17 June 1999. Actual examples of his writing were included in *Power of the Word*, curated by Chang Tsong-Zung at the Taipei Museum of Art, Taichung, Taiwan (May 22 to August 29 1999). An example of international press coverage of Tsang on the occasion of Lau's exhibit is Keith B. Richburg, '"King of Kowloon": Graffiti Artist, 76, Writes On', *International Herald Tribune*, 13 May 1997, p. 20.

24 On Hong Kong's cultural fascination with Shanghai in the pre-handover years see also Leo Lee, *Shanghai Modern: The Flowering of a New Urban Culture in China, 1930–1945*, (Cambridge, MA, 1999), Chapter 10. Lee's study of the flowering of literary modernism in Shanghai during the 1930s has some parallels with the project of the present book. In both cases the cultural expressions of a Chinese city under colonial rule are studied, and an argument is made that those expressions cannot be adequately understood as colonial, even where they make use of Western elements. Lee shows a Western-influenced modernism in the service of a national cultural project, however, whereas the present study has been more concerned to document a critique of national discourse. For a more condensed presentation of Lee's position see Leo Lee, 'Shanghai Modern: Reflections on Urban Culture in

China in the 1930s', *Public Culture*, XI/1 (Winter 1999), pp. 75–107.

25 The other post-handover 'countdown' phenomenon was of course the millennium. Perhaps because of a sense of déjà vu, it appeared to attract a lot less enthusiasm in Hong Kong than many other cities. One advert for a millennium party at the Regent Hotel seemed to recall handover parties by its playful invocation of the Joint Declaration language ('one party, two centuries').

26 Two other shortlisted designs for the flag (also featuring the Bauhinia flower) were illustrated in 'Designs for future flag leave public cold', *Hong Kong Standard*, 15 February 1990, p. 4. One of the designs showed a Bauhinia flower inside a five-pointed star. Both the other designs had red, white and blue in them, and so can be said to have contained more of a reference to Hong Kong's colonial era than the chosen design.

27 Freeman Lau's censored design was a poster for a Zuni Icosohedron performance 'Two or Three Events ... of No Significance, Hong Kong 1995', which had been presented by the Urban Council. The Bauhinia emblem is depicted as if on the hat of an enthroned Chinese Emperor.

28 See Yenni Kwok, 'Web flag "vandals" stay one click ahead of law', *South China Morning Post*, 3 October 2000, internet edition.

29 For press reports on the removal of Taiwanese flags, see 'Flap over flying Taiwan flags', *South China Morning Post*, 8 August 1997, internet edition; Ng Kang-Chung, 'Display Flouted "one country" principle and broke law, say officials. Outrage as police tear down flags', *South China Morning Post*, 11 October 1997, internet edition; Linda Choy and May Sin-mi Hon, 'Anxiety aroused by Taiwan flags: Tung', *South China Morning Post*, 14 October 1997, internet edition. On successful display of the Taiwan flag (or a representation of it) on 10 October 2000, see 'One China idea hard to accept: Taipei "Envoy"', *South China Morning Post*, 11 October 2000, p. 6 and Carmen Cheung and Joan Yip, 'Taipei envoy expected soon', *Hong Kong iMail*, 11 October 2000, p. A5 (both with photos).

30 Peter Lau's statement is quoted from Emma Batha, 'Jail before censorship, vows fashion designer', *South China Morning Post*, 17 July 1997, internet edition. On the HKFDA incident see Tsang Fan, 'Post-1997 Fashion Taboo', *Ming Pao*, 14 October 1997, p. D5.

31 Michael Suen, quoted in Wendy Lim Wan-yee, 'Laws mulled on disrespect to flag', *South China Morning Post*, 21 August 1997, internet edition.

32 On the dolphin mascot's adoption see: Linda Choy, 'White dolphin mascot leaps into 1997 role', *South China Morning Post*, 21 August 1996, internet edition.

33 A cartoon by Zunzi executed on the day after the handover shows a man at home watching the event on television, wearing an 'I love Hong Kong' T-shirt and a pair of Union Jack shorts. As the anthem is played at midnight for the ceremonial lowering of the British flag, he discovers that his shorts have also fallen to half-mast. Zunzi was one of a group of Hong Kong and Macanese artists and performers who were arrested a couple of hours after the Macau handover ceremony at midnight 19 December 1999, while staging street theatre. The arrests took place near the Leal Senado (the Municipal Council building in the ceremonial heart of Macau) as preparations were underway for a performance. At an earlier performance, which took place within about an hour of the handover near the ruins of St Paul's cathedral, Zunzi used a cardboard box mask with a cartoon face of Jiang Zemin on it. All the detained artists and performers were released without charge the next day (telephone interview with Zunzi, 5 May, 2000).

Epilogue

1 The chicken flu episode was the theme of a satirical exhibition curated by Leung Foong, Phoebe Wong and Christa Suc, *Weird Chicken Show*, Hong Kong Arts Centre, 20 December 1999 to 5 January 2000.

2 President Jiang Zemin had already made an issue of reunification with Taiwan in his Tiananmen Square address on 1 October 1999, the 50th anniversary of the founding of the People's Republic (see Vivien Pik-kwan Chan, 'Pledge on unity with Taiwan', *South China Morning Post*, 2 October 1999, p. 3). Jiang reiterated his desire to settle the Taiwan question in a speech at the Macau handover ceremony, delivered on 20 December 1999 immediately following the midnight transfer of sovereignty (see Niall Frazer and Stella Lee, 'Taiwan next, vows Jiang as Macau returns to China', *South China Morning Post*, 20 December 1999, internet edition). In earlier speeches peaceful reunification was emphasized, but following the election of Chen Shui-bian of the Democratic Progressive Party as Taiwan's new president on 18 March 2000 (he took office on 20 May) military threats were to come to the fore.

3 Young Hay, 'Travelogue', in *Bonjour, Young Hay (After Courbet)* (Hong Kong, 2000), p. 27.

4 Tiananmen Square reopened on 28 June 1999 (see *Hong Kong Standard*, 29 June 1999, p. 5 for a photo). See also Associated Press, 'Hammers and trucks replace guns, tanks', *South China Morning Post*, 4 June 1999, p. 6. The 50th anniversary of the PRC on 1 October 1999 was the occasion for the makeover of the Square. Fragments of the Square's old pavement were sent to leaders of more than 170 countries as millennium gifts.

5 On the Hong Kong clock, and Tiananmen Square after the 1989 crackdown, see Wu Hung, 'The Hong Kong Clock – Public Time-Telling and Political Time/Space', *Public Culture*, IX/3 (Spring 1997), pp. 329–54. A Macau countdown clock started running in the same location as its Hong Kong predecessor on 5 May 1998.

6 On the China Millennium Monument see Staff Reporter, 'Monument down-to-earth tribute', *South China Morning Post*, 20 June 1999, p. 6 (which also features a photo) and Jasper Becker, 'Beijing rings in new to patriotic chimes', *South China Morning Post*, 1 January 2000, internet edition. On the National Theatre see Mark O'Neill, 'National Theatre site busy despite bubble of doubt', *South China Morning Post*, 4 April 2000, internet edition and Mark O'Neill, 'National Theatre architect confident of green light', *Sunday Morning Post*, 10 December 2000, p. 7.

7 On Falun Gong protests in Tiananmen Square see for example Associated Press, 'Tiananmen police grab sect suspects', *South China Morning Post*, 30 September 1999, p. 10; Agencies and Stella Lee, 'Sect members beaten, hauled from square', *South China Morning Post*, 30 October 1999, p. 1; Jasper Becker and Agencies, 'Sect outwits police to mark sit-in', *South China Morning Post*, 26 April 2000, internet edition; Agencies, 'Flags prompt "birthday bash"', *South China Morning Post*, 12 May 2000, internet edition; Staff Reporters and Agencies, 'Cult protests upstage festivities', *South China Morning Post*, 2 October 2000; 'Harsh police action ends sect protest', Associated Press report, *South China Morning Post*, 27 October 2000, internet edition; Agence France-Presse, 'Police wade into sect followers as protests continue', *South China Morning Post*, 30 October 2000, internet edition and Agencies in Beijing, 'Tiananmen sect protest crushed', *South China Morning Post*, 2 January 2001, internet edition. On public protests on the occasion of the tenth anniversary of the Tiananmen crackdown see Staff Reporters, 'Police prevent public memorials', *South China Morning Post*, 4 June 1999, p. 6, and

Jasper Becker and Agencies, 'Protest pair defy security stranglehold', *South China Morning Post*, 5 June 1999, p. 8. Dissidents apparently called upon people to mark the tenth anniversary by minor acts such as wearing plain clothing or lighting candles. On security in the Square for the 50th anniversary of the PRC see Agence Presse-France, 'Capital transformed into forbidden city', *South China Morning Post*, 30 September 1999, p. 10. Falun Gong protests also occurred in Hong Kong: on 1 October 2000 there was a National Day protest adjacent to the Convention and Exhibition Centre Extension (on the opposite side of the 'moat' surrounding it) and on 13 January 2001 protests took place around the time of an international Falun Gong conference. More than 800 practitioners marched from Chater Garden (adjoining the Legislative Council Building) to Beijing's Liaison Office in Happy Valley, a mass meditation in Victoria Park having taken place earlier in the day (see Agnes Lam, 'Sect march on Beijing office', *Sunday Morning Post*, 14 January 2001, p. 1).

Bibliography

Abbas, Ackbar, 'Cultural Studies in a Postculture', in *Disciplinarity and Dissent in Cultural Studies*, ed. Cary Nelson and Dilip Parameshwar Gaonkar (New York and London, 1996), pp. 289–312
——, *Hong Kong: Culture and the Politics of Disappearance* (Hong Kong, 1997)
Appadurai, Arjun, *Modernity at Large: Cultural Dimensions of Globalization* (Minneapolis and London, 1998)
Apple Daily
Baker, Hugh, 'The English Sandwich: Obscenity, Punning and Bilingualism in Hong Kong Cantonese', in *Interpreting Culture Through Translation. A Festschrift for D. C. Lau*, ed. Roger Ames *et al.* (Hong Kong, 1991), pp. 37–58
Bhabha, Homi, *The Location of Culture* (London, 1994)
Blyth, Sally, and Ian Wotherspoon, *Hong Kong Remembers* (Hong Kong, 1996)
Cameron, Nigel, *Hong Kong: The Cultured Pearl* (Hong Kong, 1978)
——, 'Hong Kong: The Development of Modern Art', in *Hong Kong Art Review* ed. Oscar Ho and Eric Wear (Hong Kong, 1999), pp. 60–65
Chakrabarty, Dipesh, 'Postcoloniality and the Artifice of History: Who Speaks for "Indian" Pasts?', *Representations*, XXXVII (Winter 1992), pp. 1–26
Chan, Luis, 'The Hong Kong Artists' Group', *The Studio*, CXLVIII (July 1954), pp. 84–7
——, 'In conversation', in *Luis Chan at Eighty* (Hong Kong, Hanart 2, 1985)
Chan, Raymond, *Hong Kong. 1986–1997.1.1. The Works of Raymond Chan* (Hong Kong, 1997)
Chan Yuk-keung, 'About "Ghost Encounter"', in *Ghost Encounter*, Para/Site (Hong Kong, 1998)
Chang Tsong-zung, 'Visionaries and Icon Painters: One Aspect of Hong Kong Contemporary Art', *Renditions*, nos 29/30 ['Special Issue: Hong Kong'] (Spring and Autumn 1988), pp. 275–92
——, 'Reversing Horizons', in *Exhibition 6.30* (Hong Kong, 1997), unpaginated
——, 'The Inverted Laboratory of Ho Siu-kee', in *Hong Kong Art Review*, ed. Oscar Ho and Eric Wear (Hong Kong, 1999), pp. 104–6
——, 'The Secret Artist – Is Hong Kong Art the True Underground?', *Art Planet: A Global View of Art Criticism*, 1/0 (1999), pp. 178–81. Also published in Eric Wear and Lisa Cheung (eds), *Private Content: Public View* (Hong Kong, 1997), pp. 82–8
Cheng Miu Bing, Christina, 'Resurgent Chinese Power in Postmodern Disguise: The New Bank of China Buildings in Hong Kong and Macau', in *Hong Kong: The Anthropology of a Chinese Metropolis*, ed. Grant Evans and Maria Tam (Richmond, Surrey, 1997), pp. 102–23
Cheung, Juanita, and Andrew Yeoh, *Hong Kong: A Guide to Recent Architecture* (London, 1998)
Cheung, Martha, ed., *Hong Kong Collage. Contemporary Stories and Writing* (Hong Kong, 1998)
Chinese Painting by Irene Chou (Hong Kong, Fung Ping Shan Museum, 1986)
Chiu, Karl and Wong Kan Tai, *Beijing Story* (Hong Kong, 1999)
City Vibrance: Recent Works in Western Media by Hong Kong Artists (Hong Kong, Urban Council, 1992)
Clark, Hazel, *The Cheongsam* (Oxford/New York/Hong Kong, 2000)
——, and Agnes Wong, 'Who Still Wears the Cheungsam?', in *Evolution & Revolution: Chinese Dress 1700s–1990s*, ed. Claire Roberts (Sydney, 1997), pp. 65–73

Clark, T. J., 'Preliminaries to a Possible Treatment of *Olympia* in 1865', *Screen*, XXI/1 (Spring 1980), pp. 18–41
——, *Image of the People* (London, 1982)
Clarke, David, *The Influence of Oriental Thought on Postwar American Painting and Sculpture* (New York, 1988)
——, 'The All-Over Image: Meaning in Abstract Art', *Journal of American Studies*, XXVII/3 (1993), pp. 355–75
——, 'The Calligraphic Spirit and Modern American Art', in *Eloquent Line* (Washington, DC, International Sculpture Center, 1993)
——, *Art and Place: Essays on Art From a Hong Kong Perspective* (Hong Kong, 1996)
——, 'Art Gets in Trouble with the Law in Hong Kong', *Art AsiaPacific*, III/2 (April 1996), pp. 32–3.
——, 'Art in a Shifting Frame: Economics, Politics and Visual Culture in Hong Kong', *West Coast Line*, no. 21 (Winter 1996–7), pp. 75–9
——, 'Ellen Pau', in *The Second Asia-Pacific Triennial of Contemporary Art* (Brisbane, Queensland Art Gallery, 1996), p. 70
——, 'Art in Private and in Public (and the Public and Private in Art)', in *Private Content: Public View*, ed. Eric Wear and Lisa Cheung (Hong Kong, 1997), pp. 60–67
——, 'Hong Kong Art and the Transfer of Sovereignty', *The Journal of the Oriental Society of Australia*, XXIX (1997), pp. 1–21
——, 'Varieties of Cultural Hybridity: Hong Kong Art in the Late Colonial Era', *Public Culture*, IX/3 (Spring 1997), pp. 395–415
——, 'Found in Transit: Hong Kong Art in a Time of Change', in *Inside Out: New Chinese Art*, ed. Gao Minglu (Berkeley, 1998), pp. 175–81
——, 'Breaking Down Barriers: The Art of Kwok Mang Ho', in *Kwok – Art Life for 30 Years, 1967–1997* (Hong Kong, 1999), pp. 13–14
——, 'Painting with Words: The Forgotten Dialogue Between Art and Literature', *Postwest*, no. 15 (1999), pp. 18–22
——, 'Remembrance and Forgetting: Aspects of Art and Public Space in Hong Kong during the Handover Period', *TAASA Review* [The Journal of the Asian Arts Society of Australia], VIII/1 (March 1999), pp. 14–15
——, 'The Hong Kong Convention and Exhibition Centre Extension', *Public Culture*, XI/3 (Fall 1999), pp. 566–9
——, 'Artist-run Spaces and the Development of Hong Kong Art', *USEby Asia Pacific Artist Initiatives Project* (Melbourne, 2000), pp. 12–14
——, *Modern Chinese Art* (Oxford/New York/Hong Kong, 2000)
——, 'Para/Site Art Space: Installation and Cultural Identity in Hong Kong', *Third Text*, L (Spring 2000), pp. 73–86
——, 'The Culture of a Border Within: Hong Kong Art and China', *Art Journal*, LIX/2 (Summer 2000), pp. 88–101
——, 'Subaltern Writing. Tsang Tsou Choi: The King of Kowloon', *Art AsiaPacific*, no. 29 (2001), pp. 68–71
Cohn, Don J., ed., *Vignettes from the Chinese* (Hong Kong, 1987)
Contemporary Hong Kong Art Biennial, 1989 (Hong Kong, 1989)
Contemporary Hong Kong Art Biennial, 1996 (Hong Kong, 1996)
Eastern Express
Elizabeth Frink – Sculpture and Drawings (Hong Kong, Hong Kong Land Property Company Ltd, 1989)
Evans, Grant, 'Ghosts and the New Governor', in *Hong Kong: The Anthropology of a Chinese Metropolis*, ed. Grant Evans and Maria Tam Siu-mi (Richmond, Surrey, 1997), pp. 267–96
Exhibition 6.30 (Hong Kong, Hanart TZ Gallery, 1997)
Far Eastern Economic Review
Fisher, Jean, 'Editorial', *Third Text*, XXXII (Autumn 1995), pp. 3–7

Fong, Susan, ed., *The Art of Antonio Mak* (Hong Kong, 1995)
Gao Minglu, ed., *Inside Out: New Chinese Art* (Berkeley, 1998)
Hall, Stuart, 'Cultural Identity and Diaspora', in *Identity: Community, Culture, Difference*, ed. Jonathan Rutherford (London, 1990)
Hardt, Michael, and Antonio Negri, *Empire* (Cambridge, MA and London, 2000)
Henry, Gérard, 'César: "C'est un Symbole de liberté, un Icare en quelque sorte"', *Paroles*, no. 167 (July–August 1999), p. 35
Hinterthür, Petra, *Modern Art in Hong Kong* (Hong Kong, 1985)
Ho, Oscar, 'Installation: New Possibilities, New Crises', in *Private Content: Public View*, ed. Eric Wear and Lisa Cheung (Hong Kong, 1997), pp. 18–22
——, 'The Long Road Back Home', *Art AsiaPacific*, no. 15 (1997), pp. 48–53
——, 'Inventing History', in *Hong Kong Art Review*, ed. Oscar Ho and Eric Wear (Hong Kong, 1999), pp. 46–53
——, 'City of Make Believe', *Art AsiaPacific*, no. 25 (2000), pp. 46–9
——, and Eric Wear, eds., *Hong Kong Art Review* (Hong Kong, 1999)
Ho Siu-kee, *[Body Schema]* (Macao, 2000)
Hobbs, Robert, *Hong Kong Now!* (Seattle, 1997)
Hobsbawm, E., and T. Ranger, eds, *The Invention of Tradition* (Cambridge, 1983)
Hong Kong 1999 (Hong Kong, 2000)
Hong Kong Art, 1970–1980 (Hong Kong, 1981)
Hong Kong Artists. Volume I (Hong Kong, 1995)
Hong Kong Convention and Exhibition Centre Extension: Poised for Flight (HKCECE Project Review) (Hong Kong, Building Journal/China Building Development, 1997)
Hong Kong Economic Journal
Hong Kong iMail
Hong Kong in Ink Moods: Landscape Paintings by Lui Shou-kwan (Hong Kong, Fung Ping Shan Museum, 1985)
Hou Hanru and Hans-Ulrich Obrist, eds, *Cities on the Move* (London, 1999)
In Search of Art (Hong Kong, Hong Kong Arts Centre, 1990)
Invisible Cities (Hong Kong, Hong Kong Arts Centre, 1998)
Journey to Returnification [sic] (Hong Kong, Provisional Urban Council, 1998)
Kraus, Richard Curt, *Brushes With Power: Modern Politics and the Chinese Art of Calligraphy* (Berkeley, 1991)
Laclau, Ernesto, *New Reflections on the Revolution of Our Time* (London, 1990)
——, and Chantal Mouffe, *Hegemony and Socialist Strategy* (London, 1985)
Lai, Edwin, and Jack Lee, 'A Chronology of Visual Arts Activities in Hong Kong, 1900–1930', in *Besides: A Journal of Art History and Criticism*, The Workshop/Hong Kong Art History Research Society, no. 1 (Hong Kong, 1997), pp. 135–230
Lai Mei-lin, Eliza, *Words and Images in Contemporary Hong Kong Art: 1984–1997*, M.Phil. thesis, Hong Kong University, 2000
Lau, Freeman, *Looking Back: Freeman Lau's Poster Design* (Hong Kong, 1999)
Lau Kin Wai, ed., *Cultural Chop Shui I* (Hong Kong, 1995)
——, ed., *Cultural Chop Shui II* (Hong Kong, 1996)
——, ed., *The Street Calligraphy of Tsang Tsou Choi* (Hong Kong, 1997)
Lee Ka-sing, *Forty Poems: Photographs 1995–1998* (Hong Kong, 1998)
Lee, Leo, 'Shanghai Modern: Reflections on Urban Culture in China in the 1930s', *Public Culture*, XI/1 (Winter 1999), pp. 75–107
——, *Shanghai Modern: the Flowering of a New Urban Culture in China, 1930–1945* (Cambridge, MA, 1999)
Lee Sai Chong, Jack, *Painting in Western Media in Early Twentieth Century Hong Kong*, M.Phil. thesis, Hong Kong University, 1996
Leung Chi Wo, Warren, *Visible Invisible* (Hong Kong, 1997)
——, 'The Native Sense of History', in *Hello! Hong Kong – Part 7* (Hong Kong, 1997), pp. 32–5

Leung, Simon with Janet A. Kaplan, 'Pseudo-Languages: A Conversation with Wenda Gu, Xu Bing and Jonathan Hay', *Art Journal*, LVIII/3 (Fall 1999), pp. 86–99
Li, Tim, and Kacey Wong, eds, *Home* (Hong Kong, 1999)
Lilley, Rozanna, 'Treading the Margins: Performing Hong Kong', in *Hong Kong: The Anthropology of a Chinese Metropolis*, eds Grant Evans and Maria Tam Siu-mi (Richmond, Surrey, 1997), pp. 124–47
——, *Staging Hong Kong: Gender and Performance in Transition* (Richmond, 1998)
—— 'The Hong Kong Handover', *Communal/Plural*, VIII/2 (2000), pp. 161–80
Luis Chan and his Vision (Hong Kong, Hanart Gallery Inc. and Hanart 2, 1990)
Luis Chan: Urban Geography (Taipei, Shin Kong Mitsukoshi Department Store and Hanart (Taipei) Gallery, 1993)
Maharaj, Sarat, '"Perfidious Fidelity": The Untranslatability of the Other', *Global Visions: Towards a New Internationalism in the Visual Arts* (London, 1994), pp. 28–35
McFarlane, Scott Toguri, and Henry Tsang, eds, *City at the End of Time: Hong Kong 1997* (Vancouver, 1998)
Ming Pao
Moss, Peter, *Skylines: Hong Kong* (Hong Kong, 2000)
Museum 97: History. Community. Individual (Hong Kong, Hong Kong Arts Centre, 1997)
National Treasures – Gems of China's Cultural Relics (Hong Kong, Provisional Urban Council, 1997)
Next Magazine
Ng, Sylvia S. Y., ed., *The Metropolis – Visual Research into Contemporary Hong Kong (1990–1996)* (Hong Kong, 1996)
Papastergiadis, Nikos, 'Restless Hybrids', *Third Text*, XXXII (Autumn 1995), pp. 9–18
Paulson, Ronald, *Representations of Revolution (1789–1820)* (New Haven and London, 1983)
Power of the Word (Taichung, Taiwan Museum of Art, 2000)
Purdom, Judy, 'Mapping Difference', *Third Text*, XXXII (Autumn 1995), pp. 19–32
Reunion and Vision: Contemporary Hong Kong Art (Hong Kong, Provisional Urban Council, 1997)
Roberts, Claire, 'Fashion Cultures: Contemporary Chinese Dress', in *Evolution & Revolution: Chinese Dress 1700s–1990s*, ed. Claire Roberts (Sydney, 1997), pp. 88–102
Robertson, Philip, 'Of Mimicry and Mermaids: Hong Kong and the Documentary Film Legacy', in *Hong Kong: The Anthropology of a Chinese Metropolis*, ed. Grant Evans and Maria Tam Siu-mi (Richmond, Surrey, 1997), pp. 77–101
Scott, Ian, *Political Change and the Crisis of Legitimacy in Hong Kong* (Hong Kong, 1989)
Shen, Joanne, 'Why Does This Man See Red?', *HK Magazine*, issue 158, vol. 6, no. 35, 14 February 1997, pp. 6–11
Skov, Lise, *Stories of World Fashion and the Hong Kong Fashion World*, PhD thesis, University of Hong Kong, 2000
So Hing Keung, *This Mortal Coil: So Hing Keung's Alienated Urban Landscape Photographs* (Hong Kong, 1999)
South China Morning Post (internet edition with archive at www.scmp.com)
Steiner, Henry, and Ken Haas, eds, *Cross-cultural Design: Communicating in the Global Marketplace* (New York, 1995)
Sullivan, Michael, *Art and Artists of Twentieth-Century China* (Berkeley, 1996)
Sunday Morning Post
Szeto, Naomi Yin-yin, 'Cheungsam: Fashion, Culture and Gender', in *Evolution & Revolution: Chinese Dress 1700s–1990s*, ed. Claire Roberts (Sydney, 1997), pp. 54–64
Tang, William, and Peter Wong, *Hong Kong Fashion Allure 50 Years* (Hong Kong, 1997)

The Art of Van Lau (Hong Kong, Urban Council, 1987)
The Blues: Photographs by Alfred Ko (Hong Kong, 1997)
The Hongkong Standard
The New Face of Hong Kong (Hong Kong, University Museum and Art Gallery, 1998)
The Third Asia-Pacific Triennial of Contemporary Art (Brisbane, Queensland Art Gallery, 1999)
Tiananmen Memorial Art Exhibition (Washington, DC, Congressional Human Rights Foundation, 1990)
Tsang Tak-ping, Kith, ed., *Hello! Hong Kong – Part 7* (Hong Kong, 1997)
——, *Hello! Hong Kong*, MA thesis, De Montfort University, England, 1997
——, ed., *Ma'am's Box* (Hong Kong, 2000)
——, ed., *Terraces Topography* (Hong Kong, 2000)
Turner, Matthew, '60s/90s: Dissolving the People', in *Hong Kong Sixties: Designing Identity*, ed. Matthew Turner and Irene Ngan (Hong Kong, 1995), pp. 13–34
——, 'The Festival of Fashions 1967: Designing a Hong Kong Identity', in *Hong Kong Sixties: Designing Identity*, ed. Matthew Turner and Irene Ngan (Hong Kong, 1995), pp. 104–5
Van Over, Raymond, ed., *I Ching* (New York, 1971)
Wang Hai (Hong Kong, Alisan Fine Arts Ltd, 1994)
Wark, McKenzie, 'Vectors of Memory ... Seeds of Fire. The Western Media and the Beijing Demonstrations', *New Formations*, x (Spring 1990), pp. 1–11
Wear, Eric, and Lisa Cheung, eds, *Private Content: Public View* (Hong Kong, 1997)
Welsh, Frank, *A History of Hong Kong* (London, 1993)
Wong, Wucius, *Principles of Two-Dimensional Design* (Hong Kong, 1969)
——, 'Chinese Painting in Hong Kong', in *Twentieth-Century Chinese Painting*, ed. Kao Mayching (Hong Kong, 1988), pp. 210–23
Wucius Wong: Recent Painting (Hong Kong, Hong Kong Land Property Company Ltd, 1990)
Wu Hung, 'Tiananmen Square: A Political History of Monuments', *Representations*, xxxv (Summer 1991), pp. 84–117
——, *Monumentality in Early Chinese Art and Architecture* (Stanford, 1995)
——, 'The Hong Kong Clock – Public Time-Telling and Political Time/Space', *Public Culture*, ix/3 (Spring 1997), pp. 329–54
——, 'Ruins, Fragmentation, and the Chinese Modern/Postmodern', in *Inside Out: New Chinese Art*, ed. Gao Minglu (Berkeley, 1998), pp. 59–66
——, *Transience: Chinese Experimental Art at the End of the Twentieth Century* (Chicago, 1999)
Xpressions
Young Artist Association, eds, *Pre '97 Special Arts Zone* (Hong Kong, 1996)
Young Hay, *Bonjour, Young Hay (After Courbet)* (Hong Kong, 2000)
Yu Siu-wah, 'The Revitalization of Imperial Symbols in the 1997 Reunion of Hong Kong with China', *Hong Kong Cultural Studies Bulletin*, no. 8/9 (Spring/Summer 1998), pp. 84–91

Acknowledgements

In the writing of this book, I have incurred innumerable debts. Above all, I am grateful to the artists for their willingness to discuss their work with me, formally and informally, as well as to provide me with visual material and other documentation necessary for my study. Visual material has also kindly been provided by a number of galleries, museums and other bodies, and I would like to thank them all for their help. Full acknowledgements are given in the Photographic Acknowledgements.

During the time I worked on this manuscript, I benefited from the opportunity to exchange ideas about contemporary Hong Kong culture with a great number of people, and these interlocutors influenced my own understanding to an immeasurable extent. Among those to whom I feel a particular intellectual debt are Ackbar Abbas, Oscar Ho, Leung Ping Kwan and Matthew Turner. I also learned a lot in discussion with those of my postgraduate students who had written theses on aspects of Hong Kong art, namely Edwin Lai, Eliza Lai, Jack Lee and Eric Wear.

Efficient help with assembling the research materials I draw upon in this study was given by Chan Kuen-on. Practical support was willingly offered by Karen Leung, Edwin Leung, Grace Wong and Yan Pui Ling of the Department of Fine Arts of the University of Hong Kong; this book could not have been completed without their assistance.

Financial support to enable the research on which this book is based was given by the Committee on Research and Conference Grants of the University of Hong Kong and by the Hong Kong Research Grants Council (in the form of an Earmarked Grant for Research, project number HKU 7176/00H). The former grant enabled the initiation of this research, while the latter allowed me to bring it to completion.

Earlier versions of certain parts of this book were published in a number of journals, and I am grateful to the respective editors for giving me the opportunity to test my ideas before an audience in this way. Kind permission has been given by Duke University Press to reproduce material previously published as 'Varieties of Cultural Hybridity: Hong Kong Art in the Late Colonial Era', *Public Culture*, IX/3 (Spring 1997), pp. 395–415 and 'The Hong Kong Convention and Exhibition Centre Extension', *Public Culture*, XI/3 (Fall 1999), pp. 566–9. The College Art Association has also given permission to reproduce material used in 'The Culture of a Border Within: Hong Kong Art and China', *Art Journal*, LIX/2 (Summer 2000), pp. 88–101. I also use certain material from 'Hong Kong Art and the Transfer of Sovereignty', *The Journal of the Oriental Society of Australia*, XXIX (1997), pp. 1–21 and 'Para/Site Art Space: Installation and Cultural Identity in Hong Kong', Third Text, L (Spring 2000), pp. 73–86. A number of my ideas about Hong Kong art were first tested in pieces written for *Art AsiaPacific*, and I am grateful to the editors of that journal for their interest in my work.

Photographic Acknowledgements

The author and publishers wish to express their thanks to the following sources of illustrative material and/or permission to reproduce it:

AFP PHOTO/Robyn Beck: 78; photo courtesy John Batten Gallery, Hong Kong: 89; photos courtesy the Department of Fine Arts, University of Hong Kong/Edwin Leung: 62, 64, 67, 82; photo by Fang Fang: 135; photos courtesy Susan Fong: 10–14; photos courtesy of Hanart TZ Gallery, Hong Kong: 5, 7, 8, 17, 99; photos courtesy of Hong Kong Arts Centre: 37, 66, 114–16; photos Hong Kong Museum of Art: 2–4, 9; reproduced by permission of the Hong Kong Special Administrative Region Government (Leisure and Cultural Services Department): 15; courtesy the Information Services Department (reproduced by permission of the Hong Kong Special Administrative Region Government): 63, 83–5, 87, 95, 96, 111, 123, 131; photos courtesy Lau Kin Wai: 108, 110; photos courtesy Para/Site Art Space: 40–43, 45, 47–9, 53, 57; photo courtesy Shanghai Tang: 117; photo courtesy Young Hay: 135; photo courtesy Zuni Icosahedron: 16; the author: 36, 59–61, 65, 68, 69, 71–7, 86, 88, 90–94, 101, 104, 105, 107, 109, 112, 113, 118, 119, 124–30, 132; courtesy the artists/designers: 1, 16, 18–35, 38–58, 70, 79–81, 97–100, 102, 103, 106, 120–22, 133, 134.

Index of Personal and Place Names

Numerals in *italics* refer to pages with illustrations.

1A Space 74, 79, 98

Abstract Expressionism 18, 24, 35, 70
Artist Commune 98
Atget, Eugène 87

Bank of China Building 135-8, *135*, 152,
    163–7, 181

Central Government Offices 177, *181*,
    194, *195*, 204
Central Library 152–3, *153*
César 112–13, *113*, 114–16, 122, 140
Cézanne, Paul 24
Chan, Alan 186
Chan, Benny 163
Chan, Joseph 187
Chan, Luis 9, 10–11, 13–14, 18–25, *20*,
    21, 22–5, *23*, 34, 35, 36
Chan, Raymond 58, 214, 215
Chan Yiu Hung 58, 214
Chan Yuk-keung 43, *44*, 92–3
Cheung, Lisa 74, 80
Cheung, Lucia *165*, 166–7
Cheung, Maggie 188
Cheung, William 92
China Club 188
Ching Chin Wai 97
Chiu, Karl 129, 206, 207
Choi Yan-chi 79, *79*
Chou, Irene 33
Chu, Almond 98, *98*
Clark, T. J. 38, 149
Convention and Exhibition Centre
    Extension *137*, 138–49, *140*, *141*,
    148, 152, 154, 163, 202

Duchamp, Marcel 25

Ernst, Max 22
Exchange Square 102–5, 107, 124, 139

Fang Fang 208
Frink, Elizabeth 102, *103*, 104, 105, 107,
    109–11, *110*, 119

Galliano, John 168
Galschiot, Jens 119, *120*
Gaultier, Jean Paul 168
Go, Simon 183
Gombrich, Ernst 7
Gong Li 187, *187*
Gottlieb, Adolph 24
Government House 138, 140–41, 157–9,
    158, 180
Greenberg, Clement 7, 211

Halpern, Jacques 22
Henry, Gérard 180
Ho Chiu-fan 153
Ho, Oscar 66–7, *66*, 71, 94, 134, *134*,
    172, *174*, 184
Ho Siu Kee *51*, 52, *53*, 67, 93
Ho, Tao 153, 188
Hoertner, Sabina 97
Hon Chi-fun 33
Hong Kong and Shanghai Bank Building
    105–9, *106*, *107*, 135, 138, 152, 166–7
Hong Kong Cultural Centre 34, 43,
    112–14, *112*, 138, 152, 199
Hong Kong International Airport (Chek
    Lap Kok) 159–63, 177
Hong Kong Museum of History 140,
    152, 162
Hong Kong Stadium 152
Hou Chun-ming 65

Ju Ming 102, 104–5, *104*, 136, 139

Kan Tai-keung 196
Keung, Jimmy 65
Ko, Alfred 117, *118*, 128–9, *130*
Kum Chi-keung, Desmond 47–9, *47*
Kwan, Stanley 94, 188
Kwok, David 19
Kwok Mang-ho 95–6

Lau, Freeman *191*, 192
Lau Kin Wai 94, 181–4
Lau, Peter 193–4, *195*
Lee, Aries 33
Lee Byng 11, 18

Lee, Holly 59–62, *59*, 173–4
Lee Ka-sing 43–7, *45, 46, 60, 61, 62, 71, 183*, 184
Lee, Patrick 74, 75, 79–80, 85, 87
Legislative Council Building 110, 154–6, 162, *175*, 194, 199, *201*, 204
Leung Chi Wo, Warren 73, 74, 75, 76, 80, 81, 86–7, *88*, 89, *89*, 90–92, *91*, 94, 166
Leung Mee Ping 74, 80–81
Leung Po-shan 96, 97, 190–92, *193*
Li Shan 43
Li Tiefu 11
Li Wei Han 93
Lin, Maya 145
Ling, Wessie 168, *169*
Liu Guosong 70
Liu Yuyi 41, 43, 214
Lui Shou-kwan 10, 13, 14, 17–18, *17*, 23, 24, 26, 34, 37, 40, 70, 104, 203

Ma, Victor 96
Magritte, René 25
Mak, Antonio 9, 13–14, 19, 25–37, *26, 27, 29, 30*, 67, 68, 71, 88, 171
Mak Tai-kit, Peter 163
Man Ching Ying, Phoebe 54–5, *54*, 74, 81, *83*, 95, 97
Manet, Edouard 149
Michaux, Henri 22
Moore, Henry 102, *103*, 105

Nauman, Bruce 25, 171
New Ink Painting 10, 11, 15, 17, 37, 211
Noland, Kenneth 24

Oil Street Art Village 98–9
OP Fotogallery 74

Paik, Nam-June 62
Pan He 141
Para/Site Art Space 9, 74–98, 99, 151
Pau, Ellen 52–4, *53*, 62, 63
Paulson, Ronald 38
Pei, I. M. 135–8, *135*
Pollock, Jackson 24
Prince of Wales Barracks 156–7, *156, 157*
Pun Sing Lui 47, 52, 118–19, 122, 147

Raggi 108–9, *108*, 116–17, *117*
Remington, Frederic 27
Rodin, Auguste 25
Ruan Lingyu 188
Russell, Charles Marion 27

Shanghai Tang 67, 172–3, 187–8, *187*
So Hing Keung 58, *58*, 163–6, *163*
Soulages, Pierre 24
Sze Yuen 67–8, *67*

Tang, William 168, 184, *184*, 185
Tang Wing-cheung, David 172–3, 188
To, Hiram 79, *170*, 171
Tsang, Gerard 133
Tsang Tak-ping, Kith 74, 75–9, *77*, 81–6, *84, 85*, 87, 88, 89, 90, 91, 92, 93, 94, *94*, 97, 124–7, *126*
Tsang Tsou Choi (the 'King of Kowloon') 175–84, *178–80*
Tsing Ma Bridge 159, 161–2, *162*, 163
Tsui Hark 163
Tsui, Miranda 168

Van Lau 10, 13, 15, *16*, 33, *33*, 34, 35, 36, 104, 114, 133–4, 145
Videotage 98

Wagstaff, W. W. 107–8, *107*
Wan, Pacino 173, *176*
Wang Guangyi 42, 43
Wang Hai 12, 62–3, *64, 164*, 166
Webb and Bell 154
Wong and Ouyang (HK) Ltd 138
Wong, Faye 185
Wong, Kacey 94, 95, 97, *166*, 167
Wong Kan Tai 129, *131*, 206, 207
Wong, Sara 74, 81, *82*, 92
Wong Shun-kit 49–50, *50*, 52, 60, 190, *190*, 192
Wong Wobik 56–7, *56, 57*, 71, 72
Wong, Wucius 10, 13, 14, 15–18, *16*, 19, 23, 25, 26, 34, 35, 37, 40, 70, 104, 203
Wong, Yank 127, 128

Xu Bing 92, *93*

Yee Bon 11, 18, 34
Yim, Mandy 96
Yim Sen-kee, Rocco 153
Young Hay 96, 168, 206–8, *208*
Young, John *144*, 146–7
Yu, Vincent 117
Yu Youhan 43
Yung, Danny 39, 41–3, 47, 52, 71

Zhang Daqian 24
Zhang Yimou 187
Zhao Shao'ang 19
Zunzi 48, 49, 146–7, 192